The
Postcard
Price Guide

A Comprehensive Listing

EIN GLÜCKLICHES NEUJAHR

J. L. Mashburn

COMPLETELY UPDATED

Thousands of Prices, Representing Millions of Cards!

COLONIAL HOUSE

ENKA, NORTH CAROLINA USA

Publisher: J. L. Mashburn

Editor: Emma Mashburn

Cover Design: WorldComm®

Interior Design: Emma Mashburn

Electronic Page Assembly: WorldComm®

A Colonial House Production

Printed in the United States of America

Second Edition

10 9 8 7 6 5 4 3 2 1

ISBN 1-885940-00-9

AN IMPORTANT NOTICE TO THE READERS OF THIS PRICE GUIDE:

The comprehensive nature of compiling data and prices on the thousands of cards, sets and series in this publication gives many probabilities for error. Although all information has been compiled from reliable sources, experienced collectors and dealers, some data may still be questionable.

The author and publisher will not be held responsible for any losses that might occur in the purchase or sale of cards because of the information contained herein.

The author will be most pleased to receive notice of errors so that they may be corrected in future editions.

Contact: J.L. Mashburn, Colonial House, Box 609, Enka NC 28728 USA.

Contents

DEDICATION

This book is dedicated to all collectors and dealers whose contributions and efforts have made this hobby so wonderful and so fantastically interesting.

ACKNOWLEDGMENTS

More than 100 collectors and dealers have made valuable contributions in the preparation and publication of this Second Edition. While all cannot be acknowledged, appreciation is extended to the following contributors who have given their time and effort by creating, revising or verifying new artists and checklists, lending cards for scanning, and valuing cards.

Special thanks are given to **Vernon Ham** who worked for months editing, rearranging the format, and adding checklists and artists. He was also one of six dealers who helped value the cards that are listed.

Special thanks also to collector **Shirley Hendricks** for allowing us to use the cards of her tremendous collection of Samuel L. Schmucker, both for scanning and personal checklist, and for vital information concerning them. We hope that we have done them justice. Also to **Dale Hendricks** for his assistance and expertise concerning cards in the Santa section.

To **Gordon Gesner, Vernon Ham, Fred Kahn, Michael Leach, Jack Leach,** and **Marty Shapiro** for their support and assistance in pricing cards. We feel that this formidable group has helped to assure that values are as up-to-date and as accurate as possible.

We also thank **Nouhad A. Saleh,** for help in the Artist-Signed areas; **Alyce Thorson,** for artist additions; to **Jim Dismuke,** for cards and pricing in Roadside America and Real Photos; **Kathy Danielson,** for additions to Coles Phillips; and **Kosti Kallio** of Finland for further help on Finnish and Russian card artists.

BLUE RIBBONS

These are two of the beauties who help make postcard collecting so wonderful and so fascinating!

1

Introduction

REALITY!

It is likely that the new collector of picture postcards will not understand that the older collector has had to adjust his or her thinking as the hobby has grown and card values have increased. Gone are the days of the 60's and early 70's when beautiful Brundage, Clapsaddle, PFB children and colorful Santas were plentiful at $1-2 each; Fisher, Boileau, Christy, and Phillips' ladies could be purchased at $2-3; and almost any Halloween card was available in the $1-3 range.

In the early days, I placed ads in "Collector's News" and later "The Antique Trader," stating that I would pay 5 cents each for clean, undamaged postcards issued before 1920. Almost daily several packets arrived in the mail bringing beautiful cards, most of which I did not recognize and certainly did not know their market value. I couldn't wait to get to the post office, collect the packages and return home to open them. This continued for two years with good results, until finally only common and damaged cards arrived. Also, the boxes and albums at flea markets and antique shops disappeared. The hobby had grown, prices were elevating, and the "easy picking" ceased. **Reality!**

Soon after buying sources in the U.S. became less plentiful, I began placing display ads in European stamp, postcard, and antique publications, advertising to buy artist-signed issues. This effort brought many packets from all over Europe and was extremely successful; one man sent a package almost every week for two years. The packets, however, became smaller and less frequent and the cards became more common; many cards had to be returned because of damage.

I then began traveling to Europe to attend shows, browse in shops, and look for cards on my own. My first trip in 1984 was a huge success as every dealer and shop had many cards from which to choose; I then started going from 2 to 3 times per year. The dollar was 4.20 DM and cards were plentiful. These travels have continued until the present time. Since 1991, however, the dollar has fluctuated between 1.5 and 1.7 DM, the cards are mostly all gone except those that are damaged and very common, the prices have greatly increased, and it is now unprofitable to go to Europe to buy postcards. **Reality!**

For older collectors and dealers who went through this period of plentiful cards, it has been extremely difficult to adjust to today's "buy" prices. We have, however, come to realize that beautiful old postcard masterpieces, just like rare coins, stamps, posters, autographs, etc., are in great demand world-wide. Europeans are now buying back cards they sold to Americans over the past years. This, along with the many thousands who are entering the U.S. hobby monthly, is causing an explosion in values of better material. The values in this price guide reflect how far the hobby has come in just a few short years. If old collectors are going to stay on-board, we must realize that these values definitely reflect **REALITY.**

EVOLUTION OF THIS BOOK

When I first began selling postcards to collectors in the late 1960's, I sold many that were rare and underpriced because I didn't recognize their value ... Mucha's, Wiener Werkstätte's, Kirchner's at $5-6! Finally, I saw an advertisement by Dr. James Lowe for his "*Standard Postcard Catalog.*" What a revelation! Thanks to Dr. Lowe my education had begun. I began purchasing every book and catalog, both U.S. and foreign, that I could find. They were all worth their weight in gold. I also joined several postcard clubs who sent out monthly newsletters. For me, the best was "*What Cheer News*" from the Rhode Island Post Card Club. It was edited by Elisabeth K. Austin who, in my opinion, did the hobby a tremendous service by starting the compilation of checklists of sets, series, and various artists. This was instrumental in my publishing comprehensive postcard publications today.

I began adding to and compiling other checklists, realizing that in each set or series some cards were worth more than others. I felt that the hobby would benefit from this information, both the number of cards in each set or series as well as each card's value. With the beginning efforts of James Lowe and Elizabeth Austin, and the hundreds of collectors and dealers who have helped in the meantime, this book is the end result. I hope you enjoy it and that you benefit from the experience of an "old timer."

J. L. Mashburn
August, 1994

HOW TO USE THIS PRICE GUIDE

This price guide has been uniquely designed to serve the needs of both the beginning and advanced collector, as well as the established postcard dealer. Our attempt to provide a comprehensive guide to postcards dating from the 1890's through the 1960's makes it possible for even the novice collector to consult it with confidence and ease in finding each particular listing. The following important explanations summarize the general practices that will help in getting the most benefits from its use.

CATEGORICAL ARRANGEMENT

Cards are arranged by category, and each category is listed in the Table of Contents. All Artist-Signed cards are listed under a particular type or theme. Artists are always listed alphabetically, as are the publishers if the cards are unsigned.

Topical cards are listed alphabetically with individual listings of some of the most prominent cards and their values. Otherwise, the prices listed are for generalized cards in the particular topic or theme.

LISTINGS

Listings may be identified as follows:

1. **SECTION** (Artist-Signed, Fantasy, etc.).
2. **TOPIC** (Beautiful Women, Cats, Dogs, etc.).
3. **ARTIST** (Listed in Bold Capital Letters) when available.
4. **PUBLISHER** (Listed in Bold, Lower Case Letters).
5. **NAME OF SERIES; OR SERIES NUMBER.**

6. **NUMBER OF CARDS IN SET OR SERIES** (Enclosed in Parentheses) when available.
7. **CAPTION OR TITLE OF CARD** (Enclosed in Quotation Marks).
8. **PRICE OF 1 CARD IN VERY GOOD CONDITION**
9. **PRICE OF 1 CARD IN EXCELLENT CONDITION**

Example of above:

1. **ARTIST-SIGNED**
2. **BEAUTIFUL WOMEN**
3. **HARRISON FISHER**
4. **Reinthal & Newman**
5. 101 Series
6. (12)
7. "American Beauties"
8. $10 - 15
9. $15 - 18

CONDITION AND GRADING OF POSTCARDS

The condition of a postcard, as with old coins, stamps, books, etc., is an extremely important factor in pricing it for the collector, the dealer, and for those having found cards to sell. Damaged, worn, creased, or dirty cards —cards in less than Very Good condition—are almost uncollectible unless they are to be used as a space filler until a better one is found. **Collectors should never buy a damaged card if they expect to sell it later on.**

It is necessary that some sort of card grading standard be used so that buyer and seller may come to an informed agreement on the value of a card. Two different collectible conditions, **Very Good** and **Excellent,** are used in **THE POST CARD PRICE GUIDE.** There are, of course, higher and lower grades, but these two will be most normally seen and most normally quoted for postcards sold throughout the hobby.

The standard grading system adapted by most dealers and by the leading postcard hobby publications in the field, *Barr's Post Card News* and *Post Card Collector,* is listed below with their permission:

M—MINT. A perfect card just as it comes from the printing press. No marks, bends, or creases. No writing or postmarks. A clean and fresh card. Seldom seen.

NM—NEAR MINT. Like Mint but very light aging or very slight discoloration from being in an album for many years. Not as sharp or crisp.

EX—EXCELLENT. Like mint in appearance with no bends or creases, or rounded or blunt corners. May be postally used or unused and with writing and postmark only on the address side. A clean, fresh card on the picture side.

VG—VERY GOOD. Corners may be just a bit blunt or rounded. Almost undetectable crease or bend that does not detract from overall appearance of the picture side. May have writing or postally used on address side. A very collectible card.

G—GOOD. Corners may be noticeably blunt or rounded with noticeably slight bends or creases. May be postally used or have writing on address side. Less than VG.

FR—FAIR. Card is intact. Excess soil, stains, creases, writing, or cancellation may affect picture. Could be a scarce card that is difficult to find in any condition.

Postcard dealers always want better condition cards that have no defects. Collectors should keep this in mind if they have cards to sell. Therefore, anyone building a collection should maintain a standard for condition and stick to it. Even if the asking price is a little higher when a card is purchased, it will be worth the cost when it is resold.

VALUATIONS

The postcard values quoted in this publication represent the current retail market. They were compiled with assistance from five of the leading dealers in the U.S., dealer pricing at shows, personal dealer communications, from the author's personal purchasing world-wide, from his approval sales, and from his active day-to-day involvement in the postcard field.

Some values were also compiled from observations of listings in auctions, auction catalogs (U.S., Europe, and Great Britain), prices realized and fixed price sales in the fine hobby publications, *Barr's Post Card News* and *Postcard Collector*, and other related publications. **In most instances, listings of high and low values were taken for each observation, and these were averaged to obtain the "Very Good" and "Excellent" prices quoted.**

It must be stressed that this price guide and reference work is intended to serve only as an aid in evaluating postcards. It should not be used otherwise. As we all know, actual market conditions change constantly, and prices may fluctuate. The trend for postcards seems to always be to the upside.

Publication of this price guide is not intended to be a solicitation to buy or sell any of the cards listed.

Price ranges for cards in both **Very Good** and **Excellent** conditions are found at the end of each listing. Prices for cards in less than Very Good condition would be much lower, while those grading above Excellent might command relatively higher prices.

Without exception, prices quoted are for **one** card, whether it be a single entity or one card in a complete set or series. Note that after many entries a number is enclosed in parentheses; e.g., (6). This number indicates the total number of cards in a set or in a series. The price listed is for one card in the set and must be multiplied by this number to determine the value of a complete set.

WHY PRICE RANGES ARE QUOTED

For cards graded both **Very Good** and **Excellent**, price ranges are quoted for four major reasons. Any one, or more, of the following can determine the difference in the high or low prices in each of the listing ranges.

1. Prices vary in different geographical areas across the United States. At this time, they are somewhat higher on the Pacific coast and other western states. They tend to be a little lower in the East and somewhere in-between in the central and midwestern states. For instance, a card with a price range of $6.00-8.00 might sell for $6.00 in the East, $7.00 in the Mid-West and $8.00 in the Far West.

2. Dealer price valuations also vary. Those who continually set up at postcard shows seem to have a better feel for prices and know which cards are selling well and, therefore, can adjust their prices accordingly. Dealers who sell only by mail, or by mail auction, tend to price their cards (or list estimated values in their auctions) just a bit higher. They usually are able to get these prices because of a wider collector market base obtained by the large number of subscribers served by

the nationally distributed postcard auction publications. The publications also reach collectors who are unable to attend shows.

Cards that have been sent on approvals quite often are higher than postcard shows, etc., prices because the dealer has spent more time in selecting and handling. Quite often he is working from a customer "want list."

3. Cards that are in great demand, or "hot" topics, also have wider price ranges; as collector interests rise there is a greater disparity in values because of supply and demand. If a dealer has only a small number of big demand cards he will almost automatically elevate his prices. Those who have a large supply will probably not go as high.

4. Card appearance and the subject in a set or series can also cause a variance in the price range. Printing quality, more beautiful and varied colors, and sharpness of the image may make a particular card much more desirable and, therefore, it will command a higher price.

Cards that have a wide price range usually are those that are presently the "most wanted" and best sellers. Dealers, most often, will only offer a small discount when selling these because they know there is a good market for them. Cards listed with a narrow price range are usually those that have been "hot" but have settled down and established a more competitive trading range. Dealer discounting on these slow-movers tends to be much more prevalent than those in the wide price ranges.

GUIDELINES FOR BUYING AND SELLING CARDS

As noted above, the prices listed in this price guide are retail prices—prices that a collector can expect to pay when buying a card from a dealer. It is up to the collectors to bargain for any available discount from the dealer.

The wholesale price is the price which a collector can expect from a dealer when selling cards. This price will be significantly lower than the retail price. Most dealers try to operate on a 100% mark-up and will normally pay around 50% of a card's low retail value. On some high-demand cards, he might pay up to 60% or 75% if he wants them badly enough.

Dealers are always interested in purchasing collections and accumulations of cards. They are primarily interested in those that were issued before 1915, but may be induced to take those issued afterwards if they are clean and in good condition.

Collections: Normally, collections are a specialized group or groups of cards that a person has built over the years. They will be in nice condition, without any damage, and may contain some rarities or high-demand cards.

If the collection is a group of views from your home town or state it would be to your advantage, pricewise, to sell them to a collector or dealer near you. You might place an ad in your daily paper; you will be surprised at the interest it creates. Set your price a little high; you can always come down.

If the collection contains artist-signed, topicals, and complete sets, as well as views, etc., you may need to contact a dealer in order to dispose of them. As noted above, be prepared to sell to the dealer at around 50% of the value of the collection. If you do not know of any dealers, write the **International Federation of Postcard Dealers,** to the attention of Charles R. Collins, Secretary, 19 Empire Place, Greenbelt, MD 20770, and enclose a double-stamped, self-addressed #10 envelope for a list of members.

You might also dispose of your collection by writing to the dealers who advertise in *Barr's Post Card News,* 70 South 6th St., Lansing, IA 52151 or *Postcard Collector*, P.O. Box 5000, Iola, WI 54945. Other publications that have postcard sections are *Collectors News*, P. O. Box 156, Grundy Center, IA 50638-0156, *Paper Collectors' Market Place*, P. O. Box 128, Scandinavia, WI 54977, and *The Antique Trader*, P. O. Box 1050, Dubuque, IA 52004. Write to any of these publications and ask for information on subscriptions or sample copies.

Accumulations: Accumulations are usually groups of many different kinds, many different eras, and many different topics ... with the good usually mixed in with the bad. If you have a large accumulation that you wish to sell, your best bet is to contact a dealer as noted above. You may expect only 20% to 30% of value on a group such as this. Many low demand cards are non-sellers and are worthless to a dealer, but he may take them if there are some good cards in the accumulation.

Buying: Without doubt, the best way to buy postcards is to attend a show where there is a large group of dealers. Compare prices among dealers on cards that are of interest to you, and return to those who have the best cards at the lowest price for your purchases.

Buy from a dealer in your area if there is one. A good dealer will help you with your collection by searching for cards you need or want. If none are available, many dealers listed in *Barr's Post Card News* and *Postcard Collector* run auctions or will send cards on approval. Also, you might try joining a postcard club. It is possible to find an excellent choice of cards at these meetings because attendees bring material that they know is of interest to their fellow members.

It is also possible to find cards at Antique Shows, Flea Markets and Antique Shops. You can, however, waste a lot of time and never find suitable cards. It is best to go direct to the source and that would be a postcard dealer or auctioneer. Here you can find a great variety and almost always cards of interest to you.

IDENTIFYING THE AGE OF POSTCARDS

The dating of postcards for years or eras of issue can be accurately determined if the card is studied for identity points. Research has already been done by earlier historians and guidelines have been put into place.

There were seven eras for the postcard industry and each one has distinguishing points to help establish its respective identity. The following helps determine the era of the card in question:

PIONEER ERA (1893-1898)

The Pioneer Era began when picture postcards were placed on sale by vendors and exhibitors at the Columbian Exposition in Chicago, May, 1893. These were very popular and proved to be a great success. The profitable and lasting future of the postcard was greatly enhanced.

Pioneer cards are relatively scarce. They can be identified by combinations of the following:

- All have undivided backs.

- None show the "Authorized by Act of Congress" byline.

- Postal cards will have the Grant or Jefferson head stamp.

- Most, but not all, will be multiple view cards.

- The words "Souvenir of ..." or "Greetings from ..." will appear on many.

- Postage rate, if listed, is 2 cents.

- The most common titles will be "Souvenir Card" or "Mail Card."

- Appeared mostly in the big Eastern cities.

PRIVATE MAILING CARD ERA (1898-1901)

The government, on May 19, 1898, gave private printers permission to print and sell postcards. The cards were all issued with the inscription "Private Mailing Card," and today they are referred to as PMC's. It is very easy to identify these because of the inscription. It may be noted that many of the early Pioneer views were reprinted as Private Mailing Cards.

UNDIVIDED BACK ERA (1901-1907)

On December 24, 1901, permission was given for use of the wording "Post Card" to be imprinted on the backs of privately printed cards. All cards during this era had undivided backs and only the address was to appear on the back. The message, therefore, had to be written on the front (picture side) of the card. For this reason, there is writing on the face of many cards; this is becoming more acceptable on cards of this era.

DIVIDED BACK ERA (1907-1915)

This era came into being on March 1, 1907. The divided back made it possible for both the address and the message to be on the back of the card. This prevented the face of the card from being written on and proved to be a great boon for collectors. Normally the view colors or images filled the entire card with no white border.

WHITE BORDER ERA (1915-1930)

The White Border Era brought an end to the postcard craze era. The golden age ended as imports from Germany ceased and publishers in the U.S. began printing postcards to try to fill the void. The cards were very poor quality and many were reprints of earlier Divided Back Era cards. These are easily distinguished by the white border around the pictured area.

LINEN ERA (1930-1945)

Improvements in American printing technology brought improved card quality. Publishers began using a linen-like paper containing a high rag content but used very cheap inks in most instances. Until recently, these cards were considered very cheap by collectors. Now they are very popular with collectors of Roadside America, Blacks, Comics, and Advertising. Views are also becoming more popular as collectors realize that this era too is a part of our history, and these cards help to illustrate the changes in the geographic structure of America.

PHOTOCHROME ERA (1939 to present day)

"Modern Chromes," as they are now called by the postcard fraternity, were first introduced in 1939. Publishers, such as **Mike Roberts**, **Dexter Press, Curt Teich,** and **Plastichrome**, began producing cards that had very beautiful chrome colors and were very appealing to collectors. The growth of this group has been spectacular in recent years, so much so that there are now many postcard dealers who specialize only in chromes.

REAL PHOTO POSTCARDS (1900 to present day)

Real Photo postcards were in use as early as 1900. It is sometimes very hard to date a card unless it has been postally used or dated by the photographer. The stamp box will usually show the process by which it was printed—AZO, EKC, KODAK, VELOX, and KRUXO are some of the principal ones. Careful study of photo cards is essential to make sure they have not been reproduced.

ART DECO ERA (1910 to early 1930's)

Beautiful **Colors!** Beautiful strong, deep, vibrant **Colors!** This wording only partially describes the new Art Deco movement that began around 1910—just as the Art Nouveau era was ebbing—and continued into the early 1930's. Due to the great influx of Art Deco postcards to the U.S., there has been a great demand for them in recent years as more and more American collectors discover their beauty.

Basically, for the postcard collector there are two types of Art Deco. The first, and most sought-after, were the earlier works of Brunelleschi, Chiostri, Montedoro, Bentivoglio, Meschini and Scattini, and a small number of the works of Adolfo Busi, Colombo and T. Corbella. Most of these artists did paintings of beautiful women in their mode of dress of the era, along with beautiful scenic backgrounds, etc.

The second type was predominantly of ladies in fashionable attire starting around 1915 and continuing into the 1920's. The Italian artists were the most prolific as they produced many cards, usually in sets of six, depicting a particular theme. Beautiful ladies, smartly dressed, pictured with wild animals, sleek dogs or colorful horses played a dominant role, while those engaged in tennis and golf and other sports were a close second. Corbella, Nanni, Mauzan and Colombo seem to generate the most interest.

Unfortunately, very few minor works by American artists have become highly collectible. At the present time, Art Deco cards are in great demand by artist-signed collectors within the hobby.

ART NOUVEAU (1898-1910)

Art Nouveau postcards had their beginning at the turn of the century in Europe. Primarily, the movement began in Paris--where the great poster artists congregated--and in Vienna. This new expression of decorative art was the rage of the era, and the posters and magazines such as *"Jugend," "Simplicissimus," "Le Rire," "Le Plume,"* and *"The Poster,"* were used as a means to transmit this expression to the art lovers of the world.

The works of the great poster artists based in Paris, Alphonse Mucha (who was the most famous), Steinlen, Jules Cheret, Paul Berthon, Villon, Toulouse-Lautrec, Grasset, and many others, were also published in smaller format as beautiful and colorful postcards.

Also, in Vienna, beautiful and artistic postcards were produced by publishers such as Philipp & Kramer and Wiener Werkstätte. Artists of the "Secession" movement, led by Koloman Moser, Karl Jozsa, and Oskar Kokoschka, produced thousands of beautiful cards that are treasured by collectors world-wide.

The values of some of these cards have reached unbelievable heights as can be witnessed by the prices revealed in this book. As values of the better known artists such as Mucha, Kirchner and Toulouse-Lautrec spiral ever upward, they also bring the values of the lesser publicized artist up with them.

2 Artist-Signed

If you ask a postcard collector "What do you collect?" he will invariably answer, "I collect views of my home town," and then continues ... with a gleam in his eye ... "and cards signed by Harrison Fisher"... or Philip Boileau, or Earl Christy, Frances Brundage, Pauli Ebner, and so on.

The Artist-Signed postcard is overwhelmingly the favorite type to collect in the entire postcard field. The beauty and elegance of several cards, or a group or set of cards by a great artist, makes the pulse quicken and creates the desire to possess them.

Since Artist-Signed cards are so popular we are listing almost all major and many minor artists in the U.S.A. in all fields. Included are the complete, or near complete, checklists (with all cards priced) of Harrison Fisher, Philip Boileau, Earl Christy, Howard Chandler Christy, Clarence Underwood, Coles Phillips, and others. This is a major accomplishment and, to my knowledge, has never been attempted in the postcard field. Separate checklists have been made but never all together ... and never priced.

Listed also are major and minor foreign artists and their works in the important topics of Art Deco, Art Nouveau, Fantasy, Fantasy Nudes, Color Nudes, Nursery Rhymes, Fairy Tales, Animals, French Fashion, and others. This is the type of information today's collectors and dealers desire.

What is an Artist-Signed card? It is any card bearing an artist's signature or initials. If you have never collected them, you have much to look forward to.

BEAUTIFUL LADIES

	VG	EX
B.G. (Art Nouveau and Glamour)	$40 - 45	$45 - 50
ABIELLE, JACK (France)		
Lady/Flower Series	35 - 40	40 - 45
Art Nouveau	45 - 50	55 - 60
ALBERTARELLI (Italy) Art Deco	5 - 8	8 - 10
ALFRED, JAMES D.		
Gray Lithograph Co.		
P.C. 1 - P.C. 9	5 - 6	6 - 8
ANICHINI, E. (Italy) Art Deco and Glamour		
"Fairies" Series	20 - 25	25 - 30
Dancer Series	22 - 25	25 - 28
Silhouette Series 458	15 - 18	18 - 22
Others	15 - 18	18 - 22
ANLURNY (Art Deco and Glamour)		
Series 2590	12 - 15	15 - 18
ARMSTRONG, ROLF (U.S.A.)		
K. Co., N.Y.		
Water Color Series 101 - 112	10 - 15	15 - 20

Angelo Asti
Theo. Stroefer, Series 505, No. 2

Angelo Asti
Theo. Stroefer, Series 505, No. 6

ASTI, ANGELO   (Italy)
  Raphael Tuck
    Connoisseur Series 2731   8 - 12   12 - 16
    "Beatrice"
    "Gladys"
    "Irene"
    "Juliet"
    "Marguerite"
    "Rosalind"
    Connoisseur Series 2743   8 - 12   12 - 16
    "Helena"
    "Madeline"
    "Muriel"
    "Phyllis"
    "Portia"
    "Sylvia"
  Rotograph Co., N.Y.
    Series T. 5268   7 - 10   10 - 12
    "Beatrice"
    "Gladys"
    "Irene"
    "Juliet"
    "Marguerite"
    "Rosalind"
  T.S.N. (Theo. Stroefer, Nuremburg)
    Series 508 (8) No Captions   6 - 8   8 - 10
    Semi-Nude Real Photo Series 15 - 18   18 - 22
    "Epanouissment"
    "Fantasie"
    "Solitude"
    "Une Favorite"
    "Volupte"
    Others
AVELINE, F.
  Lindberg'in Kirjap. Oy, Helsinki Series   8 - 10   10 - 12
    Others   6 - 8   8 - 10
AXENTOWICZ   (Poland)
    Heads and full-length   8 - 10   10 - 15
    Fantasy   12 - 15   15 - 18
    Nudes   12 - 15   15 - 18
AZZONI, N.   (Italy) Art Deco and Glamour
    Series 517 (6)   15 - 20   20 - 25
    Others   12 - 15   15 - 18
BACHRICH, M.   (Art Deco and Glamour)
    Ladies/Fashion   10 - 12   12 - 15
    Ladies/Sports   12 - 15   15 - 18
    Dance Series 102   12 - 15   15 - 18
BAILEY, S.C.
  Carlton Pub. Co.

Series 674	6 - 8	8 - 10
Series 689	8 - 10	10 - 12
BAKST, LEON	20 - 25	25 - 30
Secession Exhibition	150 - 175	175 - 225
Ballet	75 - 100	100 - 150
BALESTERIERI, L. (Italy) Art Deco	7 - 8	8 - 10
BALL, H. LaPRIAK (U.S.A.)	3 - 4	4 - 5
BALLETTI, P. (Italy) Art Deco and Glamour		
Ladies/Fashion	12 - 15	15 - 18
BALOTINI (Italy)		
Ladies & Dogs Series 312	12 - 15	15 - 18
Art Deco	10 - 12	12 - 14
BARBARA, S. Art Nouveau	22 - 25	25 - 30
BARBER, COURT (U.S.A.)		
B.K.W.I.		
Series 861 (12)	8 - 10	10 - 12
Series 686 (6)	10 - 12	12 - 14
Series 1200	8 - 10	10 - 12
Others	6 - 8	8 - 10
Minerva		
Series 683 (Head Studies)	8 - 10	10 - 12
R.B.H. Series 688 (Head Studies)	8 - 10	10 - 12
J.W. & Co. Series	6 - 8	8 - 9
S.W.S.B. Series	10 - 12	12 - 14
Others	6 - 8	8 - 10
Ladies & Dogs	10 - 12	12 - 14
S.W.S.B.		
"Beauties"	8 - 10	10 - 12
1228 "Following the Race"	8 - 10	10 - 12
Anonymous		
Series 2023	8 - 10	10 - 12
Series 2024	8 - 10	10 - 12
Ladies & Horses		
"Miss Knickerbocker"	8 - 10	10 - 12
"In Summer Days"	8 - 10	10 - 12
"Thoroughbreds"	10 - 12	12 - 14
2022 "Ready to Ride"	8 - 10	10 - 12
BARBER, C. W. (U.S.A.)		
B.K.W.I.		
Series 861 (12)	8 - 10	10 - 14
Series 2128 (8)	8 - 10	10 - 14
Carlton Publishing Co.		
Series 549, 660	8 - 9	9 - 12
Series 676, 678	8 - 9	9 - 12
Series 709, 716	8 - 9	9 - 12
Series 735, 861	8 - 10	10 - 14
BARRIBAL, L. (GB)		
B.K.W.I.		
Series XIX (Fashion)	10 - 12	12 - 15

T. Axentowicz
Anczyc 109, No Caption

L. Barribal
Lindbergin Kirjapaino O.Y.

Court Barber
S.W.S.B. 1240, "My Queen"

C. W. Barber, Carlton Pub. Co.
E.C. No. 549, "Yes! if you like!"

Series 860 (Fashion)	10 - 12	12 - 15
Inter-Art Pub. Co.		
Series 3292	14 - 16	16 - 18
Artisque Series	10 - 12	12 - 15
Ladies & Horses		
Artisque		
Series 2234 (6)	12 - 15	15 - 18
Series 2236 (6)	12 - 15	15 - 18
Series 15644 (Heads)	12 - 15	15 - 18
M. Munk, Vienna (Heads)	10 - 12	12 - 15
Novitas, Germany	10 - 12	12 - 15
Valentine Co.		
"Flags of Nation" Series	12 - 15	15 - 18
"Great Britain"		
"Japan"		
"Scotland"		
"Ireland"		
"Germany"		
"Russia"		
Lindberg's Tryokeria Series (8)	10 - 12	12 - 15
Lindbergin Kirjap. O.Y., Helsinki (6)	10 - 12	12 - 15
Ladies & Dogs	15 - 18	18 - 22
H.N. & N.		
15645 Girl in Furs	10 - 12	12 - 15
BASCH, ARPAD (Hungary)		
Art Nouveau and Glamour		
Series 761 (6)	120 - 130	130 - 140
Series 769 (6)	200 - 225	225 - 250
Series 785 (6)	80 - 90	90 - 100
National Ladies (10)	120 - 130	130 - 140
"1900 Grand Femme" (6)	150 - 175	200 - 250
BENDA, WLADYSLAW T. (W.T.)		
"Rosamond"	8 - 10	10 - 12
"Reverie"	8 - 10	10 - 12
BERTHON, P. (Art Nouveau)	120 - 130	130 - 150
BENTIVOGLIO (Art Deco and Glamour)		
Lady & Greyhound	40 - 50	50 - 60
Others	25 - 30	30 - 35
BERTIGLIA, AURELIO (Italy)		
Art Deco and Glamour		
Uff. Rev. Stampa; Dell, Anna & Gasparini		
Ladies/Heads	12 - 15	15 - 18
Ladies/Fashion	12 - 15	15 - 18
Ladies/Animals	15 - 18	18 - 22
Ladies/Tennis-Golf	15 - 18	18 - 22
Harlequins	15 - 18	18 - 22
Ladies/Harlequins	18 - 22	22 - 25
Ethnic/Blacks	18 - 22	22 - 25
Series 163 Big Hats	15 - 18	18 - 20

Series 241 Semi-Nudes	20 - 22	22 - 26
Series 224 Lovers Kissing	10 - 12	12 - 15
Series 2062 Couples	10 - 12	12 - 14
Ladies & Dogs		
Series 163 (6)	12 - 14	14 - 16
Ladies & Horses		
Series 227 (6)	10 - 12	12 - 14
Series 2132 (6)	12 - 14	14 - 16
Series 2151 (6)	10 - 12	12 - 14
BETTINELLI, MARIO (Italy)		
Art Deco and Glamour		
Series 884	10 - 12	12 - 14
Others	8 - 10	10 - 12
BIANCHI, ALBERTO (Italy)		
Art Deco and Glamour		
Uff. Rev. Stampa and P.A.R.		
Series 2024, 2041 Walking (6)	10 - 12	12 - 14
Series 2154 High Fashion (6)	10 - 12	12 - 15
Ladies/Heads	10 - 12	12 - 15
Ladies/Fashion	10 - 12	12 - 15
Ladies/Animals	12 - 15	15 - 18
Ladies/Tennis-Golf	15 - 18	18 - 22
Ladies/Dogs/Horses		
Series 483 (6)	8 - 10	10 - 12
Series 2020 (6)	10 - 12	12 - 14
BIELETTO, T.	5 - 6	6 - 8
BILIBIN (Russia) Art Nouveau	75 - 100	100 - 150
BIRGER (Art Deco)	15 - 18	18 - 20
BIRI, S. (Italy) Art Deco and Glamour		
Ladies/Harlequins	18 - 22	22 - 25
Others	12 - 15	15 - 18
BLUMENTHAL, M.L.	4 - 5	5 - 6
BOCCASILE, GINO (Art Deco)	50 - 75	75 - 100
BODAREVSKY, N.K.	5 - 6	6 - 8

BOILEAU, PHILIP (Canada-U.S.A.)

Philip Boileau, born in Canada but finally settling in New York, was one of the great painters and illustrators of beautiful women. His works are collected world-wide and are in great demand.

Most of his images on postcards were published in the U.S.A. by the New York firm of Reinthal & Newman during the "postcard craze" years of 1905-1918. Other principal publishers were Osborne Calendar Co., with their printings of the rare Boileau calendar cards, National Art Co. and their advertising cards, and The Taylor, Platt Co. and their scarce flower-decorated cards and valentine head issues.

Minor issuers were advertising cards by Flood & Conklin, Soapine Mfg. Co., S.E. Perlberg Tailors, and others. These various issues, as well as his other advertising cards, are extremely hard to find and are very high priced when they surface.

British, European and Finnish publishers issued Boileau cards which are very elusive and also command high prices. The Tuck Connoisseur Series 2819 and the German K N G Schöne Frauen, along with the KOY Finnish Series, are among those sought after by collectors world-wide.

PHILIP BOILEAU

AMERICAN PUBLISHERS
Reinthal & Newman

Series 94*	15 - 20	20 - 25
"At the Opera"		
"Peggy"		
"Schooldays"		
"Sweethearts"		
"Thinking of You"		
"Twins"		

* Card with Series No. on back, add $5.

Series 95 *		
"A Mischiefmaker"	15 - 20	20 - 25
"Anticipation"	15 - 20	20 - 25
"Forever"	15 - 20	20 - 25
"Little Lady Demure"	15 - 20	20 - 25
"My Chauffeur"	15 - 20	20 - 25
"Nocturne"	10 - 15	15 - 20
"Passing Shadow"	20 - 22	22 - 26
"Spring Song"**	20 - 22	22 - 26
"Today"	15 - 20	20 - 25
"Tomorrow"	20 - 22	22 - 26
"Winter Whispers"	12 - 18	18 - 22
"Yesterday"	15 - 20	20 - 25

* Cards with Series No. on back, add $5.
** Cards distr. by Chas. H. Hauff, add $5.

Series 109*		
"Evening and You"	20 - 25	25 - 30
"Girl in Black"	20 - 25	25 - 30
"Her Soul With Purity Possessed"	22 - 27	27 - 32
"In Maiden Meditation"	22 - 27	27 - 32
"June, Blessed June"	20 - 25	25 - 30
"My Moonbeam"	20 - 25	25 - 30
"My One Rose"	20 - 25	25 - 30
"Ready for Mischief"	20 - 25	25 - 30
"The Secret of the Flowers"	22 - 27	27 - 32
"True as the Blue Above"	22 - 27	27 - 32

P. Boileau, Phillips
No. 115, "If I Could Speak!"

P. Boileau, "A Passing Shadow"
R&N, Wildt & Kray, Series 1419

P. Boileau, "Yesterday!"
R&N (Novitas), No No.

P. Boileau
R&N, No No., "To-Day?"

"Twixt Doubt and Hope"	20 - 25	25 - 30
"Waiting for You"	20 - 25	25 - 30
"With Care for None"	20 - 25	25 - 30

* Cards with Series No. on back, add $5.
  200 Series

204 "Rings on Her Fingers"	10 - 15	15 - 20
205 "Question"	10 - 15	15 - 20
205 "Chrysanthemums"	15 - 20	20 - 25
206 "The Enchantress"	10 - 15	15 - 20
207 "A Hundred Years Ago"	10 - 15	15 - 20
208 "Miss America"	12 - 16	16 - 22
209 "Youth"	10 - 15	15 - 20
210 "Joyful Calm"	10 - 15	15 - 20
211 "Chums"	10 - 15	15 - 20
212 "Sweet Lips of Coral Hue"	10 - 15	15 - 20
213 "His First Love"	10 - 15	15 - 20
214 "For Him"	10 - 15	15 - 20
215 "I Wonder"	10 - 15	15 - 20
282 "Ready for the Meeting"	12 - 16	16 - 22
283 "Miss Pat"	12 - 16	16 - 22
284 "Old Home Farewell"	10 - 15	15 - 20
285 "A Serious Thought"	10 - 15	15 - 20
286 "I Don't Care"	12 - 16	16 - 22
287 "The Eyes Say No, The Lips Say Yes"	12 - 16	16 - 22
294 "Blue Ribbons"	15 - 20	20 - 25
295 "A Little Devil" ("Good Little Rogue")	15 - 20	20 - 25
296 "Once Upon A Time"	10 - 15	15 - 20
297 "My Big Brother"	10 - 15	15 - 20
298 "My Boy"	10 - 15	15 - 20
299 "Baby Mine"	15 - 20	20 - 25

Water Color Series 369-380*

369 "Vanity"	15 - 22	30 - 40
370 "Haughtiness"	20 - 25	30 - 40
371 "Purity"	15 - 22	30 - 40
372 "Loneliness"	20 - 25	40 - 45
373 "Happiness"	20 - 25	30 - 40
374 "Queenliness"	20 - 25	30 - 40
375 "Whisperings of Love" (Annunciation)	20 - 25	30 - 40
376 "Fairy Tales" (Girlhood)	20 - 25	30 - 40
377 "Parting of the Ways" (Maidenhood)	20 - 25	30 - 40
378 "Here Comes Daddy"	15 - 20	30 - 40
379 "Lullabye" (Motherhood)	20 - 25	30 - 40
380 "Don't Wake the Baby"	15 - 20	30 - 40

* Cards without Subtitle, add $5.

445 Series*	18 - 22	25 - 30

1   "Spring Song"
2   "Today"
3   "Tomorrow"
4   "Forever"

5 "My Chauffeur"			
6 "Nocturne"			
* With German caption, add $5.			
474 Series * **		20 - 25	30 - 35
1 "Spring Song"			
2 "A Passing Shadow"			
3 "Mischiefmaker" (also "A Mischief Maker")			
4 "Anticipating"			
5 "Yesterday"			
6 "Little Lady Demure"			
* With German caption, add $5.			
** Cards are more rare than Series 95.			
700 Series*		15 - 20	20 - 25
750 "Be Prepared"			
751 "Absence Cannot Hearts Divide"			
752 "A Neutral"			
753 "The Chrysalis"			
754 "Pensive"			
755 "The Girl of the Golden West"			
756 "Pebbles on the Beach"			
757 "Snowbirds"			
758 "One Kind Act a Day"			
759 "The Flirt"			
760 "In Confidence"			
761 "The Coming Storm"			
* With German caption, add $5.			
800 Series			
820 "Devotion"		25 - 30	35 - 40
821 "Golden Dreams"		20 - 25	35 - 40
822 "Every Breeze Carries My Thoughts..."		18 - 22	22 - 26
823 "Priscilla"		25 - 30	35 - 45
824 "Fruit of the Vine"		18 - 22	22 - 25
825 "Butterfly"		25 - 30	35 - 45
826 "When Dreams Come True" *		15 - 20	20 - 25
827 "Sister's First Love" *			
828 "The Little Neighbors" *			
829 "Peach Blossoms" *			
830 "When His Ship Comes In" *			
831 "Need a Lassie Cry" *			
* With German caption, add $5.			
Water Color Series 936-941		30 - 35	35 - 40
936 "A Bit of Heaven"			
937 "Chic"			
938 "Have a Care"			
also "Hav a Care"			
939 "Just a Wearying for You"			
940 "Sunshine"			
941 "Sincerely Yours"			
2000 Series		20 - 25	25 - 30

'TWIXT DOUBT AND HOPE

P. Boileau
Russian
"Richard" 113, No Caption

P. Boileau
Applique Ribbon & Plumes
B.K.W.I, "Twixt Doubt and Hope"

2052 "Thinking of You"
2063 "Chums"
2064 "His First Love"
2065 "Question"
2066 "From Him"
2067 "The Enchantress"
2068 "Joyful Calm"
Others in Series
Unnumbered Series   20 - 25   25 - 35
"The Dreamy Hour"
"Out for Fun"
Reinthal & Newman Copyright
Distributed by **Novitas**. No Numbers.   35 - 40   40 - 45
"A Mischiefmaker"
"A Passing Shadow" (Also by Wildt & Kray)
"Anticipating"
"Forever"
"Little Lady Demure"
"My Chauffeur"
"Nocturne"
"Spring Song"
"To-Day?"
"Tomorrow"

"Winter Whispers"
"Yesterday!"
Reinthal & Newman Copyright
Distributed by **J. Beagles & Co.**, London   20 - 25   25 - 30
 No No. "Little Lady Demure"
 No No. "Nocturne"
 No No. "Winter Whispers"
A. P. Co. Advertising   75 - 85   85 - 95
First Nat. Bank, Cripple Creek, CO
 "Virginia"   65 - 75   75 - 85
Flood & Conklin   (Calendar Card Ad)   100 - 125   125 - 150
 "Girl in Blue"
 "The Girl in Brown"
 "His First Love"
 Others
Holland Magazine (Ad on Back)   90 - 100   100 - 120
 "Miss Pat"
 "Ready for the Meeting"
Metropolitan Life   Advertising   35 - 40   50 - 60
National Art Company
 17 "Spring"   70 - 80   80 - 90
 18 "Summer"   70 - 80   80 - 90
 19 "Autumn"   70 - 80   80 - 90
 20 "Winter"   70 - 80   80 - 90
 150 "The Debutantes"   65 - 70   75 - 100
 160 "Summer"   70 - 80   80 - 90
 161 "Autumn"   70 - 80   80 - 90
 162 "Spring"   70 - 80   80 - 90
 163 "Winter"   70 - 80   80 - 90
 230 "Spring"   80 - 90   90 - 100
 231 "Summer"   80 - 90   90 - 100
 232 "Autumn"   80 - 90   90 - 100
 233 "Winter"   80 - 90   90 - 100
Osborne Calendar Co.*   150 - 200   200 - 250
 459 "Winifred"
 940 "A Fair Debutante"
 941 "The Blonde"
 942 "Phyllis"
 943 "Pansies"
 944 "True Blue"
 945 "Army Girl"
 946 "Day Dreams"
 947 "Passing Shadow"
 948 "The Girl in Brown"
 949 "Goodbye"
 950 "Passing Glance"
 951 "A Winter Girl"
 1436 "Violets"   200 - 250   250 - 300
 1459 "Rhododendrons"

1489 "At Play"
1738 "Virginia"
2076 "Suzanne"
3525 "Autumn"
3625 "Chrysanthemums"
  "Carnations"
  Others
* The Osborne Calendar Cards are the
  rarest U.S. series.

S.E. Perlberg Co., Tailors (Ad on Back)	85 - 100	100 - 125

"My Moonbeam"
"My One Rose"
"Secret of the Flowers"
"True as the Blue Above"
"Twixt Doubt and Hope"

C.N. Snyder Art

"Spring Song"	85 - 100	100 - 125
Soapine Advertising	85 - 100	100 - 125

Sparks Tailoring (Ad on Back) by **R&N**

"Tomorrow"	85 - 100	100 - 125

Taylor, Platt*

"Chrysanthemums"	70 - 80	80 - 100
"Poppies"	70 - 80	80 - 100
"Violets"	70 - 80	80 - 100
"Wild Roses"	70 - 80	80 - 100

* 12 cards were supposedly issued;
  only 4 have surfaced.

Will's Embassy Pipe Tobacco Mixtures

"Nocturne"	85 - 100	100 - 125

Worthmore Tay Tailors, Chicago

"Ready for Mischief"	85 - 100	100 - 125

Unsigned, Unknown U.S. Publisher *

"Au Revoir"	30 - 35	35 - 45

"Chrysanthemums" **
(To My Sweetheart)
"Day Dreams"
"Debutantes"
"Devotion"
"Poppies"
(A Greeting from St. Valentine)
(A Token of Love) 2 types exist.
"Violets"
(A Gift of Love)
 "Wild Roses"
(To My Valentine)
*   Others may exist.
** Embossed and un-embossed varieties exist;
    possibly in all four cards.

Wolf & Co.

   "Fancy Free" (Silk) Very Rare!   200 - 250   250 - 300

FOREIGN PUBLISHERS

A.V.N. Jones & Co., London

Distributed by **B.K.W.I.**

   Series 500   125 - 150   150 - 175

   "Spring"

   "Summer"

   "Fall"

   "Winter"

Apollon Sophia

   "My Big Brother" (No. 21)   40 - 50   50 - 65

B.K.W.I., German*   125 - 150   150 - 175

   "Ready for Mischief"

   "June, Blessed June"

* Die-cuts on headbands, necklaces, foil inside.

 Others exist without die-cut holes.

Diefenthal, Amsterdam   85 - 100   100 - 110

   "The Enchantress"

   "Question"

   "A Hundred Years Ago"

   "C'est Moi"

H & S, Germany   100 - 125   125 - 135

   "Au Revoir"

   "At Home" (White border)

   "Fancy Free" (White border)

   "Paying a Call" (White border)

   "Paying a Call" (No border, rev. image)

   "I Am Late" (Unsigned; blue rev. image)

K. K. OY, Finland   150 - 175   175 - 200

   "Baby Mine"

   "Sister's First Love"

   "Snowbirds"

   "Here Comes Daddy" (Light Pastels)

KNG, Germany

   Schöne Frauen Ser. 8010   100 - 125   125 - 150

   "I am Late" (No border)

   "Paying a Call" (No border)

   "Summer Breezes" (No border)

   "Fancy Free"

   "Au Revoir"

   "At Home"

   Schöne Frauen Ser. 8011

   "I am Late" (White border)   75 - 100   100 - 125

   "Fancy Free"   100 - 125   125 - 150

   "Paying a Call" (White border)   75 - 100   100 - 125

   "Summer Breezes" (White border) 75 - 100   100 - 125

   Schöne Frauen Ser. 8012   75 - 100   100 - 125

"I am Late" (rev. image, uns., untitled)
"Fancy Free"
Schöne Frauen Series 8013
"I am Late" (reversed image, uns.)   75 - 100   100 - 125
"Paying a Call" (reversed image, uns.)   75 - 100   100 - 125
"Summer Breezes" (blue rev. image)   100 - 125   125 - 150
MEU Publisher Logo on Back
Untitled, Woman/Dark Hat, Dated 1905   65 - 75   75 - 85
Albert Schweitzer, Germany   50 - 75   75 - 85
H.S. Speelman (Probably Dutch)
"Eva" (Same as "Peggy")
Raphael Tuck
Connoisseur Series 2819   150 - 175   175 - 200
"At Home"
"Au Revoir"
"Fancy Free"
"I Am Late"
"Paying a Call"
"Summer Breezes"
Utig de Muick, Amsterdam
"His First Love"   75 - 85   85 - 100
Weinthal Co., Rotterdam   75 - 85   85 - 100
Friedrich O. Woehler, Berlin
1058 - "Studie"   75 - 85   85 - 100

RUSSIAN PUBLISHERS
AWE - Russian/Polish Back
Real Photo Series
"Miss America"   125 - 150   150 - 175
"Richard" (Rishar, Petrograde)   125 - 150   150 - 175
104 "Winter"
105 "Spring"
106 "Autumn"
108 "Poppies" (Unsigned)
109 "Wild Roses"
110 "Violets"
111 "Chrysanthemums"
112
113
114 "Warum" (Why)
116
Unknown Russian Publisher
Real-Photo Type, Russian-Polish back
"The Enchantress"   125 - 150   150 - 175
Unknown Russian Publisher
"Autumn"   125 - 150   150 - 175
Unknown Russian Publisher
5   "Rings on Her Fingers" (Unsigned)   125 - 150   150 - 175
18   "A Brotherly Kiss" (Peb. grain paper) 125 - 150   150 - 175

S. Bompard
Artistica Riservata 472-5

A. Busi
Uff. Rev. Stampa 110-4

Bonora
A.D.M. Series 18, No Caption

A. Busi
Degami 1087, No Caption

UNKNOWN PUBLISHERS

Series 682 (6)		
682-1 "Anticipation"	50 - 60	60 - 75
682-2 "True as the Blue Above"	50 - 60	60 - 75
682-3 "In Maiden Meditation"	50 - 60	60 - 75
682-4 Unknown	175 - 200	200 - 225
682-5 "Twins"	50 - 60	60 - 75
682-6 "The Girl in Black"	50 - 60	60 - 75

Unsigned

"Miss America"	50 - 75	75 - 95
"Miss America" (signed, 1910, blue ink)	50 - 75	75 - 95
"Rings on Her Fingers"	50 - 75	75 - 95

Unknown Publisher (Probably Dutch)

Series R

R.236 "Miss America"	50 - 75	75 - 95
R.238 "His First Love"	50 - 75	75 - 95
R.239 "Chums"	50 - 75	75 - 95

BOLETTA	6 - 8	8 - 10
BOMPARD, LUIGI (Italy) Glamour	12 - 15	15 - 18
BOMPARD, SERGIO (Italy)		

Art Deco and Glamour

Artistica Riservata, 472 Series	15 - 18	18 - 22

Uff. Rev. Stampa; Dell, Anna & Gasparini

208, 431, 508, 931 Fashion (6)	10 - 12	12 - 14
461 Doing Nails, Fashion (6)	10 - 12	12 - 14
464, 467, 439 Heads (6)	10 - 12	12 - 15
474 Semi-Nudes (6)	18 - 20	20 - 25
534, 914, 955, 476 Heads (6)	10 - 12	12 - 15
407, 472, 496 High Fashion (6)	10 - 12	12 - 15
506, 985 High Fashion (6)	10 - 12	12 - 15
401, 449 High Fashion (6)	15 - 18	18 - 22
971, 972, 987 High Fashion (6)	15 - 18	18 - 22
321, 940, 951 High Fashion (6)	15 - 18	18 - 22
907, 950, 956 Fashion (6)	15 - 18	18 - 22
948 Sitting, Fashion (6)	15 - 18	18 - 20
986 With Doll (6)	20 - 22	22 - 25
456, 987 With Hats (6)	15 - 18	18 - 22
994 Woman/Child, Snowing (6)	12 - 14	14 - 16
458, 498 Lovers Hugging	10 - 12	12 - 14
498, 609 Lovers Talking/Hugging	10 - 12	12 - 14
448, 988 Lovers Hugging, Flowers	12 - 14	14 - 16
433 Small Image-Kissing	8 - 10	10 - 12
462 Taking His Pulse (6)	12 - 15	15 - 18
960 Fixing His Tie (6)	12 - 15	15 - 18
Golf/Tennis	15 - 20	20 - 22
Erotic/Semi-Nude	20 - 22	22 - 25

Ladies & Dogs

Uff. Rev. Stampa; Dell, Anna & Gasparini

Series 11, 17 (6)	15 - 18	18 - 20

Chiostri, Ballerini & Fratini 166
No Caption

Chiostri, Ballerini & Fratini 359
No Caption

F. Earl Christy, Atkinson News
"Tilton Seminary"

F. Earl Christy, Ullman 1583
Variation of "Graduation"

Series 343 (6)	12 - 14	14 - 16
Series 457 (6)	15 - 18	18 - 20
Series 461 (6)	12 - 14	14 - 16
Series 637 (6) With Puppies	14 - 16	16 - 18
Ladies & Horses		
Series 343 (6)	12 - 15	15 - 18
Series 457 (6)	12 - 15	15 - 18
Series 641 (6)	12 - 14	14 - 16
Series 931 (6)	12 - 14	14 - 16
Series 556 (6)	10 - 12	12 - 14
BONORA (Italy) Art Deco and Glamour		
Ladies	15 - 18	18 - 22
Harlequins	20 - 25	25 - 30
BORRMEISTER (Germany)		
Ladies & Horses	8 - 10	10 - 12
BOTTARO (Italy) Art Deco and Glamour		
Series 135, Ladies 1900's	20 - 25	25 - 30
Series 123, Bathers 1900's	25 - 30	30 - 35
Others 1920's	12 - 15	15 - 18
BOTTOMLEY, G.	3 - 5	5 - 8
BOUTET, HENRI (Art Nouveau)	25 - 30	30 - 35
BRADLEY, W.H. (Art Nouveau)	150 - 200	200 - 250
BRAUN, W.H. (Germany)	6 - 8	8 - 10
BREDT, F.M. (Germany)	5 - 6	6 - 8
BREHM, GEORGE (U.S.A.)	5 - 6	6 - 8
BRILL, G.R. (U.S.A.) Sporting Girl Series	6 - 8	8 - 9
BRISLEY, E. C. (G.B.)	5 - 6	6 - 8
BROCK, A. (Germany)	5 - 6	6 - 8
BROWN, J. FRANCIS (U.S.A.)	4 - 5	5 - 6
BROWN, M.	3 - 4	4 - 5
BRUNELLESCHI, UMBERTO (Italy)		
Art Deco & Glamour		
Silhouettes	150 - 175	175 - 200
Advertising, La Tradotta Series (6)	90 - 100	100 - 110
R et Cie, France		
"Femmes" Series 31 (6)	150 - 175	175 - 200
Art Nouveau	70 - 80	80 - 100
BRUNING, MAX (Germany)	8 - 10	10 - 14
Erotic	12 - 15	15 - 18
BRYSON (U.S.A.)		
S.S. Porter, Chicago		
143 "Secrets"	5 - 6	6 - 8
BUHNE, BUNTE		
Deco Silhouette Series 225-228	12 - 15	15 - 18
BUKOVAC, PROF. V. (Poland)	4 - 5	5 - 6
BULAS, J. (Poland)	8 - 10	10 - 12
BUSI, ADOLFO (Italy) Art Deco and Glamour		
Dell, Anna & Gasparini		
Series 112 Diabolo (6)	18 - 22	22 - 25

Series 100 Fantasy (6)	25 - 30	30 - 35
Series 153 Pajamas (6)	15 - 18	18 - 22
Series 126 Girls/Fruit (6)	15 - 18	18 - 22
Series 110, 193, 1020 Fashion (6)	18 - 20	20 - 22
Series 628 Scarves/Heads	20 - 22	22 - 25
Series 437 Gypsy Type (6)	15 - 18	18 - 22
Series 558 Couples on Sled (6)	15 - 20	20 - 22
Series 575 Lovers in Moonlight (6)	15 - 20	20 - 25
Series 615 Couples/Autos (6)	22 - 25	25 - 28
Series 651 At the Beach (6)	18 - 20	20 - 22
Series 3038, 3540, 3555 (6)	15 - 20	20 - 25
Golf/Tennis	20 - 22	22 - 25
Harlequins	15 - 18	18 - 22
Ladies & Dogs		
C.E.I.C.		
Series 159	14 - 16	16 - 18
Dell, Anna & Gasparini		
Series 170 (6)	14 - 16	16 - 18
Series 533 (6)	15 - 18	18 - 20
Ladies & Horses		
C.E.I.C.		
Series 157 (6)	12 - 15	15 - 18
Degami		
Series 687 (6)	10 - 12	12 - 15
Series 1087 (6)	22 - 25	25 - 28
BUSSIERE, G. (Art Nouveau)	25 - 30	30 - 35
BUTCHER, ARTHUR (GB)		
Inter-Art Company		
Series 1098	8 - 10	10 - 12
Series 2510	6 - 8	8 - 10
United Six Girls Series	10 - 12	12 - 15
"Belgium"		
"Britain"		
"France"		
"Japan"		
"Russia"		
"Serbia"		
"Artisque" Series 1509 (6)	8 - 10	10 - 12
A.R.i.B. Series 1963 (6)	8 - 10	10 - 12
CADORIN, G. (Italy)		
Ladies/Fashion	10 - 12	12 - 15
CALDONA (Italy) Art Deco	10 - 12	12 - 15
CAPIELLO, L. Art Nouveau	200 - 250	250 - 300
CARSON, T. Art Nouveau	25 - 30	30 - 35
CASWELL, E. C. (U.S.A.)	6 - 8	8 - 10
CAUVY, L. Art Nouveau	40 - 45	45 - 50
CASTELLI (Italy) Art Deco	10 - 12	12 - 15
CELEBRI (Italy) Art Deco	8 - 10	10 - 12
CENNI, E. (Italy) Art Deco	8 - 10	10 - 12

CHAMBERS, C.E. (U.S.A.)	6 - 8	8 - 10
CHARLET, J.A. (Belgium)		
Delta Series 4	15 - 18	18 - 20
CHERET, JULES Art Nouveau	200 - 300	300 - 500
CHERUBINI, M. (Italy) Art Deco		
Uff. Rev. Stampa		
Series 790 National Ladies	15 - 18	18 - 22
Series 423, 977 Off-Shoulder Fash. (6)	12 - 15	15 - 18
Series 997 With Cupids (6)	12 - 15	15 - 18
Series 408 In Bubbles (6)	10 - 12	12 - 15
Series 959 Beauties (6)	12 - 15	15 - 20
French Glamour	15 - 18	18 - 22
CHIOSTRI, S. (Also SOFIA) (Italy)		
Art Deco and Glamour		
Ballerini & Fratini		
Comics, Flowers & Fruits in Deco Style	12 - 15	15 - 18
Series 320 Lady/Wild Animals	35 - 45	45 - 55
Series 220 Santas	20 - 25	25 - 35
Black Robed Santa	40 - 50	50 - 60
Series 166 Deco Fashion	32 - 35	35 - 40
Series 359 With Birds	25 - 30	30 - 35
Series 181 Bathers	25 - 30	30 - 40
Series 243 Witches	25 - 30	30 - 40
Series 316 With Animals	25 - 28	28 - 32
Series 238 Mermaids	35 - 45	45 - 55
Series 317 Mermaids	35 - 40	40 - 50
Harlequins	25 - 30	30 - 35
Others, Colored Background	25 - 30	30 - 40
Others, Seasons Greetings	12 - 15	15 - 18
Signed FOFI	10 - 15	15 - 18
CHRISTIANSEN, HANS (Art Nouveau)		
"Pari" Series, High Fashion Ladies	175 - 200	200 - 225
"Twentieth Century Women"	140 - 150	150 - 160
Darmstadt Expo, 1902		
Lady Vignettes (6)	175 - 200	200 - 225

CHRISTY, F. EARL (U.S.A.)

F. Earl Christy was one of the leading artists who depicted the beauty of the American girl, especially of the college and university varieties. Most of his early works were in this category, as he helped start the tradition of glorifying the beauties of the era.

He pictured them as high classed, always beautifully dressed, and seemingly in complete command of the situation. These were the girls who attended football games, played golf and tennis, rode in new automobiles and were gifted with musical talent. His was the *All-American Girl*.

His first College Girl series was published by the U.S.S. Postcard Co. in 1905. This series revealed an artist with promising talents, and he went on to design many of the "College Girl" series for numerous publishers. Among his most popular works were the Raphael Tuck College Queens and College Kings series.

After the college/university girl fad had run its course, Christy used his many talents to paint beautiful ladies and man/woman lover types. The Reinthal & Newman Co. of New York was his major publisher; however, he did many fine sets for the Knapp Co., Edward Gross, and others. His images were also published and distributed in Europe and Scandinavia.

F. EARL CHRISTY

Reinthal & Newman
No Number Series

"Love"	12 - 15	15 - 18
"A Sandwitch"	12 - 15	15 - 18
"Be With You in a Minute"	10 - 12	12 - 15
"Always Winning"	15 - 18	18 - 22
"Love Dreams"	10 - 12	12 - 15
"Lovingly Yours"	10 - 12	12 - 15
"Swimming"	12 - 15	15 - 18
"A Sweet Surrender" Series		
168 "A Sweet Surrender"	12 - 15	15 - 18
169 "The Pilot"	12 - 15	15 - 18
170 "My Love is Like a Red, Red Rose"	12 - 15	15 - 18
171 "Come Sit Beside Me"	10 - 12	12 - 15
172 "Come With Me"	10 - 12	12 - 15
173 "Love All"	15 - 18	18 - 22
"The Siren" Series		
228 "Masks Off!"	10 - 12	12 - 15
229 "Lovingly Yours"	10 - 12	12 - 15
232 "The Siren"	12 - 15	15 - 18
276 "The Love Song"	10 - 12	12 - 15
277 "Love Dreams"	10 - 12	12 - 15
278 "The Love Story"	10 - 12	12 - 15
279 "The Love Match"	10 - 12	12 - 15
280 "The Love Waltz"	10 - 12	12 - 15
281 "Love"	10 - 12	12 - 15
Water Color Series		
281 "Love"	12 - 15	15 - 18
Water Color Series		
363 "A Bit of Tea & Gossip"	12 - 15	15 - 18
364 "The Sweetest of All"	12 - 15	15 - 18
365 "For the Wedding Chest"	12 - 15	15 - 18

366 "The Message of Love"	12 - 15	15 - 18
367 "The Day's Work"	15 - 18	18 - 22
368 "A Finishing Touch"	12 - 15	15 - 18
Series 428-433		
428 "What Shall I Answer?"	10 - 12	12 - 15
429 "I'm Waiting for You"	10 - 12	12 - 15
430 "Tender Memories"	10 - 12	12 - 15
431 "A Message of Love"	10 - 12	12 - 15
432 "On the Bridal Path"	10 - 12	12 - 15
433 "Always Winning"	15 - 18	18 - 22
Series 618-623		
618 "The Girl I Like"	10 - 12	12 - 15
619 "The Girl I Like to Chat With"	10 - 12	12 - 14
620 "The Girl I Like to Walk With"	10 - 12	12 - 15
621 "The Girl I Like to Flirt With"	10 - 12	12 - 15
622 "The Girl I Like to Play With"	15 - 18	18 - 22
623 "The Girl I Like to Sing With"	10 - 12	12 - 15
Series 624-629		
624 "By Appointment"	12 - 15	15 - 18
625 "As Promised"	12 - 15	15 - 18
626 "What Shall I Say?"	10 - 12	12 - 15
627 "A Sandwitch"	12 - 15	15 - 18
628 "With Fond Love"	10 - 12	12 - 15
629 "Nearest Her Heart"	10 - 12	12 - 15
Water Color Series 942-947	12 - 15	15 - 18
942 "Protected"		
943 "Someone is Thinking of You"		
944 "Are You There?"		
945 "Love, Here is My Heart"		
946 "Worth Waiting For"		
947 "Not Forgotten"		
ENGLISH REPRINTS	15 - 18	18 - 22
2106 "On the Bridal Path"		
2107 "Tender Memories"		
2109 "Nearest Her Heart"		
FAS (F.A. Schneider)		
197 Horseback Riding	15 - 18	18 - 25
198 Skates	15 - 18	18 - 25
199 Tennis	20 - 25	25 - 30
200 Golf	20 - 25	25 - 30
201 In an Auto	15 - 18	18 - 25
202 "What the Waves are Saying"	15 - 18	18 - 25
203 Daisies	15 - 18	18 - 25
Edward Gross		
Series 3		
"Black Eyed Susan"	10 - 12	12 - 15
"Gold is not All"	10 - 12	12 - 15
"Her Pilot"	10 - 12	12 - 15
"In Deep Water"	10 - 12	12 - 15

"Oldest Trust Co."
"World Before Them"
Knapp Co., N.Y. W. M. Sanford
Paul Heckscher Import

Series 304		12 - 14	14 - 16
1	"Annie Laurie"		
2	"The Lost Chord"		
3	"Louisiana Lou"		
4	"The Rosary"		
5	"The Largo"		
6	"Love's Old Sweet Song"		
7	"Daughter of the Regiment"		
8	"Good Night, Beloved"		
9	"The Gypsy Maid"		
10	"Maryland, My Maryland"		
11	"Home, Sweet Home"		
12	"Wish I Was in Dixie"		

Paul Heckscher Import W. M. Sanford

Miniature Image Series 304		12 - 15	15 - 18
(Same as above but with different Nos.)			
371	"Annie Laurie"		
381	"The Lost Chord"		
391	"Louisiana Lou"		
401	"The Rosary"		
411	"The Largo"		
421	"Love's Old Sweet Song"		
431	"Daughters of the Regiment"		
441	"Good Night, Beloved"		
451	"The Gypsy Maid"		
461	"Maryland, My Maryland"		
471	"Home, Sweet Home"		
481	"Wish I was in Dixie"		

Paul Hecksher Import

1025-3 "I'm Ready"	12 - 15	15 - 18
Others	12 - 15	15 - 18
103 Girl in Sailor Blouse and Hat	12 - 15	15 - 18
105 Girl with Lace Collar	12 - 15	15 - 18
114 Girl in Sailor Blouse	12 - 15	15 - 18
115 Beauty, with Pearl Necklace	12 - 15	15 - 18
116 Sweet Girl with Long Curl	12 - 15	15 - 18
119 Blonde Girl with Black Pearls	12 - 15	15 - 18
124 "Prudence"	10 - 12	12 - 15
169 "Let's Go"	12 - 15	15 - 18
176 "Skipper's Mate"	12 - 15	15 - 18

215 "Beauty"	10 - 12	12 - 15
219 "Anna Belle"	10 - 12	12 - 15

Note: There may be cards missing from
103 through 219.

Knapp Co.   H. Import Series 318   12 - 15   15 - 18
"The Best of Chums"
"Blossoming Affection"
"Goodbye Summer"
"The Springtime of Friendship"

Knapp Co.   H. Import Series 319   12 - 15   15 - 18
"Embracing the Opportunity"
"In Sweet Accord"
"The Message of the Rose"
"Tempting Fate"

Knapp Co. by Sanford
Calendar Card, 1916
"I Wish I Was in Dixie"   15 - 18   18 - 22

Jules Bien, 1907
College Series 95   15 - 18   18 - 22
Girl and Boy on Football
950 "Yale"
951 "Harvard"
952 "Columbia"
953 "Penn"
954 "Princeton"
955 "Cornell"

Atkinson News Agency
"Tilton Seminary"   25 - 30   30 - 35

Chapman, N.Y., 1910   10 - 12   12 - 14
1032 "A Brisk Walk"
1034 "Waiting Their Turn"
1039 "At the Horse Show"

William B. Christy (His Father)
Unnumbered Series   12 - 15   15 - 18
"Harvard"
"Michigan"
"Penn"
"Princeton"
"Yale"

EAS (Ea. Schwerd Teger)
Girl on Brick Wall Series   10 - 12   12 - 14
"Columbia"
"Cornell"
"Harvard"

"Penn"
"Princeton"
"Yale"

H. Henninger Co.

40	Driving		8 - 10	10 - 12
44	In an Auto (Same as **FAS** 201)		10 - 12	12 - 15
45	Daisies		10 - 12	12 - 15

Illustrated Postal Card & Novelty Co.

Series 133*   10 - 12   12 - 15
  1 "Cornell"
  2 "Harvard"
  3 "Yale"
  4 "Penn"
  5 "Princeton"
  6 "Columbia"

* With Silk Applique Dress, add $10-15.

Series 150*   10 - 12   12 - 15
  1 "Cornell"
  2 "Harvard"
  3 "Yale"
  4 "Penn"
  5 "Princeton"
  6 "Columbia"

* With Silk Applique Dress, add $10-15.

Note: Nos. are on backs of some cards.

Series 160, 1907   10 - 12   12 - 15
160-1 "A Drama"
160-2 "A Critical Moment"
160-3 "The World was Made ..."
160-4 "An Attractive Parasol"
160-5 "Getting Acquainted"
160-6

"Sports" Series

552D	Swinging	8 - 10	10 - 12
554	Bowling		
557	Rowing		
562	Swimming		
567	Driving Old Car		
569	Four Princeton Girls in Auto		
572	Golf	12 - 15	15 - 18
574	Princeton Belles in Old Car	8 - 10	10 - 12
577	Buggy		
582	Three Yale Girls in Auto		
584	Tennis	12 - 15	15 - 18

F. Earl Christy, Unsigned
1910 Calendar Card

F. Earl Christy, Pain. Karjalan
Kirjap. Oy, N:0 6

F. Earl Christy, R&N 429
"I Am Waiting for You"

F. Earl Christy
P. Sander 304-A -- No Caption

Ill. P.C. & Novelty Co.
 Series 5006   6 - 8   8 - 10
 1
 2
 3 "Swinging"
 4
 5
 6
 7
 8 Horse & Buggy
 9 Old Car-Harvard
 10 Old Car-Yale
 11 Old Car-Princeton
 12 Old Car-Penn

Platinachrome, 1907   18 - 22   22 - 27
 Girl/Pennant form Letter, College Yell
 "Chicago"
 "Columbia"
 "Cornell"
 "Harvard"
 "Michigan"
 "Penn"
 "Princeton"
 "Yale"

Platinachrome, © 1905 F. Earl Christy
 No Numbers or Captions

Two Women in a Car	8 - 10	10 - 12
Woman Golfing	12 - 15	15 - 18
Woman Bowling	8 - 10	10 - 12
Woman-Ice Hockey	8 - 10	10 - 12

P. Sander, N.Y., 1907 (Ill. P.C. Co.)
 Series 198

1	"Is a Caddie always necessary"	12 - 15	15 - 18
2	"Is horseback riding ..."	10 - 12	12 - 15
3	"Trying to make a hit"	10 - 12	12 - 15
4	"A Good Racquet for Two"	14 - 16	16 - 20
5	"Out for a catch"	10 - 12	12 - 15
6	"Hockey is not the only game"	12 - 15	15 - 18

P. Sander, N.Y., 1908
 Series 246 (6) Large Hats*

1	Full Photo	6 - 8	8 - 12
2	1910 Calendar	10 - 12	12 - 15
3	Christmas, Silver	5 - 6	6 - 8
4	Christmas, Gold	5 - 6	6 - 8

5	Woman in Easter Egg	5 - 6	6 - 8
6	Valentine	5 - 6	6 - 8

* Full card is signed; others cropped & uns.
  Note: There are 6 different cards of
        each image!
  Series 304-A (6) Signed, 1908

1	Full Card	8 - 10	10 - 12
2	Birthday, White	6 - 8	8 - 10
3	Birthday, Gold	6 - 8	8 - 10
4	Birthday, Silver	6 - 8	8 - 10
5	Woman in Egg	6 - 8	8 - 10
6	Valentine, Checkered	6 - 8	8 - 10
7	Valentine, Gold	6 - 8	8 - 10
8	Horse Shoe, Birthday, White	6 - 8	8 - 10
9	Horse Shoe, Birthday, Gold	6 - 8	8 - 10
10	Horse Shoe, Birthday, Silver	6 - 8	8 - 10

  Note: 10 different cards of each image!

W.H. Sanford   Series 371 — 12 - 15 — 15 - 18
  "Goodbye Summer"
  "Tempting Fate"

Stecher Litho Co., N.Y.
  Series 618, Valentines — 8 - 10 — 10 - 12
  A "To My Sweetheart"
  B "Valentine Thoughts" (Unsigned)
  C "To My Valentine" (Unsigned)
  D "A Valentine Greeting"
  F "A Valentine Greeting"

Souvenir Postcard Co., © 1907 E. Christy
  Girl and Football Player with Banner — 12 - 15 — 15 - 18
  1 "Michigan"
  2 "Chicago"
  3 "Princeton"
  4 "Penn"
  5 "Cornell"
  6 "Yale"
  7 "Harvard"
  8 "Columbia"

Raphael Tuck
  University Girl Series 2453 — 20 - 22 — 22 - 25
  "Oberlin College"
  "West Point"
  "Syracuse U."
  "Georgetown"
  "U.S. Naval Academy"

F. Earl Christy
R&N 280, "The Love Waltz"

F. Earl Christy
R&N 278, "The Love Story"

"Tennessee"		
Series 2590	20 - 22	22 - 25
"Iowa"		
"U. of Arkansas"		
"Valparaiso U."		
"Ames"		
"Kentucky"		
"Penn State"		
Series 2593	15 - 18	18 - 22
"Bucknell"		
"Colby"		
"U. of Maine"		
"U. of Notre Dame"		
Series 2717		
"Mary Baldwin Seminary"	15 - 18	18 - 22
University Girl Series 2625	15 - 18	18 - 22
"Columbia"		
"Cornell"		
"Harvard"		
"Penn"		
"Princeton"		

"Yale"
Series 2626   15 - 18   18 - 22
"U. of Chicago"
"U. of Illinois"
"Indiana U."
"U. of Michigan"
"U. of Minnesota"
"U. of Wisconsin"
Series 2627   15 - 18   18 - 22
"Brown U."
"Tulane of La."
"Vanderbilt U."
"U. of Virginia"
"Williston Seminary"
"McGill College"
Series 2766 College Kings   60 - 70   70 - 80
"Columbia"
"Cornell"
"Chicago"
"Michigan"
Series 2767 College Queens   60 - 70   70 - 80
"Yale"
"Penn"
"Harvard"
"Princeton"
"Good Luck" Series 2769   10 - 12   12 - 15
"Not only for today ..."
"Good luck attend you ..."
"Good wishes greet you ..."
"May Fortune spin ..."
Series 2794, "Williston"   90 - 100   100 - 125
Ullman Mfg. Co.
College Girls, Series 24, © 1905 (Uns.)   8 - 10   10 - 12
1498 "Penn"
1499 "Columbia"
1512 "Yale"
1513 "Harvard"
1514 "Leland Stanford"
1515 "Cornell"
1516 "Princeton"
1517 "Chicago"
College Football Players
Series 24, © 1905 (Unsigned)
1464 "Harvard"   8 - 10   10 - 12

1465	"Princeton"	12 - 15	15 - 18
1466	"Penn"	12 - 15	15 - 18
1467	"Yale"	12 - 15	15 - 18
1518	"Columbia"	12 - 15	15 - 18
1519	"Leland Stanford"	12 - 15	15 - 18
1520	"Chicago"	12 - 15	15 - 18
1521	"Cornell"	12 - 15	15 - 18

Ullman 1907

Girl in Big College Letter Series	12 - 15	15 - 18

1990 "Chicago"
1991 "Cornell"
1992 "Michigan"
1993 "Columbia"
1994 "Penn"
1995 "Yale"
1996 "Princeton"
1997 "Harvard"

Other **Ullman** College Girls	8 - 10	10 - 12

569 "Princeton"
574 "Penn"
575 "Harvard"
582 "Yale"

Ullman Co., 1905, N.Y.

501	"Golf"	10 - 12	12 - 15
506	"A Pleasant Ride"	4 - 6	6 - 8
507	"In Fair Japan"	4 - 6	6 - 8
1583	"The Graduate"	8 - 10	10 - 12
1583	Var. of "The Graduate" (with verse)	12 - 15	15 - 18
Series 93		8 - 10	10 - 12

U.S.S.P.C. Co. 1905 College Seal Series	10 - 12	12 - 15

1 "Penn"
2 "Princeton"
3 "Harvard" (also leather) *
4 "Yale"
5 "Michigan"
6 "Chicago"
7 "Columbia"
8 "Cornell"
* Add $5-10 for leather cards.

Valentine & Sons

"Artotype" Series, No Numbers	15 - 18	18 - 22

"Columbia"
"Penn"

Friedman-Shelby Shoe Co.
Big Hat Series

Shoe Style 3324	20 - 25	25 - 30
Shoe Style 3332	20 - 25	25 - 30
The Style 3151	20 - 25	25 - 30
Red Goose School Shoes	25 - 30	30 - 35
Shoe Style 3339	20 - 25	25 - 30

Greenfield's Delatour Chocolates, 1911

Girl W/Big Hat, Walks Right	25 - 30	30 - 35
Bulls-Eye Overalls	25 - 30	30 - 35

UNKNOWN

© 1910 F. Earl Christy	8 - 10	10 - 12

Bust of woman w/nosegay & big hat
Blue dress and pink flowers
Blue hat and red flowers
Orange hat and yellow flowers

Water Colors	10 - 12	12 - 15

650-5 "Embracing the Opportunity"
656-5 "In Sweet Accord"
657-5 "Vacation Days"

F. Earl Christy (Silk Applique)
Ill. Postal Card Co., 150-1

F. Earl Christy, R&N 2106
"On the Bridal Path"

FINNISH ISSUES

Pain. Karjalan Kirjap. Oy, Viipuri

N:0 12 Unsigned, no caption.		
Same as R&N 173, "Love All"	30 - 35	35 - 40
N:0 6 Signed, no caption.		
Girl in white, w/big red umbrella	30 - 35	35 - 40
No Identification Series		
Unsigned, no caption. Same as		
R&N 365, "For the Wedding Chest"	25 - 30	30 - 35

W. & G. American Series N:o 7001/1-35

Girl with long stemmed roses handing		
one to man behind the chair.	30 - 35	35 - 40

CHRISTY, HOWARD CHANDLER

Moffat, Yard, & Co., N.Y., 1905

"The Christy Post Card"

1 "Arbutus" (B&W)	8 - 10	10 - 12
2 "At the Opera"	10 - 12	12 - 14
3 "A City Girl" (B&W)	8 - 10	10 - 12
Also in partial color.	10 - 12	12 - 14
4 "The Dance"	10 - 12	12 - 14
5 "The Debutante"	10 - 12	12 - 14
6 "Encore"	10 - 12	12 - 14
7 "Mistletoe" (B&W)	8 - 10	10 - 12
Also in partial color.	10 - 12	12 - 14
8 "A Moment of Reflection"	10 - 12	12 - 14
9 "Reverie" (B&W)	8 - 10	10 - 12
10 "A Suburban Girl" (B&W)	8 - 10	10 - 12
11 "The Summer Girl" (B&W)	8 - 10	10 - 12
12 "Violets" (B&W)	8 - 10	10 - 12
Also in partial color.	10 - 12	12 - 14
13 "Waiting"	10 - 12	12 - 14
14 "Water Lilies" (B&W)	8 - 10	10 - 12
15 "The Winter Girl" (B&W)	8 - 10	10 - 12
Unnumbered Series, 1908		
"The American Queen"	10 - 12	12 - 14
"American Beauties"	10 - 12	12 - 14
"At the Theater"	10 - 12	12 - 14
"Canoe Mates"	8 - 10	10 - 12
"Drifting"	8 - 10	10 - 12
"Excess Baggage"	8 - 10	10 - 12
"A Fisherman's Luck"	10 - 12	12 - 14

"The Golf Girl"	14 - 16	16 - 20
"Lilies"	8 - 10	10 - 12
"On the Beach"	10 - 12	12 - 14
"Sailing Close"	8 - 10	10 - 12
"A Summer Girl"	10 - 12	12 - 14
"Teasing"	8 - 10	10 - 12
"A Winning Hand"	10 - 12	12 - 14
Series 3, 1909		
"Black-Eyed Susan"	8 - 10	10 - 12
"Gold is Not All"	8 - 10	10 - 12
"Her Pilot"	8 - 10	10 - 12
"In Deep Water"	10 - 12	12 - 14
"Miss Demure"	10 - 12	12 - 14
"The Oldest Trust Company"	8 - 10	10 - 12
"A Plea For Arbitration"	8 - 10	10 - 12
"The Sweet Girl Graduate"	10 - 12	12 - 14
"The Teasing Girl"	10 - 12	12 - 14
Series 4, 1909	10 - 12	12 - 14
"Au Revoir"		
"Congratulations"		
"The Heart of America"		
"Her Gift"		
"Honeymoon"		
"Into the Future"		
"Life's Beginning"		
"Love Spats"		
"Mistletoe"		
"Overpowering Beauty"		
"A Rose on the Lips"		
Edward Gross		
Series of 6	10 - 12	12 - 14
Scribner's		
Series of 8	10 - 12	12 - 14
Armour & Co, Chicago, 1901 Ad Card		
"The Howard Chandler Christy Girl"		
(B&W)	15 - 20	20 - 25
Same, by German Publisher (B&W)	20 - 25	25 - 30
A & V, Jamestown Expo., 1907		
"The Army Girl"	200 - 225	225 - 250
"The Navy Girl"	200 - 225	225 - 250
H. Choate & Co.		
Djer-Kiss Rouge & Face Power Compacts		
"American Brunette"	20 - 25	25 - 30
Curt Teich & Co.		
"Boy Scout Jamboree" (Linen, 1937)	10 - 12	12 - 15

T.P. & Co.
Judge Co., N.Y., Series 751

"You Have a Wonderful Future!"	12 - 14	14 - 16
"Going Away" (Unsigned)	12 - 14	14 - 16

FOREIGN
Novitas   Series 21655

"City Girl"	12 - 14	14 - 16
"Drifting"	12 - 14	14 - 16
"Reverie"	12 - 14	14 - 16
"A Summer Girl"	14 - 16	16 - 20
"Violets"	12 - 14	14 - 18
"The World Before Them"	12 - 14	14 - 18
Series 21657 (6)	12 - 14	14 - 18

Pain. Karjalan Kirjap. Oy, Viipuri

N:O 2 3 Bathing Girls	16 - 20	20 - 25

CLAY, JOHN C. (U.S.A.)
Detroit Pub. Co.

	8 - 10	10 - 12

Rotograph Co.

Water Color Series 160	30 - 35	35 - 40
"Garden of Love" Ser. (12) Head in Flowers		

Armour & Co., Advertising Card

"The John C. Clay Girl" (B&W)	10 - 12	12 - 15
Same, by German Publisher (B&W)	12 - 15	15 - 18

CLIRIO, L. (Italy) Art Deco   Series 29   15 - 18   18 - 22
COFFIN, HASKELL (U.S.A.)
R. C. Co. - Series 205

"A Modern Eve"	15 - 18	18 - 22
"An American Queen"	15 - 18	18 - 22
"The Glory of Autumn"	15 - 18	18 - 22
"The Lure of the Poppies"	15 - 18	18 - 22
"Miss Jack Frost"	20 - 22	22 - 25
"Motherhood"		
"Queen of the Court"		
"The Spring Maid"		
"Vanity Fair"		
"Winter's Charm"		

K. Co. - Water Color Series   15 - 18   18 - 20

215 "Beauty"
216 "Sally"
217 "Ruth"
218 "Billy"

Photo Color Graph Co.
Ser. 205 "Art Studies"

1 "Bohemia"	12 - 13	13 - 16

Haskell Coffin
K. Co. Inc., N.Y. 216, "Sally"

Haskell Coffin
K. Co. Inc., N.Y., "Motherhood"

2	"Miss Knickerbocker"	12 - 13	13 - 16
3	"Her First Love Letter"	12 - 13	13 - 16
4	"The Final Touch"	12 - 13	13 - 16
5	"Sweet Sixteen"	14 - 16	16 - 18
6	"Girl From the Golden West"	12 - 14	14 - 16
8	"Pride of the Orient"	12 - 14	14 - 16
9	"News from the Sunny South"	12 - 14	14 - 16
Others		12 - 13	13 - 16
"Flower & Figure" Semi-Nude Series 280		15 - 18	18 - 22
1	Iris		
2	Violet		
3	Poppies		
4	Narcissus		
5	Goldenrod		
6	Daffodils		
7	Hollyhock		
8	Water Lily		
9	Nasturtium		
10	Rose		
11	Sweet Pea		
12	Morning Glory		
Fantasy Women Series, Semi-Nude		15 - 18	18 - 22

"Celia"
Others
Advertising Cards

A. R. & C.i.B. Co.	12 - 15	15 - 18
417 "An American Queen"		
"The Glory of Autumn"		
"The Joy of the Hunt"		
"Miss Jack Frost"		
"Ruth"		
"Winter's Charm"		
"Vanity Fair"		
Blue Bell Brand Candies (2)	15 - 18	18 - 22
ESK Co.		
02 Girl with Big Slouch Hat, No Caption	12 - 14	14 - 18
H & S Company		
1551 D 3 "A New York Belle"	10 - 12	12 - 14
1551 D 6 "Thoughtful"	10 - 12	12 - 14
Others, With Captions	10 - 12	12 - 14
Others, No Captions	8 - 10	10 - 12
Hires Root Beer Girl	25 - 30	30 - 35
COLIN, PAUL	50 - 75	75 - 100
COLOMBO, E. (Italy) Art Deco and Glamour		
Dell, Anna & Gasparini; Uff. Rev. Stampa		
416 Couples, with Umbrella (6)	10 - 12	12 - 15
436, 451, 453 Hats (6)	15 - 18	18 - 22
228, 445, 560 High Fashion (6)	20 - 22	22 - 25
443, 522 High Fashion (6)	14 - 16	16 - 18
360, 419, 981 High Fashion	18 - 22	22 - 25
Series 178, 539, 925 High Fashion	18 - 20	20 - 22
Series 948 "Egyptian" (6)	15 - 18	18 - 20
Series 459 Heads (6)	14 - 16	16 - 18
Series 478 Dancers (6)	18 - 20	20 - 22
Series 894, 936 (6)	12 - 15	15 - 18
Golf/Tennis	18 - 20	20 - 22
Harlequins	18 - 20	20 - 22
Colonial-Style Deco Ladies, Lovers	12 - 15	15 - 18
Ladies & Dogs		
Series 330 (6)	12 - 14	14 - 18
Series 530, 894 (6)	15 - 16	16 - 20
Series 1165 (6)	15 - 16	16 - 20
Series 1494 (6)	10 - 12	12 - 16
Series 1763 (6)	15 - 16	16 - 18
Ladies & Horses		
Series 202 (6)	12 - 15	15 - 18
Series 488, 813 (6)	15 - 18	18 - 22

Series 1676, 1869 (6)	15 - 18	18 - 22

COMBAZ, GISBERT (Belgium) Art Nouveau
Dietrich, Brussels

"Elements" Series (12)	140 - 150	150 - 175
"Proverbs" Series (12)	140 - 150	150 - 175
"The Fishermen" Series (12)	150 - 175	175 - 200
"Sins" Series (12)	150 - 175	175 - 200

COPPING, H.   4 - 6   6 - 8

CORBELLA, TITO (Italy) Art Deco & Glamour
Dell, Anna & Gasparini; Uff. Rev. Stampa

Miss Edith Cavell Series	20 - 25	25 - 28
Series 127-M Small Images (6)	10 - 12	12 - 15
Series 162-M Small Image, Lovers (6)	8 - 10	10 - 12
Series 162, 355 (6)	14 - 16	16 - 20
Series 160, 203 High Fashion (6)	12 - 15	15 - 18
Series 408 Fans (6)	12 - 15	15 - 18
Series Chair and Fans (6)	16 - 18	18 - 22
Series 233, 356, 546, 718 Heads (6)	12 - 14	14 - 16
Series 130, 203, 763 High Fashion (6)	12 - 15	15 - 18
Series 282, 316, 317 Fashion (6)	12 - 14	14 - 18
Series 118, 324 Hats (6)	12 - 15	15 - 18
Series 357 Bear-Cupids (6)	14 - 16	16 - 20
Series 344, 467 High Fashion (6)	15 - 18	18 - 22
Series 236, 516 (6)	15 - 18	18 - 22
Series 162, 234, 269 Lovers-Kissing (6)	8 - 10	10 - 12
Series 225, 367, 531 Lovers-Kissing (6)	8 - 10	10 - 12

Degami

Series 319 (6)	16 - 18	18 - 22
Series 2249 "Gypsy" (6)	10 - 12	12 - 14
Series 2250 In Oval (6)	8 - 10	10 - 12
Series 2072 Outside (6)	12 - 14	14 - 16
Series 2214, 2224, 2228 (6)	15 - 18	18 - 22
Series 3016, 3055 (6)	15 - 18	18 - 22
Series 617 Lovers-Kissing (6)	8 - 10	10 - 12
Colonial-Style Deco Ladies, Lovers	12 - 15	15 - 18
Golf/Tennis	20 - 25	25 - 28
Erotic/Semi-Nudes	20 - 25	25 - 28

Ladies/Dogs/Horses
Uff. Rev. Stampa; Dell, Anna
& Gasparini, Degami

Series 117 (6)	12 - 15	15 - 18
Series 230 (6)	12 - 15	15 - 18
Series 233 (6)	15 - 18	18 - 22
Series 237, 316, 330 (6)	15 - 18	18 - 22
Series 335 (6)	12 - 15	15 - 18

Series 464, 624 (6)	12 - 15	15 - 18
Series 516, 578 (6)	15 - 18	18 - 22
Series 530, 1085 (6)	12 - 15	15 - 18
Series 532 (6)	15 - 18	18 - 22
Degami		
Series 636	22 - 25	25 - 30
Series 2224, 2258 (6)	22 - 25	25 - 30
Series 4646 (6)	15 - 18	18 - 22
COSTANZA, G. (Italy)		
Ladies	12 - 15	15 - 18
Comics/Erotic	12 - 15	15 - 18
CRAMER, RIE	10 - 12	12 - 15
CRANDALL, JOHN BRADSHAW		
K. Co., N.Y.	10 - 12	12 - 15
CREMIEUX, ED. (France) French Glamour		
Delta Series 44	15 - 18	18 - 22
Series 27	15 - 18	18 - 20
CROTTA		
Uff. Rev. Stampa		
Series 3029 Lovers Kissing (6)	8 - 10	10 - 12

T. Corbella (Glamour)
Dell, Anna & Gasparini 338-4

T. Corbella (Art Deco)
Degami 1088

CYRANICUS (Italy) Series 204 (6)	12 - 15	15 - 18
Ladies/Heads	12 - 15	15 - 18
Ladies/Fashion	12 - 15	15 - 18
Ladies/Animals	15 - 18	18 - 22
Ladies Golf/Tennis	15 - 18	18 - 22
Ladies & Horses		
Series 150 (6)	10 - 12	12 - 14
Series 430 (6)	12 - 14	14 - 16
DANIELL, EVA (GB) Art Nouveau		
Raphael Tuck		
Unsigned		
"Art" Series 2524 (6)	90 - 100	100 - 110
"Art" Series 2525 (6)	80 - 90	90 - 100
DAVIS, STANLEY (U.S.A.)	8 - 10	10 - 12
DAY, FRANCES (U.S.A.)	4 - 5	5 - 6
DEDINA, JAN (Poland)	10 - 12	12 - 15
DE FEURE, GEORGES Art Nouveau	25 - 35	35 - 40
DAY, FRANCES (U.S.A.)	4 - 5	5 - 6
DE MARZO (Art Deco)	22 - 25	25 - 35
DENNISON (U.S.A.	3 - 4	4 - 5
DERNINI, D. (Italy) Art Deco		
Ladies	15 - 18	18 - 22
DERRANTI, D. (Italy) Art Deco		
"Elite" Series 2568	25 - 30	30 - 35
DESCH, FRANK (U.S.A.)		
Knapp Co. Series 303	15 - 18	18 - 22
"Annette"		
"Diana"		
"Eloise"		
"Flora"		
"Florence"		
"Grace"		
"Ida"		
"Isabel"		
"Laura"		
"Lillian"		
"Violet"		
"Virginia"		
Knapp Co.		
Series 309	12 - 15	15 - 18
Series 50	10 - 12	12 - 15
Others	12 - 15	15 - 18
Knapp Co., Calendars	15 - 18	18 - 22
9443 "Grace"		

T. Corbella
Dell, Anna & Gasparini 335-5

T. Corbella
Degami 636

9453 "Rosina"		
9493 "Lillian"		
9503 "Laura"		
9513 "Felicia		
H. Import Co. Series 300	10 - 12	12 - 15
DEWEY, ALFRED (U.S.A.)		
Boston Sunday Post		
Romantic Baseball Series 22	10 - 12	12 - 15
"Caught Stealing"		
"A Costly Error"		
"A Double Play"		
"A Sacrifice"		
"A Single"		
"A Shut-Out"		
Reinthal & Newman		
"Weather Forecast" Series 221 (12)	7 - 8	8 - 10
"Eventful Hours" Series 270-275	8 - 10	10 - 12
"Mother & Child" Series 450-455	7 - 8	8 - 10
"Love Signal" Series 456-461	7 - 8	8 - 10
"Moon" Series 462-467	8 - 10	10 - 12
"Smoke" Series 668-673	8 - 10	10 - 12
"Love & Nature" Series 807-812	7 - 8	8 - 10

Colombo
Uff. Rev. Stampa

John Bradshaw Crandall
K. Co. 137, "The Bohemian Girl"

DeYONCH, JOHN (U.S.A.)	5 - 6	6 - 7
DIEFENBACH, K.	8 - 10	10 - 12
DIETZE (Ladies & Dogs)		
Series 6026	10 - 12	12 - 14
DIHLEN, CHARLES WEBER (U.S.A.)	5 - 6	6 - 7
DILLON, C. B. (U.S.A.)	6 - 8	8 - 10
DITZLER, H. (U.S.A.)		
Gibson Art - Water Color Series	6 - 8	8 - 10
DOBROWOLSKI, A. (Poland)		
MJK Seasons Series 282 (4)	10 - 12	12 - 15
DOCKER, E. (Austria) Art Nouveau		
Raphael Neuber, Vienna		
Head Series 26	50 - 60	60 - 75
Others	10 - 12	12 - 15
DOUBEK, F.		
Ackerman Co.		
"Historic Ladies" Series	10 - 12	12 - 15
DOUKY (France)		
Fantasy Fashions	12 - 15	15 - 18
E.D.F., Paris		
Series 505 Big Skirt (6)	12 - 14	14 - 16
Others	12 - 14	14 - 16

Frank H. Desch
The Knapp Co. 303-7, "Isabel"

Frank H. Desch
The Knapp Co. 303-5, "Grace"

Alice Fidler Person
E. Gross, American Girl No. 103

Pearle Fidler LeMunyan
E. Gross, American Girl No. 53

DRESSLER, A. E. (U.S.A.)	6 - 8	8 - 10
DUDOVICH, M. (Italy) Art Deco		
"Eureka" Series IV (6)	12 - 15	15 - 20
Early Deco Series	75 - 100	100 - 150
Lovers Series (in car; picnic)	30 - 35	35 - 40
Others	30 - 35	35 - 40
DuFRESNE, PAUL	4 - 6	6 - 8
DUNCAN, FREDERICK (U.S.A.)		
Reinthal & Newman		
Water color Series 930-935	12 - 15	15 - 18
K. Co.	12 - 15	15 - 18
M. & B.		
Series 1415 On Train -- his Hat (6)	10 - 12	12 - 14
Ladies & Dogs		
Reinthal & Newman		
931 "A Reserved Seat"	10 - 12	12 - 15
934 "Call of the Country"	10 - 12	12 - 15
ELLETTI (Italy) Art Deco		
Celesque Series National Ladies	15 - 20	20 - 25
ELLIOTT, KATHRYN (U.S.A.)		
Gartner & Bender Issues	6 - 8	8 - 10
G.O.M. Series 1986	10 - 12	12 - 15
ELLKA, G.		
M. Munk, Vienna		
Head Studies	10 - 12	12 - 18
FABIANO (France) Art Deco and Glamour		
Delta Series 5	12 - 15	15 - 18
Series 7, 11, 15	18 - 22	22 - 28
Series 32, 59, 63	15 - 18	18 - 22
M.L.E., Paris Series 63 At the Beach	15 - 18	18 - 22
FAINI (Italy)	10 - 12	12 - 14
FARINI, MAY L.		
Black & White Issues	5 - 6	6 - 8
With "Feliz Dia" Caption - Lady/Dog	6 - 8	8 - 10
Color Issues	10 - 12	12 - 16
FARKAS	3 - 4	4 - 5
FERRARIS, A.V.	8 - 10	10 - 12
FIDLER, ALICE LUELLA (U.S.A.)	10 - 12	12 - 16
(Also Alice Fidler Person)		
FIDLER, PEARLE EUGENIA	10 - 12	12 - 16
(Also Pearle Fidler LeMunyan)		
FIDLER, ELSIE CATHERINE	10 - 12	12 - 16
The Fidler Works by **E. Gross** and		
Ullman Mfg.		
FINNEMORE, J.	5 - 6	6 - 7

FISCHER, C. (U.S.A.)   6 - 8   8 - 10

FISHER, HARRISON (U.S.A.)

Harrison Fisher was one of the most prolific of all American illustrators. His works, mainly of beautiful women of the era, are desired by collectors throughout the world. The values of his postcards tend to rise almost yearly.

The principal publisher of Fisher postcards was the New York firm of Reinthal & Newman. They published many of his cards in various series ranging from the No-Numbered, the 100's, and on through the rare and final 900 series, and then did the English reprints in the 1000 and 2000 series.

The Detroit Publishing Company, beginning around 1905, published a small group of Fisher cards from what were originally illustrations for stories in the old *LIFE* magazine. The cards were numbered in the Detroit 14,000 series and were printed mainly in sepia, with a few being in black and white.

The American book publishers who used Fisher's illustrations in their novels issued postcards to advertise their books. These advertising postcards usually showed a beautiful Fisher lady on one-half of the double cards and an order form on the other half. These cards are among the most sought after and most expensive of his American-published cards.

Foreign publishers also did several series which are very much in demand. Among the most elusive, and those commanding the highest prices, are the cards produced in Finland and Russia.

    Detroit Publishing Co.*   12 - 15   15 - 18
        14028 "I don't see ..."
        14036 "An Important ..."
        14037 "So you don't Kiss ..."
        14038 "Between Themselves ..."
        14039 "Can you give your Answer?"
        14040 "I suppose you Lost ..."
        14041 "It's just Horrid ..."
        14042 "Wasn't There ..."
        14043 "And shall we Never ..."
        14044 "I fear there is no Hope"
     *   2 Different Varieties: 1 -- Information
          at Top and 1 -- Information at Bottom
    Book Adv. Cards (**G&D, Dodd-Mead**, etc.)
    Double-folded Cards, Entire Card   150 - 175   175 - 200

Harrison Fisher
R&N 418, "Ready and Waiting"

Harrison Fisher
R&N 302, "Behave!"

Harrison Fisher
R&N 876, "A Lucky Beggar"

Harrison Fisher
R&N 835, "All Mine"

With Reply Section Missing	125 - 150	150 - 175
"The Bill Tippers"		
"Featherbone Girl"		
"Half A Rogue"		
"The Hungry Heart"		
"Jane Cable"		
"Jewel Weed"		
"The Man From Brodney's"		
"My Lady of Cleeve"		
"Nedra"		
"The One Way Out"		
"A Taste of Paradise"		
"The Title Market"		
"To My Valentine"		
"The Goose Girl"		
"Francezka"		
"Commencement"		
Armour & Co., U.S. (B&W), Narrow Size	50 - 60	60 - 70
Armour & Co., German (B&W), Narrow	70 - 75	75 - 80
Warren's Featherbone Corsets		
"The Featherbone Girl"	80 - 90	90 - 100
Reinthal & Newman		
Unnumbered Series		
"After the Dance"	10 - 15	15 - 18
"The Critical Moment"	10 - 15	15 - 18
"The Motor Girl"	12 - 18	18 - 22
"Over the Teacup"	12 - 18	18 - 22
"Ready for the Run"	10 - 15	15 - 18
"Ruth"	10 - 15	15 - 18
"A Tennis Champion"	15 - 18	18 - 22
"The Winter Girl"	15 - 18	18 - 22
101 Series (12)		
"American Beauties"	10 - 15	15 - 18
"Anticipation"	10 - 15	15 - 18
"Beauties"	12 - 15	15 - 18
"Danger"	10 - 12	12 - 15
"A Fair Driver"	15 - 18	18 - 22
"Odd Moments"	12 - 15	15 - 18
"The Old Miniature"	12 - 15	15 - 18
"Over the Tea Cup"	15 - 18	18 - 22
"Reflections"	15 - 18	18 - 22
"The Study Hour"	12 - 15	15 - 18
"A Thoroughbred"	15 - 18	15 - 18
"Those Bewitching Eyes"	12 - 15	15 - 1

102 Series (6)	15 - 18	18 - 20
"American Girl in England"		
"American Girl in France"		
"American Girl in Ireland"		
"American Girl in Italy"		
"American Girl in Japan"		
"American Girl in Netherlands"		
103 Series (6)		
"At Home with Art"	12 - 15	15 - 18
"The Canoe"	12 - 15	15 - 18
"Engagement Days"	12 - 15	15 - 18
"Fisherman's Luck"	12 - 15	15 - 18
"Fore"	22 - 26	26 - 30
"Wanted, an Answer"	12 - 15	15 - 18
108 Series (12)		
"An Old Song"	12 - 15	15 - 18
"The Ambush"	12 - 15	15 - 18
"The Artist"	12 - 15	15 - 18
"The Bride"	20 - 22	22 - 26
"The Debutante"	15 - 18	18 - 22
"Dumb Luck"	15 - 18	18 - 22
"He's Only Joking"	15 - 18	18 - 22
"His Gift"	15 - 18	18 - 22
"The Kiss"	12 - 15	15 - 18
"Lost?"	15 - 18	18 - 22
"Oh! Promise Me"	15 - 18	18 - 22
"Song of the Soul"	15 - 18	18 - 22
"Two Up"	18 - 22	22 - 25
123 Series (6)		
"Making Hay"	12 - 15	15 - 18
"A Modern Eve"	15 - 18	18 - 22
"Taking Toll"	12 - 15	15 - 18
"You Will Marry a Dark Man"	12 - 15	15 - 18
"The Fudge Party"	15 - 18	18 - 22
"In Clover"	15 - 18	18 - 22
180-191 Series		
180 "Well Protected"	15 - 18	18 - 22
181 "The Rose"	15 - 18	18 - 22
182 "Miss Santa Claus"	22 - 25	25 - 30
183 "Miss Knickerbocker"	15 - 18	18 - 22
184 "Following the Race"	15 - 18	18 - 22
185 "Naughty, Naughty!"	20 - 22	22 - 25
186 "The Proposal"	10 - 12	12 - 15
187 "The Trousseau"	10 - 12	12 - 15

188 "The Wedding"	12 - 15	15 - 18
189 "The Honeymoon"	10 - 12	12 - 15
190 "The First Evening ..."	10 - 12	12 - 15
191 "Their New Love"	10 - 12	12 - 15
192-203 Series		
192 "Cherry Ripe"	15 - 18	18 - 22
193 "Undue Haste"	15 - 18	18 - 22
194 "Sweetheart"	15 - 18	18 - 22
195 "Vanity"	15 - 18	18 - 22
196 "Beauties"	15 - 18	18 - 22
197 "Lips for Kisses"	15 - 18	18 - 22
198 "Bewitching Maiden"	15 - 18	18 - 22
199 "Leisure Moments"	15 - 18	18 - 22
200 "And Yet Her Eyes..."	15 - 18	18 - 22
201 "Roses"	15 - 18	18 - 22
202 "In the Toils"	15 - 18	18 - 22
203 "Maid to Worship"	20 - 22	22 - 25
252-263 Series		
252 "Dreaming of You"	15 - 18	18 - 22
253 "Luxury"	15 - 18	18 - 22

Harrison Fisher
M.J.S. 024 (The Kiss)

Harrison Fisher
R&N 2091, "Sketching"

254 "Pals"	15 - 18	18 - 22
255 "Homeward Bound"	12 - 15	15 - 18
256 "Preparing to Conquer"	15 - 18	18 - 22
257 "Love Lyrics"	15 - 18	18 - 22
258 "Tempting Lips"	15 - 18	18 - 22
259 "Good Night"	12 - 15	15 - 18
260 "Bows Attract Beaus"	15 - 18	18 - 22
261 "Girlie"	15 - 18	18 - 22
262 "Beauty and Value"	15 - 18	18 - 22
263 "A Prairie Belle"	15 - 18	18 - 22
300 Series		
300 "Auto Kiss"	18 - 20	20 - 25
301 "Sweethearts Asleep"	22 - 25	25 - 30
302 "Behave!"	15 - 18	18 - 22
303 "All Mine!"	12 - 15	15 - 18
304 "Thoroughbreds"	20 - 22	22 - 25
305 "The Laugh is on You"	15 - 18	18 - 22
Water Color Series 381-392		
381 "All's Well"	15 - 18	18 - 25
382 "Two Roses"	15 - 18	18 - 25
383 "Contentment"	15 - 18	18 - 22
384 "Not Yet - But Soon"	12 - 15	15 - 18
385 "Smile Even if it Hurts"	15 - 18	18 - 22
386 "Speak!"	15 - 18	18 - 25
387 "Welcome Home"	12 - 15	15 - 18
388 "A Helping Hand"	15 - 18	18 - 22
389 "Undecided"	15 - 18	18 - 25
390 "Well Guarded"	15 - 18	18 - 25
391 "My Lady Waits"	15 - 18	18 - 25
392 "Gathering Honey"	15 - 18	18 - 22
400-423 Series		
400 "Looking Backward"	18 - 20	20 - 25
401 "Art and Beauty"	15 - 20	20 - 25
402 "The Chief Interest"	15 - 20	20 - 25
403 "Passing Fancies"	15 - 20	20 - 25
404 "The Pink of Perfection"	15 - 20	20 - 25
405 "He Won't Bite"	15 - 20	20 - 25
406 "Refreshments"	15 - 20	20 - 25
407 "Princess Pat"	18 - 22	22 - 28
408 "Fine Feathers"	15 - 20	20 - 25
409 "Isn't He Sweet?"	18 - 22	22 - 28
410 "Maid at Arms"	18 - 22	22 - 28
411 "He Cometh Not"	15 - 20	20 - 25
412 "Can't You Speak?"	18 - 22	22 - 28
413 "What Will She Say?"	15 - 20	20 - 25

By
HAROLD
MACGRATH

The
GOOSE
GIRL

Harrison Fisher
Book Advertisement, "The Goose Girl"

414 "Music Hath Charm"	15 - 20	20 - 25
415 "Do I Intrude"	15 - 20	20 - 25
416 "My Queen"	18 - 22	22 - 28
417 "My Lady Drives"	18 - 22	22 - 25
418 "Ready and Waiting"	15 - 20	20 - 25
419 "The Parasol"	15 - 20	20 420
420 "Tempting Lips"	15 - 20	20 - 25
421 "Mary"	18 - 22	22 - 25
422 "Courting Attention"	15 - 20	20 - 25
423 "My Pretty Neighbor"	18 - 22	22 - 28
600-617 Series		
600 "A Winter Sport"	20 - 25	25 - 30
601 "Winter Whispers"	20 - 25	25 - 30
602 "A Christmas Him"	20 - 25	25 - 30
603 "A Sprig of Holly"	20 - 25	25 - 30
604 "Snow Birds"	20 - 25	25 - 30
605 "A Christmas Belle"	20 - 25	25 - 30
606 "The Serenade"	20 - 25	25 - 30
607 "The Secret"	20 - 25	25 - 30
608 "Good Morning, Mama"	20 - 25	25 - 30
609 "A Passing Glance"	20 - 25	25 - 30
610 "A Fair Exhibitor"	20 - 25	25 - 30
611 "Paddling Their Own Canoe"	18 - 20	20 - 25
612 "Tea Time"	20 - 25	25 - 30
613 "The Favorite Pillow"	20 - 25	25 - 30
614 "Don't Worry"	20 - 25	25 - 30
615 "June"	20 - 25	25 - 30
616 "Sketching"	20 - 25	25 - 30
617 "Chocolate"	20 - 25	25 - 30
700-705 Water Color Series		
"The Senses"		
700 "The First Meeting" Sight	20 - 25	25 - 30
701 "Falling in Love" Smell	20 - 25	25 - 30
702 "Making Progress" Taste	20 - 25	25 - 30
703 "Anxious Moments" Hearing	20 - 25	25 - 30
704 "To Love and Cherish" Touch	20 - 25	25 - 30
705 "The Greatest Joy" Common Sense	20 - 25	25 - 30
762-773 Series		
762 "Alone at Last"	12 - 15	15 - 18
763 "Alert"	15 - 18	18 - 22
764 "Close to Shore"	15 - 18	18 - 22
765 "Looks Good to Me"	12 - 15	15 - 18
766 "Passers By"	12 - 15	15 - 18
767 "At the Toilet"	15 - 18	18 - 22

768 "Drifting" *	12 - 15	15 - 18
769 "Her Favorite Him" *	12 - 15	15 - 18
770 "The Third Party" *	12 - 15	15 - 18
771 "Inspiration" *	15 - 18	18 - 22
772 "Dangers of the Deep" *	12 - 15	15 - 18
773 "Farewell" *	12 - 15	15 - 18

*Add $5 to prices if German caption.
Cards usually are slightly oversized
and have Universal copyright.
800 Series

819 "Here's Happiness"	15 - 18	18 - 22

800 Series
Cosmopolitan/Star Bylines, etc.

832 "Wireless"	20 - 25	25 - 30
833 "Neptune's Daughter"	20 - 25	25 - 30
834 "Her Game"	20 - 25	25 - 30
835 "All Mine"	18 - 20	20 - 25
836 "On Summer Seas"	20 - 25	25 - 30
837 "Autumn's Beauty"	20 - 25	25 - 30
838 "The Only Pebble"	20 - 25	25 - 30
839 "A Love Score"	25 - 30	30 - 35
840 "Spring Business"	20 - 25	25 - 30
841 "The King of Hearts"	20 - 25	25 - 30
842 "Fair and Warmer"	20 - 25	25 - 30
843 "Baby Mine"	20 - 25	25 - 30
844 "Compensation"	20 - 25	25 - 30
845 "Sparring for Time"	20 - 25	25 - 30
846 "Confidences"	20 - 25	25 - 30
847 "Her Future"	20 - 25	25 - 30
848 "Day Dreams"	20 - 25	25 - 30
849 "Muriel"	20 - 25	25 - 30
856 "Song of the Soul"	15 - 20	20 - 25
860 "By Right of Conquest" *	18 - 22	22 - 25
861 "The Evening Hour" *	18 - 22	22 - 25
862 "Caught Napping" *	20 - 25	25 - 30
863 "A Novice" *	20 - 25	25 - 30
864 "Winners" *	20 - 25	25 - 30
865 "A Midsummer Reverie" *	25 - 30	30 - 35
866 "When the Leaves Turn" *	20 - 25	25 - 30
867 "Over the Teacup"	20 - 25	25 - 30
868 "A Ripening Bud" *	20 - 25	25 - 30
869 "I'm Ready" *	20 - 25	25 - 30

Harrison Fisher
B.K.W.I., Austria, No Caption

Harrison Fisher
R&N Series 101, "Beauties"

Harrison Fisher, Detroit Pub.
14028, "I Don't See Why ..."

Harrison Fisher
R&N 255, "Homeward Bound"

870 "Reflections" *	20 - 25	25 - 30
871 "Peggy" *	20 - 25	25 - 30
872 "Penseroso" *	20 - 25	25 - 30
873 "The Girl He Left Behind" *	20 - 25	25 - 30
874 "A Spring Blossom" *	20 - 25	25 - 30
875 "A Study in Contentment" *	20 - 25	25 - 30
876 "A Lucky Beggar" *	20 - 25	25 - 30
877 "Roses" *	20 - 25	25 - 30
* With Cosmopolitan Print Dept. Byline, add $5.		
900-979 Series		
970 "Chums"	75 - 100	100 - 125
971 "Cynthia"	75 - 100	100 - 125
972 "A Forest Flower"	75 - 100	100 - 125
973 "The Dancing Girl"	75 - 100	100 - 125
974 "Each Stitch a Prayer"	100 - 120	120 - 130
975 "The Sailor Maid"	100 - 120	120 - 130
976 "My Man"	100 - 120	120 - 130
977 "My Hero"	100 - 120	120 - 130
978 "Her Heart's in Service"	100 - 120	120 - 130
979 "Somewhere in France"	125 - 150	150 - 175
1001-1005 Series English Reprints		
1001 "Cherry Ripe"	25 - 28	28 - 32
1002 "Beauties"	25 - 28	28 - 32
1003 "Vanity"	25 - 28	28 - 32
1004 "Maid to Worship"	30 - 32	32 - 36
1005 "And Yet Her Eyes Can ..."	25 - 28	28 - 32
2000 Series English Reprints		
2040 "Love Lyrics"	22 - 25	25 - 28
2041 "A Fair Exhibitor"	25 - 28	28 - 32
2042 "Can't You Speak"	22 - 25	25 - 28
2043 "Serenade"	25 - 28	28 - 32
2044 "Undecided"	20 - 22	22 - 27
2045 "Behave!"	20 - 22	22 - 27
2046 "Princess Pat"	25 - 28	28 - 32
2047 "Good Little Indian"	18 - 22	22 - 27
2048 "Chocolate"	25 - 28	28 - 34
2049 "Beauty and Value"	22 - 25	25 - 28
2050 "Contentment"	22 - 25	25 - 28
2051 "Preparing to Conquer"	22 - 25	25 - 28
2053 "The Kiss"	15 - 20	20 - 25
2054 "What to See in America"	22 - 25	25 - 28
2069 "Paddling their own Canoe"	22 - 25	25 - 28
2076 "Good Morning, Mama"	22 - 25	25 - 28
2086 "The Pink of Perfection"	22 - 25	25 - 28

2087 "He Won't Bite"	25 - 28	28 - 32
2088 "Following the Race"	22 - 25	25 - 28
2089 "The Rose"	22 - 25	25 - 28
2090 "Well Protected"	22 - 25	25 - 28
2091 "Sketching"	25 - 28	28 - 32
2092 "Ready and Waiting"	22 - 25	25 - 28
2093 "The Parasol"	22 - 25	25 - 28
2094 "Courting Attention"	22 - 25	25 - 28
2095 "Mary"	22 - 25	25 - 28
2096 "Refreshments"	22 - 25	25 - 28
2097 "Isn't He Sweet?"	25 - 28	28 - 32
2098 "The Old Miniature"	22 - 25	25 - 28
2100 "Odd Moments"	22 - 25	25 - 28
2101 "Tea Time"	25 - 28	28 - 32
2102 "Good Night!"	22 - 25	25 - 28
2103 "A Prairie Belle"	22 - 25	25 - 28
Others	15 - 20	20 - 25

FOREIGN ISSUES

FINNISH

All Finnish cards are very rare and extremely elusive. None have the R&N Copyright and all are untitled. Cards are titled using names from similar R&N images. Several have not appeared as postcards and are named if a title is known. Three have been entitled by the author until the true title surfaces.

30/25 Series		
"Snowbird" *	200 - 225	225 - 250
"Merry Christmas" by author *	200 - 225	225 - 250
"Welcome Home," variety *	200 - 225	225 - 250
"A Midsummer Reverie"	200 - 225	225 - 250
"Close to Shore"	140 - 165	165 - 220
"Winners"	140 - 165	165 - 220
"My Hero"	140 - 165	165 - 220
"Winifred" *	140 - 165	165 - 220
"When the Leaves Turn"	125 - 150	150 - 175
"My Man"	125 - 150	150 - 175
"King of Hearts"	125 - 150	150 - 175
"Not Yet, But Soon"	125 - 150	150 - 175
"Autumn's Beauty"	125 - 150	150 - 175
"On Summer Seas"	125 - 150	150 - 175
"Baby Mine"	125 - 150	150 - 175
"Muriel"	120 - 140	140 - 165

"Caught Napping"	120 - 140	140 - 165
"Beauty and Value"	120 - 140	140 - 165
"Day Dreams"	120 - 140	140 - 165
"Stringing Them" * **	120 - 140	140 - 165
"All Mine"	120 - 140	140 - 165
"Two Roses"	120 - 140	140 - 165
"Reflections"	120 - 140	140 - 165
"Love Lyrics"	120 - 145	140 - 165
"An Idle Hour"	120 - 145	140 - 165

Note: For unsigned cards add $20-25 each.
* Has not appeared on any R&N postcard.
** From Bowers-Budd-Budd Book,
    "Harrison Fisher"
The N:O Numbered Series

N:O 5 "Playing the Game," Unsigned	200 - 250	250 - 300
N:O 10 "Midsummer Reverie," Untitled	175 - 200	200 - 250
N:O 4 "Close to Shore" (764)	165 - 190	190 - 240
N:O 7 "A Novice"(863)	165 - 225	190 - 225
N:O 11 "At the Toilet" (767)	165 - 190	190 - 225
N:O 13 "Welcome Home" (387)	165 - 190	190 - 225

W.&G. American Series No. 7001/1-35
Unsigned, no Numbers, no Captions

"Following the Race," (184)	165 - 190	190 - 250
"American Beauties" (101)	165 - 190	190 - 250
"Alert" (763)	165 - 190	190 - 250
"Yet Some Prefer Mountains" (571)	165 - 190	190 - 250
"At the Toilet" (767)	165 - 195	190 - 250

W.&G. American Series No. 7001/36-50
Unsigned, no Numbers, no Captions

"A Sprig of Holly" (603)	165 - 190	190 - 250
"The Favorite Pillow" (613)	165 - 190	190 - 250
"Girlie" (261)	165 - 190	190 - 250

W.&G. American Series No. 7031/1-7
Unsigned, no Numbers, no Captions

"Eavesdropping" * **	225 - 250	250 - 275

* Has not appeared on an R&N postcard.
** Titled by Author.

Pain. Karjalan Kirjap. Oy., Viipuri Series
Numbered, Unsigned, no Captions

N:O 5 "Playing the Game" *	225 - 250	250 - 275
N:O 10 "A Midsummer Reverie" (865)	175 - 200	200 - 250
N:O 4 "Close to Shore" (764)	160 - 190	190 - 235
N:O 7 "A Novice" (863)	160 - 190	190 - 235

* Has not appeared on an R&N postcard.

K.K. Oy N:O 1-20 Series
Signed, no Numbers, no Captions

"Mistletoe" * **	250 - 275	275 - 300
"Thoroughbreds" (304)	200 - 225	225 - 250

* Has not appeared on an R&N postcard.
** Titled by Author.

The Publisher at Polyphot Series
Unsigned, no Numbers, no Captions

"At the Toilet" (767)	150 - 175	175 - 225
"Eavesdropping" * **	225 - 250	250 - 275
"A Sprig of Holly" (603)	150 - 175	175 - 225
"Don't Worry" (614)	150 - 175	175 - 225
"Following the Race" (184)	150 - 175	175 - 225

* Has not appeared on an R&N postcard.
** Titled by the Author.

The "No Identification" Series
Unsigned, no Numbers, no Captions

"Autumn's Beauty" (837)	175 - 200	200 - 250
"Following the Race" (184)	175 - 200	200 - 250
"Contentment" (383)	175 - 200	200 - 250

Harrison Fisher
3025 Series, "Welcome Home"

Harrison Fisher, "Welcome Home"
N:0 Numbered Series

"The Only Pebble" (838)	175 - 200	200 - 250
The S & K Kouvola Rev. Image Ser.		
Unsigned, no Numbers, no Captions		
"Snowbird" *	225 - 250	250 - 300
"Winners" (864)	225 - 250	250 - 300
"Study in Contentment" (875)	225 - 250	250 - 300
The Real Photo Card Series		
Signed, no Numbers, no Captions		
"American Beauties," Series 101	75 - 85	85 - 100
"Daydreams" (848)	75 - 85	85 - 100
"Drifting" (768)	75 - 85	85 - 100
"A Novice" (863)	75 - 85	85 - 100
The Otto Andersin, Pori Series		
Unsigned, no Numbers, no Captions		
"All's Well"	225 - 250	250 - 300
"Close To Shore" (765)	225 - 250	250 - 300
"Drifting" (768)	225 - 250	250 - 300

Untitled Series, No Publisher

(With "Stamp Here" in Stamp Box)		
"Friends"	80 - 90	90 - 100
"Homeward Bound"		
"June"		
"Love Lyrics"		
"Sport"		
"To Walk"		
"Yet Some Men Prefer Mountains"		

RUSSIAN

"Richard" (Rishar, St. Petersburg

or Petrograde) Backs	100 - 150	150 - 175
No. 54 "Vanity"		
No. 117 "Hexenaugen"		
No. 824 "Made to Worship"		
No. 828 "Teacup Time"		
No. 830 "A Faste (Taste) of Paradise"		
No. 834 "Vanity"		
"May-Time"		
"Food for Thought"		
Other		
Russian-Polish Real Photo Types		

AWE With Russian/Polish Back

"Miss Knickerbocker" (183)	75 - 100	100 - 150
"Miss Santa Clause" (182)	75 - 100	100 - 150

Extremely Rare Harrison Fisher Poster
French Editions des Petites Affiches de Normandie - Rouen
Affiches De La Grande Guerre No. 11

Harrison Fisher
Anonymous Russian Real Photo
3223

Harrison Fisher
Untitled Series, "To Walk"

Others	75 - 100	100 - 150
Russian-English Backs		
No. 24 "Sport" (Following the Race)	75 - 100	100 - 150
Others	75 - 100	100 - 150
Apollon Sophia		
No. 21 "La Musique" (The Artist)	75 - 90	90 - 125
Others	75 - 90	90 - 125
Other Russian	75 - 100	100 - 125
No. 024 "Kuss" (Kiss)	75 - 80	85 - 90
Linen, No. 192 "Cherry Ripe"	100 - 125	125 - 150

GERMAN-AUSTRIAN

B.K.W.I., Austria		
No No., No Caption "Naughty, Naughty"	125 - 140	140 - 160
MEU		
"A Critical Moment"	100 - 110	110 - 135
"In the Country" (R&N 131)	70 - 75	75 - 80
MEU/Alfred Schweizer		
Either or Both, No Captions	75 - 100	100 - 125
"Vienne" Series 806	60 - 75	75 - 80
JTK "Kron-Trier" Series	60 - 75	75 - 80
M.J.S.		
"The Kiss" (No Caption) (108 Series)	40 - 50	50 - 60
Utig de Muick, Amsterdam		
"The Honeymoon" (224)	60 - 75	75 - 90
Friedrich O. Wolter		
"Peggy" (871)	60 - 75	75 - 90

FRENCH

Affiches De La Grande Guerre, No. 11	450 - 500	550 - 600

FLAGG, JAMES MONTGOMERY (U.S.A.)

Detroit Publishing Co.		
B&W 14000 Series	8 - 10	10 - 15
14011 "The Sweet Magic of Smoke"		
14149 "Sir Charles"		
14150 "It Certainly Wasn't"		
14151 "For Heaven's Sake"		
14152 "So Sensible"		
14153 "Not Bad to Take"		
14154 "Beyond More Conjecture"		
14155 "A Cold Proposition"		

14156	"If You Get Gay"		
14157	"If You're a Perfect Gent"		
14158	"Make it Pleasant for Him"		
Henderson Litho		6 - 8	8 - 10
501	"Engaged - His Attitude"		
2503	"Something on Account"		
Reinthal & Newman			
"Miss Behaving" Series		12 - 14	14 - 16
288	"A Club Sandwich"		
289	"Putting Out the Flames"		
290	"Miss Behaving!"		
291	"The Most Exciting Moment"		
292	"The Real Love Game"		
293	"Dry Goods"		
TP & Co., N.Y.			
Series 738 Sepia			
"Trouble Somewhere"		8 - 9	9 - 10
Series 751			
"The Hypnotist"		10 - 12	12 - 14
"The Only Way to Eat an Orange"		10 - 12	12 - 14
"Say When"		10 - 12	12 - 14
Series 818-8 "Holding Hands"		10 - 12	12 - 14
Series 818-10			
"In The Hands of the Receiver"		10 - 12	12 - 14
FONTAN, LEO (France) French Glamour			
Series 17, 80		20 - 25	25 - 30
Series 23, 95, 5016		15 - 18	18 - 22
FOSTER, F.D. (U.S.A.)		4 - 5	5 - 6
FRANZONI, ROBERTO (Italy) Art Deco			
Dell, Anna & Gasparini; Uff. Rev. Stampa			
Series 44 Heads (6)		12 - 14	14 - 18
Series 78 Hands/Head		12 - 15	15 - 18
Series 4358 Fashion - Windy Day (6)		15 - 18	18 - 20
Ladies/Fashion		12 - 15	15 - 18
Erotic/Semi-Nudes		18 - 20	20 - 22
Golf/Tennis		18 - 20	20 - 22
Ladies & Dogs			
B.K.W.I.			
Series 369 (6)		10 - 12	12 - 15
Series 6309 (6)		12 - 15	15 - 18
P.R.S.			
Series 50 (6) High Fashion			
FREDILLO (France) Art Nouveau		25 - 30	30 - 35
FREIXAS, J. (U.S.A.)			
Winsch, Copyright		20 - 25	30 - 40

FREYSCHLAG, G.	3 - 4	4 - 5
FRUNDT, H. (Art Nouveau)	25 - 30	30 - 35
GALLAIS, P. (France) French Glamour		
Semi-Nude Series	20 - 22	22 - 26
GAYAC (France) French Glamour		
Series 290	18 - 20	20 - 25
GERBAULT, H. (France) French Glamour		
Series 36	15 - 18	18 - 22
GIBSON, CHARLES DANA (U.S.A.)		
Detroit Publishing Co.		
B &W 14000 Series		
14000 "Has She a Heart?"	8 - 10	10 - 12
14003 "Their Presence of Mind"	8 - 10	10 - 12
14004 "Melting"	8 - 10	10 - 12
14005 "When Hunting ..."	8 - 10	10 - 12
14006 "Last Days of Summer"	8 - 10	10 - 12
14008 "The Dog"	8 - 10	10 - 12
14009 "Who Cares"	8 - 10	10 - 12
14017 "Good Game for Two"	10 - 12	12 - 14
14019 "Here it is Christmas"	8 - 10	10 - 12
14029 "The Half Orphan"	8 - 10	10 - 12
14046 "Bathing Suits"	8 - 10	10 - 12
14048 "The Half Orphan"	8 - 10	10 - 12
14050 "America Picturesque"	8 - 10	10 - 12
14051 "The Stout Gentleman"	8 - 10	10 - 12
14052 "No Wonder the Sea Serpent ..."	8 - 10	10 - 12
14054 "Stepped On"	8 - 10	10 - 12
14055 "Mr. A Merger Hogg ..."	8 - 10	10 - 12
14057 "Ill Blows the Wind ..."	8 - 10	10 - 12
14059 "Rival Beauties"	8 - 10	10 - 12
14065 "The Gibson Girl"	12 - 15	15 - 18
14066 "Jane"	10 - 12	12 - 15
14067 "Mabel"	10 - 12	12 - 15
14068 "Amy"	10 - 12	12 - 15
14069 "Eleanor"	10 - 12	12 - 15
14070 "Margaret"	10 - 12	12 - 15
14071 "Molly"	10 - 12	12 - 15
14072 "Helen"	10 - 12	12 - 15
14074 "The Sporting Girl"	12 - 15	15 - 18
14185 "The Eternal Question"	10 - 12	12 - 15
James Henderson & Sons		
Sepia Heads	8 - 10	10 - 12
"Annie"		
"Clorinda"		

"Gladys"		
"Maude"		
"Nina"		
"Peggy"		
"Beatrice"		
"Bertha"		
"Eileen"		
James Henderson & Sons		
Comic Series (36)	5 - 6	6 - 8
Schweizer & Co.		
Embossed, Sepia Series	10 - 15	15 - 18
Pictorial Comedy Series	10 - 12	12 - 15
GIGLIO	4 - 6	6 - 8
GILBERT, C. ALLEN (U.S.A.)	5 - 6	6 - 8
Calendar, 1911	6 - 8	8 - 10
Taylor-Platt Issues	6 - 8	8 - 10
GILLEY (Art Deco)		
Paris Gravure		
Series 1961, 1971 Semi-Nudes	10 - 12	12 - 15
GNISCHAF, RUAB (Germany)	6 - 8	8 - 10
GOBBI, D. (Italy) Art Deco		
Majestic		
Series 2546, Chinese Dragon	15 - 18	18 - 22
Ladies	22 - 25	25 - 28
Gondola/Lovers	18 - 20	20 - 25
Series 1216	12 - 15	15 - 18
Series 2474 Harlequins	18 - 22	22 - 26
Series 2477	15 - 18	18 - 22
Series 2479	12 - 15	15 - 18
Series 2494	15 - 18	18 - 22
Series 2530, 2556, 2560	20 - 25	25 - 28
Elite		
Series 2631	12 - 15	15 - 18
Series 2550	18 - 20	20 - 22
GODELA, D. (Italy)		
Series 272 Head Studies	12 - 15	15 - 18
Series 296 Head Studies	12 - 15	15 - 18
D.A.G. Series 409 In Oval - Sitting (6)	8 - 10	10 - 12
GRAF, MARTE or MG		
Art Deco & Silhouettes		
Deco Silhouettes Series 733-758	8 - 12	12 - 15
Other Deco Silhouettes	10 - 12	12 - 15
GRANDE (Italy) Art Deco and Glamour		
Series 437 (6)	12 - 15	15 - 18
GRASSET, EUGENE (Swiss) Art Nouveau	100 - 110	110 - 125

Collection Cinos	125 - 135	135 - 145
Collection des Cent	500 - 550	550 - 600
GREENE, FREDERICK (U.S.A.)	5 - 6	6 - 7
GREFE, WILL (U.S.A.)		
Moffat, Yard Co.		
Playing Card Queens	15 - 18	18 - 22
"Club"		
"Diamond"		
"Heart"		
"Spade"		
Moffat, Yard Co. Series 3	10 - 12	12 - 15
GREINER, MAGNUS (U.S.A.)		
Auburn Publishing Co., Pennant Series	5 - 6	6 - 8
Anonymous German Series 1500	8 - 10	10 - 12
GRILLI, S. (Italy) Art Deco		
GRIMBALL, M.M. (U.S.A.)		
Gutmann & Gutmann	15 - 20	20 - 25
GROSS, BELLA	5 - 6	6 - 8
GROSZE, MANNI (Italy)		
Art Deco Silhouettes		
Deco Series 2041 Nudes	15 - 18	18 - 22
PFB (In Diamond)		
Series 2042, Nudes	15 - 18	18 - 22
Series 3339, Nudes	18 - 20	20 - 22
Series 2052, Dancing	12 - 15	15 - 18
Others	12 - 15	15 - 18
GUARINO, ANTHONY	4 - 5	5 - 6
GUARNERI (Italy) Art Deco		
Ladies	15 - 18	18 - 22
GUERZONI, G. (Italy)		
Art Deco and Glamour		
Ladies/Heads/Fashion	7 - 9	9 - 12
Ladies/Animals	10 - 12	12 - 15
Erotic/Semi-Nudes	10 - 12	12 - 18
Ladies & Dogs	10 - 12	12 - 15
Ladies & Horses		
B.K.W.I.		
Series 710 (6)	8 - 10	10 - 12
GUILLAUME, A. (France) Art Nouveau	75 - 100	100 - 125

GUNN, ARCHIE   (British)

Archie Gunn was born in England and began painting portraits at
an early age. His first works were very impressive, and he was
commissioned to do portraits of some important Earls and Prime

Archie Gunn
Taylor-Platt, Am. Beauty Series

Archie Gunn
Taylor-Platt, Am. Beauty Series

Ministers. Upon graduation from college and from the Art Academy in London, he began designing posters for some of London's principal theaters.

Archie migrated to New Rochelle, New York in 1888 at the age of 25. There he made his home and began illustrating magazines, did some portrait painting and magazine covers, as well as posters for some of the New York play productions. Later, during the postcard era, he painted beautiful ladies that were adapted for postcards. His postcards were published by National Art, Philip Sander, Novelty Mfg. & Art Co., and the Illustrated Postal Card Co.

Archie Gunn was not as well known as Boileau, Fisher, the Christys and Underwood, but today's collectors are finding that his work is very beautiful and they have now begun collecting his cards in earnest.

J.Bergman
Black & White Series (6)		5 - 6	6 - 7

National Art Co.
13	"Bowling Girl"	8 - 10	10 - 12
14	"Tennis Girl"	12 - 14	14 - 18
15	"Skating Girl"	8 - 10	10 - 12

16 "College Mascot"	7 - 9	8 - 9
"City Belles" Series		
33 "Miss New York"	8 - 10	10 - 12
34 "Miss Philadelphia"	8 - 10	10 - 12
35 "Miss Boston"	8 - 10	10 - 12
36 "Miss Chicago"	8 - 10	10 - 12
37 "Miss Pittsburg"	8 - 10	10 - 12
39 "Miss Toronto"	8 - 10	10 - 12
40 "Miss Washington"	8 - 10	10 - 12
41 "Miss Seashore"	8 - 10	10 - 12
71 "Miss Milwaukee"	8 - 10	10 - 12
72 "Miss Detroit"	8 - 10	10 - 12
77 "Miss Cleveland"	8 - 10	10 - 12
87 "Miss San Francisco"	8 - 10	10 - 12
90 Untitled	6 - 8	8 - 9
"Clans"	7 - 8	8 - 10
"College Belles"	10 - 12	12 - 14
"National Belles"	10 - 12	12 - 14
214 "Lady & the Bear"	8 - 10	10 - 12
217 "Devotion"	8 - 10	10 - 12
219 "Yuletide"	8 - 10	10 - 12
220 "Sables"	8 - 10	10 - 12
221 "Ermine"	8 - 10	10 - 12
223 "Automobiling"	8 - 10	10 - 12
276 "The Fencer"	8 - 10	10 - 12
277 "On Guard"	8 - 10	10 - 12
Full-Length Santa	12 - 15	15 - 20

Illustrated Postal Card & Novelty Co.

WWI Army Series 1368 (12)	6 - 8	8 - 10

"The American Spirit"
"Army, Navy, and Reserves"
"Don't Worry About Me"
"If Wishes Came True"
"Lest We Forget"
"None but the Brave Deserve ..."
"Pals"
"Parting is Such Sweet Sorrow"
"Repairing a Man of War"
"Rosemary! That's for Remembrance"
"Shoulder Arms"
"When the Last Goodbyes are Whispered"

WWI Army Series 1371 (12)	6 - 8	8 - 10

"A Parting Message"
"Hello! I Haven't Heard from You"
"Don't Worry, We're Alright"

"Guardian Spirits"
"Letters are Always Welcome"
"Liberty and Union Now and Forever"
"Pleasant Memories"
"The Rose for Remembrance"
"Sentry Moon"
"Warmth in the Camp and ..."
"We Won't Come Back Till it's Over ..."
"Worthwhile Fighting For ..."

Taylor-Platt

American Beauty Series (6)	8 - 10	10 - 12
Statler Calendar Cards, 1912 (12)	6 - 8	8 - 10

Anonymous

B&W   No Captions

Girl Holding Basketball	8 - 10	10 - 12
Girl Wading in Water	6 - 8	8 - 10
Girl at Wheel of Sail Boat	6 - 8	8 - 10
Girl Holding Golf Club	8 - 10	10 - 12
Girl Holding Golf Club, but in Color	10 - 12	12 - 14
Beautiful Lady, Red Bow, Red Dress	6 - 8	8 - 10
Beautiful Lady, Pink Bow, Pink Dress	6 - 8	8 - 10
Beautiful Lady, Bust, Holding 3 Roses	6 - 8	8 - 10
B&W/Sepia, Women, No Captions (3)	5 - 6	6 - 7

Lowney's Chocolates

Golf Girls Series (6)	12 - 14	14 - 18
HAGER, NINI (Austria) Art Nouveau	100 - 125	125 - 150

H.G.R. (Art Nouveau)

Series 316 (6)	25 - 30	30 - 35

HAMMICK, J.W. (GB)

Photocom "Celesque" Series

531 "The Motor Girl"	10 - 12	12 - 15
532 "The Society Girl"	10 - 12	12 - 14
533 "The Ball Room Girl"	10 - 12	12 - 15
534 "The Sporting Girl"	12 - 15	15 - 18
535 "The Sea Side Girl"	10 - 12	12 - 15
HAMPEL, WALTER (Austria) Art Nouveau	75 - 100	100 - 150
HARBOUR, JENNIE	12 - 15	15 - 18

HARDY, HAYWARD (G.B.) Art Deco

Ladies	8 - 10	10 - 12
Ladies/Animals	10 - 12	12 - 15
Harlequins	12 - 14	14 - 18
Erotic/Semi-Nudes	15 - 18	18 - 22

HARE, J. KNOWLES (U.S.A.)

Empire Art, Series 112	6 - 7	7 - 8
P. Heckscher, Series 1009 (6)	10 - 12	12 - 14

1 "Eugenie"		
2 "Rosamond"		
3 "Beryl"		
4 "Clarice"		
5 "Madeline"		
6 "Charmion"		
Series 1026 (6)	8 - 10	10 - 12
M&H Fine Woolens	10 - 12	12 - 15
Statler Advertising Cards, 1912 (13)	12 - 14	14 - 16
HARPER, R. FORD		
Reinthal & Newman Water color Series		
350 "Peg O' My Heart"	8 - 12	12 - 16
351 "My Summer Girl"	8 - 12	12 - 16
352 "Love's Locket"	8 - 12	12 - 16
353 "True Blue"	12 - 14	14 - 18
354 "The Favorite Flower"	12 - 14	14 - 18
355 "Miss Innocence"	8 - 12	12 - 16
Gibson Art Co. Issues	8 - 10	10 - 12
P. Herkscher		
Series 1010	10 - 15	15 - 18
Series 1013	10 - 15	15 - 18
Series 1025	10 - 15	15 - 18
P. Sander		
Lady Santa Claus (4)	35 - 40	40 - 50
HART, JOSEF (Germany) Art Nouveau	25 - 30	30 - 35
HARRISON (U.S.A.)	6 - 7	7 - 8
HARTLEIN, W.	4 - 5	5 - 6
HAVILAND, F.	4 - 6	6 - 8
HAYDEN, A.E.	3 - 4	4 - 5
HEINZE, A.	5 - 6	6 - 8
HELLI (ICART) (France) French Glamour		
Series 153 (6)	60 - 70	70 - 80
HEROUARD (France) French Glamour		
Series 55, 300	20 - 25	25 - 30
HERSCHEL, OTTO (Austria)	6 - 8	8 - 10
HERVE, G.		
Lapina		
Series 5064 "Smoker"	6 - 8	8 - 10
HILDER, G. HOWARD		
Platinachrome		
National Girl Series	6 - 8	8 - 10
HILLSON, D.		
Girl Series in Red & Black (23)	6 - 8	8 - 10
HOCK, F. (Art Nouveau)	30 - 35	35 - 40

Maude Humphrey, Unsigned
Gray Litho. Co., No. 3-A

Henry Hutt
H&S, No Caption

HOFER, A.	6 - 8	8 - 10
HOFFMAN, JOSEF (Art Nouveau)	150 - 200	200 - 300
"Ver Sacrum"	1000 - 1500	1500 - 2500
HOHENSTEIN, A. (Russia) Art Nouveau		
1901 Milano Int. Expo Series	30 - 35	35 - 40
HOLZMAN, A.	6 - 8	8 - 10
HOROWITZ, H.		
Raphael Tuck		
Series 1 "A Dream of Fair Women" (6)	8 - 10	10 - 12
HORRELL, CHARLES	4 - 6	6 - 8
HORSFALL, MARY (British)	6 - 8	8 - 10
Ladies & Horses	8 - 10	10 - 12
HUMPHREY, MAUD		
Gray Litho. Co., N.Y. (G. in Diamond)	15 - 17	17 - 22
(All her lady postcards are unsigned.)		
P.C. 10 through P.C. 16		
P.C. 18, P. C. 20, P.C. 25,		
P.C. 36, P.C. 37, P.C. 37A, P.C. 38		
P.C. 113, P.C. 135, P.C. 139, P.C. 141		
Others		

HUNT, ESTHER
   National Art Co.

9-12 Little Chinese Girls	5 - 6	6 - 7

HUNTER, LILLIAN W. (U.S.A.)   6 - 8   8 - 10
HUTT, HENRY (U.S.A.)
   Detroit Publishing Co.

B&W 14000 Series	8 - 10	10 - 12
14202 "Sincerity"		
14203 "Curiosity"		
14204 "Tired of Life"		
14205 "Expectancy"		
14207 "Frivolity"		
14208 "Courageous"		
14209 "Shy"		
14211 "Pleasure"		
14212 "Joy"		
14213 "Whimsical"		

   H & S, Germany   10 - 12   12 - 15

ICART, LOUIS (France) French Glamour

Lady & Black Dog	60 - 80	80 - 100
Series 48 (6)	60 - 70	70 - 80
"L'Eternal Feminin" (6)	125 - 150	150 - 175

ICHNOWSKI, M. (Poland)   10 - 12   12 - 15
IRIBE, PAUL   150 - 175   175 - 200
JANK, ANGELO (Germany) Art Nouveau   25 - 30   30 - 35
JANKE, URBAN
   Wiener Werkstätte   150 - 200   200 - 250
JANTSY-HORVATH, C.   5 - 6   6 - 8
JARACH, A. (France) French Glamour

Delta Series 156, 158	18 - 20	20 - 22
Series 18	18 - 20	20 - 25

JAY, CECIL   5 - 8   8 - 10
JIRASEK, A.J. (Austria)   4 - 5   5 - 7
JONES, J. (U.S.A.)
   P. Gordon, 1908

"Opera Girl"	6 - 7	7 - 8
"Vacation Girl" (Unsigned)	4 - 5	5 - 6
College Girl Series	6 - 7	7 - 8

JOSSOT, HENRI (France) Art Nouveau   100 - 200   200 - 300
JOZSA, KARL (Austria) Art Nouveau
   A. Sockl, Wien

"Femme au Coeur"	70 - 80	80 - 90
"Sirens and Circeans" Series (6)	200 - 225	225 - 250

E.S.D.B., Austria
 "Coeur Dame" Series (6)   60 - 70   70 - 80
Simon Steffans
 "Smoke Rings" Series (6)   110 - 115   115 - 120
JUNG, ORITZ (Czech) Art Nouveau
 Wiener Werkstätte
  339, Aeroplanes & Giraffes   800 - 850   850 - 900
  529, Wiener Cafe   650 - 700   700 - 800
KABY   4 - 6   6 - 8
KAINRADL, L. (Germany) Art Nouveau   75 - 100   100 - 250
KALHAMMER, G.
 Wiener Werkstätte   200 - 250   250 - 300
KALOUS, GRET   6 - 8   8 - 10
KALVACH, RUDOLPH (Austria)
 Art Nouveau (WW)   1000 - 1500   1500 - 2500
KASKELINE, F.
 Deco/Silhouettes   12 - 15   15 - 18
 S.W.S.B.
  Ladies and Horses Series 1119   10 - 12   12 - 15
KATINKA (Sweden) Art Deco   10 - 12   12 - 15
KAVAL, M. (France) Art Deco
 Lapina, Paris   12 - 14   14 - 16
  Series 5027, 5029, 5030 Hats (6)
  Series 5031, 5032 Hats (6)
  Series 5034, 5036 Hats (6)
KELLER, A.I.
 Historical Sweethearts Series   4 - 5   5 - 6
 "The Introduction"
 "The Wooing of Anne Hathaway"
 "The Proposal"
 "The Wedding"
 Others   4 - 5   5 - 6
KEMPF, TH. (Austria) Art Nouveau   30 - 40   40 - 50
KENYON, ZULA   6 - 8   8 - 12
KIEFER, E.H. (GB)
 Bamforth & Co.   6 - 8   8 - 12
  "Could You Be True"
  "Dear Heart"
  "Good Bye"
  "I'm Growing Fond of You"
  "Love a Lassie"
  "My Chum"
  "There's Nobody Like You"
  "You Know You're Not Forgotten"

"Waiting For You"
"When Dreams Come True"
"When You Feel Dreamy"
"When You Feel Naughty ..."
"When You're Traveling ..."
"When Your Heart Aches ..."
"Would You Care"
"Would You Learn to Love Me"

KIENERK, G. (Art Nouveau)		
"Cocorico"	450 - 500	500 - 600
KIEZKOW (Art Nouveau)	70 - 75	75 - 80
KIMBALL, ALONZO (U.S.A.)		
Reinthal & Newman		
Series 122, Lovers	6 - 8	8 - 10
KING, HAMILTON (U.S.A.)		
Coca Cola Girl (Advertising Card)	700 - 900	900 - 1000
Coca Cola Motor Girl	1000 - 1200	1200 - 1500
E. Gross		
American Girls	8 - 10	10 - 12
Bathing Beauties (12)	15 - 20	20 - 25
"Asbury Park Girl"		
"Atlantic City Girl"		
"Bar Harbor Girl"		
"Cape May Girl"		
"Coney Island Girl"		
"Long Beach Girl"		
"Larchmont Girl"		
"Manhattan Beach Girl"		
"Narragansett Girl"		
"Newport Girl"		
"Palm Beach Girl"		
"Ocean Grove Girl"		
KING, JESSIE M. (G.B.) Art Nouveau	60 - 70	70 - 80
KINNEYS, THE (U.S.A.)	6 - 8	8 - 10
KIRCHNER, RAPHAEL (Austria)		
Art Deco		
Reinthal & Newman		
Later Period		
"Pierrot's Lovers" (10)	80 - 90	90 - 100
Art Nouveau		
Early Period		
Au Serial Hold-to-Light (6)	250 - 300	300 - 350
A.S.W.		
"Demi-Vierges" Series 927 (6)	125 - 150	150 - 175

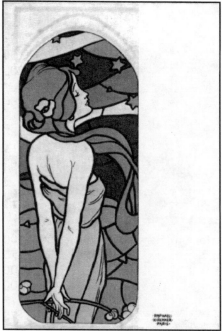

Raphael Kirchner, P.M.M., Paris
"Stained Glass Windows" Series

Raphael Kirchner
Theo. Stroefer, "Legendes" Series

Raphael Kirchner
Theo. Stroefer Series 427

Raphael Kirchner (Unsigned)
Anonymous Early Publisher

B.K.W.I.
"Sweet Fruits" Series (6)	125 - 140	140 - 150
"Noel!" Series 2049 (10)	150 - 175	175 - 200

B & S
"Fleur de Chemin" Series (6)	150 - 175	175 - 200

H.M. & Co.
"Angels" Series 184 (6)	80 - 100	100 - 125

Hirondelle
"Fleurs d'Amour" Series (6)	150 - 175	175 - 200

Kosmos
"Eisblumen" Series (10)	150 - 175	175 - 200

M. Munk, Vienna
"Continental" Series 4003 (6)		
"Sun Rays" or "Women in the Sun"	80 - 90	90 - 100
"Fleur Au Pied (10)	125 - 150	150 - 175
"Geisha" Series (10)	65 - 75	75 - 100
"Mikado" Series (6)	65 - 75	75 - 100
"Les Cigarettes Du Monde" (6)	125 - 150	150 - 175
"La Favorite" (6)	125 - 150	150 - 175

Erika
1119-1124 Japanese Faces in Flowers	150 - 175	175 - 200

Pascalis Moss & Co.
"Marionette" Series 4140 (6)	75 - 100	100 - 125
"Leda & the Swan" (10) Unsigned	150 - 175	175 - 200

P.M.M., Paris
"Stained Glass Windows" Series (6)	300 - 400	400 - 500

Raphael Tuck
"Automobile" Series 598 (6)	100 - 125	125 - 150
"Continental" Series 4024 (6)	125 - 150	150 - 175
"Salome" (6)	100 - 125	125 - 150
"Les Sylphides" Series 285 (6)	100 - 125	125 - 150

B.S., Wien
"Wiener Blut" Series 1042 (6)	150 - 175	175 - 200

A. Sockl
Bicycle Girls (10)	75 - 100	100 - 125
Delightful Perfumes (6)	100 - 125	125 - 150

R. Söhne
"Couples" Series (6)	125 - 150	150 - 175
"Enfants de la Mer" (10)	75 - 100	100 - 125
"Erika" Series 1123 (6)	150 - 175	175 - 200

E. Storch
"Cigarette Du Monde" (6)	125 - 150	150 - 175
"The Favorite" (6)	125 - 150	150 - 175
"Geisha" Series (10)	50 - 75	75 - 100

Mela Köhler
Wiener Werkstätte No. 594

Mela Köhler
Wiener Werkstätte No. 346

Maria Likarz-Strauss
Wiener Werkstätte No. 645

Maria Likarz-Strauss
Wiener Werkstätte No. 778

Theo. Stroefer

"Legendes" (6)	75 - 100	100 - 125
"Moderne Madchen" Series 1129 (6)	125 - 150	150 - 175
"Noel!" Series 184 (6)	75 - 100	100 - 125
"Noel!" Series 197 (6)	150 - 175	175 - 200
"Roma" Series 220 (10)	100 - 125	125 - 150
Santa	300 - 350	350 - 400

Anonymous

"Mikado" Series (6)	60 - 75	75 - 100
"Santoy" Series (6)	90 - 100	100 - 125
"Vieux Temps" V Series (6)	75 - 100	100 - 12

French Glamour

Series 1, 5	60 - 75	75 - 85

KNOEFEL

Novitas Illumination Series

Series 668 Nudes (4)	15 - 20	20 - 25
Series 20888 Mother/Baby	10 - 12	12 - 15
Series 15662 With Japanese Lantern	15 - 18	18 - 22
Other Illuminated	12 - 15	15 - 18

M. Munk Illumination

Series 1992 Japanese Lantern	15 - 18	18 - 22

KÖHLER, MELA (Austria)

Art Nouveau/Deco

M. Munk

1910 Era	75 - 100	100 - 125
After 1915	35 - 40	40 - 45

B.K.W.I.

620 Series (6)	40 - 45	45 - 50
1910 Era	75 - 100	100 - 125
After 1915	40 - 45	45 - 50

Wiener Werkstätte   250 - 450

KOISTER (France) French Glamour

Delta Series 71	15 - 18	18 - 22

KOKOSCHKA, OSCAR (Austria)

WW, No. 76	2000 - 2250	2250 - 2500
Others	2000 - 2250	2250 - 2500

KONOPA, RUDOLF (Austria) Art Nouveau	35 - 40	40 - 45
KOPAL Art Nouveau	30 - 35	35 - 40
KOSA (Austria) Art Nouveau	150 - 165	165 - 175

KOSEL, H.C.

B.K.W.I. Series 181	10 - 12	12 - 15
KOTAS, V.	6 - 8	8 - 10

KOVIES, K.   Art Deco

D.A.G. Series 474-1, 474-3, 474-4 (Skating)	12 - 15	15 - 18

KRATKI, F.	5 - 6	6 - 8
KRAUSZ, J.V. (Austria)	8 - 10	10 - 12
KRENNES, H. (Poland)	8 - 10	10 - 12
KUANI, C. COLAN Art Deco		
Ultra Series 2166 Shoulders (6)	10 - 12	12 - 14
KUCHINKA, JAN (Czech.)		
Praha-Podol 150 Erotic Series	25 - 30	30 - 35
H. Co. Semi-Nudes	25 - 30	30 - 35
KUDERNY		
M. Munk, Vienna		
Series 606	10 - 12	12 - 18
Series 634	8 - 10	10 - 15
Series 841, Semi-Nudes	12 - 15	15 - 18
Series 835, Tiny Men	12 - 15	15 - 18
KULAS, J.V. (Germany) Art Nouveau	35 - 40	40 - 45
KUNZLI, MAX	6 - 8	8 - 10
KURT, E. MAISON Art Deco		
P.F.B. (in Diamond)		
Fantasy Doll Series	15 - 18	18 - 22
Fantasy Dance Series (Lesbian Types)	30 - 35	35 - 40
Japanese Series	12 - 15	15 - 18
KUTUW, CHRISTO (Poland)	6 - 8	8 - 10
LAFUGIE		
Series 45	15 - 18	18 - 22
LARCOMBE, ETHEL Art Nouveau	25 - 30	30 - 35
LARRONI (Italy) Art Deco		
S.W.S.B. Series 6733 Lovers Kissing (6)	8 - 10	10 - 12
LASKOFF, F. (Poland) Art Nouveau	75 - 85	85 - 100
LASALLE, JEAN	4 - 6	6 - 8
LAURENS, P.A. (Czech.)	8 - 10	10 - 12
LAUDA, RICHARD (Denmark) Art Nouveau	40 - 50	50 - 60
LEARNED	5 - 6	8 - 10
LEBISCH, FRANZ (Austria)		
W.W.	75 - 100	100 - 150
LE DUCIS, A.		
Uff. Rev. Stampa		
Series 2039 High Fashion (6)	8 - 10	10 - 12
LeDUEI	10 - 12	12 - 14
LEINWEBER, R.	6 - 8	8 - 10
LELEE, L. (France) Art Nouveau	25 - 30	30 - 100
LENDECKE, OTTO (Poland)		
Wiener Werkstätte	125 - 150	150 - 250
LENG, MAX Art Nouveau	20 - 25	25 - 40
LENOLEM (France) French Glamour		
Meissner & Buch Series 219	18 - 20	20 - 25

LESKER, H. Art Deco	8 - 10	10 - 12
LESSIEUX, LOUIS (France) Art Nouveau	35 - 40	40 - 45
LHUER, VICTOR	15 - 18	18 - 22
LIKARZ-STRAUSS, MARIA (Austria)		
Wiener Werkstätte	250 - 300	300 - 350
No. 744, "Prosit Neujahr"	500 - 550	550 - 600
LINDSELL, L.	4 - 5	5 - 6
LIVEMONT, P. (Belgium) Art Nouveau	200 - 250	250 - 350
LLOYD, T.	4 - 6	6 - 8
LOFFLER, B. (Austria) Art Nouveau	200 - 250	250 - 300
LONGLEY, CHILTON (U.S.A.) Art Deco		
A.G. & Co. Ltd.		
Series 422	22 - 25	25 - 30
Others	22 - 25	25 - 30
Series 90 Hats (6)	10 - 12	12 - 14
LORELEY Art Deco	12 - 15	15 - 18
LORENZI, FACIO	15 - 18	18 - 22
LÖW, FRITZI (Austria)		
Wiener Werkstätte	125 - 150	150 - 250
LUDSON Series 90 Hats (6)	10 - 12	12 - 14
M.M.S.	5 - 6	6 - 8
MSM		
Meissner & Buch	15 - 18	18 - 22
MACDONALD, A.K. (G.B.) Art Nouveau	35 - 40	40 - 45
MAILICK, A.	8 - 10	10 - 12
MALUGANI, G.	15 - 20	20 - 25
MANASSE, A. (Austria)	5 - 6	6 - 8
MANNING, FREDERICK S. (U.S.A.)		
Series 117 Portraits	8 - 10	10 - 12
Others	6 - 8	8 - 10
MANNING, G.		
P.A.R. Series 144 Coat-Hat (6)	10 - 14	14 - 16
MANNING, REG (U.S.A.)	7 - 8	8 - 9
MG or MANNI GROSZE (Silhouettes)	12 - 15	15 - 20
MANUEL, HENRI (France) French Glamour		
Series 51, 55	18 - 20	20 - 25
MANSELL, VIVIAN (GB)		
"National Ladies" Series	10 - 12	12 - 14
Others	8 - 10	10 - 12
MARCOS. J. (Italy)		
Lady/Bubbles Fantasy	12 - 15	15 - 20
MARCO, M.		
Raphael Tuck		
Series 2763 (Asti-type)	6 - 8	8 - 10

MARECHAUK, C.	6 - 8	8 - 10
MARSHEL, HARRY		
Djer-Kiss Rouge	6 - 8	8 - 10
MARTIN-KAVEL		
Head Studies		
Series 5027-5036	10 - 12	12 - 15
Lapina Nudes	12 - 15	15 - 18
MARTINEAU, ALICE	6 - 8	8 - 10
MASTROAINI, D. (Italy)		
Ladies	7 - 9	9 - 12
MATALONI, G. (Italy) Art Nouveau	25 - 30	30 - 35
MAUZAN, L. A. (Italy) Art Deco & Glamour		
Dell, Anna & Gasparini; Uff. Rev. Stampa		
Series 386, 394 Lovers - Kissing (6)	10 - 12	12 - 14
Series 462, 498 Lovers-by--the-Sea (6)	10 - 12	12 - 14
Series 343, 424 Couples (6)	10 - 12	12 - 14
Series 248 Roman "Lovers" (6)	12 - 14	14 - 16
Series 42 Sport (6)	14 - 16	16 - 18
Series 301, 438 (6)	15 - 18	18 - 22
Series 279, 297 Heads - Green Ring (6)	20 - 22	22 - 25
Series 145, 252 Hat & Scarf (6)	20 - 22	22 - 25
Series 46, 230 Fashion (6)	15 - 18	18 - 22
Series 83, 250, 174 Walk, Traveling (6)	20 - 22	22 - 25
Series 247, 298 Beauties (6)	20 - 22	22 - 25
Series 53 Man Sits on Giant Shoes (6)	10 - 12	12 - 14
Series 43, 235 Shoulders Up (6)	12 - 15	15 - 18
Series 321, 343, 414 Fashion (6)	15 - 18	18 - 22
Series 8, 14, 80 High Fashion (6)	15 - 18	18 - 22
Series 201, 202, 2050 Walking (6)	10 - 12	12 - 15
Series 126 Waist-Up, in Chair (6)	18 - 22	22 - 25
Series 2, 10 With Cupid (6)	12 - 15	15 - 18
Tennis/Golf	18 - 20	20 - 25
Erotic/Semi-Nudes	20 - 22	22 - 25
Ladies & Dogs		
Uff. Rev. Stampa		
Series 316, 453 (6)	12 - 14	14 - 16
Series 491 (6)	10 - 12	12 - 15
Ladies & Horses		
Series 383 (6)	12 - 15	15 - 18
MAYER, LOU (U.S.A.)		
Reinthal & Newman		
400 Series	7 - 8	8 - 10
500 Series	8 - 10	10 - 12
Fantasy Series 878-883	12 - 15	15 - 18

Ullman Mfg. Co.

Pretty Girl Series	5 - 8	8 - 12

M.C.

Beautiful Fashions	15 - 18	18 - 25

McFALL, J.V. (U.S.A.) 4 - 5   5 - 6

McLELLAN, CHAS. A. 4 - 5   5 - 6

McMEIN, MARGIE (U.S.A.)

Novitas Series 15672

Head Studies	10 - 12	12 - 15
Osh Kosh Pennant Girls (6)	10 - 12	12 - 15

MELASSO

Series 125 Hats (6)	12 - 15	15 - 18

MERCER, JOYCE (G.B.)   Art Nouveau   10 - 12   12 - 16

MESCHINI, G. (Italy)   Art Deco

G.P.M.

Series 113 High Fur Collars, Hats (6)	30 - 35	35 - 40
Series Ars Nova	35 - 40	40 - 45

Ditta A. Guarneri, Milano

Ladies/Dogs Series	35 - 40	40 - 50
Ladies	32 - 35	35 - 40
Harlequins	30 - 35	35 - 40
Lovers	30 - 32	32 - 36

METLOKOVITZ, LEOPOLDO or LM (Italy)

Art Nouveau Works	50 - 75	75 - 125
Art Deco	15 - 20	20 - 25
Ladies/Fashion	10 - 12	12 - 14
Bathing Beauties	10 - 12	12 - 15
Couples	8 - 10	10 - 12

MEUNIER, GEORGES (France)

Cinos and Collection des Cent	150 - 200	200 - 250

MEUNIER, HENRI (Belgium) Art Nouveau   125 - 150   150 - 200

"Four Seasons" (4)	60 - 70	70 - 80
"Inspiration"	100 - 110	110 - 120
"Zodiac"	100 - 125	125 - 150

MEUNIER, SUZANNE   French Glamour

Marque L-E

No. 500-506	20 - 25	25 - 28
Series 11, 20, 22	18 - 22	22 - 26
Series 26, 42, 77	22 - 25	25 - 35
Series 29, 32, 35	20 - 25	25 - 30
Series 56, 74	18 - 22	22 - 26
Series 24, 52, 60, 99	18 - 22	22 - 26
Series 64, 96, 98	25 - 30	30 - 35
Delta Series 90	20 - 22	22 - 26

MIGNOT, VICTOR (Belgium) Art Nouveau	30 - 35	35 - 40
MIKI (Finland) Art Deco	8 - 10	10 - 12
MILLER, MARION	3 - 4	4 - 5
MILLIERE, M. (France) French Glamour		
Series 6, 21, 30, 37	18 - 22	22 - 26
Series 34, 54, 65	20 - 25	25 - 30
MOLINA, ROBERTO		
"Diabolo" Series	8 - 10	10 - 12
MONESTIER, C. (Italy) Art Deco		
E. G. Falci		
Series 27 Girl-Mask, Harlequin	14 - 16	16 - 20
Series 830 Hats (6)	14 - 16	16 - 20
Others	8 - 10	10 - 12
Ladies & Dogs		
Series 36 (6)	12 - 15	15 - 18
MONIER, MAGGY	15 - 18	18 - 22
MONTEDORO (Italy) Art Deco		
Uff Rev. Stampa		
Series A (6)	40 - 50	50 - 60
Series B (6)	50 - 60	60 - 70
MORAN, LEON (U.S.A.)	5 - 6	6 - 7

G. L. Pew
Anon., 109-4

Maurice Pepin
Delta Series 16, No. 80

G. Meschini
G.P.M., Ars Nova Series

M. Montedoro
Uff. Rev. Stampa B-4

G. Nanni
Uff. Rev. Stampa 255-4

G. Nanni
Uff. Rev. Stampa 257-4

Suzanne Meunier
Marque L-E 506

Suzanne Meunier
Marque L-E 500

MOSER, KOLOMAN (Austria) Art Nouveau

Ackerman	225 - 250	250 - 275
Gerlach & Schenk "Ver Sacum"	1000 - 1500	1500 - 2500
Philipp & Kramer		
Series I - V	200 - 250	250 - 350

MOSTYN, MARJORIE   (GB)

Raphael Tuck		
Series 108 Jewel Girls	10 - 12	12 - 15
Series 11 "Fair of Feature"	10 - 12	12 - 15
Water Color Series 2397 "A Maiden Fair"	8 - 10	10 - 12
MOUTON, G.	8 - 10	10 - 12

MUCHA, ALPHONSE (Czechoslovakia)
Isaac H. Blanchard Co., N.Y.
"Jeanne D'Arc" -- with Maude Adams as Joan.
Only 3 copies have surfaced;
advertised at $15,000.

MUCHA, ALPHONSE **(Czechoslovakia)***
Collection Cinos
Waverley Cycles Advertising Bicycles
Sold for $13,500.

"Gismonda," "Lorenzaccio," "Samaritaine"	500 - 550	550 - 600
Collection des Cent		
No. 11a "Jeune fille au trone"	1500 - 2000	2000 - 2500

No. 11b "Jeune fille bleue"	1500 - 2000	2000 - 2500
Collection JOB (Cigarettes)		
No. 6, Calendar "Femme blonde ..."	350 - 375	375 - 400
Vertical	700 - 750	750 - 800
No. 9, "Femme brune fumant"	350 - 375	375 - 400
Vertical	625 - 650	650 - 675
Vin Mariana	700 - 800	800 - 1000
F. Champenois		
"Cartes Postales Artistiques"		
First Series (C 1-12)		
The Seasons (4)	125 - 150	150 - 175
The Flowers (4)	100 - 150	150 - 175
The Ages (4)	150 - 200	200 - 250
Second Series (C 13-24)		
Byzantines (2)	125 - 150	150 - 200
The Seasons (4)	125 - 150	150 - 175
The Arts (4)	175 - 200	200 - 225
Reverie	275 - 300	300 - 325
Zodiac	250 - 300	300 - 350
Third Series (C 25-36)		
Vignettes (3)	275 - 300	300 - 325
Seasons (4)	200 - 250	250 - 300
"Salome"	200 - 225	225 - 250
"Aurore," "Crepuscule" (Dusk)	300 - 325	325 - 350
"Primevere"	325 - 350	350 - 375
"La Plume"	325 - 350	350 - 375
Fourth Series (37-48)		
The Months of the Year (12)	150 - 175	175 - 200

Alphonse Mucha, Champenois, France, Months of the Year, "Juin"

*Alphonse Mucha, Champenois
Stones Series "Topaz"*

*Alphonse Mucha
Champenois, "La Plume"*

Fifth Series (49-60)		
Sarah Bernhardt		
"La Plume"	500 - 525	525 - 550
Bienfaisance Aust.-Hung.		
(Coll. des Cent)	900 - 1000	1000 - 1200
Cocorico (with Rooster)	500 - 525	525 - 550
Cocorico (lady in oval)	250 - 275	275 - 300
Cocorico (Lady in rectangle)	250 - 275	275 - 300
Menus (4)	225 - 250	250 - 300
The Fan	475 - 500	500 - 525
Paris 1900 Exposition	400 - 450	450 - 500
Sixth Series (C 61-72)		
Calendar	325 - 350	350 - 375
Temps de la Journee (4)	250 - 300	300 - 350
"Reverie"	250 - 300	300 - 350
Young Lady with Harp	250 - 300	300 - 350
Young Lady at Dressing Table	250 - 300	300 - 350
Young Lady with Flower Bouquet	250 - 300	300 - 350
Lady with pen	250 - 300	300 - 350
"Water Lily," "Fleur de cerisier"		
(Horizontal)	400 - 450	450 - 500
Seventh Series (C 73-84)		
Autumn	500 - 550	550 - 575
Plantes (4)	400 - 450	450 - 500

Leon Peltier
Delta Series 17, No. 84

Albert Penot
Delta Series 12, No. 57

Lierre	450 - 500	500 - 550
Lygie	400 - 450	450 - 500
Gemstones (4)	500 - 550	550 - 600
The Fruit	600 - 700	700 - 800
Flower	600 - 700	700 - 800
Moet & Chandon (98-107)	250 - 300	300 - 350
Sarah Bernhardt, Extremely Rare		
Prices Estimated at $10,000-20,000.		
Gismonda		
Lorenzaccio		
Hamlet		
1916-1917		
La Samaritaine		
Lorenzaccio		
Miscellaneous		
Barcelona Expo		
Extremely Rare -- $10,000-15,000.		
1904 Lefevre-Utile Adv.	750 - 850	850 - 1000
Cognac Bisquit Adv., Vertical	800 - 1000	1000-1500
Cognac Bisquit Adv., Horizontal	600 - 650	650 - 750
"La Revue du Bien" Adv. Poster	600 - 650	650 - 700
"Vin Mariani" 1910 Wine Adv.	900 - 1100	1100 - 1500
Warner's Rust Proof Corsets, 1909	750 - 850	850 - 1000
Czechoslovakian Issues (57)	70 - 75	75 - 250

* Listings for most Mucha cards are from **Les Illustrateurs**, 1991 Edition, by **Neudin**.

MUGGIANI (Italy) Art Deco		
Ladies/Heads/Fashion	12 - 15	15 - 18
Ladies/Animals	15 - 18	18 - 22
MUHLBERG, S.	8 - 10	10 - 12
MURCH, FRANK		
Decorative Poster Co., Series HC 1-12	8 - 10	10 - 12
MUSSINO (Italy) Art Deco		
MUTTICH, C.V. (Czech.)		
Head Studies	5 - 8	8 - 10
Others	5 - 8	8 - 10
MYER (U.S.A.)	4 - 5	5 - 6
NP Art Deco	12 - 15	15 - 18
NAILLOD, C.S.	6 - 8	8 - 10
NAM, J.	8 - 10	10 - 12
NANNI, G. (Italy) Art Deco		
Uff. Rev. Stampa; Dell, Anna & Gasparini		
Series 26-A, 597 Couples Kissing (6)	12 - 14	14 - 16
Series 373 Couples Kissing (6)	14 - 16	16 - 18
Series 255 National Girls (6)	15 - 18	18 - 22
Series 529 Pajamas, Smoking (6)	15 - 18	18 - 22
Series 206, 253, 256 Hats (6)	18 - 20	20 - 25
Series 21, 304, 378 Hats (6)	18 - 20	20 - 25
Series 162 Hats and Ties (6)	20 - 22	22 - 27
Series 308, 376, 396 Heads (6)	14 - 16	16 - 18
Series 283 Fur Collar Hats (6)	18 - 20	20 - 25
Series 377, 521 Hats, Coats	14 - 16	16 - 18
Series 337 Playing Cards-Hats (6)	18 - 20	22 - 25
Series 372, 505 Heads, High Fash. (6)	12 - 14	14 - 16
Series 480 In Buggy (6)	15 - 18	18 - 22
Series 494 With Hat Boxes (6)	20 - 22	22 - 25
Series 445 Lounging Around (6)	20 - 22	22 - 25
Series 540 Heads (6)	22 - 25	25 - 28
Couples	10 - 12	12 - 14
Ladies/Animals	15 - 18	18 - 22
Harlequins	18 - 22	22 - 25
Soccer Series	18 - 22	22 - 25
Erotic/Semi-Nudes	22 - 25	25 - 30
Ladies & Dogs		
Series 205 (6)	15 - 18	18 - 22
Series 300 (6)	15 - 18	18 - 22
Ladies & Horses		
Series 116, 257 (6)	12 - 15	15 - 18
Series 307 (6)	15 - 18	18 - 22

Series 374 (6)	14 - 16	16 - 18
NASH, A. (Ladies & Dogs)		
Heckscher		
703 "Love Me, Love My Dog"	10 - 12	12 - 14
NAST, THOMAS, JR.		
Tennis "Love Game"	15 - 18	18 - 20
Others	6 - 8	8 - 10
NEFF, GUY	2 - 3	3 - 4
NEY (France) French Glamour		
Delta Series 24	20 - 25	25 - 30
NICZKY, E.	5 - 6	6 - 8
NIKOLAKI, Z.P.		
Reinthal & Newman Ladies Series	6 - 8	8 - 10
NORMAN, S.		
Reinthal & Newman Series 1000	8 - 10	10 - 12
NOURY, GASTON (France) Art Nouveau	60 - 75	75 - 150
NYSTROM, JENNY (Sweden)	10 - 12	12 - 15
OPLATEK (Ladies & Horses)	8 - 10	10 - 12
ORLANDI, V. (Italy)		
T.A.M. Series 7612 Couples Hugging (6)	8 - 10	10 - 12
OST, A. (Belgium) Art Nouveau	20 - 25	25 - 35
PAGNOTTA (Italy) Art Deco		
Series 494 High Fashion (6)	8 - 10	10 - 12
PAGONI (Italy) Art Deco	8 - 10	10 - 12
PALANTI, G. (Italy) Art Deco	8 - 10	10 - 12
PANNETT, R.	6 - 8	8 - 10
PATELLA, B. (Italy)		
Art Deco	10 - 12	12 - 15
Art Nouveau	35 - 40	40 - 45
PAYNE, G.	4 - 6	6 - 8
PELLEGRINI, E.	12 - 15	15 - 18
PELLON, A.		
Ideal Series (6)	80 - 90	90 - 100
PELTIER, L. (France) French Glamour		
Delta Series 17, 28	18 - 20	20 - 22
PENNELL (U.S.A.)		
M. Munk, Vienna		
Series 913, 1114 Sporting Girls	6 - 8	8 - 10
Ladies & Dogs "My Companion"	8 - 10	10 - 12
Ladies & Horses	8 - 10	10 - 12
PENOT, ALBERT (France) French Glamour		
Series 10, 12, 28	18 - 22	22 - 26
Series 16, 25	18 - 20	20 - 25
Series 97, 98, 109	15 - 18	18 - 22

PENTSY	8 - 10	10 - 12
PEPIN, MAURICE		
Delta Series 23 High Fashion	18 - 22	22 - 25
Delta Series 16, 21, 30 French Glamour	20 - 25	25 - 30
PERAS (France) French Glamour		
Series 68	15 - 18	18 - 22
PERINI, T. (Italy) **Ladies & Horses**	8 - 10	10 - 12
PETER, OTTO (Germany)	6 - 8	8 - 10
PETERSON, L. (U.S.A.) Cowboys/Indians		
H. H. Tammen -- Love & Life Series	5 - 6	6 - 8
PEW, C.L.		
Aquarelle Series 109, 2239	6 - 8	8 - 10
Leubrie & Elkus (L&E)		
Series 2221, 2223 (Heads)	8 - 10	10 - 12
Others	6 - 8	8 - 10

PHILLIPS, COLES (U.S.A.)

The works of Coles Phillips are some of the most elusive of the famous U.S. illustrators, and are very rarely seen in auctions. The famous Fadeaway Girls, both signed and unsigned, are among the most beautiful ever published. His renderings of ladies for Community Plate are also very popular with advertising collectors. Relatively unknown are his set of six movie stars for C.P. & Company, New York. These also are extremely hard to find.

COLES PHILLIPS
    * **Cards Listed with an asterisk are Fadeaway Girls images.**

Life Publishing Co., 1907		
Life Series 1		
"Her Choice"	35 - 40	40 - 50
Life Pub. Co., 1909		
© Coles Phillips Series	40 - 50	50 - 60
"Arms and the Man" *		
"Between You and Me ..." *		
"Home Ties" *		
"Illusion" *		
"Inclined to Meet" Series 2 *		
"The Sand Witch"		
"Such Stuff as Dreams are Made Of"		
"What Next?" Series 2		
"Which?" Series 2 *		
Life Pub. Co., 1910		
"A Call to Arms" *	45 - 50	50 - 60

"All Wool and Face Value" Series 2	40 - 45	45 - 50
"And Out of Mind as ..." Series 2	40 - 45	45 - 50
"Discarding from Strength" Series 2	45 - 50	50 - 60
"Hers"	40 - 45	45 - 50

P.F. Volland & Co., Chicago
© by Life Pub. Co.

"The Latest in Gowns, Good Night" *	35 - 40	40 - 45
"Long Distance Makes ..." *	45 - 50	50 - 55
"May Christmas Day Heap Up for You"	35 - 40	40 - 45
"Memories" *	45 - 50	50 - 55
"My Christmas Thoughts ..." *	45 - 50	50 - 55
"Pals" *	45 - 50	50 - 55
"The Survival of the Fittest" *	45 - 50	50 - 55

C.P. Co., Inc., N.Y.

Movie Star Series	50 - 55	55 - 60

"King Baggott"
"Francis X. Bushman"
"Alice Joyce"
"Blanche Sweet"
"Rosemary Theby"
"Lillian Walker"

ADVERTISING

R. Stafford Collins, N.Y.

Community Plate	40 - 45	45 - 50

Community Plate

Ad for Brunner Fl. Jeweler	40 - 45	45 - 50

Community Plate

"A Case of Love at First Sight"	40 - 45	45 - 50
"The Aristocrat of the Dining Table"	40 - 45	45 - 50
Book Advertisement	50 - 55	55 - 60

"The Dim Lantern," by Temple Bailey
"The Trumpeter Swan," by Temple Bailey

Calendar Cards, With Verse	40 - 45	45 - 50

Unsigned
Ten unsigned Fadeaway Girls have
been attributed to Coles Phillips.

Prices of these are:	25 - 30	30 - 35
PILLARD	5 - 6	6 - 7
PINKAWA, ANTON (Japan) Art Nouveau	25 - 30	30 - 35
PINOCHI (Italy) Art Deco		
Series 206 Hats (6)	10 - 12	12 - 15
Series 172 Lovers (6)	10 - 12	12 - 15
Others	8 - 10	10 - 12

Coles Phillips, Life Pub. Co.
"Between you and me and the post"

Coles Phillips, Community Plate
"The Aristocrat of the Dining ..."

PIOTROWSKI, A. (Poland)		
PLANTIKOW	8 - 10	10 - 12
Ladies & Horses	8 - 10	10 - 12
POWELL, LYMAN (U.S.A.)		
"Eventful Days" Series	8 - 10	10 - 12
"Graduation Day"		
"Engagement Day"		
"Wedding Day"		
"Birthday"		
Flower Series 783	6 - 8	8 - 10
PRESSLER, G.		
Djer-Kiss Rouge	6 - 8	8 - 10
PUTTKAMER		
Erotic Lovers Series 8027 (6)	15 - 18	18 - 22
QUINNELL, CECIL W.		
B.K.W.I. 251 "The Jewel Girls"	10 - 12	12 - 14
"Pearl"		
"Ruby"		
"Emerald"		
"Topaz"		
"Turquoise"		
"Sapphire"		
"Glad Eye" Series	8 - 10	10 - 12
RABES, MAX (German)	8 - 10	10 - 12

RALPH, LESTER (U.S.A.)
Reinthal & Newman

"Dancing" Series 801-806	12 - 14	14 - 18
"The La Furlana"		
"The Cortez"		
"The Half and Half"		
"The Tango"		
"The One Step"		
"The Maxie"		
813-818 Series*	10 - 12	12 - 14
813 "The Awakening of Love"		
814 "The Stage of Life"		
815 "Up in the Clouds"		
816 "For All Eternity"		
817 "In Proud Possession"		
818 "The Home Guard"		

* With German Caption add $2.

The Knapp Co., N.Y.
Paul Heckscher Series 392

1	8 - 10	10 - 12
2 "An Offer of Affection"	8 - 10	10 - 12
3 "Weathering it Together"	8 - 10	10 - 12
4	8 - 10	10 - 12
5 "Four-In-Hand"	8 - 10	10 - 12
6 "Her First Mate"	8 - 10	10 - 12
7 "Two is Company Enough"	8 - 10	10 - 12
8 "Fellow Sports"	8 - 10	10 - 12
10 "Diana of the Shore"	10 - 12	12 - 14

H. Import Series 308

1 "Confidential Chatter"	8 - 10	10 - 12
3 "A Social Call"	8 - 10	10 - 12
4 "A Stroll Together"	8 - 10	10 - 12
5 "The Wings of the Wind"	8 - 10	10 - 12
6 "A Surprise Party"	10 - 12	12 - 14
7 "Two is Company Enough"	8 - 10	10 - 12
9 "Fellow Sports"	10 - 12	12 - 14
Others	10 - 12	12 - 14

Series 1026

2 "Feathered Friends"	8 - 10	10 - 12
Others	8 - 10	10 - 12
Series 7*	10 - 12	12 - 14
9523 "Fellow Sports"		
9543 "Favored by Fortune"		
9563 "Two is Company Enough"		
9573 "Her First Date"		
9583 "A Challenge from the Sea"		
9593 "A Game in the Surf"		
9603 "Diana of the Shore"		
9613 "Four-in-Hand"		

9623 "Fellow Sports"		
9633 "An Offer of Affection"		
Others		
* This series also adapted as Knapp Calendars.		
Add $3-5 to prices for Knapp Calendars.		
C.W. Faulkner	10 - 12	12 - 14
Seies. 1314B "Fast Companions"		
Series 1315D "Her Proudest Moment"		
Others		
RAPPINI (Italy) Art Deco and Glamour		
Series 2016 With Hand Mirror (6)	10 - 12	12 - 14
Ladies/Heads/Fashion	12 - 15	15 - 18
Ladies/Animals	15 - 18	18 - 22
Ladies/Sports	15 - 18	18 - 22
Ladies & Horses		
Series 1002 (6)	10 - 12	12 - 15
Series 1092, 2019 (6)	9 - 11	11 - 13
RAUH, LUDWIG (Austria) Art Nouveau	25 - 30	30 - 35
READ, F.	4 - 5	5 - 6
READING	7 - 8	8 - 10
REED, MARION	3 - 4	4 - 6
RELYEA		
E. Gross Series	8 - 10	10 - 12
REYNOLDS (U.S.A.)		
Cowgirl Series	5 - 6	6 - 7
REYZNER, M.	6 - 8	8 - 10
REZSO, KISS		
"Siren Lady" Series 68-73	10 - 12	12 - 14
RICCO, CARLO (Italy) Art Deco	8 - 10	10 - 12
RICCO, LORIS (Italy) Art Deco		
Ladies	18 - 22	22 - 26
Lovers	15 - 18	18 - 22
Harlequins	20 - 22	22 - 26
ROBERTY, L.		
M. Munk, Vienna		
Bather Series 1124	10 - 12	12 - 15
RODE, G.		
Uff. Rev. Stampa		
Series 6529 On Chair (6)	12 - 14	14 - 16
RODELLA, G.	4 - 6	6 - 8
RUMPEL, F.	6 - 8	8 - 10
RUNDALZEFF, M. (Russia)	6 - 8	8 - 10
RUSSELL, MARY LA F.	6 - 7	7 - 8
RYAN, C. (U.S.A.)		
Art Nouveau		
A 633 "Folly"	10 - 12	12 - 15
A 634 "Joy"	10 - 12	12 - 15
A 638 "So Lonesome"	10 - 12	12 - 15

E. Sacchetti
F. Polenghi 19, No Caption

A. Terzi
Uff. Rev. Stampa 341-2

A 677 "Dreaming of Days Gone By"	10 - 12	12 - 15
Others	10 - 12	12 - 15
Winsch Backs		
Non-Art Nouveau, Glamour		
"Blissful Moments, etc."	5 - 6	6 - 8
RYLAND, H.	8 - 10	10 - 12
RYLANDER, CARL (Sweden) Art Deco	12 - 15	15 - 18
SACCHETTI, ENRICO (Italy)		
E. Polenghi		
Ladies & Dogs	15 - 18	18 - 22
Others	12 - 15	15 - 18
SAGER, XAVIER (France)		
French Glamour/Fantasy		
Noyer		
Series 131 -- Pajamas	15 - 18	18 - 22
Series 138 -- Lingerie	18 - 22	22 - 25
Series 156 -- Lesbian Dancers	22 - 27	27 - 35
Series 690 -- "Peaceful Shells"	18 - 22	22 - 25
Other Glamour Series	18 - 22	22 - 25
Erotic/Nudes	20 - 25	25 - 30
ST. JOHN		
National Art		
"National Girls" Series	12 - 14	14 - 16
"Foreign Girls" Series	8 - 10	10 - 12

"The Four Seasons"	10 - 12	12 - 15
"State Girl" Series	8 - 10	10 - 12
Montgomery Co., Chicago	8 - 10	10 - 12
103 "Shopping"		
104 "Promenade"		
106 "Beauties"		
SALMONI, G. (Italy) Art Deco	10 - 12	12 - 14
SALVADORI (Italy) Art Deco		
Series 168 "The Wolf" Fur (6)	15 - 18	18 - 22
SAMSON, C. W.		
Valentine & Sons Bathing Girls	8 - 10	10 - 12
SAN MARCO (Italy) Art Deco		
P.A.R.		
Series 2037, 2082 Hats	12 - 15	15 - 20
Fantasy Series - Lady/Bubbles	15 - 18	18 - 25
Others	10 - 12	12 - 15
SAND, ADINA	4 - 6	6 - 8
SANTINO, F. (Italy) Art Deco		
Uff. Rev. Stampa		
Series 131 Fashion Pose (6)	12 - 15	15 - 18
Ladies & Dogs		
Series 6783 (6)	12 - 14	14 - 16
Ladies & Horses		
Series 68 (6)	8 - 10	10 - 12
SCATTINI (Italy) Art Deco		
Ladies	15 - 18	18 - 22
Harlequins	18 - 22	22 - 25
SCHIELE, EGON (Art Nouveau)	150 - 200	200 - 250
Wiener Werkstätte	2500 - 2750	2750 - 3000
SCHILBACH	6 - 8	8 - 10
SCHLOSSER, R. (Germany)	5 - 6	6 - 8
SCHROCCHI (Italy) Art Deco		
Series 4360 Fashion (6)	10 - 12	12 - 14
SCHMUTZLER, L. (See Color Nudes)		
Moderne Kunst Series	6 - 8	8 - 9
SCHUBERT (Austria)		
M. Munk, Vienna -- Ladies & Dogs	6 - 8	8 - 10
SCHUTZ, ERIC (Austria)		
B.K.W.I. Series 128	8 - 10	10 - 12
SCHWETZ		
Wiener Werkstätte	125 - 150	150 - 200
SHAND, C.E. (Art Deco)	20 - 25	25 - 30
SHARPE	8 - 9	9 - 10
SHERIE	5 - 6	6 - 7
SICHEL, N.	5 - 6	6 - 8
SIMM, PROF. FRANZ (Germany)	5 - 6	6 - 8
SIMONETTI, A. (Italy) Art Deco & Glamour		
Ladies & Horses		
Series 41 (6)	12 - 15	15 - 18

Relyea
E. Gross Co. No. 7

Loris Ricco
Degami 2089

Series 90 (6)	10 - 12	12 - 15
SITSCHKOFF (Russia)	10 - 12	12 - 15
SCHMUCKER, SAMUEL L. (SLS) (U.S.A.)		
See New Chapter on Samuel L. Schmucker.		
SOLDINGER, A. (Poland)	8 - 10	10 - 12
SOLOMKO S. (Russia)		
Lapina, Paris		
Russian Princess 1600 Series*		
"Queen Aeviakovna"	22 - 25	25 - 28
"Wassilisa Mikoülichna"		
"Princess Apraksia"		
"Princess Warrior Nastasia"		
"Princess Mary, The White Swan"		
"Princess Zabava Poutiatichna"		
"Queen Azviakovna of the East"		
* Russian Backs - Add $4-5 each.		
T.S.N. (Theo. Stroefer, Nurnberg) *		
15 "Parisiene"	14 - 16	16 - 18
175 "Phantasy"	16 - 18	18 - 22
"Dream of Icarius"	14 - 15	15 - 18
"Pearl of Creation"	15 - 18	18 - 20
"Vanity" (Semi-nude)	15 - 20	20 - 25
"Circe" (Semi-nude)	15 - 20	20 - 25
"The Tale" (Fantasy)	15 - 16	16 - 18

S. de Solomko, Lapina 1630
"Princess Zabava Poutiatichna"

S. de Solomko, Lapina 1631
"Queen Azviakovna of the East"

P. Stanlaws
E.Gross No. 3 (No Caption)

P. Stanlaws, A.R. & C.i.B. 550,
"Fresh as the Morn"

"The Blue Bird" (Fantasy)	18 - 20	20 - 22
"Magician Circle" (Semi-nude)	15 - 20	20 - 25
154 "Temptations" (Semi-nude)	15 - 20	20 - 25
"Glow Worm" (Fantasy)	15 - 18	18 - 20
"Fortune Telling" (Fantasy)	15 - 18	18 - 20
Other **T.S.N.** (Many)	8 - 10	10 - 12
* Russian Backs - Add $4-5 to prices.		
SOMERVILLE, H.	4 - 6	6 - 8
SONREL, ELISABETH (Art Nouveau)	75 - 100	100 - 150
SPOTTI, F. (Ladies & Dogs)		
Uff. Rev. Stampa, Series 158	8 - 10	10 - 12
SPURGIN, FRED	5 - 7	7 - 9
STACHIEWICZ, P.	8 - 10	10 - 12
STAMM, MAUD	5 - 6	6 - 7
STANLAWS, PENRHYN (U.S.A.)		
Edward Gross		
Stanlaws 1-12 No Captions	14 - 16	16 - 20
Knapp Co., N.Y.		
900 Series	15 - 18	18 - 22
"A Midsummer Maid"		
"After the Matinee"		
"Daisies Won't Tell"		
"Fair as the Lily"		
"Fresh as the Morn"		
"Girl of the Golden West"		
"Kissed by the Snow"		
"The Pink Lady"		
"School Days"		
K. Co.		
Distributed by A.R. & C.i.B		
900 Series Reprints, Called Series 550	15 - 18	18 - 20
"A Midsummer Maid"		
"Daisies Wont Tell"		
"Fresh as the Morn"		
"Girl of the Golden West"		
"The Pink Lady"		
Series 551	15 - 18	18 - 20
"After the Matinee"		
"Kissed by the Snow"		
"School Days"		
"Fair as the Lily"		
Reinthal & Newman		
Military Ladies Series		
981 U.S.A.	15 - 18	18 - 22
982 Serbia	12 - 14	14 - 16
983 Belgium	12 - 14	14 - 16
984 France	12 - 14	14 - 16
985 Italy	12 - 14	14 - 16
986 Greece	12 - 14	14 - 16

J. Tam
Marque L-E 75, No. 2　　　　*J. Tam*
Marque L-E 75, No. 4

987 Great Britain	12 - 14	14 - 16
988 Russia	12 - 14	14 - 16
H. Choate & Co.		
Djer-Kiss Rouge & Face Powder Compacts		
"Silver Blonde"	22 - 25	25 - 28
STEINLEN, A.T. (Switzerland)		
Art Nouveau		
Better Issues	175 - 200	200 - 500
Others	30 - 35	35 - 45
STENBERG, AINA (Sweden) Art Deco	10 - 12	12 - 15
STOLTE, F. (Ladies & Horses)		
Series 25 (6)	8 - 10	10 - 12
TACCHI, E. (Italy) Art Deco		
Series 494 High Fashion (6)	8 - 10	10 - 12
TAM, JEAN (France) French Glamour		
Series 39, 47, 50, 70, 78, 81	18 - 22	22 - 25
Series 57, 67	20 - 25	25 - 30
TERZI, A. (Italy) Art Deco and Glamour		
Uff. Rev. Stampa; Dell, Anna & Gasparini		
Series 287, 299 Heads (6)	10 - 12	12 - 15
Series 322 Heads (6)	15 - 18	18 - 22
Series 323 Sitting (6)	10 - 12	12 - 15
Series 486 Fashion (6)	10 - 12	12 - 15
Series 454 Fashion (6)	15 - 18	18 - 22

Series 482 Small Images (6)	8 - 10	10 - 12
Golf/Tennis	14 - 16	16 - 20
Couples	10 - 12	12 - 14
Ladies/Animals	12 - 14	14 - 18
Ladies & Dogs		
Series 341, 349, 399 (6)	10 - 12	12 - 14
Series 457, 482, 973 (6)	12 - 13	13 - 16
Series 976, 559, 969 (6)	12 - 14	14 - 18
Ladies & Horses; Uff. Rev. Stampa		
Series 320 (6)	10 - 12	12 - 16
TORNROSE, ALEX		
Welles Head Series (B&W)	6 - 8	8 - 9
Others	6 - 7	7 - 8
TOULOUSE-LAUTREC, HENRI (France)		
"Cabaret Bruant"	600 - 700	700 - 900
"La Goulue au Moulin Rouge"	1500 - 1600	1600 - 1800
(Card recently sold for $1800.)		
TRAVER, C. WARD (U.S.A.)		
H & S Art Co.		
"The Beauty of the Season"	8 - 10	10 - 12
"Sweet Seventeen"	8 - 10	10 - 12
Others	8 - 10	10 - 12
TUHKA, A. (Finland) Art Deco	10 - 12	12 - 14
TURRAIN, E.D. Art Nouveau	25 - 30	30 - 35
TWELVETREES, C.	5 - 6	6 - 8

UNDERWOOD, CLARENCE

Clarence Underwood was another of the more important illustrators of magazine covers and magazine fiction who benefitted from the great postcard era. This painter of beautiful ladies did work for Reinthal & Newman of New York, but his most beautiful images were published by the R. Chapman Co. (better known as the R.C. Co., N.Y.). They did the 1400 Series Water Colors of his ladies wearing big, beautiful, and colorful hats. These will always be some of the most beautiful renderings of the era.

Marcus Munk, the famous postcard publisher of Vienna, also did many of his images on postcards. These were mainly of loving couples with colorful backgrounds, and many were sport oriented. Other foreign publishers produced some of his works, but Underwood was unable to gain the great popularity attained by his fellow American artists—Fisher, Boileau and Christy.

CLARENCE UNDERWOOD (U.S.A.)

C.W. Faulkner		
Series 5	10 - 12	12 - 14
Series 1010	10 - 12	12 - 14

1278 "A Symphony of Hearts"	8 - 10	10 - 12
"Their Search for Old China"	8 - 10	10 - 12

National Art

"Playing Card" Series	8 - 10	10 - 12
78 "Hearts" Two Men, Two Women		
79 "Poker" Five Men		
80 "Bridge" Four Women		
81 "Euchre" Five Men		

Reinthal & Newman

300 Series Water Colors		
345 "The Flirt"	10 - 12	12 - 15
346 "Pretty Cold"	10 - 12	12 - 15
347 "Her First Vote"	25 - 30	30 - 35
348 "It's Always Fair Weather"	10 - 12	12 - 15
349 "Rain or Shine"	10 - 12	12 - 15
350 "Pleasant Reflections"	10 - 12	12 - 15

R.C. CO., N.Y.

1400 Water Color Series	15 - 20	20 - 25
1436 "Constance"		
1437 "Diana"		
1438 "Vivian"		
1439 "Phyllis"		
1440 "Celestine"		
1441 "Rosabella"		
1442 "Juliana"		
1443 "Victoria"		
1444 "Aurora"		
1445 "Sylvia"		
1446 "Virginia"		
1447 "Doris"		

Frederick A. Stokes Co.

Series 1		
"A Problem of Income"	7 - 8	8 - 10
"Castles in the Smoke"	7 - 8	8 - 10
"For Fear of Sunburn"	8 - 9	9 - 12
"Knight Takes Queen"	7 - 8	8 - 10
Series 2	8 - 10	10 - 12
"Love Me, Love My Cat"		
"Love Me, Love My Dog"		
"Love Me, Love My Donkey"		
"Love Me, Love My Horse"		
Series 3	8 - 10	10 - 12
"When We're Together Fishing"		
"When We're Together at Luncheon"		
"When We're Together Shooting"		
"When We're Together in a Storm"		
Series 4	8 - 9	9 - 12
"Beauty and the Beast"		
"The Best of Friends"		

"Expectation"		
"The Promenade"		
Series 5		
"A Lump of Sugar"	8 - 9	9 - 12
"After the Hunt"	8 - 9	9 - 12
"The Red Haired Girl ..."	10 - 12	12 - 14
"Three American Beauties"	10 - 12	12 - 14
Series 6		
"Feeding the Swans"	7 - 8	8 - 10
"A Pet in the Park"	7 - 8	8 - 10
"Posing"	7 - 8	8 - 10
"A Witch"	8 - 10	10 - 12
Series 7	7 - 8	8 - 10
"An Old Melody"		
"Over the Teacups"		
"The Opera Girl"		
"The Violin Girl"		
Series 8		
"At the Races"	8 - 10	10 - 12
"Embroidery for Two"	7 - 8	8 - 10
"Out for a Stroll"	7 - 8	8 - 10
"Two Cooks"	7 - 8	8 - 10
Series 14	7 - 8	8 - 10
"Their First Wedding Gift"		
"Their Love of Old Silver"		
"Two and an Old Flirt"		
"Vain Regrets"		
Series 15		
"A Lesson in Motoring"	8 - 10	10 - 12
"A Skipper and Mate"	7 - 8	8 - 10
Series 19		
"The Only Two at Dinner"	7 - 8	8 - 10
"The Only Two at the Game"	8 - 10	10 - 12
"The Only Two at the House Party"	7 - 8	8 - 10
"The Only Two at the Opera"	7 - 8	8 - 10
Series 22		
"The Greatest Thing in the World"	7 - 8	8 - 10
"The Last Waltz"	7 - 8	8 - 10
"Lost?"	7 - 8	8 - 10
"Love on Six Cylinders"	8 - 10	10 - 12
Series 377 Untitled (4) B&W	5 - 6	6 - 8
Taylor, Platt & Co.		
Series 782	10 - 12	12 - 15
"A Fisherman's Luck"		
"A Heart of Diamonds"		
"A Modern Siren"		
"Daisies Won't Tell"		
"The Glories of March"		
"His Latest Chauffeur"		

"Indicating a Thaw"
"The Magnet"
"Let's Paddle Forever"
"Love Has It's Clouds"
"Stolen Sweets"
"True Love Never Runs Smooth"

Osborne Calendar Co.

Advertising Cards	25 - 30	30 - 35
1521 "Fancy Work"		
1561 "Mary had a Little Lamb"		
1571 "The Tongue is Mightier ..."		
1601 "The Favorite's Day"		
1621 "Music Hath Charm"		
Others		

A.R. & Co.

1283 "Des Meeres und der Liebe Wellen"	10 - 12	12 - 14

M. Munk, Vienna

Series 303 (8)		
Beautiful Ladies With Pets--No captions	8 - 10	10 - 12
Series 377, 385, 387, & 388	10 - 12	12 - 15
Ladies & Dogs		
"My Companion"	10 - 12	12 - 15
Series 742 *		
"Love Laughs at Winter"	8 - 10	10 - 12
"Love on Wings"	12 - 15	15 - 18
"Under the Mistletoe"	8 - 10	10 - 12
"The Sender of Orchids"	8 - 10	10 - 12
"The Last Waltz"	8 - 10	10 - 12
"The Greatest Thing"	8 - 10	10 - 12
Others	8 - 10	10 - 12

* Series 742 A,B,C,D,E,F,G & H.
All Same as Series 742 but with German
captions, add $3.

Series 832, 834, 837 & 860 *		
"A Penny for Thought"	8 - 10	10 - 12
"A Problem of Income"	8 - 10	10 - 12
"Cherry Ripe"	8 - 10	10 - 12
"He Loves Me ..."	8 - 10	10 - 12
"How to Know Wildflowers"	12 - 15	15 - 18
"Only a Question of Time"	8 - 10	10 - 12
"The Sweetest Flower that ..."	8 - 10	10 - 12
"Skipper and Mate"	10 - 12	12 - 15
"Love and Six Cylinders"	12 - 15	15 - 18

With German Captions, add $3.

Novitas, Germany

400 Series		
445 "Gestand nis"	8 - 10	10 - 12
447 "Einig"	10 - 12	12 - 14
449 "Zukunftplane"	10 - 12	12 - 14

Clarence Underwood
R&N 775, "Wanted - An Answer"

Clarence Underwood
R&N 779, "Help Wanted - Male"

Others	10 - 12	12 - 14
Others, No Captions	8 - 10	10 - 12
20000 Series	8 - 10	10 - 12
20391 No Caption		
20392 No Caption		
20451 "Wer Wird Siegen"		
20452 "Dem Fluck Entgegen"		
20453 No Caption (Lovers of Beauty)		
20454 "Liebe Auf Eis"		
20455 "Abwesend, Aber Nicht Vergessen"		
20456 No Caption		
20457 "Zwei Seelen und ein Genankt"		
20458 "Zukunpt Straune"		
20459 No Caption		
20460 "Glucklicht Tagt"		

FINLAND
  W. & G.   (Weilin & Goos)

American Series N:0 7001 1-35		
6 Cards with No Captions	20 - 22	22 - 25

RUSSIAN
  Richard (Rishar)

"The Last Waltz Together"	20 - 25	25 - 35

Others	20 - 25	25 - 35
UNIERZYSKI, J. (Poland)	5 - 6	6 - 8
UPRKA, JOZA (Czech.)	6 - 8	8 - 10
USABAL, L. (Italy)		
P.F.B. (in Diamond) Series 3796 (6)	12 - 14	14 - 16
Ladies & Dogs		
Series 3968 (6)	12 - 14	14 - 16
E.A.S.B.		
Series 111 Lovers under the Mistletoe	8 - 10	10 - 12
Series 103 Lovers Dancing	8 - 10	10 - 12
Series 114 Lovers Dancing	10 - 12	12 - 14
Erkal		
Series 301, 308, 367 Hats (6)	8 - 10	10 - 12
Series 303 Smoking Ladies (6)	10 - 12	12 - 14
Series 336 Tennis (6)	15 - 18	18 - 22
Series 343 Skiing (6)	10 - 12	12 - 14
Series 318, 356 Lovers (6)	10 - 12	12 - 15
Series 339 On Toboggan Sled (6)	10 - 12	12 - 14
Series 347 Gypsy Heads (6)	8 - 10	10 - 12
Series 330, 337, 357 Dancing/Kissing (6)	8 - 10	10 - 12
Series 1318 Lovers on Couch (6)	10 - 12	12 - 15
G. Kuais Series 1393 Hats	6 - 8	8 - 10
Gurner & Simon		
Series 2027 Lovers at the Bar (6)	6 - 8	8 - 10
S. & G.		
Series 694 Couples, Man in Uniform	5 - 6	6 - 7
S.W.S.B.		
Series 128 Lovers Kissing	8 - 10	10 - 12
Series 1007, 1068 Couples Dancing	8 - 10	10 - 12
Series 1070 Lesbian Dancers	20 - 22	22 - 25
Series 1108 Nude in Fur	12 - 15	15 - 18
Series 1256 Couples Dancing	8 - 10	10 - 12
Series 1295-1300 Dancing/Blacks	18 - 20	20 - 22
Series 1356 Heads/Smoking	10 - 12	12 - 14
Series 303 "Ladies Smoking"	10 - 12	12 - 14
Series 4668, 4669, 4670 (6)	10 - 12	12 - 14
Ladies & Dogs		
S.W.S.B.		
Series 4989	8 - 9	9 - 10
Series 1336 (6)	8 - 10	10 - 12
Ladies & Horses		
S.W.S.B.		
Series 257, 328, 345 (6)	8 - 10	10 - 12
Series 320 (6)	7 - 8	8 - 10
Series 1201 (6)	7 - 8	8 - 10
Series 4700 (6)	8 - 10	10 - 12
Series 1180, 1181 (6)	6 - 8	8 - 10
Erkal		
Series 307, 320, 335 (6)	10 - 12	12 - 14

S.W.S.B.
Women in Uniform	8 - 10	10 - 12
Series 1091, 6380, 6383 Dancing (6)	6 - 8	8 - 10

Anonymous
Series 20468 Couples Dancing	8 - 10	10 - 12

Art Deco

Erkal
Series 324 "Gypsy"	10 - 12	12 - 14
Series 363 Butterfly Ladies (6)	18 - 22	22 - 26

P.F.B. in Diamond
Series 6073 Beauties on Pillows (6)	12 - 14	14 - 16

S.&G.S.iB.
Series 6378, 6379, 6381 Dancing (6)	10 - 12	12 - 14
Series 6382, 6384 Dancing (6)	10 - 12	12 - 14
Series 6387, 1071, 1091 Dancing (6)	10 - 12	12 - 14
Series 1058, 1330, 1333 Dancing (6)	10 - 12	12 - 14
Series 1207, 1208 Dancing (6)	12 - 14	14 - 16

Guner & Simon
Series 2027 Lovers Kissing	8 - 10	10 - 12

UZLEMBLO, HENRY (Poland)   6 - 8   8 - 10

Clarence Underwood
Novitas 20457 "Two is Company"

Georges Wambach
Looy & Muygan, "Bonne Annee"

VALLET, L. (France) French Glamour		
Lapina Nude "La Douche" Series	18 - 22	22 - 25
VASSALO, A. (Italy) Art Deco	12 - 14	14 - 16
VEITH, E.	5 - 6	6 - 8
VENTURA, R.	10 - 12	12 - 14
VERNON, EMILE	3 - 4	4 - 5
VILLON, JACQUES (France) Art Nouveau		
Coll. des Cent and **Monnier**	400 - 500	500 - 800
VINCENT, RENE Art Deco	15 - 18	18 - 22
VINNOY (France) Art Deco	12 - 14	14 - 18
VOGLIO, BENITO (France)		
VOIGHT, C.A.	3 - 4	4 - 5
WACHTEL, WILHELM (Germany)	6 - 8	8 - 10
WALLACE (U.S.A.)		
Ladies & Horses	8 - 10	10 - 12
WANKE, ALICE (Austria) Art Nouveau	25 - 50	50 - 100
WAPALLOKA (Russia)	6 - 8	8 - 10
WASILKOWSKI, K. (Poland)	8 - 10	10 - 12
WASKO, EDWIN G.	5 - 6	6 - 8
WENNERBERG, B. (Sweden) Art Nouveau	12 - 15	15 - 25
WEZEL, A. (Austria)	8 - 10	10 - 12

K. Wasilkowski
Polish, J.C. 10

W. Wimbush, R. Tuck 3603
Sporting Girls, "Bathing ..."

WFA
  Ladies & Horses

Series 204 (6)	6 - 8	8 - 10

WICHERA, R.R.
  M. Munk, Vienna

Series 112, 322, 411 (6)	8 - 10	10 - 12
Series 224, 450, 530, 683 (6)	10 - 12	12 - 15
Series 229, 633, 1101 (6)	10 - 12	12 - 15
Series 1163 (6)	8 - 10	10 - 12
Series 559, 5590 Big Hats (6)	12 - 14	14 - 18
Series 684 Semi-Nudes (6)	12 - 15	15 - 20

WIEDERSEIM, GRACE (also G. Drayton)
  Armour & Co.
    "American Girl" Series

"The Wiederseim Girl"	30 - 35	35 - 40
"The Wiederseim Girl" (German Pub.)	35 - 40	45 - 50

WIMBUSH, WINIFRED
  Raphael Tuck

Sporting Girls, Series 3603	10 - 12	12 - 15
Others	8 - 10	10 - 12

WUYTS, A.   4 - 6   6 - 8

ZABCZINSKY
  C.B.B.

Series 21-1 Dancing (6)	15 - 18	18 - 22
Series 21-2 Standing (6)	18 - 20	20 - 25
Series 21-3 Dancing (6)	15 - 18	18 - 22
Series 21-4 Dancing (6)	15 - 18	18 - 22
Series 21-5 Dancing (6)	15 - 18	18 - 22
Series 21-6 Dancing	15 - 18	18 - 22

ZABCZOMSLU, W.   Art Deco   8 - 10   10 - 12

ZANDRINO, A.   (Italy) Art Deco

Series 18 Nude With Wild Animals (6)	20 - 25	25 - 30
Series 17 Fans (6)	12 - 15	15 - 17
Series 23, 24, 30 Fashion (6)	12 - 15	15 - 17
Series 94 Hats (6)	12 - 15	15 - 17

ZELECHOWSKI, K. (Poland)   8 - 10   10 - 12
ZENISER, JOSEF   6 - 8   8 - 10
ZEUMER, BRUNO (Germany)   5 - 6   6 - 8
ZINI, M.

Ladies	10 - 12	12 - 15

ZIRKA   4 - 6   6 - 8
ZMURKO, FR. (Poland) Color Nudes
  ANCZYC Series   8 - 10   10 - 12

BEAUTIFUL CHILDREN

ALANEN, JOSEPH (Finland)

Easter Witch Children	8 - 10	10 - 12

Miniature Easter Witch Cards	15 - 18	18 - 20
ALYS, M.	2 - 3	3 - 4
ANDERSON, ANNE	4 - 6	6 - 8
ANDERSON, V.C. (U.S.A.)	5 - 6	6 - 7
R. Tuck Series 7 -- Leap Year (12)	8 - 10	10 - 12
ETA (E. T. ANDREWS)		
Early Chromo-Lithographs	25 - 30	30 - 40
ANTTILA, EVA (Finland)	6 - 8	8 - 10
ATWELL, MABEL LUCIE (G.B.)		
Early Period, Pre-1915	12 - 15	15 - 18
Middle Period, 1915-1930	10 - 12	12 - 15
1930's-1950 Period	6 - 8	8 - 10
Valentine & Sons		
Series 748 Golliwogs	18 - 20	20 - 25
Series A561 Golliwogs	15 - 18	18 - 22
Series A579 Golliwogs	18 - 20	20 - 25
Suffragette "Where's My Vote"	18 - 20	20 - 25
See Blacks		
AZZONI, N. (Italy) Art Deco		
Dell, Anna & Gasparini		
Series 517 (6)	12 - 14	14 - 16
BARBER, C.W.		
Carlton Publishing Co.	6 - 8	8 - 10
BARHAM, SYBIL (G.B.) See Fairies/Fairy Tales		
C. W. Faulkner		
Series 502	5 - 6	6 - 7
Series 701	5 - 6	6 - 7
Series 964	5 - 6	6 - 7
BARKER, C.M.	6 - 8	8 - 10
BARNES, G.L. See Fairy Tales/Nursery Rhymes		
BARROWS, ELIZABETH	5 - 6	6 - 7
BAUMGARTEN, FRITZ FB		
See Fairy Tales/Nursery Rhymes		
Meissner & Buch	6 - 8	8 - 10
Other Publishers	6 - 8	8 - 10
BAYER, CHARLES A.	2 - 3	3 - 4
BEM, E. (Russia)		
Lapina Series	12 - 15	15 - 18
Russian Backs	18 - 22	22 - 25
Russian Alphabet Series	15 - 18	18 - 22
BERTIGLIA, A. (Italy) Art Deco		
Series 155 & 1053 Dutch Kids (6)	8 - 10	10 - 12
Series 1010 Playing War (6)	12 - 14	14 - 18
Series 1069 (6)	7 - 8	8 - 10
Series 2114 With Dolls (6)	10 - 12	12 - 16
Series 2428 Making Movies (6)	12 - 15	15 - 18
Series 2444 (6)	8 - 10	10 - 12
Series 2461 (6)	10 - 12	12 - 15

*Mabel Lucie Atwell
Valentine, "Pals"*

*Mabel Lucie Atwell
Valentine, "I'se Engaged - Dears!"*

*ETA (E. T. Andrews)
Theo. Stroefer, Series 27*

*A. L. Bowley, R. Tuck C1757
"A Happy Christmas"*

BLODGETT, BERTHA
  AMP Co.

Series 209, Easter	6 - 7	7 - 8
Series 410, Christmas	5 - 6	6 - 7
Little Girls/Huge Hats Series	6 - 8	8 - 10

BOMPARD, L. (Italy) Art Deco

Series 379 (6)	8 - 9	9 - 10
Series 454 (6)	8 - 9	9 - 10
Series 497 (6)	8 - 9	9 - 10
Series 523 (6)	8 - 10	10 - 12
Series 567 (6)	8 - 10	10 - 12
Series 906 (6)	8 - 10	10 - 12
Series 993 (6)	8 - 10	10 - 12

BONNE, SIGRID   5 - 6   6 - 7
BONORA (Italy)

Boy Scout Series 760	20 - 25	25 - 28

BORISS, MARGRET (Art Deco)   10 - 12   12 - 15
  Armag Co.

"Occupation Series" (6)	8 - 10	10 - 12
See Fairy Tales/Nursery Rhymes		

BOWDEN, DORIS   6 - 8   8 - 10
BOWLEY, A.L.

Early Unsigned Chromo-Lithographs	25 - 30	30 - 35
Raphael Tuck Series C3782	15 - 18	18 - 25

BOWLEY, MAY

Early Unsigned Chromo-Lithographs	20 - 25	25 - 30
Others	15 - 18	18 - 20

BRETT, M. See Fairy Tales/Nursery Rhymes
BRISLEY, NORA   6 - 8   8 - 10
BRUNDAGE, FRANCES (U.S.A.)
  Sam Gabriel

New Year		
Series 300, 302, 316 (10)	10 - 12	12 - 14
St. Patrick's Day		
Series 140 (10) (Unsigned)	8 - 10	10 - 12
Memorial Day		
Series 150	10 - 12	12 - 15
"In that instant o'er his ..."		
"Would I could duly praise ..."		
"Enough of Merit has each ..."		
"Brave minds, howe'er at war ..."		
"One Flag, one Land, one Heart ..."		
"By fairy hands their knell ..."		
Valentine's Day Series 413 (6)	8 - 10	10 - 12
Halloween		
Series 120, 121 (10)	20 - 22	22 - 25
Series 123 (10)	12 - 15	15 - 20
Series 125 (6)	20 - 22	22 - 25

May Bowley
R. Tuck Christmas Series E3657

Frances Brundage (Unsigned)
Jos. Engelman, Chromo-Litho.

Thanksgiving		
Series 130, 132, 133 (10)	8 - 10	10 - 12
Series 135 (6)	6 - 8	8 - 10
Christmas Series 200, 208, 219	10 - 12	12 - 15
Santas	15 - 18	18 - 22
Raphael Tuck		
New Year		
Series 601 (Uns.)	8 - 10	10 - 12
Series 1036	10 - 12	12 - 15
Valentine's Day		
Series 11 (4) (Uns.)	8 - 10	10 - 12
Series 20, 26 (Uns.)	10 - 12	12 - 15
Series 100, 101 (6) (Uns.)	10 - 12	12 - 14
Series 107 and 117	10 - 12	12 - 15
Blacks	22 - 25	25 - 28
Series 102 (6)	12 - 15	15 - 18
Blacks	25 - 30	30 - 35
Series 115 (4)	8 - 10	10 - 12
Blacks	25 - 28	28 - 32
Series 118 (4)	10 - 12	12 - 14
Blacks	22 - 25	25 - 28
Easter Series 1049 (3)	8 - 10	10 - 12
Memorial Day		
Series 173 (12) (Uns.)	8 - 10	10 - 12

Frances Brundage (Unsigned)
Wezel & Naumann

Frances Brundage (Unsigned)
Theo. Stroefer Series 84-V

E. Bem (Russian Artist)
Lapina 116, "An Old Friend ..."

Ellen H. Clapsaddle (Unsigned)
Int. Art Publishing Co.

Ellen H. Clapsaddle (Unsigned)
Anonymous German Publisher

Halloween (See Halloween Greetings)		
Christmas		
Series 4 (12)	12 - 15	15 - 20
Series 165 (2)	10 - 12	12 - 15
Blacks	18 - 20	20 - 25
Series 1035 (2)	10 - 12	12 - 15
Blacks		
Series 2723 "Colored Folks" (6)	50 - 60	60 - 70
Series 4096 "Funny Folks" (4)	25 - 30	30 - 35
Early Foreign Publishers		
Carl Hirsch, W.H.B.,		
Theo. Stroefer (T.S.N.), Wezel &		
Naumann, C. Baum, & Anon.		
Large Images	30 - 35	35 - 40
Small Images	20 - 25	25 - 30
BURD, C.M. (U.S.A.)		
Rally Day Series	6 - 8	8 - 10
Birthday Series	6 - 8	8 - 10
BUSI, A. (Italy) Art Deco		
Series 500 (6)	12 - 14	14 - 16
Boy Scout Series	16 - 20	20 - 25
CARR, GENE		
Rotograph Co.		
Series 219 (4th of July)	8 - 10	10 - 12
CASTELLI, V. (Italy) Art Deco		
Ultra		
Series 533 (6)	8 - 10	10 - 12
C.B.T.	2 - 3	3 - 4
CENNI, E. (Italy) Art Deco	5 - 6	6 - 7
CHAMBERLIN (U.S.A.)		
Campbell		
310 "Suffrage First"	60 - 70	70 - 80
312 "Let's Pull ..." Suffrage	60 - 70	70 - 80
CHIOSTRI, Sofia (Italy) Art Deco		
Ballerini & Fratini		
Series 184 Japanese (6)	10 - 12	12 - 15
Series 188 (6)	10 - 12	12 - 15
Series 319	15 - 18	18 - 20
CLAPSADDLE, ELLEN H. (U.S.A.)		
International Art. Publishing Co.		
Angels, Cherubs	4 - 6	6 - 8
Animals	4 - 5	5 - 6
Young Ladies, Women	5 - 6	6 - 8
Bells, Florals, Crosses, Sleds, etc.	2 - 3	3 - 4
Good Luck, Thanksgiving	2 - 3	3 - 4
Thanksgiving Children	5 - 6	6 - 9
Indians	6 - 7	7 - 9
Transportation	2 - 3	3 - 4
Christmas Children	10 - 12	12 - 14

Santas	12 - 16	16 - 20
Easter Children	7 - 9	9 - 14
Valentine Greetings	5 -6	6 - 8
Valentine Children	6 - 8	12 - 18
Series 941, 942, 944	8 - 10	10 - 15
Series 952, 953	8 - 10	10 - 15
Series 1034, 1081 (Uns.)	6 - 8	8 - 10
Valentine Mechanicals	30 - 35	35 - 50
Series 16190 (4)		
"To My Valentine"		
"St. Valentine's Greeting"		
"To My Sweetheart"		
"Love's Fond Greeting"		
Series 51810	20 - 25	25 - 30
Memorial Day		
Series 973, 2444, 4397 (6)	8 - 9	9 - 12
Series 2935 (6)	12 - 14	14 - 16
Washington's Birthday		
Series 16208, 16209 (4)	5 - 8	8 - 10
Series 16250 (6)	5 - 8	8 - 10
Series 51896 (6)	5 - 8	8 - 10
Lincoln's Birthday	5 - 8	8 - 12
St. Patrick's Day	6 - 9	9 - 12
Independence Day		
Series 2443, 4398	8 - 12	12 - 14
Halloween (See Halloween Greetings)		
Wolf & Co.		
Add $2-4 to Int. Art Publishing prices.		
Suffragettes		
"Love Me, Love My Vote"	60 - 70	70 - 80
"Woman's Sphere is in the Home"	40 - 45	45 - 50
Foreign Publishers, add $3-4.		
CLARK, A. (U.S.A.)	5 - 6	6 - 7
CLOKE, RENE (G.B.) See Fairies		
C. W. Faulkner Series (1930's)	8 - 10	10 - 12
Valentine's Series (1930's-40's)	6 - 8	8 - 10
Salmon Bros.		
Series (1930's-40's)	6 - 7	7 - 8
1950's Series	3 - 4	4 - 5
Medici Society Series (1950's-60's)	1 - 2	2 - 3
COLBY, V.	2 - 3	3 - 4
COLEMAN, W.S.	6 - 8	8 - 10
COLOMBO, E. (Italy)		
A. Guarneri (Milano)		
Series 234 (6)	7 - 8	8 - 9
Series 454 (6)	8 - 9	9 - 10
Series 618 (6)	8 - 10	10 - 12
Series 665 Child With Dog (6)	8 - 10	10 - 12
Series 960, 1764, 1905, 1964 (6)	8 - 10	10 - 12

Series 1968 (6)	10 - 12	12 - 14
Series 2007, 2140, 2141 (6)	6 - 8	8 - 10
Series 2033 (6)	8 - 10	10 - 12
Series 2044 (6)	8 - 10	10 - 12
Series 2181 (6)	8 - 10	10 - 12
Series 2223 (6)	10 - 12	12 - 14
Series 2252, 2426 (6)	6 - 8	8 - 10

G.P.M.

Series 1693-2	8 - 10	10 - 12
Series 1964 (6)	8 - 10	10 - 12

Ultra

Series 2039 (6)	8 - 10	10 - 12
COOK, A. M.	8 - 10	10 - 12

COOPER, PHYLLIS (GB) Art Deco

Raphael Tuck

Series 3463, 3464 "Happy Land" (6)	18 - 22	22 - 25
Doll-Toy Series (6)	18 - 22	22 - 25
CORBELLA, A.	8 - 10	10 - 12

CORBETT, BERTHA (U.S.A.)

J.I. Austin

Sunbonnet Children	8 - 10	10 - 15
CORY, F.Y.	2 - 3	3 - 4
COTTOM, C.M.	3 - 4	4 - 6
COWDEREY, K.	4 - 6	6 - 8
COWHAM, HILDA	6 - 8	8 - 10
CRAMER, RIE	15 - 18	18 - 22

CURTIS, E. (U.S.A.)

Raphael Tuck

Garden Patch 2	8 - 10	10 - 12

"Apple"	"Peach"
"Beet"	"Radish"
"Cantelope"	"Red Pepper"
"Carrot"	"Watermelon"

Raphael Tuck

Series 7 -- Leap Year (12)	8 - 10	10 - 12
"Valentine Maids" Series D12		
PC 1 "School Slates" (12)	6 - 7	7 - 8
PC 3 "Love's Labors" (12)	6 - 7	7 - 8
PC 4 "From Many Lands" (12)	6 - 7	7 - 8

CZEGKA, B. (Polish)

W.R.B. & Co.

Series 22 (6)	8 - 10	10 - 12
DAWSON, MURIEL	4 - 6	6 - 8
DeGARMES	1 - 2	2 - 3

DEWEES, ETHEL, E.D., EHD (U.S.A.)

AMP Co.	6 - 8	8 - 9
Ernest Nister Series 2543	8 - 10	10 - 12
DEXTER, MARJORIE	4 - 5	5 - 6

DIXON, DOROTHY
   Ullman Mfg. Co.
      Sunbonnet Babies (6)   8 - 10   10 - 12
DRAYTON, GRACE - (Wiederseim) (U.S.A.)
   Reinthal & Newman

306 "A Button Sewed on ..."	20 - 25	25 - 28
488 "Lambey Dear"	15 - 20	20 - 25
489 "Oh Dear Me"	15 - 20	20 - 25
492 "Gee up Dobin" (Unsigned)	15 - 20	20 - 25
493 Skipping Rope	15 - 20	20 - 25
495 Teacher & Children	15 - 20	20 - 25
496 "Do you, or don't you?"	15 - 20	20 - 25
497 "I should worry"	15 - 20	20 - 25
500 "More of All"	15 - 20	20 - 25
502 "Love at first sight"	20 - 25	25 - 30
503 "The Trousseau"	20 - 25	25 - 30
504 "The Wedding"	20 - 25	25 - 30
505 "The Honeymoon"	20 - 25	25 - 30
506	20 - 25	25 - 30
507 "Their New Love"	20 - 25	25 - 30

   Raphael Tuck
      Series 223 (6) (Unsigned)   15 - 20   20 - 25

E. Colombo
A. Guarneri (Milano), 2426

E. Colombo
G.P.M. 1693-2

DO YOU OR DON'T YOU?

REISTHAL & NEWMAN, PUBS., N.Y.

Phyllis Cooper
R. Tuck, Happy Land - I, 3463

G. G. Drayton, R&N 496
"Do You or Don't You?"

Series 241 "Bright Eyes" (Uns.) (6)	20 - 25	25 - 30
"I'se Awful Sweet ..."		
"I'm Your Little Darling Boy ..."		
"The Boys About Me Rant ..."		
Others		
Series 242 (Unsigned) (6)	15 - 20	20 - 25
Series 243 "Love Message" (Uns.) (6)	20 - 25	25 - 30
Series 1002 "Happy Easter" (Uns.) (6)	20 - 25	25 - 28
See Blacks		
Davis Co.		
34 Baby Girl in Sled	25 - 30	30 - 35
B.B. London (Unsigned) (6)	25 - 30	30 - 35
DUDDELA, JOSEPHINE	8 - 10	10 - 12
DULK, M.		
Gibson Art Series 252		
Fantasy Flower Girls, Birthday	10 - 12	12 - 16
"Daffodil" "Rose"		
"Pansy" "Sweet Pea"		
"Forget me Not" "Violet"		
"Poppy" "Red Rose"		
"Pussy Willow" "Tulip"		
Valentine Series - Girls (6)	8 - 10	10 - 12
EBNER, PAULI (Germany)		
Early - Signed PE	15 - 18	18 - 22

Pauli Ebner
M. Munk, 878

Pauli Ebner
A.R., 1416

Santas	18 - 22	22 - 25
M. Munk, Vienna		
Series 878 Toys	15 - 17	17 - 20
Series 1126 Victorian Children	10 - 12	12 - 14
Series 1129 Birthday	10 - 12	12 - 15
Series 403, 986, 1019 New Year	12 - 15	15 - 18
Series 550, 1136, 1269 New Year	15 - 17	17 - 20
Series 1044 Winter	12 - 14	14 - 16
Series 1158, 1263	12 - 14	14 - 16
Series 1106 Christmas	12 - 14	14 - 16
August Rokol, Vienna or AR		
Series 1428 Birthday	12 - 14	14 - 18
Series 1375, 1440 Toys	15 - 17	17 - 20
Series 1321	12 - 14	14 - 16
"Puppet Marriage Series"	18 - 22	22 - 26
E.F.D. or ELLEN F. DREW		
M.A.P. Co.	3 - 4	4 - 6
Ernest Nister	5 - 6	6 - 8
EGERTON, LINDA	6 - 8	8 - 10
ELLAM, WILLIAM (G.B.)	5 - 6	6 - 8
ELLIOTT, KATHRYN (U.S.A.)	4 - 5	5 - 6
Gibson Art Co.		
Halloween Series (10)	6 - 8	8 - 10
F.B. (not Brundage)	5 - 6	6 - 8

F.S.M.
Heininger "Courtship & Marriage" Series	8 - 10	10 - 12
FEDERLEY, ALEXANDER (Finland)	5 - 6	6 - 8
FEIERTAG, K. (Austria)		
B.K.W.I.	5 - 6	6 - 8
FIALKOWSKA, WALLY (Germany)		
Large Children, Comical	10 - 12	12 - 14
Small Children & Babies	6 - 8	8 - 10
Black Children	12 - 15	15 - 18
FLOWERS, CHARLES (U.S.A)	5 - 6	6 - 7
FOLKARD, CHARLES		
A & C Black		
"Nursery Rhymes & Tales"		
Series 91 (6)	12 - 15	15 - 18
"Beauty and the Beast"		
"Cinderella"		
"Little Bo Peep"		
"Tom, Tom, the Piper's Son"		
"Red Riding Hood"		
"Sleeping Beauty"		
FRANK, E.	5 - 6	6 - 7
GASSAWAY, KATHERINE (U.S.A)		
Raphael Tuck		
Series 113 Bridal, Valentines (6)	6 - 8	8 - 10
Series 130 Easter Series (12)	6 - 7	7 - 8
Series 22495 "The New Baby" (6)	6 - 8	8 - 10
Rotograph Co.		
"Age" Series	8 - 10	10 - 12
117 "1 Year"		
118 "2 Years"		
119 "3 Years"		
120 "4 Years"		
121 "5 Years"		
National Girls		
220 "America"	8 - 10	10 - 12
221 "Ireland"	7 - 8	8 - 10
222 "England"	7 - 8	8 - 10
223 "Germany"	7 - 8	8 - 10
224 "France"	7 - 8	8 - 10
225	7 - 8	8 - 10
226 "Italy"	7 - 8	8 - 10
227 "Sweden"	7 - 8	8 - 10
American Kid Series (6)	5 - 6	6 - 8
Black Children	8 - 10	10 - 12
Others	5 - 6	6 - 8
GEORGE, MARY ELEANOR		
Ernest Nister	20 - 22	22 - 25
GILSON, T. (U.S.A.)		
Black Children Comics	8 - 10	10 - 12

Wally Fialkowska
A.V.M. 1148 , German Caption

Katherine Gassaway (Uns.)
K&N, Hamburg, No. 6

GOLAY, MARY	3 - 4	4 - 5
GOODMAN, MAUDE		
Raphael Tuck		
Series 824-833	10 - 12	12 - 15
Early Chromo-Lithographs	20 - 25	25 - 30
GOLIA, E. (Italy) Art Deco		
Series 102 War-time Children	18 - 20	20 - 25
GOVEY, A (G.B.)		
Humphrey Milford, London		
"Dreams and Fairies" Golliwogs	12 - 14	14 - 18
GRASSETTI (Italy) Art Deco	6 - 8	8 - 10

GREENAWAY, KATE (KG) (G.B.)

Kate Greenaway was one of the first well-known illustrators of children.   Her earliest works were of Valentines, Birthday and Christmas non-postcards. Later came her famous children's books and almanacs. She did many fine illustrations that were used in the "Mother Goose" and "Old Nursery Rhymes" books printed by Rutledge and Sons.

Postcards were produced in limited quantities from these illustrations. They are rarities, and are very hard to find in any condition. Kate died in 1901 before the postcard-craze era of 1905-1918 began.

The works that were adapted for postcards are signed "KG" and have undivided backs. They depict well-known children types and a verse from the "Mother Goose" book which she illustrated.

KATE GREENAWAY

Multilingual Backs with Verse	60 - 75	75 - 90
Without Verse (Unsigned)	30 - 40	40 - 50
From *Mother Goose* and *Old Nursery*		
Rhymes (B&W) *	60 - 75	75 - 95

Signed KG, With Verse
"A diller, a dollar ..."
"As Tommy Snooks, and Bessie Brooks ..."
"Billie Boy Blue ..."
"Cross Patch, lift the latch ..."
"Elsie Marley has grown so fine ..."
"Girls and boys come out to play ..."
"Goosey, goosey, gander ..."
"Hark! Hark! The dogs bark ..."
"Here am I, little jumping Joan ..."
"Humpty Dumpty sat on a wall ..."
"Jack and Jill went up the hill ..."
"Johnny shall have a new bonnet ..."
"Little Betty Blue, lost her ..."
"Little Jack Horner sat in the corner ..."
"Little lad, little lad ..."
"Mary, Mary, quite contrary ..."
"Polly put the kettle on, ..."
"Ride a cock-horse to Banbury-cross ..."
"Ring-a-ring-a-roses ..."
"Rock-a-bye baby ..."
"There was an old woman ..."
"Tom, Tom, the piper's son ..."
Listing is incomplete.
* From article by Don & Judy McNichol in
    "What Cheer News," R. Island P.C. Club

GREINER, MAGNUS (U.S.A.)   See Blacks
International Art Pub. Co.

Dutch Children Series 491, 692 (6)	6 - 7	7 - 8
"Molly & the Bear" Series 791	10 - 12	12 - 15

GRIGGS, H.B. (also H.B.G.)
L & E (Leubrie & Elkus)

Christmas Series 2224, 2264, 2275	6 - 8	8 - 10
New Year's		
Series 2225, 2266, 2276	6 - 8	8 - 10
Easter Series 2226, 2254, 2271	6 - 8	8 - 10
Valentine's Day		
Series 2218, 2243, 2244, 2267	8 - 10	10 - 12
Series 2217, 2219, 2248	10 - 12	12 - 14
Blacks	15 - 18	18 - 20

M. Grimball, Russian "Richard"
No. 453, "The Grand Finale"

B. C. (B. P.) Gutmann
"Richard" 138, "Falling Out"

Bessie Pease Gutmann
G&G 1204, "Feeling"

B. P. Gutmann, Novitas
20607/4, "The First Lesson"

St. Patrick's Day
Series 2230, 2232, 2253, 2269 — 8 - 10 — 10 - 12
Thanksgiving
Series 2212, 2213, 2233, 2263, 2273 — 6 - 8 — 8 - 10
George Washington's Birthday
Series 2268 — 8 - 10 — 10 - 12
Halloween
Series 2214, 2216, 2262 — 10 - 12 — 12 - 14
Series 2263, 2272 — 12 - 14 — 14 - 16
Series 2231, 7010 — 15 - 16 — 16 - 18
Birthday
Series 2232 — 6 - 8 — 8 - 10

Anonymous Publisher Series
Series 2215, 7010 — 12 - 14 — 14 - 16

GRILLI, S. (Italy) Art Deco — 6 - 8 — 8 - 10
GRIMBALL, Meta M.
    Gutmann & Gutmann — 15 - 18 — 18 - 22
    Reinthal & Newman — 12 - 15 — 15 - 20

    FOREIGN ISSUES
    Novitas — 25 - 30 — 30 - 35
      Series 10726
      "Puppen Mutterchen's Einkauf"
      "Storenfried"
      "Leckerbissen"
      Series 10930
      "Say Das Nicht Noch Mal!"
      "Kinderdieb" Series 10966
      "Delighted" Series 20607
      1 - "He Won't Bite" (German Caption)
      4 - "The First Lesson" (German Caption)
      Series 20608
      "Music Hath Charm"
      Series 2168 "Fired"
      Other German Captions
      "Love at First Sight"

GROSS, O. — 2 - 3 — 3 - 4
GUARINO, ANTHONY — 3 - 4 — 4 - 5
GUASTA (Italy) Art Deco — 6 - 8 — 8 - 10
GUTMANN, BESSIE PEASE (U.S.A.)
BESSIE PEASE GUTMANN
    Gutmann & Gutmann
    200 Series - Children
      200 "The New Love" — 25 - 30 — 30 - 35
      201 "The Lone Fisherman"
      Others
    500 Series - Beautiful Women
      500 "Rosebuds" — 35 - 40 — 40 - 45
      501 "Senorita"

502 "Waiting"
503 "Daydreams"
504 "Poppies"
505 "I wish you were here"

800 Series - Young Girls
  800 "Margaret"   35 - 40   40 - 45
  801 "Betty"
  802 "Virginia"
  803 "Alice"
  804 "Lucille"
  805 "Dorothy"

900 Series - Babies
  900 "Contentment"   32 - 35   35 - 38
  901 "Come play with me"
  902 "All is Vanity"
  903 "His Majesty"
  904 "Dessert"

1000 Series - Baby/Mother
  1000 "Sunshine"   30 - 35   35 - 40
  1001 "I love to be loved by a baby"
  1002 "In Slumberland"

FSM, Henry Heininger Co.
"May End in a Tie"

Florence Hardy
BD 378, No Caption

1003 "Baby mine"
1004 "The Sweetest Joy"

1100 Series - Young Women

1100 "Repartee"	35 - 40	40 - 45

1101 "Sweeheart"
1102 "Sweet Sixteen"
1103 "Speeding"
1104 "Happy Dreams"

1200 Series - The Five Senses

1200 "Tasting"	35 - 40	40 - 45

1201 "Seeing"
1202 "Smelling"
1203 "Hearing"
1204 "Feeling"

1300 Series - A Woman's Life

1300 "The Baby"	30 - 35	35 - 40

1301 "Off to school"
1302 "The Dubutante"
1303 "The Bride"
1304 "The Mother"

FOREIGN
Novitas - N in Circle
Series 20360 (6)

Same as G&G 1300 Series, "A Woman's Life"	45 - 50	50 - 55
Series 20361 - Sunshine Series	35 - 40	40 - 45

Series 20607

"The First Lesson"	45 - 50	50 - 55

"Love at First Sight"
"The New Love"

Series 20697 (6)

Same as G&G 200 Series	45 - 50	50 - 55

Series 20608 (6)

"The Lone Fisherman"	45 - 50	50 - 55

"Music Hath Charm"
"Ragtime"
"My Bruzzer has a fever..."

Others

20556 Images in Water	40 - 45	45 - 50

20558 Mother on knees kisses boy
"All is Vanity"
"Feeling"
"Delighted"
"The Foster Mother"
"Guess Who?" Unsigned
"Love is Blind"
"Margaret"

"*Benjamin Franklin...*," 576   "*Boston Tea Party*," 577

"*Bunker Hill*," 578   "*Washington's Courtship*," 579

Terrific Discovery! Now there are four signed Maud Humphrey images by the V.O. Hammond Publishing Company.

"Stolen Sweets" Unsigned
"Strenuous"
Others

Russian
M.J.S.

011 Images in Water		50 - 55	55 - 60

Richard (Rishar, Petrograde
or St. Petersburg)

91 "The New Love"		50 - 55	55 - 60
137 "Making Up"		50 - 55	55 - 60
155 Girl with many dolls		55 - 60	60 - 65
Others			
Other Foreign Publishers & Distributors		40 - 45	45 - 48

Advertising
Brown & Bigelow Calendars

120-131 Months of year (12)		45 - 50	50 - 55
HALLOCK, RUTH		5 - 6	6 - 8

HARDY, FLORENCE (G.B.)

C.W. Faulkner & Co.		8 - 9	9 - 10
Dancing Series 914 (6)		12 - 14	14 - 16
M. Munk, Vienna			
Series 352 (6)		8 - 10	10 - 12
Others		6 - 8	8 - 10

HAYS, MARGARET G. (U.S.A.)

Ernest Nister

Big Eyes Series		25 - 30	30 - 35
"Miss Polly Pigtail" Series (6)		25 - 30	30 - 35
2748 Dressed in Pink			
2749 Dressed in Green			
2750 Dressed in Purple			
2751 Dressed in Red			
2752 Dressed in Yellow			
2753 Dressed in Blue			
Series 3059 Valentine Children		15 - 17	17 - 20
Series 3061 (6) Large Images		15 - 17	17 - 20

The Rose Co.

Christmas Series (6)		15 - 17	17 - 20

Anonymous

Paper Doll Series 3 (6)		75 - 85	85 - 100
Paper Doll Series 6 (6)		75 - 85	85 - 100

HEINMULLER, A.
International Art Pub. Co.

Series 1002, Halloween (6)		12 - 14	14 - 16
Series 1003, St. Patrick's Day (6)		4 - 6	6 - 7
Series 1004, Thanksgiving (6)		4 - 5	5 - 6
Series 1620, Valentines (6)		5 - 6	6 - 7
HOLLYER, EVA		6 - 8	8 - 10
HORSFALL, MARY		4 - 6	6 - 8

HUMMEL
Pre-1950	12 - 15	15 - 18
Later Period	5 - 6	6 - 7

HUMPHREY, MAUD (U.S.A.)
V. O. Hammon Pub. Co.	125 - 150	150 - 175
576 "Benjamin Franklin Entering Phila."		
577 "Boston Tea Party"		
578 "Bunker Hill"		
579 "Washington's Courtship"		
R. L. Conwell Co. (Unsigned)	10 - 12	12 - 15
Anonymous Publisher		
Signed M.H. -- "The Four Seasons" (4)	50 - 60	60 - 75
Gray Lithograph Co. (Unsigned)		
43, 44, 45, 46, 47, 48, 49, 50, 54	12 - 15	15 - 20
Others	12 - 15	15 - 20
Rotograph		
Series F457	12 - 15	15 - 20

HUMPHREYS, L. G. 2 - 3   3 - 4

HUTAF, AUGUST (U.S.A.)
Ullman Mfg. Co.		
"A Little Odd Fellow"	6 - 8	8 - 10
"A Little Shriner"	6 - 8	8 - 10
Other	6 - 8	8 - 10
Other Publishers	4 - 6	6 - 8

I.M.J. (I.M. JAMES) (G.B.)
M. Munk		
Children Series	6 - 8	8 - 10

JACKSON, HELEN (See Fairy Tales)
Others	10 - 12	12 - 15

JACOBS, HELEN 6 - 8   8 - 10

K.V.
LP Co.		
Kewpie-like Children	8 - 10	10 - 12
Black Children (or Mixed)	12 - 15	15 - 18

KASKELINE, FRED
Silhouette Series 9033 (6)	6 - 8	8 - 9
Others	6 - 7	7 - 8

KEMBLE, E.B.   See Blacks
Comic Children	3 - 4	4 - 5

KENNEDY (See Fairy Tales)

KIDD, WILL 3 - 5   5 - 6

KER, MARY SIGSBEE 4 - 5   5 - 6

KING, HAMILTON 8 - 10   10 - 12

KINSELLA, E.P.
Tennis Series	18 - 20	20 - 25
Others	12 - 15	15 - 18

KIRK, M.L.
National Art Co.		
Birthday Signs (7)	8 - 10	10 - 12

KNOEFEL
  Illuminated Appearance
  Novitas

Series 664 (6)	6 - 8	8 - 10
Series 656 With Phones (6)	10 - 12	12 - 14
Series 15834, 20887 (Mother/Child) (6)	8 - 10	10 - 12

KÖHLER, MELA (Austria) Art Deco   25 - 30   30 - 35
LeMAIR, H. WILLEBEEK (G.B.)
  Augener, Ltd.

Children's "Pieces of Schumann"	12 - 15	15 - 18

    "Catch Me if You Can"
    "Dreaming"
    "Perfect Happiness"
    "Melody"
    "The Merry Peasant"
    "First Loss"
    "The Poor Orphan"
    "Romance"
    "Roundelay"
    "Sicilienne"
    "Soldier's March"
    "Vintage"

The Children's Corner	6 - 8	8 - 10

    "Baby's Fright"
    "Dreadfully Busy"
    "Fishing Boats"
    "Greedy"
    "Hair Cutting"
    "Last Year's Frock"
    "Out of the Snow"
    "Preserving Dickey"
    "Poor Baby"
    "Queen of the Birds"
    "The Dove's Dinner Time"
    "The Garden City"
    "The Invalid's Birthday"

LEVI, C.

Suffragette	20 - 22	22 - 25
Series 210, 3308 "Komical Koons"	12 - 15	15 - 18

LEWIN, F.G. (See Blacks)
  Bamforth Co.

Children Comics	6 - 8	8 - 10

LINDEBERG

Head Studies	6 - 8	8 - 10

LD
  Meissner & Buch   6 - 8   8 - 9
LANDSTROM, B. (Finland)

Fairy Tales	6 - 8	8 - 9

M.S.M.
A.V.M. 1351, German Caption

Irene Marcellus
E. Nister 3215, "This Dear ..."

H. G. C. Marsh, "Family Cares"
C. W. Faulkner Ser. 962-D

Anonymous German
"First Day of School"

MAILICK, R. (German)
    Angels, Children   8 - 10   10 - 15
MAISON-KURT
    Fantasy Bear Set with Girl (4)   12 - 15   15 - 18
MALLET, BEATRICE (G.B.)
    R. Tuck
        "Cute Kiddies" Oilette Series
          3567, 3568, 3628, 3629   (6)   8 - 9   9 - 10
MARCELLUS, IRENE
    E. Nister
        Ser. 3215, Child's Head in Pie, etc.   14 - 15   15 - 18
        Ser. 736, 737   15 - 18   18 - 20
        Ser. 1885, 3097   15 - 18   18 - 20
MARGOTSON, H.   6 - 8   8 - 10
MARSH, H.G.C. (G.B.)
    BD
        Child and Teddy Bear   10 - 12   12 - 15
        "Wee Willie Winkle"   8 - 10   10 - 12
        "Curly Locks"   7 - 8   8 - 10
    C. W. Faulkner, Series 962   10 - 12   12 - 15
MARSHALL, ALICE   8 - 10   10 - 12
MART, L.   5 - 6   6 - 7
MARTINEAU, ALICE   6 - 8   8 - 10
MAYBANK, THOMAS (See Fairies)   8 - 10   10 - 12
McCUTCHEON, JOHN T. (U.S.A.)   4 - 6   6 - 8
MAUZAN, L.A. (Italy) Art Deco
    Series 45 With Dogs   10 - 12   12 - 15
M.D.S. (U.S.A.) See Blacks and Teddy Bears
M.E.P. (see MARGARET EVANS PRICE, MP)
    Others   6 - 7   7 - 8
M.M.S.
    G.K. Prince
        Series 421   5 - 6   6 - 8
M.S.M.
    A.V.M. Series   10 - 12   12 - 15
    Meisner & Buch Series   12 - 15   15 - 18
MERCER, JOYCE   12 - 15   15 - 18
MILLER, HILDA T.   12 - 15   15 - 18
MITCHELL, SADIE   4 - 5   5 - 6
NASH, A. (U.S.A.)
    Heckscher
        Series 704   6 - 8   8 - 10
NIXON, K. See Fairy Tales
NORFINI (Italy) Art Deco   8 - 10   10 - 12
NOSWORTHY, FLORENCE (G.B.)   6 - 8   8 - 10
    See Fairy Tales
NUMBER, JACK
    PFB (in Diamond) German Captions
        Series 2068 (4)   8 - 10   10 - 12

Series 2070 (4)	8 - 10	10 - 12
Series 2076 (4)	8 - 10	10 - 12
NYSTROM, JENNY (Sweden)	10 - 12	12 - 15
See Fairy Tales		
NYSTROM, KURT (Sweden)	6 - 8	8 - 12

O'NEILL, ROSE (U.S.A.)

One of the most popular of all the signed artists is Rose O'Neill, who created and drew the lovable Kewpie doll. The Kewpies delighted children and adults during the period after World War I through the Depression of the thirties.

Her first works were for advertising, covers and inside illustrations for some of the leading magazines. All showed the adorable Kewpies collection. Rose O'Neill's Kewpie cards continue to be among the her in various activities. The Gibson Art Company published many of O'Neill's designs on postcards for most of the holiday seasons. Her best and most popular were probably those of Christmas.

The Edward Gross Co. did a great set of six large image Kewpies, while Campbell Art and National Woman Suffrage each issued a card on Women's Suffrage that have become the most famous of all her works. She also did two series of blacks that were published by Raphael Tuck. These are very scarce and are avidly pursued by many collectors.

These jolly Kewpies say "How-do-you-do," and wish you a happy Easter season.

Rose O'Neill, Gibson Art 69077, "These Jolly Kewpies ..."

L. Mart
Graf. N. Moneta, Milano

Susan P. Pearse
M. Munk 856, "A-B-C-School"

Rose O'Neill also did illustrations for advertisements as well as illustrated books. The book signatures sometimes used her married name, Latham.

ROSE O'NEILL

Gibson Art		
Greetings with Kewpies	30 - 35	35 - 40
Edward Gross, N.Y.		
Large Image Kewpies	85 - 100	100 - 110
Campbell Art Co.		
Klever Kards		
Dated 1914 (26)	55 - 60	60 - 65
Dated 1915 (20)	60 - 65	65 - 70
228 "Votes for Women ..."	200 - 225	225 - 250
National Woman Suffrage		
"Votes for our Mothers"	300 - 350	350 - 400
Raphael Tuck		
See Blacks		
Rock Island Line, Advertising	45 - 50	50 - 60
Parker-Bruaner Co. Ice Cream Ad.	100 - 150	150 - 200
OUTCAULT, R. (U.S.A.)	8 - 10	10 - 12
See Artist-Signed Comics		

OUTHWAITE, IDA R. (See Fairies)	10 - 12	12 - 15
PALMER, PHYLLIS (U.S.A.)	4 - 6	6 - 8
PARKINSON, ETHEL (G.B.)		
BC		
Series 745 (6)	8 - 10	10 - 12
BD		
Series 475 (6)	10 - 12	12 - 14
C. W. Faulkner		
Series 951	12 - 14	14 - 16
M. Munk, Vienna		
Series 132, 380, 488 (6)	10 - 12	12 - 15
Series 232, 502, 554 (6)	8 - 10	10 - 12
Series 191, 234 (6)	8 - 10	10 - 12
Series 531 (6)	8 - 10	10 - 12
Days of the Week (Dutch Children)	12 - 15	15 - 18
Others	8 - 10	10 - 12
PARTLETT, HARRY (COMICUS) (G.B.)	5 - 6	6 - 7
PATERSON, VERA	6 - 7	7 - 8
PEARSE, S.B. (Susan) (G.B.)		
M. Munk, Vienna		
Series 563, 727, 728 (6)	10 - 12	12 - 15

Chloe Preston, R. Tuck 3461
"Quaint Little Folk"

Chloe Preston, R. Tuck 3461
"Quaint Little Folk"

M.E.P. (Margaret Evans Price), Stecher Series 417C

Series 635 (6) Dolls	14 - 18	18 - 22
Series 679, 712, 713 (6)	12 - 14	14 - 16
Series 758 (6) Dancing	12 - 14	14 - 18
Series 844, 922, 925 (6)	12 - 14	14 - 18
Series 856 (6) With Toys	14 - 18	18 - 22
Series 862 (6)	8 - 10	10 - 12
Others	8 - 10	10 - 12

PEASE, BESSIE COLLINS
See Bessie P. Gutmann

PETERSEN, HANNES (Belgium)	5 - 6	6 - 8
PHILIPP, FELICIEN	8 - 10	10 - 12
PIATTOLI, G. (Italy) Art Deco	6 - 8	8 - 10
PINOCHI, E. (Italy) Art Deco	6 - 8	8 - 10
PITTS, JOHN E. J.E.P. (U.S.A.)	5 - 6	6 - 10
POWELL, LYMAN	5 - 6	6 - 8

PRESTON, CHLOE (British)   Art Deco
   B.R. Co.

Series E (Black Background) (6)	12 - 15	15 - 18
Raphael Tuck, 461	12 - 15	15 - 18

PRICE, MARGARET EVANS   M.E.P & MP
  (U.S.A.)
  Stecher Litho Co.

Series 413, 415, 417 Christmas (6)	6 - 8	8 - 10
Series 648, 656, 657, 749, 875 Christmas (6)	8 - 10	10 - 12
Series 517, 628, 821 Valentine's (6)	8 - 10	10 - 12
Series 503, 750, 783 Easter (6)	8 - 10	10 - 12
Series 98 Flower Children (6)	8 - 10	10 - 12
Series 403 St. Patrick's (6)	6 - 8	8 - 10
Girl Scouts	12 - 15	15 - 18

Eugenie Richards, R&N 2072,
"None But the Brave ..."

Agnes Richardson, R. Tuck
C1421, "A Happy Christmas"

Agnes Richardson, R. Tuck
C1420, "A Happy Christmas"

Agnes Richardson, R. Tuck
C1422, "Christmas Greetings"

See Halloween		
Note: Many of the Stecher Series were reprinted in the 40's & 50's.	2 - 3	3 - 4
R.R.		
M. Munk, Vienna		
Series 1030	8 - 10	10 - 12
RACKHAM, ARTHUR (G.B.)	12 - 15	15 - 20
RICHARDS, EUGENIE	6 - 8	8 - 10
RICHARDSON, AGNES (G.B.)		
Charles Hauff		
No No. Series	8 - 10	10 - 12
C. W. Faulkner		
Series 126, 6126 (6)	10 - 12	12 - 14
M. Munk, Vienna		
Series 706 (6)	8 - 10	10 - 12
Others	8 - 10	10 - 12
International Art Co.		
1958 "My Love is Like ..."	6 - 8	8 - 10
1959 "I'll Take Care of Mummy"	6 - 8	8 - 10
Raphael Tuck		
Series C3609 (6)	8 - 10	10 - 12
Series 8670 (6)	8 - 10	10 - 12
Series 1262, 1281 "Art" (6) Golliwogs	18 - 22	22 - 25
Series 1232 "Rescued" (6) Golliwogs	18 - 22	22 - 25
Series 1397 (6) Golliwogs	18 - 22	22 - 25
Series C-1420, C-1421, C-1422	15 - 18	18 - 22

R. Sgrilli, G.P.M. 2260 (No Caption)

Valentine & Sons		
Series C2006 (6) Golliwogs	15 - 18	18 - 20
Others	8 - 10	10 - 12
See Blacks		
ROBINSON, ROBERT (U.S.A.)		
Edward Gross		
Series 205 Boy Ball Player	15 - 20	20 - 25
ROWLES, L. Art Deco	8 - 10	10 - 12
RUSSELL, MARY LA FENETRA (U.S.A.)		
Sam Gabriel Co.		
Children	4 - 6	6 - 8
Halloween	8 - 10	10 - 12
Salke		
"Brick Wall" Children	6 - 8	8 - 10
SANDFORD, H.D. (G.B.) See Blacks		
SANFORD, M. (G.B.)		
Raphael Tuck		
See Blacks		
SAUNDERS, E.H. (U.S.A.)	5 - 6	6 - 8
S.K. Art Deco	8 - 10	10 - 12
SGRILLI (Italy) Art Deco	8 - 10	10 - 12
SMITH, JESSIE WILCOX (U.S.A.)		
Reinthal & Newman		
"Garden" Series 100	18 - 18	18 - 22
"Among the Poppies"		
"Five O'Clock Tea"		
"The Garden Wall"		

M. Sowerby, B.D. No. 130 (Beautiful Art Deco)

"The Green Door"		
"In the Garden"		
"The Lily Pool"		
SMITH, MAY	6 - 8	8 - 10

SOWERBY, AMY MILLICENT (G.B.)

Amy Millicent Sowerby was an English artist who illustrated several wonderful children's books. Her most famous was Lewis Carroll's "Alice in Wonderland," and then Robert Lewis Stevenson's "A Child's Garden of Verse." Her illustrations also appeared on picture postcards that were intended for children.

Her cards all have precise detail. Colors are exceptionally bright and the lithography is excellent. Most of Sowerby's cards were published in England and Europe. The American Post Card Co. and Reinthal & Newman, of New York, published several series for distribution in the U.S.

AMY MILLICENT SOWERBY

B.D. (Art Deco)	12 - 15	15 - 18
Reinthal & Newman		
Unnumbered Series	12 - 15	15 - 18
"Cold"		
"Fair"		
"Wet"		
"Dry"		
"Cloudy"		
"Dull"		
Series 2001	15 - 18	18 - 22
"Peggy"		
"Phoebe"		
"Phyllis"		
"Priscilla"		
Humphrey Milford, London (See Fairy Tales)		
Name of Series		
"Favorite Children" (6)	12 - 15	15 - 18
"Flower Children" (6)	12 - 15	15 - 18
"Flowers & Wings" (6)	12 - 15	15 - 18
"Merry Elves" (6)	12 - 15	15 - 18
"Old Time Games" (6)	10 - 12	12 - 15
"Sky Fairies" (6)	12 - 15	15 - 18
No Publisher		
Little Jewels Series	12 - 15	15 - 18
"Amethyst"		
"Emerald"		
"Pearl"		

"Ruby"		
"Sapphire"		
"Turquoise"		
Woodland Games (6)	10 - 12	12 - 15
SPARK, CHICKY (Germany)	5 - 6	6 - 8
SPURGIN, FRED (G.B.)	4 - 5	5 - 6
See Blacks		
STENBERG, AINA (Sweden)	12 - 15	15 - 18
STOCKS, M.		
H.K. & Co.		
"Jack in the Box" (Golliwogs)	12 - 14	14 - 16
SURR, RUTH WELCH (U.S.A.)	2 - 3	3 - 4
R.T.	2 - 3	3 - 4
TARRANT, MARGARET (G.B.)	6 - 8	8 - 15
(See Nursery Rhymes)	6 - 8	8 - 12
TEMPEST, DOUGLAS (G.B.)		
Bamforth Co.		
See Blacks		
Comic Kids and Animals (30's)	3 - 4	4 - 6
Raphael Tuck		
Series 3 (6) "Dainty Dimples"	6 - 8	8 - 10
TEMPEST, MARGARET	4 - 6	6 - 8
THOMAS, V.	4 - 5	5 - 6
TWELVETREES, CHARLES (U.S.A.)		
Ullman Mfg. Co.		
"National Cupid" Series 75	10 - 12	12 - 14
1877 "United States"		
1878 "England"		
1879 "Ireland"		
1880 "Scotland"		
1882 "Mexico"		
1883 "Holland"		
1884 "Spain"		
1885 "Canada"		
1887 "China"		
1888 "Italy"		
Edward Gross, N.Y.		
Comical Kids	6 - 8	8 - 10
Wedding Series	10 - 12	12 - 15
1050 "Infant Series"	6 - 7	7 - 8
"Am I crying..."		
"I'm a war baby, but..."		
"I'm the family darling..."		
"Folks all say..."		
"Our baby can't talk..."		
"Watch your step..."		
National Art		
Days of the Week Series	6 - 7	7 - 8
Morning-Noon-Night Series	6 - 8	8 - 10

Millicent Sowerby
R&N 2001, "Pamela"

C. Twelvetrees, Ullman
National Cupid Ser. 75, No. 1877

UPTON, FLORENCE K.
  Raphael Tuck
    Golliwog Series

Series 1791, 1792	20 - 25	25 - 30
Series 1793, 1794	20 - 25	25 - 30
VOIGHT, C.A.	3 - 4	4 - 5
VON HARTMAN, E.	2 - 3	3 - 4

WALL, BERNHARDT C. (U.S.A.) See Blacks
  Ullman Mfg. Co.

"Overall Boys"	6 - 8	8 - 10
92 "Young America"		
93 "Me and Jack"		
94 "Leap Frog"		
95 "A Rough Rider"		
"The Senses"	8 - 10	10 - 12
1716 "Feeling"		
1717 "Smelling"		
1718 "Tasting"		
1719 "Hearing"		
1720 "Seeing"		
"Nursery Rhymes" Series (Unsigned)	8 - 10	10 - 12
1664 "Little Bo Peep"		
1665 "To Market, To Market"		

1666 "Rain, Rain Go Away"		
1667 "See Saw, Marjorie Daw"		
1668 "Goosey, Goosey, Gander"		
1669 "Come, let's go to bed"		
Sunbonnet Months of the Year		
Unsigned, 1633-1644	8 - 9	9 - 12
Sunbonnet Girl's Days of the Week		
Unsigned, 1408-1410, 1491-1494	10 - 12	12 - 15
Sunbonnet Seasons	10 - 12	12 - 14
1901 Spring		
1902 Summer		
1903 Autumn		
1904 Winter		
"Mary and Her Lamb" Sunbonnets		
1759-1762	8 - 10	10 - 12
Sunbonnet Twins	10 - 12	12 - 15
1645 "Give us this Day ..."		
1646 "The Star Spangled ..."		
1647 "Should Auld Acquaintance ..."		
1648 "A Good Book is ..."		
1649 "Now I Lay Me Down ..."		
1650 "Be It Ever So Humble ..."		

Grace Wiederseim
R&N No Number, "Blow"

Grace Wiederseim, R. Tuck
"Cunning Cupids" Series 2914

Sunbonnet Girls	10 - 12	12 - 14
1765 "6 A.M., Milking Time"		
1766 "7 A.M., Breakfast Time"		
1767 "10 A.M., Mowing Time"		
1768 "12 N., Noon Time"		
1769 "3 P.M., Haying Time"		
1770 "6 P.M., Home, Sweet Home"		
Sunbonnet Girls Nursery Rhymes	10 - 12	12 - 15
1664 "Little Bo Peep"		
1665 "To Market, to Market"		
1666 "Rain, Rain, Go Away"		
1667 "See Saw, Marjorie Daw"		
1668 "Goosey, Goosey, Gander"		

Bergman
Suffragettes

"Votes for Women" Series	30 - 35	35 - 40
Unnumbered Sunbonnet Series	8 - 10	10 - 12

No Publisher

Animated Fruit & Vegetable Set	7 - 8	8 - 9

"Apple"	"Cabbage"
"Karat"	"Ears"
"Cucumber"	"Lemon"
"Melon"	"Onion"
"Pair"	"Peach"
"Pine"	"Potato"
"Pumpkin"	"Turnip"

WANKE, ALICE	8 - 10	10 - 12
WHEELER, DOROTHY (See Fairy Tales)		
WHITE, FLORA (See Fairy TalesNursery Rhymes)		
WICHERA, R.R.	6 - 8	8 - 10
WIEDERSEIM, GRACE (also Grace Drayton)		

Reinthal & Newman

No Number	20 - 25	25 - 30
"A button sewed on..."		
"Blow"		
"I think I'd rather..."		
"The more I see ..."		
"You're going to get ..."		
98 "Nothing doing"		
99 "Where's oo hanky"		
110 "What you don't know ..."		
112 "No Ma'am, we ain't ..."		
113 "So near & yet so far"		
115 "Curfew shall not ..."		
116 "I'm so discouraged ..."		
117 "Courage"		
120 "I hate a spanking ..."		
121 "Stung!"		
174 "Here's How"		

175	"Don't wake me up ..."		
176	"I wish somebody was ..."		
177	"And what did Mamma ..."		
249	"Gee! but this is ..."		
250	"Wanted! Somebody ..."		
308	"I'd rather say Hello ..."		
493	Skipping Rope		
496	"Do you or don't you"		

Raphael Tuck

Series 242, Unsigned	20 - 25	25 - 30
"In Arcady"	25 - 30	30 - 35
Series 2914 "Cunning Cupids"	25 - 28	28 - 32

Armour & Co.

American Girl Series		
"The Wiederseim Girl"	25 - 30	35 - 40

A.M. Davis, Boston

Series 34 Christmas Messages	20 - 25	25 - 30
Series 143 Birthday Messages		
Series 357 Easter Messages		

Anonymous

Series 38 "Days of Week" (Uns.)		

Campbell Art Co.

	30 - 35	35 - 40

Campbell Soup Co.

Campbell Soup Kids (10¢ a can) -- 24	100 - 120	120 - 150
Copyright, Large Images (4)	30 - 35	35 - 40
Copyright, With Jingles	40 - 50	50 - 60

Swift & Co.

With Ads on Reverse (6)	30 - 35	35 - 40

Schweizer Co.

Series 10596		
Boy/Girl under Mistletoe	30 - 35	35 - 40
"Beware of Dog" Sign		
"Choose Me"		
"Help the Poor"		
"You mustn't kiss me!"		

WOODWORTH, JULIA	3 - 4	4 - 5
WUYTS, A. (Austria)	4 - 6	6 - 8

COMICS

ANDERS, O. (G.B.)	5 - 6	6 - 8
ANDERSON, M. (CYNICUS) (G.B.)	6 - 8	8 - 10
ARIS, ERNEST (G.B.)	5 - 6	6 - 8
BAIRNSFATHER, BRUCE (G.B.)	6 - 8	8 - 10
BARNES, G.L. (G.B.)	2 - 3	3 - 4
BATEMAN, H.M. (G.B.)	4 - 5	5 - 6
BIGGAR, J.L. (G.B.)	4 - 5	5 - 6
BIANCO, T. (Italy)	4 - 5	5 - 6

Tom Browne
Davidson Brothers, "Seaside Comforts" Series 2575-3
"Off to the Seaside"

Tom Browne
Davidson Brothers, "Joy to the Ocean" Series 2642-4
"Did You Say a Coffee or a Coffin, Sir?"

Political Comics	12 - 15	15 - 20
BISHOP, P. (U.S.A.)		
"Ginks" Series	8 - 10	10 - 12
Others	4 - 5	5 - 6
BLACK, W.M. (W.M.B.) (G.B.)	5 - 6	6 - 8
BOULANGER, M. (See Animals)	10 - 12	12 - 15
BRADSHAW, P.V. (G.B.)	6 - 8	8 - 10
BRILL, GEORGE (U.S.A.)	6 - 7	7 - 10
"Ginks"	12 - 15	15 - 18
BROWNE, TOM (G.B.)		
Davidson Bros.		
Each Series Contains 6 Cards:		
Series 2575 "Seaside Comfort"	6 - 8	8 - 10
Series 2578 "Billiards Made ..."	8 - 10	10 - 12
Series 2585 "Amateur Photographer"	10 - 12	12 - 15
Series 2587 "Cycling"	10 - 12	12 - 15
Series 2594 "Kissing"	10 - 12	12 - 15
Series 2598 "Are We Downhearted ..."	5 - 8	10 - 15
Series 2618 "Baseball III"	15 - 18	18 - 22
Series 2619 "Baseball III"	15 - 18	18 - 22
Series 2627 "Diabolo"	10 - 12	12 - 15
Series 2637 "New Compensation Act"	8 - 10	10 - 12
Series 2642 "Joys of the Ocean"	6 - 8	8 - 10
BUCHANAN, FRED (G.B.)	4 - 5	5 - 6
BULL, RENE (G.B.)	5 - 6	6 - 7
BUXTON, DUDLEY (G.B.)	4 - 5	5 - 6
CADY, HARRISON (U.S.A.)		
"QUADDY" Series 10	30 - 35	35 - 40

E. Chandler, Joseph Asher & Co., No. A-724

CARMICHAEL (U.S.A.)
Series 668 "Anybody Here Seen Kelly"	6 - 7	7 - 8
Series 565 "I Love My Wife But ..."	7 - 8	8 - 10
Series 261 "Would You?" (6)	6 - 7	7 - 9

Bamforth Co.
Series 262 "If"	6 - 7	7 - 8
Others	6 - 7	7 - 8

CARR, GENE (U.S.A.)

Rotograph Co., N.Y.
4th of July Series (5)	8 - 9	9 - 10
St. Patrick's Series (6)	4 - 6	6 - 8

CARTER, REG (G.B.)
Early Issues	6 - 8	8 - 10
After 1920 Issues	3 - 4	4 - 5

CARTER, SYDNEY (G.B.)	8 - 10	10 - 12
CAVALLY, F. (U.S.A.)	2 - 4	4 - 6
CHANDLER, E.	5 - 6	6 - 8
CHRISTIE, G.F. (G.B.)	6 - 8	8 - 10
COCK, STANLEY	4 - 5	5 - 7
COMICUS (HARRY PARTLETT) (G.B.)	2 - 3	3 - 4
COLBY, V.	1 - 2	2 - 3
COOK, C.K.	6 - 8	8 - 10
COWHAM, HILDA (G.B.)	4 - 5	5 - 6

CROMBIE, CHARLES (G.B.)

Valentine
"Rules of Golf" Series	15 - 18	18 - 22
"Rules of Cricket" Series	10 - 12	12 - 15

Charles Crombie, Valentine, "Rules of Golf" Series

Craig Fox, Tichnor Brothers (Linen)

"Humors of Fishing" Series	10 - 12	12 - 15
Others	4 - 6	6 - 8
DARLING, JAY	10 - 12	12 - 15
DAVEY, GEORGE (G.B.)	4 - 5	5 - 6
DENSLOW, W.W. (U.S.A.)	10 - 12	12 - 15
DIRKS, GUS (G.B.) Comic Insects	6 - 7	7 - 8
DIRKS, R. (Germany)		
American Journal Examiner		
Katzenjammer Kids	6 - 8	8 - 10
DISNEY, WALT (U.S.A.)		
Foreign Issues		
French, 30's era	15 - 20	20 - 25
German, 30's era	20 - 25	25 - 30
Czech., 30's era	20 - 25	25 - 30
Hungarian, 30's era	20 - 25	25 - 30
Other 30's era issues	15 - 20	20 - 25
DONADINI, JR. (Italy) (See Blacks)		
Auto Driver Series (6)	10 - 12	12 - 15
Horse Racing Series (6)	10 - 12	12 - 15
DUNCAN, HAMISH	3 - 4	4 - 6
DWIG (C.V. DWIGGINS) (U.S.A.)		
C. Marks (See Halloween)		
Raphael Tuck		
"Cheer Up" Series (24)	6 - 8	8 - 10
"Don't" Series (24)	6 - 8	8 - 10
"Everytime" Series (24)	6 - 8	8 - 10
"Follies" Series (12)	6 - 8	8 - 10
"If" Series (24)	6 - 8	8 - 10
"Ophelia" Series (24)	6 - 8	8 - 10

"Help Wanted" Series (12)	6 - 7	7 - 8
"Never" Series (24)	6 - 7	7 - 8
"Jollies" Series (12)	6 - 8	8 - 10
"School Days" Series (24)	6 - 8	8 - 10
"Smiles" Series (24)	8 - 10	10 - 12
"Toast" Series (12)	8 - 10	10 - 12
"Zodiac" Series (12)	12 - 16	16 - 22
Charles Rose		
"Baby" Series (6)	8 - 10	10 - 12
"Moon" Series (6)	6 - 8	8 - 10
"Moving" Series (6)	8 - 10	10 - 12
"New York" Series (6)	8 - 10	10 - 12
"Oyster Girl" Series (6)	10 - 12	12 - 14
"Sandwich" Series (6)	8 - 10	10 - 12
"Superstition" Series (6)	8 - 10	10 - 12
"What are Wild Waves ..." Series (6)	10 - 12	12 - 14
"The Wurst Girl" Series (6)	10 - 12	12 - 14
"The Frankfurter Girl" Series (6)	10 - 12	12 - 14
R. Kaplan		
"Fortune Teller" Series (12)	8 - 9	9 - 10
"How Can You Do It?" Series (24)	6 - 7	7 - 8
"Mirror Girl" Series (24)	8 - 10	10 - 12
Sam Gabriel		
"If's & And's" Series (24)	6 - 7	7 - 8
"Leap Year" Series 401 (12)	9 - 10	10 - 12
"Fortune Teller" Series 55 (12)	6 - 8	8 - 10
Edward Gross		
"What's the Use?" (6)	6 - 7	7 - 8
EDWARDS, LIONEL	4 - 6	6 - 8
ELLAM (W.R.) (See Teddy Bears)		
"Breakfast in Bed" Series	15 - 20	20 - 25
Others	10 - 12	12 - 15
FOX, CRAIG	1 - 2	2 - 3
FISHER, BUD (U.S.A.)		
Mutt and Jeff (Unsigned)	12 - 15	15 - 20
FLEURY, H.	4 - 6	6 - 7
FULLER, EDMUND	5 - 7	7 - 8
GIBBS, MAY	18 - 22	22 - 26
GIBSON, CHARLES DANA (U.S.A.)		
Henderson Co.		
Sepia Comics (36)	5 - 6	6 - 7
Detroit Publishing	8 - 10	10 - 12
GILL, ARTHUR (G.B.)	4 - 5	5 - 6
GILSON, T.	4 - 5	5 - 6
GLADWIN, MAY	4 - 5	5 - 6
GOLDBERG, RUBE (U.S.A.)		
Albie the Agent	8 - 10	10 - 12
Barton & Spooner		
Series 212 "The Ancient Order"	6 - 8	8 - 10

H. B. Griggs (H.B.G.)	*Myer*	
L. & E. Series 2271	*Aurochrome Series A-22*	

Series 213 "Foolish Questions"	5 - 6	6 - 8
Dreamland Skating Rink - Advertising	15 - 18	18 - 22
GOODYEAR, ARCHIE	4 - 5	5 - 6
GRIGGS, H.B. and HBG		
L & E		
Halloween (See Halloween)		
Suffrage Series	70 - 80	80 - 90
Others	6 - 8	8 - 12
HAMISH	4 - 5	5 - 6
HARDY, DUDLEY (G.B.)	5 - 6	6 - 8
HASSALL, JOHN	6 - 7	7 - 8
HORINA, H. and **H.H.** (U.S.A.)		
Illustrated P.C. Co.	5 - 6	6 - 8
HURST, HAL	4 - 5	5 - 6
HUTAF, AUGUST (U.S.A.)		
P.C.K.		
"Advice to Vacationists"	5 - 6	6 - 7
IBBETSON, ERNEST	6 - 8	8 - 10
KENNEDY, A.E.	5 - 6	6 - 8
KINSELLA, E.P. (See Sports)		
Others	6 - 8	8 - 12
KYD, J.C.C. (G.B.)		
Raphael Tuck		
Charles Dickens Characters	8 - 10	10 - 12

R. F. Outcault, H. H. Tammen, "Buster Brown" Series 1002

"The Artful Dodger" -- Oliver Twist
"Mrs. Bardell" -- Pickwick Papers
"Bill Sikes" -- Oliver Twist
"Bumble" -- Oliver Twist
"Captain Cuttle" -- Dombey & Sons
"Dick Swiveller" -- Old Curiosity Shop
"Fat Boy" -- Pickwick Papers
"Mr. Jingle" -- Pickwick Papers
"The Little Marchioness" -- Old Curiosity Shop
"Mr. Micawber" -- David Copperfield
"Mr. Pecksniff" -- Martin Chuzzlewit
"Mr. Peggotty" -- David Copperfield
"Mr. Pickwick" -- Pickwick Papers
"Quilp" -- Old Curiosity Shop
"Sam Weller" -- Pickwick Papers
"Samson Brass" -- Old Curiosity Shop
"Mrs. Sarah Gamp" -- Martin Chuzzlewit
" Sergeant Buzfuz" -- Pickwick Papers
"Toots" -- Dombey & Sons
"Trotty Veck" -- The Chimes
"Uriah Heep" -- David Copperfield
"Mr. Weller" -- Pickwick Papers
"Whackford Squeers" -- Nicolas Nickleby

LEWIN, F.G. (See Blacks)	5 - 6	6 - 8
LEVI, C. (See Blacks)	4 - 5	5 - 6
LUDOVICI, A.	4 - 5	5 - 6
MARTIN, ABE (U.S.A.)		
Illustrated P.C. Co.	5 - 6	6 - 7

"Leap Year"	6 - 8	8 - 10
Other "Leap Year" Issues	6 - 8	8 - 10
F.L.		
"Comical Types" (The Strong Man, etc.)	6 - 8	8 - 10
Others	5 - 6	6 - 8
HYDE, GRAHAM	5 - 6	6 - 8
MASON, GEORGE W.	5 - 6	6 - 8
MAY, PHIL (G.B.)	6 - 8	8 - 12
Raphael Tuck		
Series 1295 (6)	8 - 10	10 - 12
Series 1775 (6) Drunks	6 - 8	8 - 10
McCAY, WINSOR (U.S.A.)		
Raphael Tuck		
"Little Nemo" Series	25 - 30	30 - 35
McGILL, DONALD (G.B.) See Blacks		
Pre-1914	6 - 8	8 - 10
Others	2 - 3	3 - 4
McMANUS, GEORGE (U.S.A.)		
"Bringing Up Father" Series	35 - 40	40 - 45
MORELAND, ARTHUR	5 - 6	6 - 8
MUNSON, WALT (Linens of 30's and 40's)	1 - 2	2 - 3
MYER		
Aurochrome Series	4 - 5	5 - 6

R. F. Outcault, Calendar Card Series 1907
Buster Brown Company

NEWELL, PETER (U.S.A.)
  Detroit Publishing Co.
    Series 14169-14178

"Bigger-than-Weather-Boys"	10 - 12	12 - 15

OPPER, FRED (U.S.A.)

"Happy Hooligan" Series	8 - 10	10 - 12
"Alphonse & Gaston" Series	6 - 8	8 - 10
"And Her Name Was Maud" Series	6 - 8	8 - 10
Others	5 - 6	6 - 8

    Add $3 for Tuck Issues.

OUTCAULT, R.F. (U.S.A.)
  The American Journal Examiner
    Buster Brown Series (8)

"Look at Santa Claus"	15 - 18	18 - 22
"Oh, See the Sea Serpent"	12 - 15	15 - 18
"Resolved: Nothing Can Stop Us"	10 - 12	12 - 15
"Say! Mary Jane ..."	12 - 15	15 - 18
"What Enormous Bill on Legs ..."	10 - 12	12 - 15
"Who is Buster Posing?"	15 - 18	18 - 22
"Who is Buster Getting Away From?"	12 - 15	15 - 18
"Who is the Laugh On?"	12 - 15	15 - 18

  Bloomingdale Brothers, 1902

Buster Brown Adv. Series (6)	70 - 80	80 - 90

  Bloomingdale Brothers

Buster Brown Santa Claus Card	85 - 90	90 - 100

  Brown Shoe Co., 1909
    Buster Brown Blue Ribbon Shoes

Months of Year (12)	15 - 20	20 - 25

  Burr-McIntosh, 1903
    Buster Brown and His Bubble (10)]

"A Quiet Day in Town"	15 - 20	20 - 25
"Hands Up"	15 - 20	20 - 25
"Black or White?" (Blacks)	20 - 25	25 - 30
"Looking for Trouble"	15 - 20	20 - 25
"A Good Bump"	15 - 20	20 - 25
"Over the Bounding Main" (Blacks)	20 - 25	25 - 30
"A Rise in Bear"	15 - 20	20 - 25
"A Smooth Bit of Road" (Blacks)	20 - 25	25 - 30
"The Constable"	20 - 25	25 - 30
"All Over"	15 - 20	20 - 25

  Kaufmann and Strauss, 1903
    Advertising Cards with Imprints of

Various Firms (16+)	12 - 15	15 - 18

  J. Ottman, 1905

Comic Series (40+)	10 - 12	12 - 15

  J. Ottman, 1906

Christmas Card Set (4?) Unsigned	12 - 15	15 - 18

  F. A. Stokes, 1906

Buster Brown Outcault Cartoon Lectures	15 - 18	18 - 22
"Come on Tige"		
"Gee, What's Playing?"		
"Give it to Mary Jane, Buddy"		
"If Tige Would Only Go Away"		
"Where Are You Going?"		

H. H. Tammen, 1906

Buster Brown Series (Embossed) *	15 - 18	18 - 22
"Come and Join Us in a Blowout"		
"I Ain't Got no Time ..."		
"Hurry Back with the Answer"		
"It was de Dutch"		
"Way Down in My Heart ..."		
* Reduced Series of Above Set, 1908	20 - 25	25 - 30

Raphael Tuck, 1903

Valentine Series (12)	10 - 12	12 - 15

Raphael Tuck, 1904

Valentine Scroll Series (6)	10 - 12	12 - 15
"Can you Guess the One ...?"		
"Don't Monkey with this Heart of Mine"		
"Here's a Wireless Telegram ..."		
"I am Perfectly Willing ..."		
"Why Don't Someone Ask ...?"		
"Won't You be my Honey ...?"		

Raphael Tuck

Obverse Trademark Valentines (6)	10 - 12	12 - 15
"I Adore You"		
"I Think I've Made a Lovely Start ..."		
"O! Will I be Your Valentine?"		
"I Want You to be My Valentine"		
"Resolved that there's a Certain Party"		
"Wouldn't that there's ..."		

Raphael Tuck

Valentine Series 106 (6)	10 - 12	12 - 15
Valentine Series 111 (6)	10 - 12	12 - 15
Valentine Series 112 (6)	10 - 12	12 - 15
"For you February 14th"		
"Resolved that Without my Heart ..."		
"Still Now"		
"There's a Certain Person ..."		
"Will you be my Valentine ...?"		

Raphael Tuck

New Outcault Series 7		
Valentine Postcards	12 - 14	14 - 16
Buster Brown		
Series 8 Valentine Postcards (10)	10 - 12	12 - 15
"Bear, Bear, Don't Go Away"		
"Honey, How Your Eyes Do Shine"		
"I Am Perfectly Willing ..."		

"I Dreams Erbout Yo' Eb'ry Night ..."
"Laugh, Laugh and be Merry ..."
"Love Me, and the World is Mine"
"Now How Do Little Birdies Know ..."
"Of All the Days in the Year ..."
"Oh, Maid, Take Pity ..."
"Someone Has Asked Someone ..."

Buster Brown Postcards	12 - 15	15 - 18
Love Tributes Series 5	12 - 15	15 - 18

Ullman Mfg. Co., 1906

"Darktown" Series 76 (4)	20 - 22	22 - 25

"Darktown Doctors"
"Darktown Dames"
"Deed, I Dun Eat No Chicken"
"Koontown Kids"

Buster Brown Co., Chicago, 1906

Buster Brown 1906 Calendars	15 - 18	18 - 22
Buster Brown 1907 Calendars	15 - 18	18 - 22

Outcault Adv. Co., Chicago, 1907

Buster Brown 1908 Calendars	15 - 18	18 - 22
Buster Brown 1909 Calendars	15 - 18	18 - 22
Buster Brown 1910 Calendars	15 - 18	18 - 22
Buster Brown 1911 Calendars	15 - 18	18 - 22

R. F. Outcault, New York, 1907

Little House Maid 1908 Calendars	12 - 15	15 - 18
Little House Maid 1909 Calendars	12 - 15	15 - 18
Little House Maid 1910 Calendars	12 - 15	15 - 18
Little House Maid 1911 Calendars	12 - 15	15 - 18
Mr. Swell Dresser 1908 Calendars	15 - 18	18 - 22
Mr. Swell Dresser 1909 Calendars	15 - 18	18 - 22
Mr. Swell Dresser 1910 Calendars	15 - 18	18 - 22

R. F. Outcault, N.Y., 1908-11

Bank Series 1909-11 Calendars	12 - 14	14 - 16

R. F. Outcault, N.Y., 1909

Bank Series 1912-13 Calendars	12 - 14	14 - 16
Rockford Watch 1909-10 Calendars	20 - 25	25 - 30

R. F. Outcault, N.Y., 1911

Yellow Kid 1910 -12 Calendars	70 - 80	80 - 100
Yellow Kid 1913 Calendars	70 - 80	80 - 100

R. F. Outcault, Copyright

Blue Boy 1912-14 Calendars	12 - 15	15 - 18
Buster Brown 1912-15 Calendars	12 - 15	15 - 18
Furniture 1912-15 Calendars	12 - 15	15 - 18
Mary Jane 1911-13 Calendars	12 - 15	15 - 18
Yellow Kid Look-a-Like 1914-15 Calendars	12 - 15	15 - 18

PARLETT, HARRY (G.B.)
  Taylor's Orthochrome

Series 2830 (6) Roller Skating	8 - 10	10 - 12
PHIZ (H.K. BROWNE)	8 - 10	10 - 12

PIPPO

Big Eyed Man Series	8 - 10	10 - 12
Barber		
Blacksmith		
Cook		
Doctor		
Gambler		
Musician		
Rich Man		
Sculptor		
POULBOT, F. (France)	10 - 12	12 - 15
RAEMAKERS, LOUIS (Netherlands)	6 - 8	8 - 10
REYNOLDS, FRANK	5 - 6	6 - 8
REZNICEK (Denmark)	12 - 15	15 - 18
ROBERTS, VIOLET	12 - 15	15 - 18
ROBIDA (France)	10 - 12	12 - 15
ROBINSON, W. HEATH	6 - 8	8 - 10
ROUNTREE, HARRY	6 - 8	8 - 10
SANDFORD, H. DIX (See Blacks)		
Others	6 - 7	7 - 8
SCHONFLUG, FRITZ	8 - 10	10 - 12
SCHULTZ, C.E. (Bunny)		
"Foxy Grandpa" Series	6 - 8	8 - 10
SHEPHEARD, GEORGE E.	5 - 6	6 - 7
SHINN, COBB and **TOM YAD** (U.S.A.)		
See Art Nouveau		
H.A. Waters Co.		
"Foolish Questions" Series	3 - 4	4 - 5

Fred Spurgin, "Leap Year" Series, No. 956

Lance Thackeray
Raphael Tuck & Sons, "Weather Reports" Series, No. 9088

"Ford" Comics	6 - 8	8 - 10
"Charlie Chaplin" Cartoons	8 - 10	10 - 12
SPURGIN, FRED (G.B.) See Blacks		
"Leap Year" Series 956	8 - 10	10 - 12
Others	5 - 6	6 - 8
STUDDY, G.E.		
"Bonzo"	8 - 10	10 - 12
Others	4 - 5	5 - 6
SWINNERTON		
American Journal Examiner	6 - 7	7 - 10
TAYLOR, A.	1 - 2	2 - 3
TEMPEST, D. (See Blacks)		
Others	2 - 3	3 - 4
THACKERAY, LANCE (G.B.)		
Raphael Tuck		
"At the Seaside" (6)	8 - 9	9 - 12
"Game of Golf" (6)	15 - 18	18 - 22
Series 9088, "Weather Reports" (6)	7 - 8	8 - 10
THIELE, ARTHUR See Blacks		
L & P		
Fat Lady Series	10 - 12	12 - 14
Bathing Girls Series	12 - 14	14 - 16
Others	12 - 14	14 - 16
UPTON, FLORENCE (G.B.)		
Golliwogs	30 - 35	35 - 40
See Golliwogs		
WAIN, LOUIS		
"Charlie Chapman Cats"	200 - 225	225 - 250

Bernhardt Wall
Anonymous Publisher, "I'll bring you back some Souvenirs"

WALL, BERNHARDT
Many Sets and Series	5 - 6	6 - 10

WARD, DUDLEY | 3 - 4 | 4 - 5

WEAVER, E. (U.S.A.)
Ford Comics	8 - 10	10 - 12
Others	1 - 2	2 - 3

WELLMAN, WALTER (U.S.A.)
"Try Dan Cupid" Series (32)	5 - 6	6 - 8
"Merry Widow Wiles" (8)	5 - 6	6 - 8
"Last Will & Testament" Series (8)	6 - 8	8 - 10
"Weaker Sex" Series (12)	6 - 8	8 - 10
"Hand" Series (12)	5 - 6	6 - 8
"The Suffragette" Ser. (16) See Suffragettes		
"Life's Little Tragedies" (16)	5 - 6	6 - 8

"Beau, Dough, No"
"Bell, Tell, H___"
"Bliss, Kiss, Hiss"
"Blow, O__, Woe"
"Bore, Bore More, Snore"
"Call, Gall, That's All"
"Dance, Chance, Pants"
"Date Late, Fate"
"Dine, Wine, Fine"
"Eyed, Tried, Tied"
"Fairy, Marry, Carry"
"Grins, Wins, Twins"
"Knock, Doc, Rock"

"Optimistic Miss"
Gartner & Bender Publishers

P.F.B. Comic
Series 5677

"Sea, See, Gee!"		
"Skirt, Flirt, Hurt"		
"Stare, Hair, Prayer"		
Linen Comics (See Blacks)	1 - 1.50	1.50 - 2
WELLS, C.		
Lounsbury		
Series 2025 "Lovely Lilly"	6 - 7	7 - 8
WITT		
"Ford Booster" Comics (10)	7 - 8	8 - 10
WOOD, LAWSON (G.B.)		
Chimps, Parrots, etc.	6 - 8	8 - 10
See Suffragettes		
YAD, TOM (Also **COBB SHINN**)	1 - 2	2 - 3
ZIM	4 - 5	5 - 6

PUBLISHERS

Bauman (Unsigned)		
Ugly Girls - Days of the Week (6)	6 - 8	8 - 9
Gartner & Bender		
Water Color Sets (6)	6 - 8	8 - 10
"Amy Bility"		

"Antie Quate"
"Gee Whiz"
"Gee Willikins"
"Jimmy"
"Optimistic Miss"
"Phil Os Opher"

Irwin Kline (Unsigned)

Masonic (No Numbers) (6)	6 - 7	7 - 8

P.F.B. (Unsigned)

Series 5897 Mother-in-Law (6)	8 - 10	10 - 12
Series 6307 Comic Lovers (6)	8 - 10	10 - 12
Series 6538 Domestic Riot (6)	8 - 10	10 - 12
Many Others	6 - 8	8 - 10

SILHOUETTES

ALLMAHER, JOSEFINE	6 - 8	8 - 9
BECKMAN, JOHANNA	5 - 7	7 - 8
BURKE, PAUL	5 - 7	7 - 8
BORRMEISTER, R.	6 - 8	8 - 10
BRENING, H.	10 - 12	12 - 15

*Felicien Philipp, Vouga &
Cie. 46, German Caption*

*K.M.H.
Kleiner, Berlin, No. 3345*

DIEFENBACH, K. W.
  B. G. Teubner
    Fantasy Children   7 - 10   10 - 15
FORCK, ELISABETH   6 - 7   7 - 8
GRAF, MARTE
    Art Deco Series 1, 2, 3, 4 (743-754)   8 - 10   10 - 14
    Others   8 - 10   10 - 12
GROSS, CH.   5 - 7   7 - 8
GROSZE, M.
  P.F.B. (IN DIAMOND)
    Deco Series 2041 "After Bath"   12 - 15   15 - 18
    Nude Series 2042   12 - 15   15 - 18
    Series 2043   10 - 12   12 - 15
    Nude Series 3339   12 - 15   15 - 18
    Series 3341 & 3342   10 - 12   12 - 15
    Others   10 - 12   12 - 14
  K.M.H.   8 - 10   10 - 12
KASKELINE
    Art Deco, Ladies/Children   8 - 10   10 - 12
LAMP, H.
    Series 3, Deco Dancing   12 - 15   15 - 18
    Series 4, Bathing   12 - 15   15 - 18
PHILIPP, FELICIEN   8 - 10   10 - 12
PEANITSCH, LEO   10 - 12   12 - 14
ROBA (Deco Fantasy)   12 - 15   15 - 18
SACHSE-SCHUBERT, M.   10 - 12   12 - 14
SCHIRMER (See Fairy Tales/Nursery Rhymes) 10 - 12   12 - 14
SCHONPFLUG, FRITZ   10 - 12   12 - 15
SCHMIDT, GERDA LUISE (Germany)   8 - 10   10 - 12
STUBNER, LOTTE   8 - 10   10 - 12
S.K.
  Meissner & Buch   8 - 10   10 - 12
SUSS, PAUL   10 - 12   12 - 15

BLACKS, SIGNED

ATWELL, MABEL L.
  Valentine & Sons
    Series 745, A331 (6)   12 - 15   15 - 18
    Series 614, 615 (6)   16 - 18   18 - 22
    Series A550   10 - 12   12 - 15
  Others
    Early Period, Pre-1915   16 - 18   18 - 20
    Middle Period, 1915-30   14 - 16   16 - 18
    Late Period, 1930-50   8 - 10   10 - 12
BRUNDAGE, FRANCES
  Raphael Tuck
    Series 2723 "Colored Folks" (6)   40 - 45   45 - 50
    "Church Parade"

"The Christening"		
"De Proof of de Puddin' "		
"Don't took de las' piece"		
"The Village Choir"		
"You is a Chicken"		
Series 100, 102 (1), (2) Unsigned	20 - 22	22 - 26
Series 108 (4) Unsigned	25 - 30	30 - 35
Series 115 (Unsigned)	25 - 30	30 - 35
Series 118 (2) Unsigned	30 - 35	35 - 40
"Waiting fo' Mah Sweetheart"		
"To Greet Mah Valentine"		
Series 4096 "Funny Folk" (4)	30 - 35	35 - 40
Other Signed Brundage	15 - 18	18 - 22
Unsigned	12 - 15	15 - 18
BUCHANAN, FRED		
Raphael Tuck Series 9309 (6)	10 - 12	12 - 15
CARTER, SYDNEY (G.B.)		
Hildesheimer & Co.		
Series 5232 "The Dance" Series	12 - 15	15 - 18
CLAPSADDLE, ELLEN H.		
Int. Art. Pub. Co.		
Mechanical Series 1236		
"A Jolly Halloween" Black Child	300 - 350	350 - 400
No Number Valentine	14 - 16	16 - 18
Girl Sits on Box	10 - 12	12 - 14
Boy Offers Girl Ice Cream	12 - 14	14 - 16
Stewart & Woolf, London		
Black Boy Walking Left	20 - 25	25 - 30
Others	20 - 25	25 - 30
COCKRELL	6 - 8	8 - 10
COOK, A. M.		
ZAHC "In Erwartung"	12 - 15	15 - 18
CRANE	8 - 10	10 - 12
CURTIS, E.	6 - 8	8 - 10
DONADINI, JR. Series 454	12 - 15	15 - 18
FLC		
F. A. Moss	6 - 8	8 - 10
FUL		
M. Munk, Black Series	15 - 18	18 - 22
FYCH, C.D.		
Valentine & Sons	8 - 10	10 - 12
GASSAWAY, KATHERINE		
Rotograph Co.		
105 "I Scared I'll Get Sunburned"	10 - 12	12 - 14
123 "I Wish I was in Dixie"	10 - 12	12 - 14
Others	8 - 10	10 - 12
GILSON, T. (G.B.)		
E. J. Hey & Co.		
Series 262	10 - 12	12 - 15

Mabel Lucie Atwell
Anon. Spanish Publisher

Ellen H. Clapsaddle (Uns.)
Int. Art Publishing Co.

A. M. Cook
ZAHC, "Picaninies"

T. Gilson
"Hoping for the Best"

Series 410		
Mama and Child	10 - 12	12 - 15
"Rats"	10 - 12	12 - 15
Series 151 "Le's 'av a puff"	8 - 10	10 - 12
J. Salmon		
Series 2571	10 - 12	12 - 14
British Manufacturer Series	8 - 10	10 - 12
GREINER, MAGNUS (U.S.A.)		
International Art Black Series 701-710	12 - 14	14 - 18
701 "A Darktown Trip"		
702 "The Serenade"		
704 "A Lad and a Ladder"		
707 "A Darktown Idyl"		
708 "A Feast"		
709 "A Darktown Lover"		
710 "A Darktown Philosopher"		
HERMAN, H.		
Ullman Co.		
Series 106 (4)	10 - 12	12 - 15
HUTAF, AUGUST (U.S.A.)		
Ullman Mfg. Co.		
Seris 113 "Blacktown Babies"	10 - 12	12 - 14
K.V.		
L.P. Series 206 Black Kewpies	10 - 12	12 - 15
KEMBLE Black & White Comics	6 - 8	8 - 10
KINSELLA, E.P.		
Langsdorf Series 713 (6) "Diabolo"	18 - 20	20 - 26

Rastus always is de puffec' gentleman !

F. G. Lewin
J. Salmon No. 2257, "Rastus always is de puffec' gentleman!"

Reg Maurice, Regent, "Dat Love Stuff Makes Me Sick!"

LEVI, C.
  Ullman Co.

Series 165	8 - 10	10 - 12
Series 210, 3308 "Suffragette"	25 - 30	30 - 35

LEWIN, F.G. (G.B.)

Artisque	12 - 14	14 - 16
Inter-Art Co.	8 - 10	10 - 12

  J. Salmon

Series 2257	10 - 12	12 - 15
Series 2756	10 - 12	12 - 14
"A Little Light on a Dark Subject"		
"I's a Waiting for You"		
"Love Will Find a Way"		
Series 2583	8 - 10	10 - 12
"I's is Jus' Nuts on You"		
(Boy and Girl Near Tree Hut)		
Boy with Flowers for Pickaninny Girl	10 - 12	12 - 14

  Bamforth Co.
    Black Kid Comics"

"Just We Two - in Our Little Canoe"	8 - 10	10 - 12
"I Love the Sea When You Are in it"	8 - 10	10 - 12
"I's Just Bilin' Ober ..." Unsigned	6 - 8	8 - 10
"Two Lovin' Hearts"	6 - 8	8 - 10

LONG, F.G. (U.S.A.)

Kaufmann & Strauss, 1904	10 - 12	12 - 14

LUZE (France)   10 - 12   12 - 14

MAURICE, REG (G.B.)
  Regent

Series 4137	12 - 14	14 - 16

T.R., *"Dis-am-fine"*
A. M. Davis & Co. Series 521

Ethel Parkinson
B. Dondorf (German Caption)

H. Dix Sandford
Raphael Tuck, Seaside Coons Series 9318, "So Polite"

FUL
M. Munk, Vienna, No. 242

Agnes Richardson
Celesque, "Love at First Sight"

Series 501	12 - 14	14 - 16
McGILL, DONALD (G.B.)		
Bamforth	6 - 8	8 - 10
D. Constance, Ltd.	6 - 8	8 - 10
MINNS, B.E. (G.B./Australia)		
Carlton Publishing Co.		
"Glad Eye" Series (6)	12 - 14	14 - 16
O'NEILL, ROSE		
Raphael Tuck		
Series 2483		
"Pickings from Puck"	60 - 70	70 - 80
"One View"		
"Better than a Sermon"		
"A Brain Worker"		
"Ne Plus Ultra"		
Series 9411		
"High Society in Coontown" (6)	100 - 110	110 - 120
"All that was Necessary"		
"Taken"		
"A Provisional Finance"		
"A Misunderstanding"		
"Finis"		
"His Limited Provisioning Capacity"		

Series 9412		
"Coontown Kids" (6)	80 - 90	90 - 100
OUTCAULT, RICHARD F.		
Ullman Mfg. Co.		
"Darktown" Series 76	16 - 18	18 - 20
Raphael Tuck		
Und/Back Valentines	10 - 13	13 - 18
Buster Brown and His Bubble (3, 6 & 8)	20 - 25	25 - 30
A.S.		
Hildesheimer & Co.		
Series 5268 (No Captions)	8 - 10	10 - 12
PARKINSON, ETHEL		
B. Dondorf	12 - 15	15 - 18
SANDFORD, H. DIX (or H.D. or H.D.S.)		
Raphael Tuck		
Ser. 9049 "Happy Little Coons" (6)	12 - 14	14 - 16
Ser. 9050 "Sand Coons" (6)	10 - 12	12 - 15
Ser. 9093 "Curley Coons" (6)	12 - 14	14 - 16
Ser. 9227 "Happy Little Coons" (6)	10 - 12	12 - 14
Ser. 9228 "Happy Little Coons" (6)	10 - 12	12 - 14
Ser. 9229 "Happy Little Coons" (6)	14 - 16	16 - 18
Series 9318 "Seaside Coons" (6)	10 - 12	12 - 15
Series 9427 "More Coons" (6)	10 - 12	12 - 15
Series 9428, 9489		
"Dark Girls & Black Boys" (6)	10 - 12	12 - 15
Series 9457 "Happy Little Coons" (6)	10 - 12	12 - 15
Series 9968, 9969 "Seaside Coons" (6)	10 - 12	12 - 15
Hildesheimer & Co.		
Series 5268 "Negroes"	8 - 10	10 - 12
SANFORD, M.		
Raphael Tuck Series	10 - 12	12 - 15
A.S.		
Hildesheimer & Co.		
Series 5268 (No Captions)	8 - 10	10 - 12
SANFORD, M.		
Raphael Tuck Series	10 - 12	12 = 15
SHEPHEARD, GEORGE E. (G.B.)		
Raphael Tuck		
Series 9068 "Coon's Cooning" (6)	10 - 12	12 - 14
SPARKUHL		
AVM		
Series 636 White/Black	10 - 12	12 - 14
SPURGIN, FRED (Latvia/G.B.)		
J & A Co.		
"Coon Series" 405	12 - 14	14 - 16
"Am My Nose Still Shiny?"		
"Golly! You are Looking Pale"		
"Things are Looking Black"		
Others	10 - 12	12 - 14

T.R.
  A.M. Davis Co.   10 - 12   12 - 15
TEMPEST, DOUGLAS (G.B.)
  Bamforth Co.
    "Look me over, buddy ..."   8 - 10   10 - 12
    "Oh, Honey! If ..."   8 - 10   10 - 12
    "I'se Black all over ..."   6 - 8   8 - 10
    "Full on top -- cooler than riding inside!"   8 - 10   10 - 12
    "Here's a Quaint Coon"   8 - 10   10 - 12
    Others   6 - 8   8 - 10
THIELE, ARTHUR (Germany)
  FED
    Head Studies, Series 386 (6)   20 - 25   25 - 30
    Black Jockeys Series 871 (6)   20 - 25   25 - 28
TWELVETREES, CHARLES   (U.S.A.)
  Edward Gross
    61   "Doe you tink ...?"   6 - 8   8 - 10
    151 "She do, she don't"   8 - 10   10 - 12
    864 Two Black Boys in Basket   6 - 7   7 - 8
    "Woman, Kiss Me"   6 - 8   8 - 10
    Others   6 - 8   8 - 10
TYRRELL, E.R. (U.S.A.)
  S. S. Porter   8 - 10   10 - 12
USABAL, LOTTE (Germany)
    Series 1295-1300   1-8 - 20   20 - 22
WALL, BERNHARDT (U.S.A.)
  Ullman Mfg. Co.
    Series 59 "Little Coons"   10 - 12   12 - 14
    1660 "You all can hab de Rine"
    1661 "Deed, I didn't steal um"
    1662 "Who's dat say chicken?"
    1663 "Just two Coons"
    Series 70 "Cute Coons"   10 - 12   12 - 14
    1852 "A chip off the old Block"
    1853 "Whose Baby is OO?"
    1854 "He lubs me"
    1855 "I's so happy"
WIEDERSEIM, GRACE
  Raphael Tuck
    Series 2723 "Colored Folks"   35 - 40   40 - 50
    "Church Parade"
    "Don't Took the Last Piece"
    "The Christening"
    "De Proof of de Puddin' "
WUYTS, A.   (Austria)
  A. Noyer Series 76 (6)   10 - 12   12 - 14
ZAHL
  Poster Series   12 - 14   14 - 18

"Othello"
"Be's Jst Du?"

BLACKS, UNSIGNED

Albertype Co.
PMC

"Greetings from the Sunny South" (12)	30 - 35	35 - 40

Detroit Pub. Co.

Black Series	10 - 12	12 - 14

G. B. Co.

Series G Husband & Wife (6)	8 - 10	10 - 12

Franz Huld

Cake Walk, "Darkey Series" (PMC)	12 - 15	15 - 18

Ill. P.C. Co.

"Darkies" Series 78	8 - 10	10 - 12

Langsdorf

"Greetings from the Sunny South"	10 - 12	12 - 15

P.F.B. Series 7148 (6)

P.F.B. Series 7148 (6)	12 - 14	14 - 18
Series 7179 (6)		
Black Gents & Ladies (6)	20 - 25	25 - 30
Series 7942 (6)	12 - 14	14 - 18
Series 7946 (6)	12 - 14	14 - 18

Taggart

Red Background Series 24 (6)	10 - 12	12 - 15
Thanksgiving Series 608 (6)	8 - 9	9 - 10

Raphael Tuck

Oilette Series 9297 (6)		
"Among the Darkies"	10 - 12	12 - 14
"Negro" 1819 (6)	8 - 10	10 - 12
"Coon Studies" Series 2087, 2088 (6)	10 - 12	12 - 14
"Coon Studies" Series 9094, 9542 (6)	10 - 12	12 - 14
"Coontown Kids" Series 2843, 9092 and 9412 (6)	10 - 12	12 - 14
"Happy Darkies" Series 2363 (6)	10 - 12	12 - 14
"Happy Little Coons" Series 8438, 9049 (6)	10 - 12	12 - 14
"High Society in Coontown" Oilette Series 9411 (6)	15 - 18	18 - 22
Calendar Series 1043, Black Couples (6)	8 - 10	10 - 12
Negro Melodies Series 2398, 6909 (6)	12 - 14	14 - 16
Sunny South Coon Studies Ser. 2181 (6)	10 - 12	12 - 14
Negro Series 4400, 4401 (6)	10 - 12	12 - 14

Ullman Mfg. Co.

"Little Coons," Series 59 (6)	10 - 12	12 - 15
"Kute Koon Kids," Series 1065 (6)	10 - 12	12 - 14
Mechanical - "Pick the Pickaninnies" Puzzle	50 - 55	55 - 60

John Innis
MacFarlane Publishing Company, Troilene Series, "The War Canoe"

W. F. Cody (Buffalo Bill)
H. H. T. Company, No. 1696

C. W. Russell, Ridgley Cal. Co.
"Lone Wolf -- Piegan"

Valentine & Sons		
"Coonville" (6)	8 - 10	10 - 12
White Border, Real Life	5 - 7	7 - 10
Linen Cards		
1930-1949	2 - 3	5 - 8

COWBOYS & INDIANS

CRAIG, CHARLES (U.S.A.)		
Williamson-Hafner		
Indian Series	8 - 10	10 - 12
CURTIS, E. S. (U.S.A) Sepia		
Indian Series	35 - 40	40 - 45
DAVENPORT, R.A.		
Cowboys	6 - 7	7 - 9
FELLER, FRANK (U.S.A.)	8 - 10	10 - 12
GOLLINS	8 - 10	10 - 12
GREGG, PAUL		
H. H. Tammen Co.		
Cowboy Series	8 - 10	10 - 12
INNES, JOHN		
Western Art Series (6)	10 - 12	12 - 15
"The Bad Man"		
"Pack Train"		
"The Portage"		
"Prairie Schooner"		
"Roping Bronco"		
"Warping the Fur Barge ..."		
MacFarlane Pub. Co.		
Troilene Series	10 - 12	12 - 15
"Cattle Girl"		
"Indians in a Snow Storm"		
"Indian Pony Race"		
"Fur Canoe"		
"Roping a Steer"		
"The Town Marshall"		
"The War Canoe"		
"Warping the Air Barge Upstream"		
LARSEN, DUDE AND DOT (U.S.A.)		
Linens of 30's and 40's	1 - 2	2 - 3
MAY, KARL (Germany)		
Cowboys and Indians	10 - 12	12 - 15
PAXSON, E.S.		
McKee Printing Co.		
Northwest Postcard and Souvenir Co.	10 - 12	12 - 15
"Apache"		
"Crow"		
"Curley, Custer's Scout"		
"Flathead"		

"Mis-sou-la"
"A Nez Perce"
"Northern Indian"
"Sioux"
PAYNE, HARRY (G.B.)
  Raphael Tuck

"The Wild West" Series	10 - 12	12 - 14
"A Scamper Across the Prairie"		
"The Head of the Column"		
"Sounding the 'Turn Out' "		

PETERSON, L. (U.S.A.)
  H.H. Tammen Co.
    Indian Series

3420 "Chief Sitting Bull"	10 - 12	12 - 15
3421 "Chief Geronimo"	10 - 12	12 - 15
3422 "Chief Yellow Hawk"	8 - 10	10 - 12
3423 "Chief Eagle Feather"	8 - 10	10 - 12
3424 "Chief High Horse"	8 - 10	10 - 12
3425 "Starlight"	8 - 10	10 - 12
3426 "Chief Big Feather"	8 - 10	10 - 12
3427 "Sunshine"	8 - 10	10 - 12
3428 "Fighting Wolf"	8 - 10	10 - 12
3429 "Minnehaha"	10 - 12	12 - 14
3430 "Hiawatha"	10 - 12	12 - 15
3431 "Chief Red Cloud"	10 - 12	12 - 15
3432 "Eagle Feather & Squaw"	8 - 10	10 - 12
3433 "Chief Black Hawk"	10 - 12	12 - 14
Unsigned Series	8 - 10	10 - 12

  H. H. Tammen Co.

"Cow Girl Series"	6 - 8	8 - 10

REISS, WINOLD (U.S.A.)   10 - 12   12 - 15
REMINGTON, FREDERIC (U.S.A.)
  Detroit Publishing Co.

14179 "Evening on a Canadian"	35 - 45	45 - 55
14180 "His First Lesson"	30 - 35	35 - 45
14181 "A Fight for the Water Hole"	35 - 45	45 - 55
14182 "An Argument with the Marshal"	35 - 45	45 - 55
14183 "Calling the Moose"	30 - 35	35 - 45

  Taylor Publishing

1012 "Pony War Dance"	80 - 90	90 - 100
1022 "The Sun Fisher"		
1027 "The Punchers"		

REYNOLDS

Cowboy Series 4400	5 - 6	6 - 8
Cowgirl Series 4406	5 - 6	6 - 8

RHINEHART, F.A.

Indian Series	8 - 10	10 - 12
"Rain in the Face," Sioux		
"Big Man"		

"Chief Wolf Robe," Cheyenne
"Chief Red Cloud," Sioux
"Chief Sitting Bull," Sioux
"Eagle Feather & Papoose"
"Two Little Braves," Sioux & Fox
"Chase-in-the-Morning"
"Hattie Tom," Chiricahua, Apache

ROLLINS, W. E. (U.S.A.)	6 - 8	8 - 10
RUSSELL, CHARLES M. (U.S.A.)		
Ridgley Calendar Co. (In Color)	25 - 30	30 - 35

"All Who Know Me ..."
"Antelope Hunt"
"Are You the Real Thing?"
"A Bad Bronco"
"The Bear in the Park ..."
"Better than Bacon"
"Blackfeet Burning ..."
"Bold Hunters ..."
"Boss of the Herd"
"Cowboys Off for Town"
"Elk in Lake McDonald"
"The First Furrow"
"Have One on Me"
"I Savvy These Folks"
"Jerked Down"
"Lassoing a Wolf"
"Lone Wolf - Piegan"
"Powderface -- Arapahoe"
"Rainy Morning in a ..."
"Red Cloud"
"Roping a Grizzly"
"Roping a Wolf #2"
"The Round Up #1"
"The Round Up #2"
"Scattering the Riders"
"The Scouts"
"Stay With Him!"
"Sun Shine and Shadow"
"A Touch of Western ..."
"Waiting for a Chinook"
"Where Ignorance is Bliss"
"White Man's Skunk ..."
"Wild Horse Hunters #1"
"Wild Horse Hunters #2"
"Women of the Plains"
"Wound Up"
"A Wounded Grizzly"

(In Sepia or Black and White)	10 - 12	12 - 15

"The Buffalo Hunt #28"

Buffalo Calf (Jicarilla Apache)
Detroit Pub. Co. No. 13943

Montera Cabezon (Apache)
Detroit Pub. Co. No. 13941

"Buffalo Protecting Calf"
"The Christmas Dinner" (B/W)
"Cowboys off for Town"
"Gnome with Lantern"
"Holding up the ... Stage" (B/W)
"Indian Dog Team"
"Initiated" (B/W)
"The Initiation of ..." (B/W)
"The Last of the Buffalo" (B/W)
"Nez Perce"
"An Old Fashioned ..."
"Painting the Town" (B/W)
"Powderface -- Arapahoe"
"A Roper"
"The Shell Game" (B/W)
"The Trail Boss" (B/W)
Printed Photograph (Head in Oval)   6 - 8   8 - 10
(Black ink on pale green silk)
a. "A Christmas Dinner"
b. "The Initiation of the Tenderfoot"
c. "The Last of the Buffalo"
d. "Painting the Town"
e. "The Shell Game"

f. "The Trail Boss"

A. Selige, St. Louis   8 - 10   10 - 12
    Indian Chief Series
      "Chief Black Hawk"
      "Chief Afraid of Eagle"
      "Chief Fleet of Foot"
      "Chief Bear Goes Inwoods"
      "Chief Yellow Hair"
      Others

Raphael Tuck
    Series 2171 "Indian Chiefs" (12)   10 - 12   12 - 15
      "Chief Charging Bear"
      "Chief Yellow Thunder"
      "Chief Yellow Horn"
      "Chif White Swan"
      "Chief Shooting Hawk"
      "Chief Black Thunder"
      "Chief Eagle Track"
      "Chief Red Owl"
      "Chief Black Chicken"
    Series 9131   10 - 12   12 - 15
      "Chief Charging Bear"
      "Chief Not Afraid of Pawnee"
      "Chief Black Chicken"
      "Chief Eagle Track"

Maurice Boulanger (Uns.), Raphael Tuck, "Humorous Cats" Series 122

B. Cobbe, Raphael Tuck 3563, "Let the Poor Thing Go"

"Chief Black Thunder"		
"Chief White Swan"		
Series 9011 "Hiawatha" (6)	10 - 12	12 - 15
Series 1330 "Hiawatha" (6)	10 - 12	12 - 15
Cowboy Series 2499	5 - 6	6 - 8
C. A. Read Co.		
"Hold Her Zeb, I'm Coming"	6 - 8	8 - 10
Roberts, Helena, Montana		
"Waiting for a Chinook"	6 - 8	8 - 10
Souvenir of Military Circus and Wild West		
Show, Southampton, L.I., July 2-4, 1910.	10 - 12	12 - 14
SCHUTZ, F.W. (U.S.A.)		
Cowboy Series 1728-1746	8 - 10	10 - 12
1728 "The Outlaw"		
1730 "Alkalai Ike"		
1741 "Roping the Bull"		
"Shooting up the Town"		
Others		

PUBLISHERS

Weiners, Ltd. "Buffalo Bill's Wild West" (6)	20 - 25	25 - 30

ANIMALS

CATS

ALDIN, CECIL (G.B.)	6 - 7	7 - 8
BARNES, G.L. (G.B.)		
Raphael Tuck		
Series 9301 "Cat Studies" (6)	8 - 10	10 - 12

Louis Wain, Davidson Brothers Series 6086, "We dine early, so ..."

Series 6495 "Cat Studies" (6)	8 - 10	10 - 12
Fairy Tale/Nursery Rhymes Series	12 - 14	14 - 16
"Little Boy Blue"		
"Red Riding Hood"		
"Tom, Tom, Piper's Son"		
Others		

BOULANGER, MAURICE (France)
International Art Publishing Co.

Series 586 (6)	6 - 8	8 - 10
Series 472 Large Image (6)	12 - 15	15 - 20
Series 473 Large Image (6)	15 - 18	18 - 22

K.F. Editeurs Series 586 — 18 - 20 — 22 - 25
Kopal Series 417 — 12 - 15 — 15 - 18
Raphael Tuck

Series 122 "Humorous Cats" (6) (Uns.)	12 - 15	15 - 18

BROWNE, TOM
Davidson Brothers

Series 2509 (6) "Funny Cats"	8 - 10	10 - 12
Series 2528 (6) "Comic Cats"	8 - 10	10 - 12

CLIVETTE — 6 - 8 — 8 - 10
COBBE, B. (G.B.)
Raphael Tuck

Series 9099, 9157 Oilettes (6)	10 - 12	12 - 14
Series 9436 Oilettes	10 - 12	12 - 14

DAWSON, LUCY — 5 - 6 — 6 - 8
ELLAM, WM. HENRY (G.B.)
Raphael Tuck

"Mixed Bathing" Series	10 - 12	12 - 15

"Mrs. Caudle's Curtain Lectures"	12 - 15	15 - 20
Series 9321 (6) "Breakfast in Bed"	12 - 15	15 - 20
Series 9685 (6) "Tales of the Seaside"	8 - 10	10 - 12
Illustrated P. C. Co.	8 - 10	10 - 12
FEIERTAG (Austria)	4 - 6	6 - 8
FREES, H.W.		
Rotograph Co.		
Real Photo Cat Comics	6 - 8	8 - 10
GEAR, MABEL		
Valentine & Sons	4 - 5	5 - 6
HOFFMAN, A.	5 - 6	6 - 8
KASKELINE		
S.W.S.B. Series 4370	5 - 6	6 - 8
LANDER, EDGAR (G.B.)		
Raphael Tuck		
Real Photo Studies Series 5088, 7006 (6)	4 - 5	5 - 6
MAC or HENRY SHEPHEARD		
Valentine & Sons		
Cat Studies	6 - 8	8 - 10
SCHWAR		
Cat Studies	6 - 8	8 - 9
SPERLICH, T. (G.B.)	6 - 7	7 - 8
German-American Novelty Co.		
Series 648 (6)	6 - 8	8 - 10
Langsdorf Co.		
Series 3047	8 - 10	10 - 12
STOCK, A.	5 - 6	6 - 7
STOCKS, M.	6 - 8	8 - 10
H.K. Co.		
Series 217, 3237, 381 (6)	6 - 8	8 - 10
THIELE, ARTHUR		
TSN		
Series 129 Dancing (6)	10 - 12	12 - 15
Series 134 Large Heads (6)	18 - 20	20 - 25
Series 710, 1015 (6)	15 - 18	18 - 22
Series 896 Large Heads (6)	25 - 28	28 - 30
Series 915 Comic Cats (6)	12 - 15	15 - 18
Series 995 Large Cupid Cats (6)	25 - 30	30 - 35
Series 1002 At Home (6)	10 - 12	12 - 15
Series 1015, 1007 Cat Families (6)	10 - 12	12 - 15
Series 1015, 1077, 1175 (6)	10 - 12	12 - 15
Series 1326 In Kitchen (6)	10 - 12	12 - 15
Series 1412 Large Image (6)	20 - 22	22 - 26
Series 1423 In School (6)	10 - 12	12 - 15
Series 1424 Large Image (6)	28 - 30	30 - 35
"Big Cleanup"		
"Big Washday"		
"Dressmaking"		
"Going to Bed"		

Norah Drummond, Raphael Tuck 3599, "All Scotch"

"Kitty Traveling"
"Writing"

Series 1602 Comical Cat Kids (6)	10 - 12	12 - 15
Series 1825 & 1826 Cat Kids (6)	10 - 12	12 - 15
Series 1827 & 1852 Cat Kids (6)	12 - 15	15 - 18
Series 1882 & 2030 In School (6)	10 - 12	12 - 15

THOMAS, PAUL
Raphael Tuck

Series 1196 (6)	8 - 10	10 - 12

WAIN, LOUIS
Raphael Tuck
Oilette Series 3385

Series 5 Paper Doll Cats (6)	200 - 250	250 - 275
"Dick Whittington"	350 - 400	400 - 450
Calendar Series 298, 304 (6)	35 - 40	40 - 45
Series 331 (6)	30 - 35	35 - 40
Series 644 Japanese (6)	35 - 40	40 - 45
Series 1003 "Write Away" (6)	40 - 45	45 - 50
Oilette Series 1412, 6444 (6)	40 - 45	45 - 50
Series 8515 (6)	30 - 35	35 - 40
Series 6084, 6723, 6724, 6727 (6)	30 - 35	35 - 40
Series 9563 "Diabolo" (6)	35 - 40	40 - 45
Series 8819, 9396 (6)	30 - 35	35 - 40

Davis

Series	25 - 30	30 - 35

Ettinger

Series 5376 Santa (Unsigned)	150 - 175	175 - 200
C. W. Faulkner Series	30 - 35	35 - 40

Aug.Specht
Stuttgart
Bernhardiner

Aug Specht, Anonymous Publisher, "Bernhardiner" (St. Bernard)

National Series	25 - 30	30 - 35
E. Nister Series	30 - 35	35 - 40
J. Salmon Series	30 - 35	35 - 40
Wrench Series	25 - 30	30 - 35
Santa Claus Cats (6)	175 - 200	200 - 225

DOGS

BARTH, KATH	6 - 8	8 - 10
BUTONY		
B.K.W.I. Series 859 (6)	8 - 10	10 - 12
C.A.	6 - 8	8 - 10
CORBELLA, TITO (Italy)		
Series 378 (6)	12 - 15	15 - 18
Others	10 - 12	12 - 15
DONADINI, JR. (Italy)		
Dog Studies (6)	10 - 12	12 - 15
Series 235 (6)	12 - 14	14 - 16
DRUMMOND, NORAH (G.B.)		
Raphael Tuck		
Series 3599 (6) "All Scotch"	8 - 10	10 - 12
Series 9105 (6)		
"Sporting Dogs"	12 - 14	14 - 16
"Faithful Friends"	7 - 8	8 - 12
Series 772 Dachshunds	8 - 10	10 - 12
FEIERTAG (Austria)	4 - 5	5 - 6
Dressed, Doing People Things	8 - 10	10 - 12

"Favorite Dogs: The Japanese Spaniel," Knight Brothers 1701

FREES, H.W.
  Rotograph Co.
    Comic Dog Photos   4 - 6   6 - 7
GREINER, A.
    Series 726 (Dog Studies) (6)   8 - 10   10 - 12
    Series 727 (6)   8 - 10   10 - 12
GROSSMAN, A.   6 - 8   8 - 10
GROSSMAN, M.   8 - 10   10 - 12
HANKE, H.
    Series 4056 Dressed Dachshunds   12 - 15   15 - 18
HANSTEIN
  Raphael Tuck
    Series 4092 "Favorite Dogs" (6)   8 - 10   10 - 12
HARTLEIN, W.   6 - 7   7 - 8
HERZ, E.W. (Austria)   7 - 8   8 - 10
KENNEDY, A.E.
  C. W. Faulkner
    Series 1424   8 - 10   10 - 12
KIENE   10 - 12   12 - 15
KIRMBE
  Raphael Tuck
    Series 3586 "Racing Greyhounds" (6)   12 - 15   15 - 18
KLUGMEYER (Austria)   6 - 8   8 - 10
MAC or HENRY SHEPHEARD
  Valentine & Sons
    "Tailwagger" Dog Series   10 - 12   12 - 15
MacGUIRE
    Head Studies (Pastels)   8 - 10   10 - 12

MAILICK, R.
    Dog Studies   10 - 12   12 - 15
MOODY, FANNIE   6 - 8   8 - 10
MULLER, A.
    Series 3956 (6) Dachshunds   12 - 15   15 - 18
    Other Dressed Series   10 - 12   12 - 15
    Others   6 - 8   8 - 10
OHLER, J.
    Comical Dogs   6 - 8   8 - 10
P.O.E. (Austria)   6 - 8   8 - 10
PANKRATZ
    Comical Dachshunds   10 - 12   12 - 15
REICHERT, C. (Austria)
  T.S.N.
    Series 923, 1280 (6)   7 - 8   8 - 10
    Series 1336, 1337 (6)   8 - 10   10 - 12
    Series 1851 (6)   8 - 10   10 - 12
SCHNOPLER, A. (Austria)
    Comical Dachshunds   10 - 12   12 - 18
SCHONIAN
  German American Art
    Series 1961   8 - 10   10 - 12

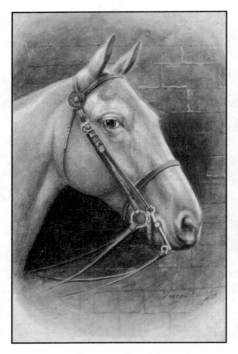

George Rankin
J. Salmon, 3354

C. Reichert
T.S.N. Series 1605

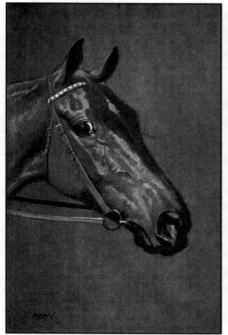

O. Merté
A.M.S. Series 589

M. Veit
CAFS Series 2028

T.S.N.		
Series 1961	8 - 10	10 - 12
SPERLICH, SOFIE (Germany)	5 - 6	6 - 7
STOLZ, A. (Austria)		
Series 772 Dachshunds	8 - 10	10 - 12
STUDDY (G.B.)		
"Bonzo" Issues	8 - 10	10 - 12
With Tennis or Golf	12 - 14	14 - 18
With Black Dolls	12 - 15	15 - 18
THIELE, ARTHUR (Germany)		
Raphael Tuck		
Series 9799 (6)	15 - 18	18 - 22
T.S.N.		
Series 843 (6)	18 - 22	22 - 25
Series 946 (6) Large Hunting Dogs	20 - 22	22 - 25
Series 1128, 1893 (6)	10 - 12	12 - 15
German American Novelty Co.		
Series 806 (Large Image)	18 - 22	22 - 25
THOMAS (G.B.)		
Raphael Tuck		
Series 6990 "French Poodles" (6)	10 - 12	12 - 14

WAIN, LOUIS (G.B.)
  Raphael Tuck

Series 6401 Comical Dogs (6)	35 - 45	45 - 55
Series 6402 (6)	35 - 45	45 - 55
Series 9376 (6)	35 - 40	40 - 45

WATSON, MAUDE WEST
  Raphael Tuck
    "Dog Sketches"

Series 3346, 8682, E8837, 9977 (6)	8 - 10	10 - 15
Series 3103 (6)	10 - 12	12 - 15

WEBER, E.

Dachshund Comics	8 - 10	10 - 12

WOMELE
  M. Munk, Vienna
WUNDERLICH, A.

Dachshunds	12 - 15	15 - 18

HORSES

ADAMS

Meissner & Buch	8 - 10	10 - 12
BARTH, W.	8 - 10	10 - 12
BRAUN, LOUIS	8 - 10	10 - 12

CASTALANZA

Series 342	8 - 10	10 - 12

CORBELLA, TITO (Italy)

Series 316 (6)	12 - 14	14 - 16

DONADINI, JR. (Italy)

Series 237 Racing Comics	10 - 12	12 - 15

DRUMMOND, NORAH
  Raphael Tuck

Series 9065, 9138 (6)	8 - 10	10 - 12
Series 9561 (6)	12 - 15	15 - 18
Series 3109, 3194, 3603 (6)	8 - 10	10 - 12

FENNI (Racing Series)	10 - 12	12 - 15

FRIEDRICH, H.

Series 464 (6)	6 - 8	8 - 10

HANSTEIN
  Raphael Tuck

Series 810 Steeple Chase (6)	8 - 10	10 - 12

HERMAN
  Raphael Tuck Oilettes
    "The Horse" (6)

	10 - 12	12 - 14

KOCH, A.
  B.K.W.I.

Series 473 Trotters (6)	12 - 15	15 - 18
Series 377, 566 (6)	8 - 10	10 - 12

Series 660, 739, 865 (6)	10 - 12	12 - 14
Series 966 Circus Studies (6)	12 - 14	14 - 18
KOCH, LUDWIG (Austria)		
B.K.W.I.		
Series 493, 948 (6)	10 - 12	12 - 15
Series 830, 865 (6)	12 - 14	14 - 16
Series 1447, 1470 (6)	10 - 12	12 - 14
Series 372, 377, 473 (6)	12 - 14	14 - 18
Series 566, 660, 739	12 - 14	14 - 18
Series 966 Circus Studies (6)	12 - 14	14 - 18
O.F.Z.-L		
Series 280-285	10 - 12	12 - 15
KOCH, PROF. G.		
Raphael Tuck		
Series 588B (6)	10 - 12	12 - 15
KOLB		
Raphael Tuck		
Series 4084 Oilette (6)	10 - 12	12 - 14
KROMBACK	10 - 12	12 - 14
MATHEUSON	8 - 10	10 - 12
MAUZAN		
Series 383 (6)	10 - 12	12 - 14
MERTÉ, O.		
A.M.S.		
Series 589, 599, 660 (6)	10 - 12	12 - 15
Series 623 - Circus Horses (6)	10 - 12	12 - 15
Series 729 (6)	8 - 10	10 - 12

Aug. Müller, H.K. Company, Series 411

Raphael Tuck		
Series 9946 - Circus Horses (6)	10 - 12	12 - 15
MÜLLER		
T.S.N.		
Series 128, 133 (6)	8 - 10	10 - 12
Series 333, 411, 509 (6)	10 - 12	12 - 15
S.W.S.B.		
Series 6919 (6)	6 - 8	8 - 10
NANNI		
Series 257, 307 (6)	8 - 10	10 - 12
PAYNE, HARRY		
Raphael Tuck	12 - 15	15 - 18
R.K.		
B.K.W.I.		
Series 350, 380, 386 (6)	6 - 8	8 - 10
RANKIN, GEORGE (G.B.)	6 - 8	8 - 10
REICHERT, C.		
T.S.N.		
Series 934, with dogs (6)	10 - 12	12 - 14
Series 1359 (6)	10 - 12	12 - 14
Series 1605, 1606, with dogs (6)	8 - 10	10 - 12
Series 1732, with dogs (6)	8 - 10	10 - 12
Series 1782, 1870 (6)	10 - 12	12 - 14
Series 1422, Unsigned (6)	6 - 8	8 - 10
M. Munk, Vienna		
Series 268, 771 (6)	8 - 10	10 - 12
Series 1165 (6)	10 - 12	12 - 14
SCHILLING, F.	8 - 10	10 - 12

Early Pig Chromo-Lithograph Comic

Anonymous, 2545-1
German Easter Greeting

Anonymous
German New Year's Greeting

SCHONIAN
  T.S.N.

Series 1838, 5826 (6)	10 - 12	12 - 15
Series 1935, with dogs (6)	12 - 14	14 - 16
Series E1935 (6)	10 - 12	12 - 14

SCHUTZ

Series 972 (6)	6 - 8	8 - 10

  Alfred Stiebel Company

Series 430, 438 (6)	10 - 12	12 - 15

SHILLING, F.
  A.R. & C.i.B.

Series 1136 (6)	8 - 10	10 - 12

STOKES, VERNON
  Photochrom Co.

"Celesque" Series (6)	7 - 8	8 - 9

TENNI

Harness Racing Series	8 - 10	10 - 12

TERZI, A.

Series 320 (6)	10 - 12	12 - 14

THAMSE
  Raphael Tuck

	6 - 8	8 - 10

THOMAS, J.
  Raphael Tuck

Series 353, 529 (6)	10 - 12	12 - 14

Anonymous, R.P. 8068
Early Chromo-Lithograph

Anonymous
Early Chromo-Lithograph

Series 1182, 9254 (6)	12 - 14	14 - 16
Series 575-B - Trotters (6)	10 - 12	12 - 15
Series 579 - Steeplechase (6)	8 - 10	10 - 12
Racing Series	10 - 12	12 - 15
Series 9254 (6)	8 - 10	10 - 12
W&L, Berlin		
Series 1182	10 - 12	12 - 14
TRACHE, E.		
Series 464, 466, 788 (6)	8 - 10	10 - 12
Series E463, 1175 (4)	8 - 10	10 - 12
VELTEN		
A.B.D.		
Series 775	8 - 10	10 - 12
W.F.A.	7 - 8	8 - 10
WALKER		
Raphael Tuck		
Series 9544 (6) "Chargers"	8 - 10	10 - 12
WRIGHT, ALAN		
Series 12219 (6)	10 - 12	12 - 14
WRIGHT, GEORGE		
E. W. Savory, Ltd.		
Series 2118 (6)	8 - 10	10 - 12

OTHER ANIMALS

BARNES-AUSTIN, EDGAR (G.B.)		
Raphael Tuck		
"Piggie-Wiggie" Series	10 - 12	12 - 14
BAUMGARTEN, FRITZ (Bunny Rabbits)	8 - 10	10 - 12
CANTLE, J.M. (G.B.)	6 - 7	7 - 8
COBBS, B. (G.B.)		
Raphael Tuck		
Series 9539 (6) "Bunnies"	5 - 6	6 - 7
CRITE		
"Billy Possum" Series (See Political)		
DONADINI, JR. (Italy)		
Animal Studies	8 - 10	10 - 12
DRUMMOND, NORAH (G.B.)		
Raphael Tuck		
Series 9507 (6) "Famous British Cattle"	7 - 8	8 - 10
Series 3297 (6) "Faithful Friends"	7 - 8	8 - 12
EARNSHAW, HAROLD C.		
Millar & Lang (Comic Animals)	4 - 6	6 - 8
Gottschalk, Dreyfus & Davis	4 - 6	6 - 8
ELLAM		
Raphael Tuck		
Series 9684 (6) "Dressed Elephants"	15 - 18	18 - 22
GEAR, MABEL (U.S.A.)	5 - 8	8 - 10
GREEN, ROLAND (G.B.)	5 - 6	6 - 7
HORINA, H.		
Ullman Mfg. Co.		
Series 91 (Jimmy Pig)	10 - 12	12 - 15
1967 "This little pig went to market"		
1968 "This little pig went bathing"		
1969 "This little pig stayed home"		
1970 "This little pig went to school"		
1971 "This little pig went to a party"		
1972 "This little pig went to war"		
1973 "This little pig went fishing"		
1974 "This little pig worked in garden"		
1975 "This little pig went sailing"		
1976 "This little pig was a drummer boy"		
HUDSON, G.M.		
Raphael Tuck		
Series 8648 "Guinnepins"	8 - 10	10 - 12
JAMES, FRANK (G.B.)	4 - 5	5 - 6
KEENE, MINNIE (G.B.)	4 - 5	5 - 6
KENNEDY, A.E. (G.B.)	5 - 8	8 - 10
LANDSEER, SIR EDWIN (G.B.)	8 - 10	10 - 15
LESTER, A. (G.B.)	4 - 5	5 - 6
MAGUIRE, HELENA (G.B.)	5 - 6	6 - 7

Raphael Tuck
Series 6713, 6714 (6)
    "Animal Studies" .... 7 - 8   8 - 10
MÜLLER, A. (Germany) .... 5 - 6   6 - 8
PERLBERG, F.
Raphael Tuck
    Art Series 991 (6) .... 6 - 7   7 - 8
POPE, DOROTHY (G.B.) .... 4 - 5   5 - 6
RANKIN, GEORGE (G.B.) .... 4 - 5   5 - 6
SCRIVENER, MAUDE (G.B.) .... 6 - 7   7 - 10
STEWART, J.A. (G.B.) .... 4 - 5   5 - 6
THIELE, ARTHUR
German-American Novelty Art Co.
    Series 789 Pigs, Large Image .... 20 - 25   25 - 30
T.S.N.
    Series 919 Dressed Ducks .... 15 - 20   20 - 25
    Series 1165 Dressed Chicks .... 15 - 20   20 - 25
    Series 1352 Dressed Chicks .... 12 - 15   15 - 18
    Series 1452 Dressed Chicks .... 15 - 20   20 - 25
    Series 1020, 1021 Dressed Bunnies .... 15 - 20   20 - 25
    Series 781 Dressed Monkeys .... 20 - 22   22 - 26
VALTER, EUGENIE (G.B.) .... 5 - 6   6 - 7
WAIN, LOUIS (G.B.)
    Frogs .... 35 - 40   40 - 45
WARDLE, ARTHUR (G.B.) .... 4 - 5   5 - 6
WEALTHY, R.J. (G.B.) .... 4 - 5   5 - 6
WEST, A.L. (G.B.) .... 5 - 6   6 - 7

3

Fantasy

Fantasy, according to **Webster,** means imagination or fancy; wild visionary fancy; an unnatural or bizarre mental image; illusion, phantasm; an odd notion, whim, caprice; a highly imaginative poem, play; mental images as in a daydream ... all of these definitions come to life on beautiful and wonderful fantasy postcards.

Most of the fantasies bring to life the days of our youth ... of fairies and fairy tales, of frog kings and sleeping princesses, of dolls and teddy bears and dressed animals doing people things ... of mermaids and sea creatures, of vixens and voluptuous nudes ... which came later. These make a wonderful fantasy world for us all!

Before the influx of foreign cards to the U.S. in the late 70's and 80's, collectors of fantasy had to be content with the works of Dwig and a handful of other artists, a few nursery rhymes and fairy tales, some exaggerations of big fish, mosquitoes and farm produce, etc.—not too great for a fantasy collector.

Slowly the beautiful and desirable imports began appearing in auctions and finally in dealer stocks, and now everyone has discovered them. Prices have spiraled and most all types are in great demand. The most desirable are listed in these pages. Have a Fantasy time!

FAIRIES

The Fairy family includes Brownies, Elves, Gnomes, Goblins, Fairies, Leprechauns, Pixies, and Sprites.

	VG	EX
BARHAM, SYBIL (G.B.)		
C. W. Faulkner		
Series 1859 (6) "Fairies"	$10 - 12	$12 - 14
BAUMGARTEN, FRITZ (Germany)		
Oppel & Hess, Jena		
Series 1509	10 - 12	12 - 15
Other Series	10 - 12	12 - 15
Other Publishers	10 - 12	12 - 15
BERGER		
Series 116 (B&W)	15 - 20	20 - 25
CLOKE, RENE		
Valentine & Sons "Fairies" (6)	8 - 10	10 - 12
Series 1002		
Series 1183		
Series 1848		

C.M.C., "The Serenade"
C. W. Faulkner, 1855

Josephine Duddla
G. A. & Company, 136

Beryl Haig, "Fairy Whispers"
A. & M. Davis & Co., Ser. 949

Phyllis M. Purser
Salmon 5158, "A Sleeping Boy"

J. Salmon		
Series 4626 (6)	6 - 8	8 - 10
Series 4627 (6)	8 - 10	10 - 12
COWHAM, HILDA (GB)		
C.W. Faulkner		
"The Fairy Glen" Series (6)	10 - 12	12 - 15
DAUSTY		
C. & P. & Co.		
Series 704 "Nymphs" (6)	8 - 10	10 - 12
GIRIS, CESAR		
Raphael Tuck		
Series 2365 "Madame Butterfly" (6)	18 - 20	20 - 25
HAIG, BERYL (G.B.)	12 - 15	15 - 18
MARSH, H.G.C. (G.B.)		
C.W. Faulkner		
Series 1510 (6)	12 - 15	15 - 18
MARSHALL, ALICE (G.B.)		
Raphael Tuck		
Series 3490 "Fairyland Fancies" (6)	15 - 18	18 - 25
Series 3489 (6)	18 - 20	20 - 26
MAUSER, PHYLLIS		
P. Salmon		
Series 5159 "Brownies & Fairies" (6)	8 - 10	10 - 12

I. R. & G. Outhwaite, A.& C.
Black, "The Witch's Sister ..."

H. Peyk
R. H. F. 758

MAYBANK, THOMAS
  Raphael Tuck
    Series 6683 "Midsummer Dreams" (6)   20 - 22   22 - 25
MILLER, HILDA (GB)
  C.W. Faulkner
    Series 1690 "Fairies"   12 - 15   15 - 18
    Series 1693 "Fairies"   12 - 15   15 - 18
    Series 1822 "Peter Pan"   15 - 18   18 - 20
MÜLLER, PAUL LOTHAR (Germany)
  Oscar Heierman, Berlin (Novitas)
    Series 550 "Gnomes"   8 - 10   10 - 12
OUTHWAITE, IDA R. (G.B.)
  A. & C. Black, London
    Series 71-A "Fairy Frolic"   15 - 18   18 - 22
    Series 72 "Elves & Fairies"   15 - 18   18 - 22
    Series 75 "Elves & Fairies"   15 - 18   18 - 22
    Series 76 "Elves & Fairies"   12 - 15   15 - 18
    Series 79 "Elves & Fairies"   15 - 18   18 - 22
    Mermaid "Playing With Bubbles"   20 - 25   25 - 30
PEYK, H.   10 - 12   12 - 15
PURSER, PHYLLIS M. (G.B.)   8 - 10   10 - 12
RICHARDSON, AGNES
  Raphael Tuck
    Series 1649 "Fairies"   20 - 25   25 - 30

Series 3447	16 - 18	18 - 20

SCHMUCKER, SAMUEL L.
(See Schmucker Section)

SCHUTZ, E. (Austria)

B.K.W.I.

Series 391 (6)	18 - 20	20 - 25

M. Munk, Vienna

Series 1363 (6)	15 - 18	18 - 22
Series 1364 (6)	15 - 18	18 - 22
Series 1365 (6)	15 - 18	18 - 22
Series 435 (6) Uns. Andersen's Fairy Tales	18 - 20	20 - 25

SHERBORNE

Salmon & Co.

Series 4239 "Fairies of the Wood"	10 - 12	12 - 15

SOWERBY, MILLICENT (G.B.)

Humphrey Milford, London

"Woodland Games" Fairies (6)	18 - 20	20 - 25
"Fairies Friends" Series (6)	22 - 25	25 - 28
"Flowers & Wings" Elves (6)	12 - 15	15 - 18
"Merry Elves" (6)	12 - 15	15 - 20
"Fairy Frolic" Series (6)	12 - 15	15 - 20
"Favorite Children" (6)	10 - 12	12 - 15

M. Sowerby
H. Milford, "The Summer Elves"

Margaret W. Tarrant
Medici, "The Poppy Fairies"

"Flower Children" (6)	12 - 15	15 - 18
"Old Time Games" (6)	18 - 20	20 - 25
"Sky Fairies" (6)	15 - 18	18 - 22

STEELE, L.R. (GB)
   Salmon & Co.

Series 5050-5055 "Famous Fairies"	6 - 8	8 - 10

SYMONDS, CONSTANCE (G.B.)

C. W. Faulkner Series 1645 (6)	15 - 18	18 - 20

TARRANT, MARGARET (G.B.)
   Medici Society

PK 120 "The Fairy Troupe"	8 - 10	10 - 12
PK 184 "The Enchantress"	8 - 10	10 - 12
Others	8 - 10	10 - 12

UNTERSBERGER, ANDREAS (Germany)
   Emil Kohn, Munchen

Fairy and Gnome Series (12)	12 - 14	14 - 18

WATKINS, DOROTHY (GB)
   Valentine & Sons

Series 6 "The Dance of the Elves"	8 - 10	10 - 12

WHEELER, DOROTHY (G.B.)
   Bamforth & Co.

Series 1 "Fairy Secret" (6)	8 - 10	10 - 14

WEIGAND, MARTIN

Gnomes, Mushroom Series (12)	15 - 18	18 - 20

   Raphael Tuck

Oilette Series 6683 (6)	15 - 18	18 - 22
"Mid-Summer Dreams" (6)	15 - 20	20 - 25

   Valentine & Sons

Series 108 (6)	10 - 12	12 - 14

ANONYMOUS

Elves	5 - 8	8 - 15
Fairies	8 - 10	10 - 15
Gnomes	6 - 8	8 - 12
Goblins (Usually Halloween)	6 - 8	8 - 12
Leprechauns	5 - 7	7 - 12
Pixies	8 - 10	10 - 15
Sprites	7 - 8	8 - 10

FAIRY TALES AND NURSERY RHYMES

ANDERSEN, HANS

"The Little Mermaid"	15 - 20	20 - 25

BARHAM, SYBIL (G.B.)

Series 1734 "The Pied Piper of Hamelin"	10 - 12	12 - 14

BARNES, G.L.
   Raphael Tuck Series 9301

Cats -- Fairy Tales/Nursery Rhymes	12 - 14	14 - 16
"Little Boy Blue"		
"Red Riding Hood"		

H. Dockal, "Rumpelstilzchen"
Uvachrom, Series 407

Linda Edgerton
V. Mansell & Co., No. 1111

"Tom, Tom, Piper's Son ..."		
Others		
BAUMGARTEN, FRITZ (FB) Germany		
Series 1487, 1516	10 - 12	12 - 14
BORISS, MARGRET		
"Hansel and Gretel" (6)	8 - 10	10 - 12
"Pied Piper of Hamelin" (6)	8 - 10	10 - 12
"Puss in Boots" (6)	8 - 10	10 - 12
BRETT, MOLLY		
The Medici Society, Ltd., London		
Series 1, 145, 147, 155, 168, 179, 185	5 - 6	6 - 8
BURD, C.M.		
Series 18 "Nursery Rhymes"	10 - 12	12 - 15
CALDECOTT, RANDOLPH		
F. Warne & Co. 48-card Set	4 - 6	6 - 8
COMMIEHAU, A.		
Series 48	6 - 8	8 - 10
DOCKAL, H.		
UVACHROM Series 407	8 - 10	10 - 12
EDGERTON, LINDA		
Mansell & Company Series 1111	10 - 12	12 - 15
GREENAWAY, KATE (See Beautiful Children)		

HERRFURTH, OSCAR (Germany)
UVA Chrom, Stuttgart
Brothers Grimm Fairy Tales (6 per Series)

125 "Hansel & Gretel"	6 - 7	7 - 8
128 "Rotkappchen"		
(Little Red Riding Hood)	7 - 8	8 - 9
139 "Frau Holle" (Lady Hell)	4 - 5	5 - 6
140 "Dornroschen" (Sleeping Beauty)	7 - 8	8 - 9
147 "Schneewittchen" (Snow White)	7 - 8	8 - 9
154 "Aschenbrodl" (Cinderella)	6 - 7	7 - 8
223 "Der Gestiefelte Kater" (Puss in Boots)	5 - 6	6 - 7
241 "Die Gansemagd" (The Goose Maid)	5 - 6	6 - 7
242 "Der Rattenfanger von Hameln"		
(Pied Piper)	7 - 8	8 - 9
252 "Der Schweinhirt" (The Pig Herdsman)	5 - 6	6 - 7
254 "Siebenschon" (Seven Lovelies)	5 - 6	6 - 7
264 "Der Tannenbaum" (The Fir Tree)	4 - 5	5 - 6
265 "Der Wolf und die Sieben Geisslein"		
(The Wolf and the Seven Goats)	4 - 5	5 - 6
266 "Marienkind"	4 - 5	5 - 6
267 "Tischlein deck dich"	4 - 5	5 - 6
268 "Die Sieben Schwaben"	5 - 6	6 - 7
269 "Bruderchein und Schwesterchen"	6 - 7	7 - 8
285 "Die Bremer Stadtmusikanten"	5 - 6	6 - 7
298 "Hans im Gluck" (Jack & Jill)	5 - 6	6 - 7
299 "Das Tapfere Schneiderlein"	5 - 6	6 - 7
311 "Der Kleine Daumling" (Tom Thumb)	6 - 7	7 - 8
319 "Hase und Igel - Das Lumpengesindel"	5 - 6	6 - 7
320 "Die Sieben Raben" (The Seven Ravens)	6 - 7	7 - 8
324 "Munchhausen I"	4 - 5	5 - 6
325 "Munchhausen II"	4 - 5	5 - 6
354 "Das Schlaraffenland"		
(Milk & Honey Land)	4 - 5	5 - 6
355 "Der Frosch Konig" (The Frog King)	6 - 7	7 - 8
363 "Die Heinselmannchen"	5 - 6	6 - 7
369 "Till Eulenspiegel" (12 cards)	4 - 5	5 - 6
376 "Schneeweifchen und Rosenrot --		
Die Sterntaler"	6 - 7	7 - 8
379 "Konig Drosselbart"	4 - 5	5 - 6
387 "Caliph Stork"	4 - 5	5 - 6
388 "Aus Flem deutschen Marchenwald I"	4 - 5	5 - 6
406 "Aus Flem deutschen Marchenwald II"	4 - 5	5 - 6
407 "Rumpelstilken"	6 - 7	7 - 8
413 "Marchen-Elfen"	5 - 6	6 - 7

Tales (Sagen) Other than Grimm (6-Card Series)
Sage - A fantastic or incredible tale.

127 "Die Nibelungen - Sage"	6 - 7	7 - 8

141 "Parsival" (Parsifal)	7 - 8	8 - 9
157 "Rubezahl I"	4 - 5	5 - 6
158 "Wilhelm Tell" (12)	5 - 6	6 - 7
161 "Rubezahl II"	4 - 5	5 - 6
239 "Die Tristan - Sage"	6 - 7	7 - 8
247 "Die Parsival - Sage I"	6 - 7	7 - 8
HUTAF, AUGUST W. (U.S.A.)		
Series 105 (Little Bakers)	6 - 8	8 - 10
2089 "Pat-a-Cake"		
2090 "Make Me a Cake ..."		
2091 "Criss It and Cross It ..."		
2092 "Put It in the Oven ..."		
2093 "Put on the Chocolate ..."		
2094 "Icing and Candles ..."		
JACKSON, HELEN		
Raphael Tuck Series 6749 (6)	10 - 12	12 - 14
JUCHTZER	7 - 8	8 - 10
KENNEDY		
C. W. Faulkner Series 1633 (6)	8 - 10	10 - 12
KUBEL, O.		
Brothers Grimm Tales	10 - 12	12 - 14
KUTZER, E.		
Der. Sudmark Poster Series	12 - 15	15 - 18
248 "Walther von der Vogelweide"		
253 "Die Parzival - Sage II"		
258 "Die Lohengrin - Sage"		
259 "Die Tannehauser - Sage"		
263 "Aus der Zeit der Minnesanger"		
361 "Der Lichtenstein" (12)	4 - 5	5 - 6
Bund Der Deutschen		
373 "Rotkäppchen" (Red Riding Hood)	12 - 15	15 - 18
Others	12 - 15	15 - 18
LANDSTROM, B. (Finland)	6 - 8	8 - 10
LEETE, F. (Germany)		
H.K. & M. Co.		
"Siegfried" Poster Cards (6)	12 - 15	15 - 18
LeMAIR, WILLIBEEK		
Augener, Ltd.		
Our Old Nursery Rhymes (12)	10 - 12	12 - 15
"Baa Baa Black Sheep"		
"Hickory, Dickory, Dock"		
"Georgy Porgy"		
"Here We Go Round the Mulberry Bush"		
"I Love Little Pussy"		
"Little Bo Peep"		
"Mary Had a Little Lamb"		
"Oranges and Lemons"		
"O Where is My Little Dog Gone"		
"Pat a Cake"		

Flora White, J. Salmon, Ltd.
"Red Riding Hood"

M. Sowerby, H. Milford
"Little Miss Muffet"

"Pussy Cat, Pussy Cat"
"Sing a Song of Sixpence"
Old Rhymes With New Pictures (12)   10 - 12   12 - 15
"Humpty Dumpty"
"Little Boy Blue"
"Little Miss Muffet"
"Lucy Locket"
"Polly Put the Kettle on ..."
"Twinkle Twinkle"
"Jack & Jill"
"Little Jack Horner"
"Little Mother"
"Mary, Mary ..."
"Three Blind Mice"
"Yankee Doodle"
Little Songs of Long Ago (12)   10 - 12   12 - 15
"Dame Get Up and Bake Your Pies"
"I Had a Little Nut Tree"
"I Saw Three Ships a Sailing"
"Little Polly Flinders"
"Little Tom Tucker"
"London Bridge Has Broken Down"
"Old King Cole"
"Over the Hills and Far Away"

"There Came to My Window"
"The North Wind Doth Blow"
"Young Lambs to Sell"
"Simple Simon"
Little People (6)   10 - 12   12 - 15
"Evening Prayer"
"In the Garden"
"Good Evening, Mr. Hare"
"Little Culprit"
"In the Belfrey"
"Time to Get Up"
More Old Nursery Rhymes (12)
"A Frog He Would a Wooing Go"
"A Happy Family"
"Bed Time"
"Curley Locks"
"Girls and Boys Come Out to Play"
"Hush-a-by Baby"
"Ride a Cock Horse"
"The Crooked Man"
"There Was a Little Man"
"Three Little Kittens"
Old Dutch Nursery Rhymes   10 - 12   12 - 15
"Follow the Leader"
"Our Baby Prince"
"Polly Perkin"
"The Little Sailor"
"The Marionettes"
"The Tiny Man"
"Turn Round, Turn Round"
Small Rhymes for Small People   8 - 10   10 - 12
"Dance-a-Baby Ditty"
"Dance to Your Daddy"
"Goosey Gander"
"Lavender Blue"
"Lazy Sheep"
"Little Jumping Joan"
"Sleep, Baby, Sleep"
"The Babes in the Woods"
"Three Mice Went to a Hole to Spin"
MÜHLBERG   8 - 10   10 - 12
MILLER, HILDA T.
   C. W. Faulkner & Sons
     Fairy Tale Series 1784   15 - 20   20 - 25
MILLER, MARION
   Ernest Nister   10 - 12   12 - 15
NIXON, K.
   C. W. Faulkner & Co.
     "Alice in Wonderland" (6)   12 - 15   15 - 18

Hilda T. Miller
C. W. Faulkner, No. 1784, "Jack and Jill"

NOSWORTHY, FLORENCE E.		
F. A. Owen Series 160	10 - 12	12 - 14
NYSTROM, JENNY (Sweden)		
Signed Issues	20 - 22	22 - 25
Unsigned Issues	10 - 12	12 - 14
PAYER, E.	7 - 8	8 - 10
PINGGERA		
Posters	12 - 15	15 - 18
239 "Sans Daumling" (Tom Thumb)		
240 "Schneewittchen"		
245 "Aschenpuitel"		
251 "Jung Frau"		
"Rubezahl"		
SCHIRMER	8 - 10	10 - 12
SCHUTZ, E. (Austria)		
B.K.W.I.		
Poster Cards		
Series 435 (6) Andersen's Fairy Tales	15 - 18	18 - 22
Deutscher Schulverein		
Poster Cards		
319 "Rumpelstilzchen"	15 - 18	18 - 25
320 "Schneewittchen" (Snow White)	18 - 20	20 - 25
321 "Rotkäppchen" (Red Riding Hood)	18 - 20	20 - 22
322 "Die Sieben Raben" (Seven Ravens)	15 - 18	18 - 22
564 "Aschenbrodel" (Cinderella)	20 - 22	22 - 25
653 "Der Frotchkonig" (The Frog King)	20 - 22	22 - 25
862 "Dornroschen" (Sleeping Beauty)	18 - 20	20 - 22

SOWERBY, AMY MILLICENT (G.B.)
Humphrey Milford, London

"Favourite Nursery Rhymes" (6)	18 - 20	20 - 22
"Favourite Nursery Stories" (6)	12 - 15	15 - 20

TARRANT, MARGARET (G.B.)
T. P. & Company, N.Y.

"Story Book Series"	6 - 8	8 - 10

TYPO, Boston

"Tell Me a Story"	6 - 8	8 - 10
VALENTINE's Series (6)	6 - 8	8 - 10

WAIN, LOUIS (G.B.)
Raphael Tuck

"Oilette" Series 3385 "Paper Doll Cats"	200 - 250	250 - 275
"Aladdin"		
"Beauty and the Beast"		
"Cinderella"		
"Little Red Riding Hood"		
"Robinhood"		
"Dick Whittington"	300 - 350	350 - 400

WALL, BERNHARDT
Ullman Mfg. Co.

"Nursery Rhymes" Series 1664-1668	10 - 12	12 - 15
"Red Riding Hood" Series	10 - 12	12 - 15
1752 "Take Some Cakes ..."		
1753 "On the Way to Grandmother's ..."		
1754 "Arrives at Grandmother's ..."		
1755 "Comes to Bed ..."		
1756 "Innocently Lay Down in Bed ..."		
1757 "Hears the Wolf Say ..."		
"Mary and Her Lamb" Series 1759-1762	10 - 12	12 - 15

WHEELER, DOROTHY
Humphrey Milford

"Snow Children" Series (6)	8 - 10	10 - 12

WHITE, FLORA (GB)

Ilfracombe Mermaid, "Who are You?"	20 - 25	25 - 30
J. Salmon Poster Series	10 - 12	12 - 15
"Cinderella"		
"Dick Whittington"		
"Goose Girl"		
"Hop-O-My-Thumb"		
"Peter Pan"		
"Puss in Boots"		

WINKLER

	7 - 8	8 - 10

Anonymous
Paper Doll Cut-outs

Series 3382 "Little Bo-Peep"	50 - 60	60 - 70
Series 3383 "Little Boy Blue"	50 - 60	60 - 70

PUBLISHERS

Bien, Jules Series 40 (6)	8 - 10	10 - 12
Clark, C.S. Series 2	6 - 8	8 - 10
F.H.S. Co. Series 9 (6)	6 - 8	8 - 10
Finkenrath, Paul (P.F.B.)		
Series 6943	12 - 14	14 - 16
Series 8666	12 - 15	15 - 18
German-American Novelty Art		
Series 397 (6)	8 - 10	10 - 12
Gottschalk & Dreyfuss (German)		
Series 2114 and 2115	8 - 10	10 - 12
Mansell, A. Vivian & Co., London		
Series 1067, 2106	8 - 10	10 - 12
Misch & Stock		
Series 120 "Fairy Tales & Pantomines"	8 - 10	10 - 12
National Art Company		
Series 308 - 314 (6)	8 - 10	10 - 12
Newman, Wolsey & Co.		
Nursery Rhymes, Signed MMH	8 - 10	10 - 12
P.F.B.		
Fairy Tale Series	22 - 25	25 - 28
"Cinderella"		
"The House of Sweets"		
"Little Red Riding Hood"		
"Sleeping Beauty"		
"Snow White"		
"Tom Thumb"		
Salmon & Company		
Fairy Tale Series	10 - 12	12 - 15
Tuck, Raphael		
Series IX Glosso "Happy Childhood" (B/W)	6 - 8	8 - 10
Series 9 "Little Nursery Lovers" (12)	12 - 15	15 - 18
Series 12 "Nursery Don'ts" (12)	12 - 15	15 - 18
Series 3376 "Nursery Rhymes" (6)	10 - 12	12 - 18
Series 3328, 3379, 3488 (6)	10 - 12	12 - 18
Series 132 "Lovers in Nursery Land"	8 - 10	10 - 12
Series 5579 "Happy Childhood"	8 - 10	10 - 12
Series 5600 "Cat Studies" (6) B/W	12 - 15	15 - 18
Series 5629 "Pussy in Fairyland"	10 - 12	12 - 14
Series 6496 "Landor's Cat Studies" (B/W)	6 - 8	8 - 10
Series 8484 Oilette "Aesop's Fables" (6)	15 - 18	18 - 20
Tullar-Meredith		
"This Little Pig" (5)	8 - 10	10 - 12
Ullman Mfg. Co.		
1752-1757 "Little Red Riding Hood"	8 - 10	10 - 12
1759-1762 "Mary & Her Lamb"	8 - 10	10 - 12

E. Wessel (Bruxelles), Anonymous, No. 426

DRESSED ANIMALS, INSECTS, BIRDS

BEARS (See Teddy Bears)		
TEMPEST, MARGARET		
Medici Society Series 61	6 - 8	8 - 10
BIRDS	5 - 6	6 - 8
BUGS	10 - 12	12 - 15
CATS See Artist-Signed Cats		
COWS, BULLS, ETC.	10 - 12	12 - 15
DOGS See Artist-Signed Dogs		
P.F.B. Ser. 8168 (6)	15 - 18	18 - 22
Ullman Mfg. Co.		
"Br'er Rabbit" Series 112	8 - 10	10 - 12
"Bunny Girl" Series 84	6 - 8	8 - 10
"Jungle Sports" Series 72	8 - 10	10 - 12
"Monkey Doodle" Series 196	8 - 9	9 - 10
ELEPHANTS	15 - 20	20 - 22
FROGS	15 - 20	20 - 25

   Rotograph Company
   F.L. 379   "Officer Stout Frog"
   F.L. 380   "Dew-Drop Frog"
   F.L. 381   "Will B. Stout Frog"
   F.L. 382   "Mrs. Hoppin' Frog ..."
   F.L. 383   "Leap Frog"
   F.L. 384   "Hammersly Frog,
     the 'Village Smith' ..."
   F.L. 385   "Grandmother Bullsie"
   F.L. 386   "Lily-Pad Frog"

Unsigned C. Baumgarten, Dondorf, No. 951, "Frohliche Pfingsten"

F.L. 387 "Professor Singer Frog"
F.L. 388 "Captain Skippin' Frog, of the
    Froghurst Volunteer Hose Co."
F.L. 389 "Brassie Frog"
F.L. 390 "I. M. De Bull Frog"

GOATS	12 - 15	15 - 18
GRASSHOPPERS	10 - 12	12 - 15
HIPPOPOTAMUSES	15 - 20	20 - 25
HORSES	12 - 15	15 - 18
MAY BUGS (MAIKAFIRS)	12 - 15	15 - 22
OPOSSUMS (See Political)		
PIGS	10 - 12	12 - 18
PIG CHIMNEY SWEEPS	12 - 15	15 - 20
RABBITS	6 - 8	8 - 15
RATS/MICE	10 - 12	12 - 15

MISCELLANEOUS FANTASY

AUTOS FLYING ABOVE CITY	8 - 10	10 - 12
BUSI, ADOLFO		
Series 3059, Women/Snowmen (6)	18 - 20	20 - 25
P/Kaplan		
Series 57 Women's Heads in Clouds (12)	12 - 15	15 - 20
CORBELLA, TITO		
Uff. Rev. Stampa, Milano Series 268		
Death and Edith Cavell	15 - 20	20 - 25

    1 - "Cavell Standing over the Conquered
        Figure of Death ..."
    2 - "Death Offering Head of Cavell ..."

Big Hat Fantasy
A.R. & C.i.B. 4030

Gnome and Red-Headed
Mushroom Child, EAS 774

3 - "Death and Arrogant German Officer ..."
4 - "Cavell Standing Before Death ..."
5 - "Death Hovers as Cavell Gives Water ..."
6 - "Death Plays Piano as Cavell Lies ..."

DEATH HEADS	8 - 12	12 - 18
ELVES, GNOMES	5 - 6	6 - 10
FACES IN MOUNTAINS	10 - 12	12 - 18
FLOWER FACES	6 - 8	8 - 12
Ernest Nister, London	10 - 12	12 - 15
The Standard, London (Multi-Baby)		
Series 67	6 - 8	8 - 10
GIANT PEOPLE	5 - 6	6 - 7
GOLLIWOGS		
Humphrey Milford, London		
"Dreams & Fairies" Signed A. Govey	12 - 14	14 - 18
H.K. & Co.		
"Jack in the Box" Signed M. Stocks	12 - 14	14 - 18
Raphael Tuck Signed F.K. Upton		
Series 1793, 1794 (6)	30 - 35	35 - 40
Series 1791, 1792 (6)	30 - 35	35 - 40
Series C2006 Signed A. Richardson (6)	18 - 22	22 - 25
Raphael Tuck		
"Art" Series 1281 (6)	15 - 18	18 - 20
Rescued Series 1282 (6)	18 - 20	20 - 22

Oilette Series 1397 (6)	15 - 18	18 - 25
"Art" Series 1262 (6)	15 - 18	18 - 22
Valentine & Sons Signed Mabel L. Atwell		
Series A561 (6)	12 - 15	15 - 18
Series A579 (6)	12 - 15	15 - 20
Series 748 (6)	15 - 18	18 - 22
John Winsch		
1910 Issue	15 - 18	18 - 20
1912 Issue (Santa)	18 - 22	22 - 26
1913 Issue (Santa)	40 - 50	50 - 60
DEPICTING THE FUTURE	7 - 8	8 - 10
MAN IN THE MOON	5 - 8	8 - 10
MAPS-BODIES MAKING UP COUNTRIES	8 - 9	9 - 10
METAMORPHICS See Topicals		
MUSHROOMS, GIANT	6 - 8	8 - 12
MUSHROOM PEOPLE	8 - 10	10 - 15
NUDES/ANIMALS		
R.S.M. Series 784		
S/Zandrino (6)	15 - 18	18 - 22
SKELETONS, DEPICTING DEATH	8 - 10	10 - 12
SNOWMEN	6 - 10	10 - 20
S/A. Thiele Snowman Series 1297 (6)	15 - 18	18 - 22
SOLOMKO		
UN		
1015 "Dream of Icarius"	12 - 15	15 - 18
1019 "Blue Bird"	15 - 18	18 - 20
STICK OR WOOD PEOPLE	6 - 8	8 - 10

WAGNER OPERA FIGURES

AIGNER		
Series 259	8 - 10	10 - 12
BAUFCHILD		
"Lohengrin" (6)	8 - 10	10 - 12
BERGMULLER, C.W.	8 - 10	10 - 12
DOUBEK		
Ackerman	8 - 10	10 - 12
ERLAND, P.V.	7 - 8	8 - 9
GLOTZ, A.D.		
"Parsival" Series	10 - 12	12 - 15
Series 22	8 - 10	10 - 12
GOETZ		
M. Munk, Vienna		
Series 861		
"Die Feen"	8 - 10	10 - 12
"Die Meistersinger"	8 - 10	10 - 12
"Die Walkure"	8 - 10	10 - 12
"Gotterdammerung"	10 - 12	12 - 14
"Lohengrin"	8 - 10	10 - 12

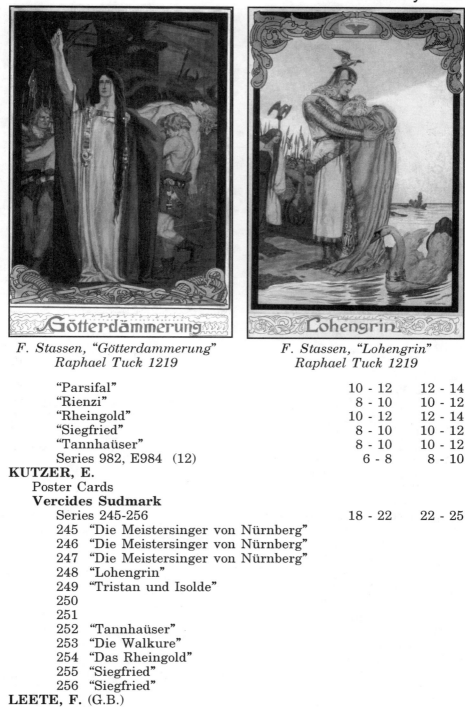

F. Stassen, "Götterdammerung"
Raphael Tuck 1219

F. Stassen, "Lohengrin"
Raphael Tuck 1219

"Parsifal"	10 - 12	12 - 14
"Rienzi"	8 - 10	10 - 12
"Rheingold"	10 - 12	12 - 14
"Siegfried"	8 - 10	10 - 12
"Tannhaüser"	8 - 10	10 - 12
Series 982, E984 (12)	6 - 8	8 - 10

KUTZER, E.
Poster Cards
Vercides Sudmark

Series 245-256	18 - 22	22 - 25

245 "Die Meistersinger von Nürnberg"
246 "Die Meistersinger von Nürnberg"
247 "Die Meistersinger von Nürnberg"
248 "Lohengrin"
249 "Tristan und Isolde"
250
251
252 "Tannhaüser"
253 "Die Walkure"
254 "Das Rheingold"
255 "Siegfried"
256 "Siegfried"

LEETE, F. (G.B.)
Poster Cards

Anonymous, E.S.D. No. 8159, "Das Rheingold"

L. Pernitzch
    "Wagner's Heldengestalten" (24)   12 - 15   15 - 18
LUDVIG
    Series 718   6 - 8   8 - 10
NOWAK, OTTO
    B.K.W.I.
        Series 1412 "Parsival"   8 - 10   10 - 12
        Series 2352   8 - 10   10 - 12
PETER, O.
    Series 399   8 - 10   10 - 12
PILGER
    "Tannhaüser" (With Music)   8 - 10   10 - 12
PINGGERA
    Poster Cards
    Deutches un Niederosterrich
        Series 242-252   15 - 18   18 - 22
        242 "Siegfried"
        248 "Herrolof"
        250 "Tannhaüser"
        750 "Gotterdammerung"
        751 "Die Walkure"
        752 "Tannhaüser"
ROWLAND
    Series 258   8 - 10   10 - 12
SCHLIMARSKI
    Series 420   8 - 10   10 - 12
SCHUTZ, E.
    B.K.W.I.
        Series 438 Posters   18 - 22   22 - 26

"Der Fiegende Hollanders"
"Tristan & Isolde"
"Rienzi"
"Lohengrin"
Others

SPIELZ, A.
Series 247

"Parsival"	10 - 12	12 - 14

STASSEN, FRANZ
Raphael Tuck

Series 1219	15 - 20	20 - 25

PUBLISHERS

B.K.W.I.

Series 438 (6)	12 - 15	15 - 18

E.S.D.
German Series

8157 "Die Walkure" (6)	10 - 12	12 - 15
8158 "Siegfried" (6)	10 - 12	12 - 15
8159 "Das Rheingold" (6)	15 - 18	18 - 22
8160 "Gotterdammerung" (6)	8 - 10	10 - 12
8161 "Die Meistersinger" (6)	8 - 10	10 - 12
8162 "Tristan und Isolde" (6)	10 - 12	12 - 15
8163 "Der Fliegende Hollander" (6)	8 - 10	10 - 12
8164 "Lohengrin" (6)	10 - 12	12 - 15

M. Munk, Vienna
Wagner's Series 28

Ladies in Wagner's Operas	10 - 12	12 - 14

T.S.N.

Series 141 "Lohengrin" (6)	8 - 10	10 - 12

Raphael Tuck
"Wagner" Series

690 "Siegfried" (6)	12 - 15	15 - 20
691 "Lohengrin" (6)	12 - 15	15 - 20
692 "Gotterdammerung" (6)	10 - 14	14 - 18
693 "Tristan and Isolde" (6)	12 - 15	15 - 20
694 "The Rheingold" (6)	15 - 20	20 - 25
695 "The Flying Dutchman" (6)	10 - 14	14 - 18
Series XX, 1219 "Modern Meister" (6)	12 - 15	15 - 18

Ottmar Zieher

Wagner's Operas (6)	25 - 28	28 - 32

DEATH FANTASY

CIEZKIEWKZ, E.

"Girl in Red"	8 - 10	10 - 15

"Lettre d'Adieu," P.F.B. 226   *Jos. Strnad, "Nymphe"*

"Woman & Skull"	8 - 10	10 - 12
CHOPIN, FR.		
Series 116 "Playing Death"	8 - 10	10 - 12
LAMM, E.		
Death in the Field	8 - 10	10 - 12
MANDLI, JOSEPH		
"The End"	8 - 10	10 - 12
PETER, O.		
400 Burning Nudes	10 - 12	12 - 14
PODKOWINSKI		
Nude on Fiery Horse	12 - 14	14 - 16
WACHSMUTIF		
PFB		
"Die Beute"	10 - 12	12 - 14
WOLFF, H.		
PFB		
4480 Death Rides a Horse	10 - 12	12 - 15
PFB Series 226	15 - 20	20 - 25

FANTASY NUDES

BENDER		
"La Femme" (Snakes)	12 - 15	15 - 18

BEROUD, L.
  Salon 1901
    Series 201-20 "Fantasie"   12 - 15   15 - 18
BOCKLIN, A.
  Bruckmann A.G.
    21   "Triton & Nereide" (Merman)   10 - 12   12 - 15
    6   "The Nereid" (Snake)   12 - 15   15 - 18
BRAUNE, E.
  Amag Kunst
    63   "Walkure" (Horse)   10 - 12   12 - 15
CABANEL, A.
  Salon J.P.P.
    2206 "Nymph & Faun" (Man-Goat)   12 - 15   15 - 18
COURSELLES-DUMONT
  Lapina
    564 "In der Arena" (Lion)   12 - 15   15 - 18
DUSSEK, E.A.
  J.K.
    69   "Froschkonigs Braut" (Frog)   15 - 18   18 - 22
FISCHER-COERLINE
  M.K.
    2475 "Salome" (Severed Head)   12 - 15   15 - 18
GEIGER, C.A.
  Marke J.S.C.
    6109 "Liebeskampf" (Man-Sea Beast)   15 - 18   18 - 22
    6112 "Salome" (Severed Head)   12 - 15   15 - 18
GIOVANNI, A.
  ARS Minima
    119 "Salome" (Severed Head)   12 - 15   15 - 18
GLOTZ, A.D.
  B.K.W.I.
    1009 "Lebensluge" (Ghost of Dead)   10 - 12   12 - 15
HIRSCH   10 - 12   12 - 14
HOESSLIN, GEORGE
  NPG
    491 "Die Schaumgebstene"
         (Nude in Oyster Shell)   10 - 12   12 - 15
KELLER, F.
  Russian Publisher
    076 "Finale" (Death Head)   12 - 15   15 - 18
KOMINEL   10 - 12   12 - 14
KORPAL   10 - 12   12 - 14
LAMM   10 - 12   12 - 14
LEETE, F. (G.B.)
  Munchener Kunst
    3113 "Nidre und Wasserman"
         (Water Creature)   10 - 12   12 - 15
    3114 "Gefangene Nymphe" (Dwarfs)   10 - 12   12 - 15
    3117 "Triton Belaufde Nereide" (Merman)   10 - 12   12 - 15

A. Piotrowski, Anonymous, 505

LENOIR, CH.
  Lapina
    5122 "Victory" (Octopus)   15 - 18   18 - 22
LEOPAROVA
  KV
    1183 "Salome" (Severed Head)   10 - 12   12 - 15
LINS, ADOLF
  EAS
    607 "Faun and Nymphe"   12 - 15   15 - 18
MANDL, J.
  Minerva
    177 "Printemps" (Wings)   10 - 12   12 - 15
MASTAGLIO
  Galerie Munchener Meister
    380 "Duell" (Nudes Fencing)   10 - 12   12 - 15
MASTROIANNI, C.
    198 "Fievre d'Amore" (Waterfall)   10 - 12   12 - 15
MEUNIER, SUZANNE (France)
  MARQUE L.E.
    Series 64 (6)   28 - 32   32 - 40
MUHLBERG, GEORG (Germany)
    Nude Riding a Seahorse.   12 - 15   15 - 18
MULLER-BAUMGARTEN
  FEM
    161 "Faun & Nymphe" (Man-Goat)   8 - 10   10 - 12
MUTTICH, C.V. (Czech)
  V.K.K.V.
    2077 "Sulejka" (Peacock)   10 - 12   12 - 15

PENOT, A.
  Lapina
    1340 "Red Butterfly" (Red-Winged Nude)   12 - 15   15 - 18
PIOTROWSKI, A.
  Minerva
    505 Woman/Children/Serpent   10 - 12   12 - 15
    1028 "Salome" (Severed Head)   10 - 12   12 - 15
  Manke JSC
    6082 "Charmeuse de Serpents" (Snake)   15 - 18   18 - 22
REINACKER, G.
  PFB
    6032 "Schlangen-Bandigerin" (Snake)   12 - 15   15 - 18
ROTHAUG
  LP
    2815 "Pan and Psyche" (Man-Beast)   15 - 18   18 - 22
  W.R.B. & Company
    No. 4 "Nymphe"   12 - 15   15 - 18
ROWLAND, FR. (G.B.)
  SVD
    379 "Sirenen" (Snakes)   12 - 15   15 - 18
ROYER, L.
  Salon de Paris
    374 "La Sirene" (Death Head)   12 - 15   15 - 18
RÜDISÜHLI, EDUARD
  K.E.B.
    "The Demon of Love"   12 - 15   15 - 18
SAMSON, E.
  A.N., Paris
    243 "Diane" (Wolf Dogs)   10 - 12   12 - 15
SCALBERT, J.
  S.P.A.
    48 "Leda & the Swan"   10 - 12   12 - 15
SCHIFF, R.
  W.R.B. & Co.
    22-74 "Leda & the Swan"   15 - 18   18 - 22
    22-74 "Head in Clouds"   12 - 15   15 - 18
SCHIVERT, V.
  Arthur Rehn & Co.
    "Die Hexe"   15 - 18   18 - 22
SCHMUTZLER
  Russian Publisher, Richard
    245 "Salome" (Severed Head)   12 - 15   15 - 18
SCHUTZ, E.
  Poster Cards
  B.K.W.I.
    41 "The Frog King" (Big Frog)   15 - 18   18 - 22
    885 Goethe's "Der Fischer" (Mermaid)   30 - 35   35 - 38
    885 "God & the Baiadere"   18 - 20   20 - 25
    979 "Die Forelle" (Mermaid)   30 - 35   35 - 38

205 Wagner's "Parsival"	15 - 18	18 - 22
557 "Lotusblume" (Nude in flower)	18 - 20	20 - 25
Series 165 (6) (Nudes on Giant Flowers)	22 - 25	25 - 30

SOLOMKO, S.
   TSN

Nude in Peacock Feathers	18 - 20	20 - 22

STELLA, EDUARD
   BRW

354 "Diane" (Dogs)	18 - 20	20 - 22

STRNAD, JOS.

Anonymous 255 "Nymphe"	12 - 15	15 - 18
STUCK	10 - 12	12 - 14

STYKA, JAN
   Lapina

810 "Good Friends" (Horse)	10 - 12	12 - 15

SZYNDIER, P.
   Mal. Polske

22 "Eve" (Snakes)	20 - 22	22 - 25

VEITH, E.
   B.K.W.I.

1101 "Teasing" (Man-Goat)	10 - 12	12 - 15
WACHSMUTH, M.	10 - 12	12 - 14

WARZENIECKI, M.

WILSA

90 "Une Nouvelle Esclave" (Death)	10 - 12	12 - 15

WOLLNER, H.
   B.K.W.I.

1101 "Sadismus" (Death Head)	10 - 12	12 - 15

ZANDER
   S.S.W.B.

4790 "Sieg der Schonheit" (Tiger)	10 - 12	12 - 15

ZATZKA, H. (The Netherlands)
   Panphot, Vienne

1284 "La Lerle" (Nude in Large Oyster Shell)	12 - 15	15 - 18

MERMAIDS

ATWELL, MABEL LUCIE
   Valentine & Sons

951 (With Black Doll)	12 - 15	15 - 18

BENEZUR

"Der Kampf"	16 - 18	18 - 22

BOCKLIN, A.
   F. Bruckmann AG

"Play of Naiads"	12 - 15	15 - 18
"Im Spiel der Wellen"	12 - 15	15 - 18

CARTER, REG.
   Max Ettinger & Co.

Copyright 1910, M.N.
Anonymous Publisher

Series 649, "Wassernixen"
Chromo-Lithograph

Walt (Walt Munson)
Tichnor Bros. Linen, No. NH15

Series 4453 (Diver Series) (6)	15 - 20	20 - 25
CHIOSTRI, S.		
Ballerini & Fratini		
Series 238 (6) Deco	40 - 50	50 - 60
Series 317 (6) Deco	40 - 50	50 - 60
GILLAUME		
Art Moderne		
Series 764 "Seetrift"	18 - 20	20 - 25
GOHLER, H.		
Richard-Rischar		
"Du Nixlein Wunderhold ..."	15 - 18	18 - 22
KASPARIDES		
"Bath of Water Fairy"	15 - 18	18 - 22
LEETE, F. (G.B.)		
Munchener Kunst		
3116 "De Taufe des Fawn"	14 - 16	16 - 18
LIEBENWEIN, M.		
B.K.W.I.		
1028 "Der Verrufene Weiher"	15 - 18	18 - 22
OUTHWAITE, IDA (Australia)		
A & C Black, London		
Series 73 "Playing with Bubbles"	22 - 26	26 - 30
SAGER, XAVIER		
Big Letter Card		

Kirsten Wiwel
Mermaid in Silhouette

Chiostri
Ballerini & Fratini, 317

"Un Baiser D'Ostende"	22 - 25	25 - 30
SCHMUTZLER, L.		
Hanfstaengl Co.	12 - 15	15 - 18
SCHUTZ, E.		
B.K.W.I.		
Poster Cards		
203 "Flame of Love"	20 - 25	25 - 28
391-3 Heine - "Der Mond ist ..."	20 - 22	22 - 25
434-4 Andersen's Marchen	25 - 28	28 - 30
766-2 Schubert - "Das Wasser ..."	25 - 28	28 - 32
885-5 Goethe - "Der Fischer"	30 - 35	35 - 38
979-5 Schubert - "Die Forelle"	30 - 35	35 - 38
SOLOMKO, SERGE (Russia)		
T.S.N.		
93 "The Tale"	15 - 18	18 - 25
WHITE, FLORA (G.B.)		
W. E. Mack, Hampstead		
Poster - "The Little Mermaid"	18 - 20	20 - 25
WIWEL, KIRSTEN	12 - 15	15 - 18

PUBLISHERS

S. Hildeshimer & Co.		
Andersen's "The Little Mermaid"	20 - 25	25 - 30

MN Co., 1910
Unsigned and Unnumbered (10)   20 - 22   20 - 25
M.&L.G.
National Series, Untitled
Art Nouveau -- With Seashell   25 - 30   30 - 35
Raphael Tuck
Series 6822, Mermaid Series (6)   25 - 30   30 - 35
Series 694, Wagner Series (6)
"The Rheingold"   20 - 25   25 - 30
Anonymous
Art Nouveau Series 643 (6)   50 - 55   55 - 65

SUPERIOR WOMEN/LITTLE MEN FANTASY

COLLINS
"Little Men" Series   10 - 12   12 - 15
FASCHE
M. Munk, Vienna
"Diabolo" (6)   15 - 18   18 - 22
KYOPINSKI
Little Men (6)   12 - 15   15 - 18
KURDNEY
M. Munk, Vienna
Series 606 (6)   12 - 15   15 - 18
Series 699 (6)   12 - 15   15 - 18
N.F.
Series 160-165 (6)   8 - 10   10 - 12
MAUZAN
Series 83, Little Men (6)   12 - 15   15 - 18
PENOT, A.
Lapina
Little Men Series (6)   15 - 18   18 - 22
SAGER, XAVIER
Series 43, Soldiers/Little Women (6)   18 - 20   20 - 25
SCHONPFLUG
B.K.W.I.
Series 4132 (6)   10 - 12   12 - 15

PUBLISHERS

B.G.W.
Series 123/1233 (6)   8 - 10   10 - 12
Marks, J.
Series 155 "Summer Girl" (8)   8 - 10   10 - 12
B.K.W.I.
Series 136 (6)   8 - 10   10 - 12
WBG
Series 123 (6)   7 - 8   8 - 10

TEDDY BEARS

Teddy Bears are very much in demand by collectors, both artist-signed, unsigned and real-photo types. Many great sets and series were published and are extremely popular. Many were unsigned and, because of inadequate records, the artists have not been identified.

BUSY BEARS (12)
    J.I. Austen Co.   10 - 12   12 - 15
        427 Monday, Hanging the Wash
        428 Tuesday, Ironing Clothes
        429 Wednesday, Sweeping
        430 Thursday, Mopping the Floor
        431 Friday, Baking Bread
        432 Saturday, Darning
        433 "Learning to Spell"
        434 "Playing Leap Frog"
        435 "Off to School"
        436 "Getting it in the Usual Place"
        437 "Something Doing"
        438 "Vacation"
WALL, BERNARDT
    Ullman Series 79   8 - 10   10 - 12
        1905 Sunday
        1906 Monday
        1907 Tuesday
        1908 Wednesday
        1909 Thursday
        1910 Friday
        1911 Saturday
CAVALLY BEARS (Nursery Rhymes)
    Thayer Publishing Co., Denver   15 - 17   17 - 20
        "See-saw, Margery Daw"
        "Rain, rain, go away"
        "To make your candles last for aye"
        "Cock crows in the morn"
        "Little Red Snooks was fond ..."
        "What are little Ted Boys made of?"
        "As I went to Bonner"
        "Nose, nose, jolly red nose"
        "Dame Bear made a curtsy"
        "Wash me, and comb me"
        "Ding dong bell"
        "Little Ted Grundy"
        "Teddy be nimble"
        "Multiplication is vexation"
        "Tell Tale Tit!"

"Little Ted Horner"
CRACKER JACK BEARS (16)
Rueckheim & Eckstein

1	At the Lincoln Zoo	30 - 35	35 - 40
2	In Balloon		
3	Over Niagara Falls		
4	At Statue of Liberty		
5	At Coney Island		
6	In New York		
7	Shaking Teddy's Hand (Roosevelt)		
8	At Jamestown Fair		
9	To the South		
10	At Husking Bee		
11	At the Circus		
12	Playing Baseball	40 - 45	45 - 50
13	Cracker Jack Time	30 - 35	35 - 40
14	Making Cracker Jacks		
15	At Yellowstone		
16	Away to Mars		

ROSE CLARK BEARS (12)
CLARK, ROSE

Rotograph Co., N.Y.		12 - 15	15 - 18
307	"Bear Town Cadet"		
308	"Is That You Henry?"		
309	"Henry"		
310	"The Bride"		
311	"The Groom"		

Ellam, "At the Seaside," Tuck 9793

312 "A Bear Town Sport"
313 "A Bear Town Dude"
314 "I'm Going a Milking"
315 "I Won't be Home ..."
316 "C-c-come on in"
317 "Fifth Avenue"
318 "Hymn No. 23"

DOGGEREL DODGER BEARS
WHEELAN, A.
    Paul Elder Co.   6 - 8   8 - 10
CRANE BEARS
CRANE, D.P.
    H.G.Z. Co.
      "Days of the Week"   12 - 15   15 - 18
      "Months of the Year"   10 - 12   12 - 15
ELLAM BEARS
    Raphael Tuck
      Series 9793 (6)   12 - 15   15 - 18
      Series 9794 (6)   12 - 15   15 - 18
HEAL DAYS OF THE WEEK
HEAL, WILLIAM S.   6 - 8   8 - 10
    "Sunday" Going to Church
    "Monday" Washing Clothes
    "Tuesday" Ironing
    "Wednesday" Mending
    "Thursday" Baking
    "Friday" House Cleaning
    "Saturday" Shopping
    Same Series in Leather   8 - 10   10 - 12
HILLSON DAYS OF THE WEEK
HILLSON, D .   6 - 8   8 - 10
    Leather   10 - 12   12 - 15
KENNEDY, A.E.   12 - 15   15 - 18
LITTLE BEARS
    Raphael Tuck
      Series 118 (12)   12 - 15   15 - 18
      "A Morning Dip"
      "A Very Funny Song"
      "Breaking the Record"
      "Kept in at School"
      "Missed Again"
      "Oh! What a Shock"
      "Once in the Eye"
      "The Cake Walk"
      "The Ice Bears Beautifully"
      "The Jolly Anglers"
      "Tobogganing in the Snow"
      "Your Good Health"

McLAUGHLIN BROS. BEARS
   McLaughlin Bros.   8 - 10   10 - 12
MOLLY & TEDDY BEARS (6)
GREINER, M.
   International Art Co.
     Series 791 (6)   8 - 10   10 - 12
OTTOMAN LITHOGRAPHING BEARS
   Ottoman Lithographing Co., N.Y.   8 - 10   10 - 12
     "Come Birdie Come"
     "Good Old Summertime"
     "Is Marriage a Failure?"
     "Many Happy Returns"
     "Never Touched Me"
     "Please Ask Pa"
     "Right Up-To-Date"
     "Well, Well, You never can Tell"
     "Where am I at?"
     "Will She Get the Lobster"
ROMANTIC BEARS
   M.D.S.
   Ullman
     Series 88 (4)   6 - 8   8 - 10
     1950 "Too Late"

Ottoman Lithograph
"Is marriage a failure?"

Ottoman Lithograph
"Many happy returns"

Ottoman Lithograph
"Come, birdie come"

Ottoman Lithograph
"Good old summer time"

Russian Richard, No. 913
"Nobody Loves Me"

D.P. Crane, H.G.Z. & Co.
"Saturday"

1951	"Who Cares?"		
1952	"The Lullaby"		
1953	"A Letter to My Love"		

ROOSEVELT BEARS
   Stern

1	"At Home"	20 - 25	25 - 30
2	"Go Aboard the Train"		
3	"In Sleeping Car"		
4	"On A Farm"		
5	"At a Country School"		
6	"At the County Fair"		
7	"Leaving the Ballroom"		
8	"At the Tailors"		
9	"In the Department Store"		
10	"At Niagara Falls"		
11	"At Boston Public Library"		
12	"Take an Auto Ride"		
13	"At Harvard"		
14	"On Iceberg"		
15	"In New York City"		
16	"At the Circus"		
17	"Shooting Firecrackers" (2 versions)	30 - 35	35 - 40
20	"Dancing"		
22	"In New York"		

25 "Swimming"		
29 "Go Fishing"		
30 "Bears on a Pullman"		
31 "Hunters"		
32 "At Washington"		
No Numbers	80 - 90	90 - 100
ROUNDTREE, HARRY		
Williston Press	15 - 18	18 - 22
SPORTY BEARS		
M.D.S.		
Ullman		
Series 83 (7)		
1923 "Love All"	10 - 12	12 - 14
1924 "Here's for a Home Run"	12 - 14	14 - 16
1925 "Out for a Big Game"	10 - 12	12 - 15
1926 "King of the Alley"	8 - 10	10 - 12
1927 "A Dip in the Surf"	8 - 10	10 - 12
1928 "An Unexpected Bite"	8 - 10	10 - 12
ST. JOHN BEARS		
ST. JOHN		
Western News Co.	8 - 10	10 - 12
161 "Spring"		
162 "Summer"		
163 "Autumn"		
164 "Winter"		
TOWER TEDDY BEARS		
Tower M. & N. Co. (30)	8 - 10	10 - 12
"Beary Well, Thank You"		
"But We Are Civilized"		
"Did You Ever Wear..."		
"Don't Say a Word"		
"Hurrah for - Eagle"		
"Hurrah for the..."		
"I'm Waiting For You"		
"Our Birth, You Know"		
"We Wear Pajamas"		
"You Don't Say"		
Others		
T.P. & CO. TEDDY BEARS		
T. P. & Co.	8 - 10	10 - 12
"Out for Airing"		
"I Wonder if He Saw Me?"		
"Isn't He a Darling"		
"How Strong He Is"		
"Oh! My! - He's Coming!"		
"Off for the Honeymoon"		
"Little Girl w/Teddy"		
"Dolly Gets an Inspiration"		
"Lost, Strayed, or Stolen"		

TWELVETREES BEARS
TWELVETREES, CHARLES
    National Art Co. (6)   8 - 10   10 - 12
        206 "Little Bear Behind"
        207 "Stung"
        208 "The Bear on Dark Stairway"
        209 "How can you Bear this Weather?"
        210 "A Bear Impression"
        211 "The Seashore Bear"
    National Art Co.
        271 "It's Up to You"   10 - 12   12 - 15
WALL, BERNHARDT
DAYS OF THE WEEK
    Ullman Mfg. Co., Series 79
        "Busy Bears" Series   10 - 12   12 - 15
        "Little Bears" Series   10 - 12   12 - 15
WELLS BEARS (7)   8 - 10   10 - 12
REAL PHOTO TEDDY BEARS
        With Children (Large Bears)   25 - 35   35 - 45
        With Children (Small Bears)   20 - 25   25 - 30
        With Ladies (Large Bears)   18 - 22   22 - 28
        With Ladies (Small Bears   12 - 15   15 - 20
        Bears Alone (Large)   15 - 20   20 - 25
        Bears Alone (Small)   12 - 14   14 - 16
        Bears and Movie Stars   10 - 12   12 - 15
OTHER ARTIST-SIGNED TEDDY BEARS
        With Children (Large Bears)   10 - 15   15 - 20
        With Children (Small Bears)   8 - 12   12 - 15
        With Ladies (Large Bears)   10 - 12   12 - 18
        With Ladies (Small Bears)   8 - 12   12 - 15

Meissner & Buch, "Eine Erfrifchung"

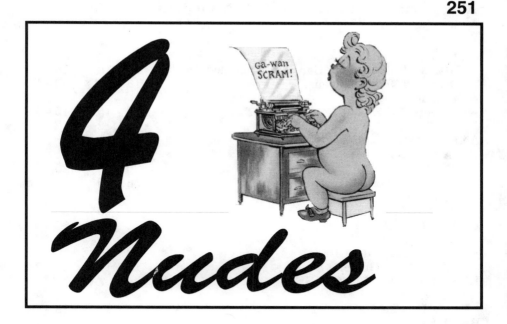

COLOR NUDES

Color nudes have now been discovered. For many years color nudes were completely neglected by the American postcard collector. Until recently, the only issues available were those of the Great Masters' reproductions of paintings from big museums and art galleries throughout the world. Stengel Art Co. of Dresden, Germany was the major publisher.

This gave color nudes a poor impression and repressed their growth until it was finally realized that there were hundreds of beautiful nudes and semi-nudes that were not museum reproductions. During postcards' Golden Years, European artists—especially the French and Germans—painted beautiful nudes relating to mythical, historical, Biblical, fairy tales, and fantasy motifs that were adapted to postcards. These cards have become highly collectible and are pursued by many American deltiologists.

Since there was no demand in the United States from 1900 to 1920, color nudes by American artists are very rare. Therefore, most all of the nudes listed here are from Europe. Many artists painted only single entities; therefore, very few sets or series are available.

ALLEAUME, L.	VG	EX
Lapina		
59 "In the Rose"	$12 - 15	$15 - 18
201 "Offering"	10 - 12	15 - 18

ASTI, A.
    JL & W 36/25, No Caption, Unsigned   15 - 18   18 - 22
    Salon 1897, "Songeuse"   18 - 22   22 - 25
AUER, R.
    Salon J.C.Z. 4 "Tender Flower"   12 - 15   15 - 18
    1 "Delight"   10 - 12   12 - 15
AXENTOWICZ, T.
    ANCZYC
        10 "Noc"   20 - 25   25 - 30
        110 "Noc"   18 - 20   20 - 25
    D.N.
        29 "Studjum"   18 - 20   20 - 25
BARBER, COURT
    S.& G.S.i.B
    1283 "Nach dem Bade"   12 - 15   15 - 18
    1284 "Der Goldene Schal"   12 - 15   15 - 18
BEAUFEREY, M. LOUISE
    H.M.
        "La Femme" Series   15 - 18   18 - 22
BENDER, S.
    H.M., "La Femme" Series (12)   15 - 18   18 - 25

Jean Gabriel Domergue
A. N., Paris, 6528, "Antonia"

Jean Gabriel Domergue
A.N., Paris, 6466, "The Parasol"

BECAGLI, P.		
Salon de Paris "Paressguse"	12 - 15	15 - 18
BERNHARD, LEO		
"Bachante"	10 - 12	12 - 15
BIESSY, GABRIEL		
Salon de Paris		
"The Model"	10 - 12	12 - 15
BORRMEISTER, R.		
Herman Wolff		
1128 "Morgengruss"	10 - 12	12 - 15
1093 "Wald Marchen"	10 - 12	12 - 15
BOTTINGER, H.		
J.P.P. 1074 "Marchen"	12 - 15	15 - 18
BOULAND, M.		
A.N., Paris 446 "Femme a l'echape"	12 - 15	15 - 18
BRICHARD, X.		
A.N., Paris 404 "After the Bath"	12 - 15	15 - 18
BUBNA, G.		
Hermann Wolff 1135 "Ein Neugierger"	10 - 12	12 - 15
BUKOVAC, V.		
Minerva		
21 No Caption	10 - 12	12 - 15
28 "Koketa"	10 - 12	12 - 15
BUSMEY, S.		
Lapina 825 "The Dream of Love"	10 - 12	12 - 15
BUSSIÈRE, GASTON (France)		
Salon de Paris 744 "Salome"	10 - 12	12 - 15
CAYRON, J.		
Lapina 5433 "Repose"	12 - 15	15 - 18
CHANTRON, A.J.		
Salon de Paris 993 "The Bind Weed"	12 - 15	15 - 18
A.N., Paris 38 "Spring"	12 - 15	15 - 18
CHAPIN		
Stengel 29920 "Souvenirs"	8 - 10	10 - 12
CHERY		
"The Source"	10 - 12	12 - 15
COLLIN, R.		
Lapina 408 "Floreal"	8 - 10	10 - 12
COMERRE, LEON		
Palais des Beaux Arts "The Golden Rain"	10 - 12	12 - 15
A.N., Paris 164 "While the Artist ..."	8 - 10	10 - 12
Musee de Luxembourg		
411 "The Spider"	8 - 10	10 - 12
COURTOIS, G.		
Lapina 526 "La Lecture"	8 - 10	10 - 12
CROZAT		
Galerie d'Art 117 "Apres le bal"	12 - 15	15 - 18
CUNICEL, EDW.		
O.F.Z.-L "Coquetry"	8 - 10	10 - 12

CZECH, E.
   "Apollon Sophia" 70 "Temptation"   8 - 10   10 - 12
DE BOUCHE
   E.K.N. 1050 "The New Ornament"   8 - 10   10 - 12
DERVAUX, G.
   Lapina 5412 "Naughty"   10 - 12   12 - 15
DEWALD, A.
   Emgre-Sabn 229 "Eve"   10 - 12   12 - 15
DOLEZEL-EZEL, P.
   F.H. & S. 5221 No Caption   10 - 12   12 - 15
DOMERGUE, JEAN GABRIEL
   A. N. Paris
      Art Deco Nudes   30 - 35   35 - 40
DUPUIS, P.
   Hanfstaengel 199 "The Wave"   12 - 15   15 - 18
DUSSEK, ED. ADRIAN
   KPHOT Co.
      JK18 "Das Neue Modell"
      JK25 "Modelpause"   12 - 15   15 - 18
      JK51 "In Gedanken"   15 - 18   18 - 22
      JK52 "Im Atelier"   20 - 22   22 - 25
      JK53 "Studie"   20 - 22   22 - 25
      JK54 "Das Model"   12 - 15   15 - 18
      JK55 "The Hat"   15 - 18   18 - 22
      JK56 "Studie"   18 - 20   20 - 25
      JK57 "The Model"   12 - 15   15 - 18
      JK58 "The Hat"   15 - 18   18 - 22
      JK59 "In Gedanken"   15 - 18   18 - 22
      JK60 "Schwuller Tag"   12 - 15   15 - 18
      JK61 "Koketterie"   15 - 18   18 - 22
      JK62 "Die Gold Gube"   15 - 18   18 - 22
      JK63 "Vertraumt"   15 - 18   18 - 22
      JK64 "Jugendstil Akstudie"   18 - 20   20 - 22
      JK65 "Im Abendlicht"   15 - 18   18 - 22
      JK66 "Halbakt"   25 - 28   28 - 32
      JK67 "Erwachen"   18 - 22   22 - 25
      JK68 "Blonder Akt"   20 - 22   22 - 25
      JK69 "Frosch Koenigs Bride"   22 - 25   25 - 28
      JK70 "Gross Toilette am Land"   12 - 15   15 - 18
EICHLER, MAX
   O.G.Z-L 291 "Nach Dem Bade"   10 - 12   12 - 15
EINBECK "Nana"   10 - 12   12 - 15
ENJOLRAS, E.
   Lapina
      718 "Repose"   12 - 15   15 - 18
      "Ruth"   10 - 12   12 - 15
      "Rest"   8 - 10   10 - 12
EVERART, M.
   A.N., Paris 7 "The Woman With Ribbons"   10 - 12   12 - 15

A. Faugeron
Lapina, 5913, "Nayade"

Gabriel Hervé
Lapina, 5039, "Nudity"

SPA
Paris 4059 "The Woman With Lamp"   10 - 12   12 - 15
Paris 76 "Young Woman at Mirror"   12 - 15   15 - 18
FAR-SI
A.N., Paris "Oriental Perfume"   12 - 15   15 - 18
FAUGERON, A.
Lapina, Paris
5913 "Nayade"   12 - 15   15 - 18
FEIKL, S.
J.K.P. 236 "Akt"   10 - 12   12 - 15
FENNER-BEHMEL, H.
Hanfstaengel's 194 "Ysabel"   15 - 18   18 - 22
FERRARIS, A.
B.K.W.I. "Leda"   12 - 15   15 - 18
FOURNIER
"Woman Bathing"   10 - 12   12 - 15
FREAND, E.
Lapina 5415 "Familiar Birds"   8 - 10   10 - 12
FRIEDRICH, OTTO
B.K.W.I. 1541 "Eitelkeit"   10 - 12   12 - 15
FRONTE, M.
Lapina
"Woman Lying Down"   12 - 15   15 - 18

Max Eichler
O.G.Z.-L, 291, "Nach dem Bade"

A. Penot
Lapina, 1225, "Repose"

Knoefel
Novitas, 886-4

Knoefel
Novitas, 668-1

FUCHS, RUDOLPH		
W.R.B. & Co.		
738 "Blaue Augen"	10 - 12	12 - 15
GALAND, LEON		
Salon de Paris "A Sleeping Woman"	12 - 15	15 - 18
GALLELLI, M.		
P. Heckscher		
143 "The First Pose"	10 - 12	12 - 15
GEIGER, C. AUG.		
NPG 453 "Eva"	10 - 12	12 - 15
GERMAIN		
"First Session"	12 - 15	15 - 18
GERVEX, HENRI (France)		
Palais des Beaux-Arts		
261 "Birth of Venus"	10 - 12	12 - 15
GITTER, H.		
Galerie Munchen Meister		
"Morgen"	8 - 10	10 - 12
"Tag"	6 - 8	8 - 10
GLUCKLEIN, S.		
Hanfstaengel's 202 "Reposing"	10 - 12	12 - 15
GODWARD, J.W.		
Russia Richard		
295 "A Fair Reflection"	10 - 12	12 - 15
GOEPFART, FRANZ		
301 "Ruhender Akt"	10 - 12	12 - 15
GOROKHOV		
N.P.G., Berlin "Wassernixe"	12 - 15	15 - 18
GRENOUILLOUX, J.		
Lapina		
"The Fair Summer Days"	12 - 15	15 - 18
"The Nymph with Flags"	12 - 15	15 - 18
Apollon		
78 "Speil der Wellen"	8 - 10	10 - 12
Salon de Paris		
"The Nymph with Flags"	12 - 15	15 - 18
GUETIN, V.		
Lapina 799 "Das Bad"	8 - 10	10 - 12
GUILLAUME, R.M.		
Lapina		
1400 "The Repose of the Model"	8 - 10	10 - 12
1083 "Rapid Change"	10 - 12	12 - 15
Soc. des Artistes 58 "The Fly"	8 - 10	10 - 12
A.H.		
K.th W.II 636 "Lybelle"	10 - 12	12 - 15
HERVÉ, GABRIEL		
Lapina		
44 "Resting"	12 - 15	15 - 18
813 "Farniente"	12 - 15	15 - 18

"My Model and My Dog"	8 - 10	10 - 12
HEYMAN, RICHARD		
Heinrich Hoffman "Psyche"	10 - 12	12 - 15
HILSER		
Minerva		
83 No Caption	10 - 12	12 - 15
1130 "Siesta"	10 - 12	12 - 15
JANUSZEWSKI, J.		
ANCZYC		
185 "Akt"	8 - 10	10 - 12
455 No Caption	8 - 10	10 - 12
KASPARIDES, E.		
B.K.W.I.		
161-4 "A Warm Summer Morning"	8 - 10	10 - 12
164-3 "The Airbath"	10 - 12	12 - 15
164-10 "Forest Silence"	8 - 10	10 - 12
Others	8 - 10	10 - 12
KIESEL, C.		
A.R. & C.i.B 463 "Salome"	8 - 10	10 - 12
KLIMES		
Minerva 1227 "Nymphe"	10 - 12	12 - 15
KNOBLOCH, J.R.		
O.G.Z.-l 1700 "Tired"	10 - 12	12 - 15
KNOEFEL		
Novitas		
668 (4) Illuminated Nudes	15 - 18	18 - 22
866 (4) Illuminated Nudes	15 - 18	18 - 22
KORPAL, T.		
ANCYZ 16 Bather "Au Ete"	10 - 12	12 - 15
KOSEL, H.C.		
B.K.W.I.		
181-3 "Kungstgeschlchte"	8 - 10	10 - 12
181-8 "Nach im Bade"	8 - 10	10 - 12
181-9 "Lekture"	8 - 10	10 - 12
181-10 "Skaoin"	10 - 12	12 - 15
KRENES, H.		
C1-12 "Danse"	8 - 10	10 - 12
KRIER, E.A.		
Salon de Paris		
5379 "Folly at Home"	8 - 10	10 - 12
KUTEW, CH.		
Frist		
Series 90, 8 No Caption	8 - 10	10 - 12
Series 90, 10 No Caption	12 - 15	15 - 18
A.F.W.		
111-2 "Ondine"	10 - 12	12 - 15
"Nymph"	12 - 15	15 - 18
LANZDORF, R.		
R. & J.D. 501 "Young Bedouin Girl"	8 - 10	10 - 12

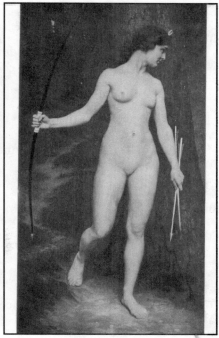

J. Scalbert
Lapina, 795, "The Toilet"

P. Seiffert
Salon de Paris, 746, "Diana"

LAUREN, P.A.
    Lapina 2032 "Didon" 8 - 10 10 - 12
LEETE, F.
    Munchener Kunst
        3114 "Bad de Bestalin" 12 - 15 15 - 18
    Hans Koehler & Co.
        76 "Bacchantalin" 12 - 15 15 - 18
LENDIR
    P. Heckscher 366 "Die Zofe" 7 - 8 8 - 10
LEFFEBURE, J.
    Musee de Luxembourg
        500 "Woman Warming Herself" 6 - 8 8 - 10
LENOIR, CH.
    Lapina 853 "Stream Song" 12 - 15 15 - 18
    A.N., Paris 19 "Tanzerin" 8 - 10 10 - 12
L'EVEIL
    Salon 1914 304 "The Awakening" 12 - 15 15 - 18
LIEBERMAN, E.
    Emil Kohn 890 "At the Window" 8 - 10 10 - 12
LINGER, O.
    G. Liersch & Co.
        537 "Susses Nichtshen" 10 - 12 12 - 15
LUCAS, H.
    Lapina 890 "Happy Night" 10 - 12 12 - 15

MAKOVSKY, C.
  Russia 539 "Dans ie Boudoir"   10 - 12   12 - 15
MALIQUET, C.
  Lapina
    "Voluptuousness"   10 - 12   12 - 15
  Salon de Paris
    56 "At the Hairdresser"   10 - 12   12 - 15
MANDL, JOS.
  Salon J.P.P. 2056 "L'Innocence"   8 - 10   10 - 12
MARECEK
  KV 1335 "Nach dem Bade"   8 - 10   10 - 12
  VKKA 1201 "Toileta"   6 - 8   8 - 10
MARTIN, F.
  AR & CiB 395 "Vom dem Spiegel"   8 - 10   10 - 12
MARTIN-KAVEL
  Lapina
    "Nude on Tiger Rug"   8 - 10   10 - 12
    934 "Surprised"   8 - 10   10 - 12
MAX, G.
  Apollon Sophia 68 "Bacchante"   10 - 12   12 - 15
MENZLER, W.
  NPG   512 "Akt"   8 - 10   10 - 12
MERCIER
  Art Moderne
    748 "Nymphe Endormie"   10 - 12   12 - 15
    "Nymph Reclining"   10 - 12   12 - 15
MERLE, K.
  Moderner Kunst 2355 "After the Bath" 8 - 10 10 - 12
MIASSOJEDOW, J.
    224 Russian "Arabian Tanzerin"   12 - 15   15 - 18
MOHN, ROTER
  Moderner Kunst
    245 "Feuerlilien"   8 - 10   10 - 12
    246 No Caption   8 - 10   10 - 12
MORIN
  Salon J.P.P. 1124 "Feu Follet"   8 - 10   10 - 12
MULLER, RICH.
  Malke & Co.
    25 "My Models"   18 - 22   22 - 25
  SPGA
    251 "Gold Fish"   18 - 22   22 - 25
    252 "Der Rote Ibis"   18 - 22   22 - 25
  Others   18 - 22   22 - 25
NAKLADATEL, J.
  J.P.P.
    440-445 (6) Semi-Nudes   15 - 18   18 - 22
NEJEDLY
  Salon J.P.P. "Erwachen"   10 - 12   12 - 15

NEMEJC, AUG.
  Polish "Tragedie"   8 - 10   10 - 12
NISSL, RUDOLF
  Novitas 388 "Akt im Mantel"   10 - 12   12 - 15
NONNENBRUCH, M.
  Salon J.P.P. 2187 "La Sculpture"   10 - 12   12 - 15
  O.G.Z.-L. 1174 "After Dancing"   10 - 12   12.- 15
  Hanfstaengel's 49 "Flora"   10 - 12   12 - 15
OSTROWSKI, A.J.
  Russian, **Rischar** 2172 "The Model" 12 - 15   15 - 18
OTTOMAN
  Lapina "The Sleeping Courtesan"   8 - 10   10 - 12
PAPPERITZ, G.
  Apollon
    84 "Boa Neuf"   12 - 15   15 - 18
    237 "Bayadere"   12 - 15   15 - 18
  Hanfstaengel's 197 "Chrysanthemums" 12 - 15   15 - 18
PAUSINGER
  Russian 063 "Salome"   15 - 18   18 - 22
PENOT, A.
  Lapina
    "Water Flower"   12 - 15   15 - 18
    "Bayadera"   12 - 15   15 - 18
    "A Young Girl"   10 - 12   12 - 15
    "The Charm of Spring"   12 - 15   15 - 18
    "Libelle"   10 - 12   12 - 15
    1225 "Repose"   10 - 12   12 - 15
    1340 "Red Butterfly"   12 - 15   15 - 18
  Salon de Paris
    229 "Repose"   10 - 12   12 - 15
PERRAULT
  Salon de Paris
    727 "Der Erste Mai"   10 - 12   12 - 15
PETER, O.
  S.V.D.
    292 "Das Kunstler Modell" 12 - 15   15 - 18
PRICE, J.M.
  Hanfstaengel's
    117 "Odaliske"   12 - 15   15 - 18
R.R.
  M. Munk
    Series 684 (6)   18 - 22   22 - 25
    Series 873 (6)   18 - 22   22 - 25
REINACKER, G.
  Marke JSC
    6054 "Am Morgen"   10 - 12   12 - 15
    6055 "Verkauft"   12 - 15   15 - 18
    6083 "Der Neue Schmuck" 12 - 15   15 - 18
  PFB 6034 "Die Favoritin"   10 - 12   12 - 15

REIFENSTEIN, LEO
    Galzburger Kunst 45 "Schönhut"   10 - 12   12 - 15

RETTIG, H.
    Munchener Meister 568 "Im Spiegel"   10 - 12   12 - 15

RIESEN, O.
    A. Sch. & Co. 7152 "Unschuld"   10 - 12   12 - 15
    S. & G. S.i.B. 1471 "Am Morgen"   12 - 15   15 - 18

RITTER, C.
    Novitas 397 "Im Gotteskleid"   10 - 12   12 - 15

ROUSSELET, E.
    Lapina
        1129 "Bathing"   12 - 15   15 - 18
        "The Dream"   8 - 10   10 - 12

ROUSTEAUX-DARBOURD
    Salon 1912 571 "Am Feuer"   10 - 12   12 - 15

SAIZEDE
    Lapina "A Woman & Statuette"   8 - 10   10 - 12

SALIGER
    Haus der D. Kunst "Die Sinne"   10 - 12   12 - 15

SCALBERT, J.
    A.N., Paris 422 "The Shift"   8 - 10   10 - 12
    Lapina
        795 "The Toilet"   10 - 12   12 - 15
        5158 "Hesitation"   10 - 12   12 - 15
    SPA 30 "Satisfaction"   8 - 10   10 - 12
    Salon de Paris
        1570 "Five O'Clock Tea"   10 - 12   12 - 15
        5085 "The Looking Glass"   10 - 12   12 - 15

SCIHLABITZ, A.
    NPGA 30 "Akstudie"   10 - 12   12 - 15

SCHIVERT, V.
    TSN 801 "Der Liebestraube"   6 - 8   8 - 10
    NPG
        237 "Susanne"   10 - 12   12 - 15
        238 "Akt"   12 - 15   15 - 18
    Munchener Kunst
        193 No Caption   12 - 15   15 - 18
        199 No Caption   12 - 15   15 - 18
    PFB 42291 "Das Modell"   15 - 18   18 - 22
    Arthur Rehn & Co.
        "Die Quelle"   15 - 18   18 - 22
        "Die Rivalin"   12 - 15   15 - 18

SCHLEMO, E.
    TSN
        888 "Schonheit ist alles"   12 - 15   15 - 18
        889 "Beauty"   10 - 12   12 - 14

SCHLIMARSKI, H.
    B.K.W.I. 1805 "Vanity"   10 - 12   12 - 15

SCHMUTZLER, L.		
O.G.Z.L. 364 "Courtezan"	15 - 18	18 - 12
E.N. 810 "Passion"	15 - 18	18 - 22
Others	12 - 15	15 - 18
SCHNEIDER, E.		
"Die Windsbraut"	10 - 12	12 - 15
NPGA 54 "Halbakt"	10 - 12	12 - 15
AMAG Kunst 51 "Bacchantin"	10 - 12	12 - 15
SCHUTZ, E.		
B.K.W.I.		
Series 165 (4)	22 - 25	25 - 28
885-1 "Gothe's Der Got und Baidere"	15 - 18	18 - 22
SEEBERGER, J.		
A.N., Paris		
466 "After the Bath"	10 - 12	12 - 15
470 "Smit with Love"	12 - 15	15 - 18
SEIGNAC, G.		
A.N., Paris		
"Gachucha"	8 - 10	10 - 12
597 "A Sprightly Girl"	10 - 12	12 - 15
760 "Indolence"	10 - 12	12 - 15
Lapina "The Birth of Venus"	12 - 15	15 - 18
SEZILLE, D.E.		
Lapina 913 "Annoying Accident"	12 - 15	15 - 18
SIEFERT, PAUL		
A.N., Paris "Diana"	15 - 18	18 - 22
Salon de Paris 746, "Diana"	15 - 18	18 - 22
SKALA		
Minerva 1117 "Eva"	10 - 12	12 - 15
SOLOMKO, SERGE (Russia)		
TSN 153 "Circe"	15 - 18	18 - 22
SOUBBOTINE		
NPG 87 "Studie"	15- 18	18 - 22
Granbergs, Stock. 577 "Im Harem"	15- 18	18 - 22
STACHIEWICZ, P.		
Wydann. Salon		
152/23 "Kwiat Olean"	15 - 18	18 - 22
152/24 "Zloty Zawoj"	12 - 15	15 - 18
"Ruth"	12 - 15	15 - 18
STELLA, EDUARD		
BRW		
353 "Madame Sans Gene"	18 - 20	20 - 22
354 "Diana"	18 - 20	20 - 22
STEMBER, N.K.		
Richard (Rishar) 1078 "Elegie"	18 - 20	20 - 25
Hanfstaengel's 56 "Jugend"	18 - 20	20 - 25
STYKA, TADE		
Lapina 183 "Cinquecento"	6 - 8	8 - 10

SUCHANKE
  VKKA 1336 "Fruhlingslied"   6 - 8   8 - 10
SYKORA, G.
  G.Z. 032 "Der Necker"   8 - 10   10 - 12
TARDIEU, VICTOR
  Salon de Paris
      168 "Study in Nude"   10 - 12   12 - 15
URBAN, J.
  D.K. & Co. 678   12 - 15   15 - 18
  J.P.P. 42   12 - 15   15 - 18
VACHA, L.
  Minerva 1170 "Suzanne"   8 - 10   10 - 12
VALLET, L.
  Lapina
      2498 "The Gourmet"   15 - 18   18 - 22
      2506 "Luxury"   15 - 18   18 - 22
      2507 "Pride"   15 - 18   18 - 22
      Others   12 - 15   15 - 18
VASNIER, E.
  Lapina 779 "The Toilet"   12 - 15   15 - 18
VASSELON, H.
  A. Noyer
      "The Spring"   12 - 15   15 - 18
VOLKER, ROB.
  Munchener Kunst
      385 No Caption   10 - 12   12 - 15
      386 No Caption   10 - 12   12 - 15
VOWE, P.G.
  MBK 2546 No Caption   8 - 10   10 - 12
WALLIKOW, F.B.
  GK. v., Berlin 432 "Reifers Obst"   6 - 8   8 - 10
WEBER, E.
  B.K.W.I. 2363 "Akt"   10 - 12   12 - 15
WITTING, W.
  S.V.D. 358 "Auf Freier Hohe"   12 - 15   15 - 18
  Dresdner KK "Jugend"   10 - 12   12 - 15
WOBRING, F.
  S.W.S.B. 4771 "Morgentau"   8 - 10   10 - 12
ZIER, ED.
  Russian, **Richard** "La Siesta"   12 - 15   15 - 18
ZMURKO, FR.
  ANCZYC
      291, 297, 355, 448, 516   12 - 15   15 - 18
      280, 347, 449, 510, 648   10 - 12   12 - 15
ZOPF, C.
  O.G.Z.-L 865 "Curious"   8 - 10   10 - 12
ZWILLER, A.
  Salon de Paris "The Rest"   10 - 12   12 - 15

E. Schutz	*FR. Urban*
B.K.W.I., 165-2	*J.P.P. 42*

PUBLISHERS

STENGEL NUDES
   Various Artists   8 - 10   10 - 12

REAL PHOTO NUDES

Real photo nude postcards were first made famous by French publishers who selected bountiful beauties of the day to pose sans clothes. The more important publishing Salons were **AN, Corona, Noyer, PC, SAPI,** and **Super.** Others such as **AG, BMV, CA, ER, GP, JA, JB, JOPA, J.R., Leo, Lydia, MAH, SDK, S.I.C., S.O.L., Star, VC,** and **WA** added to the many cards produced.

Although not always the norm, many publishers used airbrushing to obliterate any pubic or underarm hair from the photos and painted on lingerie for the prudish buyers in some markets. Tinting, especially those by **S.O.L., Paris,** enhanced the eye appeal and quality of selected series but, for today's collector, these are not quite as popular as the untouched material.

Professionally Posed
No Publisher

Professionally Posed
No Publisher

The cards were usually published and sold in sets of 6, 10 or 12, and from these many classical nudes exist. Various studio props were used for background affect. Chairs, tables, chests with mirrors, hanging tapestries, vases, and statues were among the favorites.

The most popular nudes, however, are those that were not professionally posed...were not airbrushed...and therefore left nothing to the imagination. Although the French did their share, cards of this particular type were produced mainly in Germany and Austria, and normally do not have publisher bylines. A small number of cards in this group may also have been done in the U.S.

Non-Professionally Posed

Full Frontal, w/pubic hair	30 - 35	35 - 40
Semi-Nude, w/underarm hair	20 - 25	25 - 30
Semi-Nude, no underarm hair	18 - 22	22 - 27
Rear View	15 - 18	18 - 22
Lesbian Types	25 - 30	30 - 35
Tinted	12 - 15	15 - 18

Deduct $2 for non-postcard backs.

Professionally Posed
P.C., Paris, 2216

Professionally Posed
S.O.L., Paris, 3412

Lesbian Tendencies, Professionally Posed
J.R., Paris, Series 076

Non-Professionally Posed   *German Nude, No Air Brushing*

AFRICAN AND ASIAN SEMI-NUDES

Ethnic African and Asian nude postcards have become very popular in recent years. A quality group entitled "Afrique Occidental" seems to be the most popular. Cards are lightly colored and numbering has been seen from 1 up into the 1400's. The name of the particular tribe and whether the pictured semi-nude is a maiden (fille) or a woman (femme) is usually captioned on each card.

The publishers **L & L** produced a colorful numbered series of Arabians, Algerians, Tunisians, etc., that are also very collectible. Others, titled "Scenes et Types," "Egyptian Types," and a group of "Deutsch Sud West Africa" natives by **Albert Aust**, are also commanding good prices from collectors interested in this type material.

Black and white or sepia copies of many series were also produced. These are not as popular and prices are around 50% less than those produced in color. Real photo types, if original, are priced higher.

Afrique Occidental

Filles	12 - 14	14 - 18
Femmes	10 - 12	12 - 14
Others	8 - 10	10 - 12

Eqyption
"Jeune Egyptienne"

Mayomi
Danzatrice del Caffé Arobo

L & L	8 - 10	10 - 12
Scenes et Types	8 - 10	10 - 12
Egyptian Types	8 - 10	10 - 12
P/Albert Aust	12 - 14	14 - 18
Others	6 - 8	8 - 15

Charley Garry, A.N. Paris No. 6052, "White Woman"   (Blacks/White)

SAMUEL L. SCHMUCKER

The beautiful works of Samuel L. Schmucker, or SLS as shown on the few cards he actually signed, are among the elite and most collectible cards in the hobby. Recent additions to the Raphael Tuck series 556 of "Long Ago Children," the very rare Halloween series 100, the "Quaint Dutch" series, and the Whitney sets have helped make his works the most sought after cards in the hobby.

The fantastic early fantasy cards, issued by The Detroit Publishing Co., are extremely rare, and are among the all-time favorites of the collecting fraternity. Equally outstanding are his works of beautiful ladies and children of Halloween, Christmas, New Year, Valentine's Day, Easter, Thanksgiving and St. Patrick's day by John Winsch. The workmanship and fine quality of John Winsch set the standard for other publishers. Postcard collectors and historians have also concluded that a group of cards by National Art Company, as well as those of Whitney, are the works of Schmucker, and these are also listed in this chapter.

We thank Shirley Hendricks for so graciously allowing us to scan the beautiful cards from her fabulous collection, and for permitting the use of her personal Samuel L. Schmucker checklist. According to Shirley, there are reprint variations of the cards where slight changes were made as promotional efforts by the publishers. This is particularly true in the Valentines, where many silk inserts, booklets and die-cuts were issued using the original image.

Detroit Publishing Co., No No.
Butterfly Series, "Sensibility"

Detroit Publishing Co., No. 1
Childhood Days Ser., "Baby"

Detroit Publishing Co., No No.
Drink Series, "Claret"

Detroit Publishing Co., No. 6
Gnome Series, "Owl"

Detroit Publishing Co., No No.
Int. Girls Series, "Italy"

Detroit Publishing Co., 14660
Fairy Queen Series, "Harmony"

Detroit Pub. Co., Mermaid Series
"Fish and Girl Facing Front"

Detroit Publishing Co., No No.
Smoke Series, "Laughing Waters"

For example, a collector who has the six Winsch copyright 1911 Halloween series of ladies has the basic images from which three other sets were developed ... using smaller images, different captions, different borders, or different printing techniqus. Since this is true with most all Winsch Holiday Schmucker cards, it makes a very interesting quest to find all of them. These variations tend to have a higher value than the originals. Hopefully, we will be able to list them in future editions.

SCHMUCKER, SAMUEL L. (SLS)

		VG	EX
DETROIT PUBLISHING COMPANY			
"Butterfly Series," Copyright 1907			
Actual title is "Woman--Some Reasons			
Why the Butterfly Doth Woman ..."			
"Beauty" -- Girl in blue		$150 - 200	$200 - 250
"Elusoriness" -- Girl in yellow			
"Fragility" -- Girl in blue-green			
"Inconstancy" -- Girl in red			
"L'Envoi" -- Girl in gray			
"Sensibility" -- Girl in pink			
"Childhood Days," No Copyright Date (6)			
I	"Baby Days"	200 - 250	250 - 300
II	"The Runaway"		
III	"Among the Flowers"		
IV	"Fairy Tales"		
V	"Off to School"		
"Drink" Series, Copyright 1907 (6)			
"Champagne"		150 - 200	200 - 250
"Claret"			
"Creme de Menthe"			
"Manhattan"			
"Martini"			
"Sherry"			
"Gnome" Series, Copyright 1907 (6)*			
1	Hummingbird	150 - 175	175 - 200
2	Bee		
3	Mouse		
4	Frog		
5	Beetle		
6	Owl		

* Same series with short quotation instead of one-word title. Value: $1500 - 1650.

"International Girl" Series (10 are known)
    Also known as "Cosmopolitan" Series

	VG	EX
"England"	150 - 200	200 - 250
"France"		

National Art Company
"Write"

National Art Company
"A Letter A Day Keeps the ..."

"Italy"
"Netherlands"
"Norway"
"Russia"
"Spain"
"Switzerland"
"Turkey"
"United States"
"Mottos" Series, No Copyright date (6)
Also known as "Fairy Queen" Series
14659 "Roses" - by Rosseth   225 - 250   250 - 300
14660 "Harmony" - by Thomas Moore
14661 "Captive" - by Coleridge
14662 "Youth's Garden" - by Herrick
14663 "Unafraid" - by Shakespeare
14664 "Philomeis" - By Byron
"Mermaid" Series, Copyright 1907 (6)
Fish and girl facing front   225 - 250   250 - 300
Trout and girl facing left
Seahorse and head of beautiful girl
Fish and girl facing right
Lobster and head of beautiful girl
Goldfish and head of beautiful girl
"Smoke" Series, Copyright 1907 (6)
Beautiful Girl's Head in Smoke   175 - 200   200 - 250
"Clarice" - Cigarette

Winsch, Copyright 1911
"My Valentine"

Winsch, Copyright 1911
"My Valentine" (Rare Variation)

"Laughing Waters" - Indian Pipe
"Lucinda" - Cigar
"Maude Miller" - Corncob Pipe
"Molly" - Clay Pipe
"Virginia" - Brier Pipe

NATIONAL ART COMPANY

WWI Soldier's Letter Series (Unnamed) (10)
"A letter a day keeps the blues away"
"A letter from you looks big as this to me"
"I wasn't so happy last night..."
"Oh! Let this dream come true"
"Three Cheers and Hip Hip Hooray..."
"You'll send me away with a smile..."
"Your letter today was a treat..."
"When of me you sometimes think..."
"When time hangs heavy on my hands..."
"Write"

WINSCH VALENTINE'S DAY

Copyright, 1910 - Vertical (6)

Girl in purple w/2 red heart faces	50 - 55	55 - 60
"St. Valentine's Greeting"		

Winsch, Copyright 1910
"My Valentine ... Think of Me"

Winsch, Copyright 1911
"Valentine's Plea"

Winsch, Copyright 1913
"A Valentine Reminder"

Winsch Back, No Copyright
"Be my Valentine"

Side view of blonde, gold halo and hearts	30 - 35	35 - 40
"My Valentine, think of me"		
Red head, large green heart behind	30 - 35	35 - 40
"I Greet Thee, Valentine"		
Red head wearing blue, green heart	30 - 35	35 - 40
"To my Valentine"		
Lady wearing white chiffon hat	30 - 35	35 - 40
"Be my Valentine"		
Blond wearing chiffon scarf	30 - 35	35 - 40
"A Valentine Message"		

Copyright, 1910 - Green Heart, Vertical (4)

Irish lady and Irish cupid	30 - 35	35 - 40
"Be my Valentine"		
Oriental lady and oriental cupid		
"To my Valentine"		
Indian maid and Indian cupid		
"A Valentine Message"		
Spanish Girl and Spanish cupid		
"St. Valentine's Greeting"		

Copyright, 1910 - Sports Cupid, Horiz. (4)

Fishing Cupid	25 - 30	30 - 35
"To My Valentine"		
Football Cupid		
"A Valentine Message"		
Golfing Cupid		
"To My Valentine"		
Tennis Cupid		
"To My Valentine"		

Copyright, 1910 - Vertical (4)

Blonde holding large red heart	30 - 35	35 - 40
"My Valentine think of me"		
Blonde Sleeping - purple-pink flowers	40 - 45	45 - 50
"Valentine Greetings"		
Blonde lady wearing ermine hat	40 - 45	45 - 50
"To my Valentine"		
Lady in red sitting on flower heart	30 - 35	35 - 40
"St. Valentine's Greeting"		

Copyright, 1911 - Gold Heart, Vertical (4)

Golf Girl	35 - 40	40 - 45
"Valentine Greeting"		
Fishing Girl		
"To my Valentine"		
Football Girl		
"My Valentine"		
Tennis Girl		
"Greeting to my Valentine"		
Girl in red sweater kicking football		
heart - Very Rare	70 - 80	80 - 90
"Valentine Greeting"		

Winsch-Back, Non-Copyright (6)

Nurse bandaging a broken heart	35 - 40	40 - 45
"A Valentine Message"		
Side view of blonde with hearts in hair	35 - 40	40 - 45
"I greet thee Valentine"		
Spider web background, w/hearts entangled	45 - 50	50 - 55
"My Valentine, think of me" Signed SLS		
Dark-haired lady, spider web background	55 - 60	60 - 65
"Be my Valentine"		
Blonde lady holds red heart, spider web	40 - 45	45 - 50
"To my Valentine"		
Lady floating in water with hearts	40 - 45	45 - 50
"St. Valentine's Greeting"		

Copyright, 1911 - Vertical (4)

Lady in blue holding green umbrella	30 - 35	35 - 40
"A Prayer to Valentine"		
Blonde lady in pink carrying basket		
"Gathering Hearts"		
Lady in yellow catching butterfly hearts		
"Your Valentine"		
Lady in green playing heart guitar		
"Valentine Plea"		

WINSCH EASTER

Copyright, 1910 - Flower Faces, Vertical (6)

4 Ladies' faces in red and pink flowers	30 - 35	35 - 40
"A Happy Easter"		

Winsch, Copyright 1910, "To My Valentine"

5 Children's faces in pink flowers
"Welcome Easter Morning"
4 Ladies' faces in pansies
"A Joyful Eastertide"
5 Ladies' faces in tulips
"Best Easter Wishes"
5 Ladies' faces in daffodils
"Glad Easter Greeting"
5 Ladies' faces in Easter Lilies
"Easter Greeting"

WINSCH ST. PATRICK'S DAY

Copyright, 1911 - Vertical (4)

Pretty lady sitting in shamrock wreath	25 - 30	30 - 35
"Erin Go Bragh"		
Lady sitting atop map of Ireland		
"St. Patrick's Day Greetings"		
Lady sitting on Irish hat		
"The Scots man loves ..."		
Lady at window, Horizontal		
"St. Patrick's Day in the morning"		

Copyright, 1912 - Transportation, Vertical (4)

Man/woman riding shamrock sailboat	40 - 45	45 - 50
"St Patrick's Day Souvenir"		
Man/lady riding in shamrock cart	35 - 40	40 - 45
Lady sitting atop map of Ireland		
"St. Patrick's Day Greetings"		
Man swinging lady on shamrock swing	35 - 40	40 - 45
"Erin Go Bragh"		
Man/lady riding in shamrock airship	45 - 50	50 - 55
"St Patrick's Day Greeting"		

Copyright, 1912 - Named Views, Horiz. (4)

Lady playing harp	20 - 25	25 - 30
"Erin Go Bragh"		
Lady wearing shamrock hat, with harp	20 - 25	25 - 30
"St. Patrick's Day Greetings"		
Lady on map of Ireland	15 - 20	20 - 25
"St. Patrick's Day Souvenir"		
Lady and man dancing	20 - 25	25 - 30
"St. Patrick's Day Greetings"		

Winsch Backs, No Copyright (9 known)

Lady with pig, wreath behind	25 - 30	30 - 35
"Erin Go Bragh"		
Lady standing in front of crossed pipes	25 - 30	30 - 35
"St. Patrick's Day Souvenir"		
Lady sitting on bouquet of shamrocks	25 - 30	30 - 35
"St. Patrick's Day"		
Lady with pig, wreath behind	20 - 25	25 - 30

Winsch, Copyright 1910
"A Happy Easter"

Winsch, Copyright 1911
"Erin Go Bragh"

"Erin Go Bragh"		
Lady in shamrock dress, holds big pipe	20 - 25	25 - 30
"St. Patrick's Day Greetings"		
Lady riding big white pipe	20 - 25	25 - 30
"St. Patrick's Day Souvenir"		
Lady sitting on big harp, mesh background	25 - 30	30 - 35
"Erin Go Bragh"		
Lady holds big pipe, mesh background	25 - 30	30 - 35
"St. Patrick's Day Greetings"		
Lady at the window - Horizontal	25 - 30	30 - 35
"The Top of the Mornin' to you..."		

WINSCH THANKSGIVING

Copyright, 1910 - Vertical (4)

Kneeling Pilgrim w/basket beside her	15 - 20	20 - 25
"A Peaceful Thanksgiving"		
Lady holding pumpkins	15 - 20	20 - 25
"Hearty Thanksgiving Greetings"		
Lady feeding grain to turkey	15 - 20	20 - 25
"With Thanksgiving Greeting"		
Pilgrim man/woman preparing to eat	15 - 20	20 - 25
"Best Wishes for a Happy Thanksgiving"		

Winsch Back, No Copyright
"St. Patrick's Day Souvenir"

Winsch Back, No Copyright
"St. Patrick's Day Greetings"

Winsch, Copyright 1911
"St. Patrick's Day Greetings"

Copyright, 1911 - Vertical (8)

Girl in purple picks fruit, turkey	10 - 15	15 - 20
"With Thanksgiving Greeting"		
Pilgrim lady in field, corn/pumpkins	15 - 20	20 - 25
"A Peaceful Thanksgiving"		
Pilgrim girl w/turkey, big moon	15 - 20	20 - 25
"Hearty Thanksgiving Greeting"		
Lady carrying tray with turkey	10 - 15	15 - 20
"Best Wishes for a Happy Thanksgiving"		
Lady holding armful of wheat	15 - 20	20 - 25
"A Peaceful Thanksgiving"		
Pilgrim lady, dead turkey	15 - 20	20 - 25
"Best Wishes for a Happy Thanksgiving"		
Pilgrim lady with basket on arm	15 - 20	20 - 25
"A Peaceful Thanksgiving"		
Indian maid driving fantasy turkey wagon	15 - 20	20 - 25
"A Thanksgiving Bounty be Thine" - Horiz.		

Copyright, 1912 - Indian Maids, Vertical (6)

Indian in green dress	25 - 30	30 - 35
"Sincere Thanksgiving Greeting"		
Indian holding white turkey	20 - 25	25 - 30
"All Thanksgiving Bounty be Thine"		
Indian walking with turkey	20 - 25	25 - 30
"Glad Thanksgiving Wishes"		
Indian and Pilgrim with turkey	20 - 25	25 - 30
"Hearty Thanksgiving Greeting"		

Copyright, 1913 -- Vertical (4)

Pilgrim with turkey behind her	15 - 20	20 - 25
"All Thanksgiving Bounty be Thine"		
Pilgrim with turkey platter in front		
"Thanksgiving Greeting"		
Pilgrim girl sitting on wishbone		
"A Peaceful Thanksgiving"		
Indian girl sits on ear of corn		
"Best Wishes for a Happy Thanksgiving"		

WINSCH HALLOWEEN

Copyright, 1911 - Vertical* (6)

Head & shoulders of blonde, black hood	75 - 100	100 - 125
"A Happy Hallowe'en"		
Lady riding broom, moon behind		
"All Hallowe'en"		
Lady in long white hooded robe		
"On Hallowe'en"		
Lady in red dress, owl on head		
"Hallowe'en Greeting"		
Lady in black evening gown		

Winsch, Copyright 1911
"Best Wishes for a Happy ..."

Winsch, Copyright 1912
"Glad Thanksgiving Wishes"

"Greetings at Hallowe'en"		
Lady asleep, 3 fairies		
"Hallowe'en Time"		
* 3 different sets of variations of 1911 series show smaller same design images but with different captions		60 - 150
Copyright, 1912 - Vertical* (6)		
Lady witch in front of big cauldron	75 - 100	100 - 125
"The Hallowe'en Cauldron"		
Lady in black, leering moon behind		
"The Hallowe'en Lantern"		
Lady in white-hooded cape, JOL's		
"The Magic Hallowe'en"		
Lady in red elfin costume		
"The Hallowe'en Witch's Wand"		
Lady in white clown suit, owls		
"A Hallowe'en Morning"		
Lady in green dress, JOL man		
"A Hallowe'en Wish"		
* 4 different sets of variations of 1912 series (one same size images and 3 smaller; 3 are copyrighted; 2 are vertical and 2 are horizontal)		75 - 150

Winsch, Copyright 1911
"Tonight upon your pillow ..."

Winsch, Copyright 1912
"The Hallow'en Cauldron"

Copyright, 1913 "Mask Series" - Horiz.* (4)
    Clown in red and Jack-in-the Box   75 - 100   100 - 125
    "Hallowe'en Surprises"
    Witch and clown hold jump rope
    "Hallowe'en Gambols!"
    Woman in long white hooded robe
    "Hallowe'en Faces"
    Girl in white dress, huge masks
    "Hallowe'en Faces"
*   One other set of variation of 1913 series
    has embossed design, black/gold stars
    border, different captions and cards
    are not copyrighted (#4972 on reverse)   100 - 125   125 - 150
Copyright, 1913 -- Horizontal* (4)
    Girl in white dress with pink dress   75 - 100   100 - 125
    "A Starry Hallowe'en"
    Girl in dotted dress sits on pumpkin
    "Hallowe'en Night"
    Boy surrounded by big JOL's
    "Hallowe'en Pumpkins"
    Girl in white between owl and vegetable
    "Hallowe'en Jollity"
*   4 other sets of variations of 1913 series
    and all are copyrighted 1913.

Winsch, Copyright 1913
"The Magic Hallowe'en ..."

Winsch Back, No Copyright
"Hallowe'en Friends"

Winsch, Copyright 1913
"Hallowe'en Faces"

Winsch Back, No Copyright
Embossed, "All Hallowe'en"

Winsch Back, No Copyright
No. 4972, "The Hallowe'en"

Winsch Back, No Copyright
"A Hallowe'en Wish"

Winsch, Copyright 1913
Embossed, "Hallowe'en Jollity!"

Winsch Back, No Copyright
"The Hallowe'en Witch's Wand"

Winsch Back, No Copyright
Pink Border, "Hallowe'en Jollity!"

German, Non-P.C. Back
"A Happy Hallowe'en"

Winsch Back, No Copyright
"A Merry Christmas"

Winsch, Copyright 1910
"With Best New Year Wishes"

Winsch, Copyright 1911
"A Happy New Year"

Winsch, Copyright 1910
"To Wish You a Happy ..."

WINSCH CHRISTMAS

Copyright, 1910 - Vertical* (4)
    Lady in poinsettia dress and background   20 - 25   25 - 30
    "Christmas Wishes"
    Lady in green dress, poinsettia coat
    "Christmas Greeting"
    Lady in yellow dress, holly background
    "A Merry Christmas"
    Lady in white dress and red jacket
    "A Joyful Christmas"
* Smaller images reprinted in 1915
with different captions, Vertical   25 - 30   30 - 35
Copyright, 1911 - Vertical (4)
    Girl in red hugs big snowman   45 - 50   50 - 60
    "A Merry Christmas"
    Girl in blue with dark red scarf
    "Christmas Greetings"
    Girl in green with yellow scarf
    "Merry Christmas"
    Girl with red mittens and snowballs
    "A Joyful Christmas"
Winsch Backs, No Copyright (4)
    Glamour blonde with Santa mask   45 - 50   50 - 60
    "A Joyful Christmas"
    Blonde lady with ermine fur
    "A Merry Christmas"
    Blond lady sleeps, Santa watches
    "A Merry Christmas"
    Lady in red sitting on gold bell
    "Christmas Greeting"

WINSCH NEW YEAR

Copyright, 1910 - Vertical (4)
    Reprints of 1910 Christmas issue
    with New Year Captions, Vertical   20 - 25   25 - 30
    Silks, with no copyright   25 - 30   30 - 35
Copyright, 1910 - Father Time, Vertical (4)
    With lady in purple   45 - 50   50 - 60
    "Jan. 1st."
    With lady in gold
    "Jan. 1st.
    With lady in pink flowered dress
    "Jan. 1st."
    With lady in red
    "Jan 1st."
Copyright, 1910 - 1911 Year - Vertical (4)
    1911 Baby New Year rides big bell   30 - 35   35 - 40
    "To wish you a Happy New Year"

Winsch, Copyright 1910
"Christmas Greetings"

Winsch, Copyright 1911
"Christmas Greetings"

Stork carrying Baby New Year
"A Happy New year"
Baby New Year/Father Time
"Best New Year Wishes"
Baby New Year sits on trunk
"A Happy New Year to You"

Copyright, 1911 - Vertical* (4)
Girl in red hugs snowman   35 - 40   40 - 45
"A Happy New Year"
Girl in Blue with dark red scarf
"With Best New Year Wishes"
Girl in green with yellow scarf
"A Happy New Year to You"
Girl with red mittens and snowballs
"To Wish you a Happy New Year"
* Reprints of 1911 Christmas Series as New Year

R. TUCK & SONS, LTD. -- New York

Series 100 -- Halloween (9 known)
Girl dressed in sheet, many JOL's   100 - 125   125 - 150
"Bats and owls and witch-y capers ..."
Girl pixie dressed in black, 3 JOL's
"Hallowe'en Greetings ..."

Girl with cape and Japanese lanterns
"Hallowe'en Wishes"
Girl with mask, 5 big masks behind
"This maid will mask on Hallowe'en"
Boy with Japanese lanterns, big moon
"Sing a Song of Hallowe'en"
Girl wears checked dress and JOL man
"This maiden here is dancing with ..."
Girl wears JOL cloak, with JOL on stick
"Were you this maid on Hallowe'en"
Girl dressed as clown, JOL on a stick
"Witches, Fay's and Sprites unseen ..."
Boy with flute sits on big JOL
"When you're away on Hallowe'en"

Series 198, Birthday (10) **"Quaint Dutch"**	70 - 80	80 - 90
Series 556, Christmas (8) **"Long Ago Children"**	30 - 35	35 - 40
Series 618, New Year's (6) **"Joyous"**	40 - 45	45 - 50
Series 619, New Year's (6) **"Ye Olden Days"**	30 - 35	35 - 45

WHITNEY HALLOWEEN (6)

Boy and girl with lantern, green imps	80 - 90	90 - 100

"Be brave and bold on Hallowe'en night ..."
Three children w/pumpkins, JOL, imp/owl
"Hallowe'en Greetings to You"
Three children with clown on a stick
"Just a wish for a Happy Hallowe'en"
Dutch boy, girl in flowered dress, goblins
"May you be Jolly and Gay ..."
Two girls watch flying witch, big moon
"On Hallowe'en watch and you may see ..."
Boy and girl meet big vegetable man
"Since I am here and you are there ..."

Halloween Fold-Outs	100 - 125	125 - 150
WHITNEY NEW YEAR (6)	50 - 60	60 - 75
WHITNEY CHRISTMAS (6)	50 - 60	60 - 75

Tuck Series 100

(1) "This maid will mask on Hallowe'en ..."
(2) "Were you this maid on Hallowe'en ..."
(3) "This maiden here is dancing with ..."
(4) "Bats and owls and witch-y capers ..."

Whitney Series (No Number)

(5) "Just a wish for a happy Hallowe'en ..."
(6) "Since I am here and you are there ..."
(7) "Be brave and bold on Hallowe'en
night ..."

6 Santas

Probably the most avidly collected postcards during the past year were the high quality and beautifully printed issues of our American Santa Claus and his counterparts, the German Father Christmas, St. Nicholas, and Nicolo. In greatest demand were the early Chromo-Lithographs and embossed issues of German origin with robes of colors other than red. Prices for outstanding examples of large, full-figure images with yellow, black, purple, blue, orange, gray, blue, brown, tan, green, striped, and Art Deco types of 1915-30 have simply gone through the roof. According to reports from many collectors, robes of yellow, orange, black and gray are in the "most rare" group.

Others that have also greatly increased in value are the European artist-signed issues, led by the outstanding works of A. Mailick and all Hold-To-Light issues, especially Uncle Sam Santas. The PFB and Winsch issues are also in great demand, as well as those involving transportation. On the other hand, the small or upper body figures, and those poorly printed or less brilliantly colored, have created very little interest.

SANTAS, ST. NICHOLAS AND KRAMPUS

ARTIST-SIGNED

	VG	EX
BOWLEY, A.L.		
Raphael Tuck		
Series C1758 (6)	$25 - 30	$30 - 35

Series C2099 (6)	25 - 30	30 - 35
BRUNDAGE, FRANCES		
Raphael Tuck		
Series 4 (12)	20 - 25	25 - 28
Series 525, Santa Scroll Series (6)	12 - 15	15 - 18
Series 1822 (6)	30 - 35	35 - 40
Sam Gabriel		
Series 200	12 - 15	15 - 18
Series 230	10 - 12	12 - 15
CHIOSTRI, S.		
Ballerini & Fratini		
Series 220 Black Robes	50 - 60	60 - 75
Others	30 - 35	35 - 45
GASSAWAY, KATHERINE		
Raphael Tuck		
Series 501	15 - 18	18 - 20
HBG (H.B. GRIGGS)		
L & E		
Series 2224		
Black Robe	30 - 35	35 - 40
Green Robe	25 - 30	30 - 35
Others	20 - 22	22 - 25

Blue Robed German Santa
Chromo-Lithograph

Blue Robed German Santa
Chromo-Lithograph

Series 2264		
Black Robe	30 - 35	35 - 40
Others	20 - 22	22 - 25
Series 2275		
Brown Robe	25 - 30	30 - 35
Others	18 - 20	20 - 22
HARPER, R. FORD		
Lady Santas (4)	30 - 35	35 - 45
KIRCHNER, RAPHAEL	325 - 350	350 - 400
KÖHLER, MELA (WW)	500 - 525	525 - 575
MBH		
Raphael Tuck		
Series 549 "Santa Claus" (6)	12 - 15	15 - 18
MEG		
Raphael Tuck		
Series 535 "Santa Claus" (6)	10 - 12	12 - 15
MAILICK, A.		
Hold-To-Light		
Red Robe	150 - 175	175 - 200
Robes of other Colors	250 - 275	275 - 300
Early Chromo-Lithographs		
Red Robe	40 - 50	50 - 65
Robes of other Colors	65 - 75	75 - 100
St. Nicholas & Krampus Series	35 - 40	40 - 45
MAUFF, S.A. (Stengel Art Nouveau)	200 - 225	225 - 275
SANDFORD, H. D.		
Raphael Tuck		
Series 8247, 8248 (6)	15 - 18	18 - 22
SHEPHEARD, E.		
Raphael Tuck		
Series 8415, 8421 (6)	15 - 18	18 - 22
WAIN, LOUIS		
Ettinger, Cat Santa Series 5376	150 - 175	175 - 200
Wrench, Cat Santa Series	175 - 200	200 - 225
GERMAN SANTAS		
FULL FIGURES		
Black Robe	50 - 60	60 - 75
Gray or White Robe	40 - 45	45 - 50
Blue, Tan or Purple Robe	35 - 40	40 - 45
Yellow or Orange Robe	45 - 50	50 - 60
Brown or Wine Robe	30 - 35	35 - 40
Striped, Two-color or Art Deco	45 - 50	50 - 60
Red Robe	15 - 20	20 - 25
HEADS, UPPER BODY OR SMALL IMAGE		
(Valued at 50%, or less, than Full Figures.)		
HOLD-TO-LIGHT		
FULL FIGURES		
Red Robes	125 - 150	150 - 165
Robes colored other than red	175 - 200	200 - 250

HEADS, UPPER BODY OR SMALL IMAGE		
Red Robes	90 - 100	100 - 125
Robes colored other than red	125 - 150	150 - 165
TRANSPARENCIES	60 - 70	70 - 85
MECHANICALS		
Honeycomb Folders	50 - 60	60 - 70
Pop-outs	30 - 35	35 - 40
Pull-tabs	25 - 30	35 - 40
Stand-ups	20 - 25	25 - 30
Wheel-type	30 - 35	35 - 40
SILK APPLIQUE		
FULL FIGURES		
Langsdorf	40 - 50	50 - 60
AMB	35 - 40	40 - 45
Others	25 - 30	30 - 35
SMALL FIGURES	15 - 20	20 - 25
UNCLE SAM SANTAS		
(1) Flat-Printed	550 - 600	600 - 700
(2) Embossed	600 - 700	700 - 800
(3) Squeakers	1500 - 1600	1600 - 1750
(4) Hold-to-Light		
a. Santa Knocking on Door	2000 - 2250	2250 - 2500
b. Santa Trimming the Tree	2000 - 2250	2250 - 2500
c. Santa Walking Upstairs	2500 - 2750	2750 - 3000
d. Santa at Window (bag of toys)	2800 - 3100	3100 - 3400
OTHER SANTAS		
Child Santas	10 - 15	15 - 25
Santa W/Christ Child - Add $5.		
Santa W/Switches - Add $3 to $5.		
Santa Switching Child - Add $5 - $10.		
Santa W/Odd Transportation - Add $5 - $8.		
Santa W/Krampus - Add $10 - $15.		
PUBLISHERS		
AA (Anglo American)		
Series 705, 708, 709 (6)	12 - 15	15 - 18
AMB Silks	35 - 40	40 - 45
B.W., Germany		
Series 291, 296, 305, 324	15 - 18	18 - 20
MAB	12 - 15	15 - 18
Jules Bien	10 - 12	12 - 15
Langsdorf		
Series 1320	20 - 22	22 - 28
Silks	40 - 50	50 - 60
M.M.B.		
J. Marks Series 538 (6)	4 - 5	5 - 6
E. Nash	10 - 12	12 - 15
PFB (Paul Finkenrath, Berlin)		
Series 5431, 7933 (6)	40 - 45	45 - 50
Series 7312, 6481 (6)	25 - 30	30 - 35

Uncle Sam Santa
"Hold-to-Light"

"Hold-to-Light" Santa
Purple Suit

Series 7930	20 - 22	22 - 25
Series 9593, 6434 (6)	35 - 40	40 - 45
Series 6439, 8935 St. Nicholas (6)	35 - 40	40 - 45
Other St. Nicholas Series	30 - 35	35 - 40
Other Santas	25 - 30	30 - 35
Samson Bros.		
Series 31, 705 (6)	12 - 15	15 - 20
Series 3102	25 - 28	28 - 32
Sander, P.		
Lady Santas (4) -- Signed Harper	35 - 40	40 - 50
Raphael Tuck*		
Series 1, 8000, 8619	30 - 35	35 - 40
Series 5, "Kris Kringle"	10 - 12	12 - 15
Series 55, 1029	25 - 30	30 - 35
Series 102, 136, 501	10 - 12	12 - 15
Series 512, 535, 806	12 - 15	15 - 18
Series 505, "The Christmas Series"	25 - 30	30 - 35
Series 8263	25 - 30	30 - 35
Series 8320	15 - 18	18 - 22
No Number Series "Christmas Postcards"	10 - 12	12 - 15

* Most series contain cards of children.
WINSCH, JOHN *
Copyright, 1912 - Vertical (4)

Red Robe, yellow/gold background	25 - 30	30 - 35

R. Ford Harper, Lady Santa
P. Sander 751

Brown Robed German Santa
Chromo-Lithograph

John Winsch, Copyright 1913
"Christmas Greetings"

John Winsch, Copyright 1914
"A Merry Christmas"

John Winsch, Copyright 1912
"A Joyful Christmas"

John Winsch, Copyright 1913
"A Joyful Christmas"

"A Joyful Christmas"
Red Robe, green background
"A Merry Christmas"
Santa on gold background
"I Wish You a Merry Christmas"
Orange Robe, blue background
"May Your Christmas be Bright..."

Copyright, 1912 - Vertical (4)
Children watch Santa in plane   18 - 22   22 - 26
"A Merry Christmas"
Child watching Santa's shadow
"A Joyful Christmas"
Child watching Santa around chimney
"Best Christmas Wishes" (Horizontal)
Children see Santa coming from chimney
"A Joyful Christmas"

Copyright, 1912 - Vertical (2)
Red Robed Santa with Teddy Bear and   35 - 40   40 - 45
     Golliwog at chimney
"Best Christmas Wishes"
Santa in red jacket, blue-striped
     pants flying bi-plane
"A Happy Christmastide"

John Winsch, Copyright , No. 4164, "Christmas Wishes"

Copyright, 1913 - Horizontal (4)
    Red Robe, Teddy Bear, Smokes pipe   40 - 50   50 - 60
    "Best Christmas Wishes"
    Red Robe, teddy bear, jack-in-box"
    "Christmas Greetings"
    Red Robe, with arm-load of dolls
    "Christmas Wishes"
    Red/Pink Robe carrying bag of fruit
    "Merry Christmas"
Copyright, 1913 - Horizontal (4)
    Santa in airplane tosses toys to
        children on balcony   25 - 30   30 - 35
    "A Joyful Christmas"
    Santa in airplane tosses toys to
        children on ground
    "A Joyous Christmas"
    Children watch Santa in balloon basket
    "A Merry Christmas"
    Children on balcony watch Santa with
        toys in airplane
    "A Christmas Greeting"
Copyright, 1913 - Vertical (2)
    Red Robe, driving car, big clock   25 - 30   30 - 35
    "Christmas Greetings"
    Red Robe, driving double-deck bus
    "A Christmas Greeting"
Copyright, 1914 - Gold Borders, Horizontal (4)
    Red Robe, with two girls under umbrella   40 - 45   45 - 55
    "Christmas Greeting"

Red Robe, two Children...one on back
"Best Christmas Wishes"
Red Robe, kissing one of two children
"A Joyful Christmas"
Red Robe, one of two children whispers
"A Merry Christmas"

No Copyright Date
Red & Gold Borders, Horizontal
Children greet Red Robe Santa at door   50 - 55   55 - 60
"Christmas Wishes" -- No. 4164
Children greeting Santa from bed
"A Merry Christmas"
* With Silk or Ribbon Inserts add $3-5.

REAL PHOTOS

French & European

Black & White	10 - 15	15 - 18
Tinted	15 - 18	18 - 20
St. Nicholas	10 - 15	15 - 18
U.S. Real Photos	10 - 15	15 - 20
Tinted	15 - 18	18 - 25

John Winsch, Copyright 1913
"A Christmas Greeting"

St. Nicholas
PFB Series 6439

W. H. Braun
W.R.B. & Company, No. 22-31

GRUSS VOM KRAMPUS!

H. G., H.H.I.W. No. 568
"Gruss vom Krampus!"

SAINT NICHOLAS, NICOLO

PFB Series 6439	25 - 30	30 - 35
Real Photo Types	10 - 12	12 - 15
Wearing Red/white Robe		
Full Figure	20 - 25	25 - 30
Small Figure, Head or Upper Body	10 - 12	12 - 15
Wearing Robes other than Red/White		
Full Figure	25 - 30	30 - 35
Small Figure, Head or Upper Body	15 - 18	18 - 22

KRAMPUS

European		
Red Background - pre-1915		
Full Figure	15 - 18	18 - 22
Small Figure	10 - 12	12 - 15
Printed, Color - pre-1915		
Large Figure	20 - 25	25 - 30
Small Figure	12 - 15	15 - 18
W/Crying Children - add $4-5		
W/Children in Bucket - add $5-6		
W/Erotic Women - add $5-10		
W/Cloth Applique - add $5-6		
1915-1930, Red Background	10 - 12	12 - 15
1915-1930, Printed-Color	15 - 18	18 - 20
After 1930	3 - 4	4 - 6

Greetings

Greeting cards are those sent to recognize a Holiday, Birthday, or just to say "Hello." These were, by far, the largest single type of early postcards printed; there are millions still available today.

Many were beautifully printed and very desirable, while others were poorly designed and bland, unwanted by collectors, and destined today to postcard dealers' "25 cent" boxes. The majority of cards in huge accumulations or the remnants of a dealer's stock are represented in this group. Easter, Birthday, Thanksgiving, and common flowered greetings make up the greater proportion.

On the other hand, there are high quality Greeting cards by Signed Artists such as Ellen H. Clapsaddle, Rose O'Neill, Frances Brundage, S.L. Schmucker, H.B. Griggs, Dwig, Grace Drayton/Wiederseim and others. Outstanding cards were also produced by publishers such as Winsch, Paul Finkenrath (PFB), Raphael Tuck, Nash, Santway, and Gabriel.

NEW YEAR

	VG	EX
Common	$0.50 - 1	$1 - 1.50
With Children, unsigned	2 - 3	3 - 5
With Pig	4 - 6	6 - 8
With Dressed Pigs	7 - 8	8 - 12
With Chimney Sweeps	7 - 8	8 - 12
With Pigs/Chimney Sweeps	8 - 10	10 - 15

German Chromo-Lithograph   *Mailick*
New Year   *Anonymous German Publisher*

With Elves/Mushrooms/Gold, etc.	3 - 6	6 - 10
With Big Snowmen	5 - 8	8 - 15
WithYear Date - See Year Dates		
With Dressed Mushrooms, Gnomes	5 - 8	8 - 12
Sam Gabriel S/Brundage		
Series 300, 302, 316 (10)	10 - 12	12 - 14
International Art Pub. Co. S/Clapsaddle		
Common	4 - 5	5 - 6
With Children	7 - 8	8 - 12
L & E S/H.B.G.		
Series 2225, 2227, 2266 (6)	8 - 9	9 - 10
Series 2276 (6)	8 - 9	9 - 10
P.F.B.		
Series 9501 Children/Auto (6)	6 - 8	8 - 10
Raphael Tuck Various Series		
Simple	0.50 - 1	1 - 2
With Children	2 - 3	3 - 4
Series 601 (Unsigned Brundage)	8 - 10	10 - 12
Raphael Tuck (American)		
Series 618, 619	2 - 3	3 - 4
Wolf S/Clapsaddle, Uns./Clapsaddle		

Add $3-5 per card to **Int. Art Pub. Co.** prices.

EASTER

Common	0.50 - 1	1 - 1.50
With Children, Unsigned	2 - 3	3 - 6
With Chicks, Lambs, Bunnies	2 - 3	3 - 5
With Dressed Chicks	3 - 5	5 - 7
WithDressed Bunnies	4 - 6	6 - 12
With Transportation	3 - 6	6 - 10
Easter Witches (Scandinavian) Normal	8 - 10	10 - 15
Easter Witches (Scandinavian) Small	10 - 12	12 - 18
(See Artist-Signed)		

International Art. Pub. Co. S/Clapsaddle

Children	7 - 8	8 - 12

P.F.B.

Series 5837 (6)	5 - 6	6 - 8
Series 8270 (6)	6 - 7	7 - 9
Series 8684 (6)	6 - 7	7 - 9

Wolf S/Clapsaddle, Uns./Clapsaddle
Add $2-3 per card to **Int. Art Pub. Co.** prices.

PFINGSTEN (WHITSUN)

Common	3 - 5	5 - 7
With Children	4 - 6	6 - 8
With Miakafirs (May Bugs)	8 - 10	10 - 16
With Dressed Miakafirs	10 - 12	12 - 20
With Bugs, Insects	7 - 10	10 - 12
With Frogs	10 - 12	12 - 16
With Dressed Frogs	12 - 18	18 - 25

Pfingsten cards have become very popular.

ST. PATRICK'S DAY

Common	1 - 1.50	1.50 - 2
With Children, Ladies	3 - 5	5 - 7
With Comics	2 - 3	3 - 5
With Uncle Sam or Ethnic Slurs	4 - 6	6 - 8
With Flags, Pipes	2 - 3	3 - 5

ASB

Series 340 (6)	3 - 4	4 - 5

Anglo American (AA)

Series 776, 815 (6)	3 - 4	4 - 5

Jules Bien

Series 740 (6)	3 - 4	4 - 5

Sam Gabriel

Series 140 Unsigned/Brundage (10)	8 - 10	10 - 12
Series 141 (10)	3 - 4	4 - 5

Gottschalk, Dreyfus & Davis

Series 2040, 2092, 2190, 2410	3 - 4	4 - 6

International Art Pub. Co. S/Clapsaddle		
Children	6 - 9	9 - 12
Others	4 - 5	5 - 7
L & E S/H.B.G.	8 - 10	10 - 12
(See Artist-Signed)		
Wolf S/Clapsaddle, Uns./Clapsaddle		
Add $2-3 per card to **Int. Art Pub. Co.** prices.		

VALENTINE'S DAY

Common	1 - 1.50	1.50 - 2
With Children, Ladies	3 - 4	4 - 6
With Comics	2 - 3	3 - 4
With Animals	2 - 3	3 - 4
A.S.B.		
Series 227, 229, 267 (6)	1 - 2	2 - 3
B.B. London		
Series 1501 (6)	1 - 2	2 - 3
B.W. Many Series (6)	1 - 2	2 - 3
S. Bergman Many Series (6)	1 - 2	2 - 3
Jules Bien		
Series 335 (6)	1 - 2	2 - 3

"Herzliche Pfingstgrüsse"
(May Bugs at Play)

John Winsch, Copyright 1912
"St. Valentine's Greeting"

R. Tuck & Sons' "Garden Truck" Series of Valentine Post Cards No. 2
"A Pretty Pickle!"

Int. Art Publishing Company
"Love's Greeting"

H. Wessler, No. 536
"Pray don't decline My Valentine."

F.B. (Fritz Baumgarten), "Fröhliche Ostern!"

L.R. Conwell Ser. 329, 409 (6)	1 - 2	2 - 3
Sam Gabriel		
S/J. Johnson, Series 407 (6)	4 - 5	5 - 6
Uns./Brundage Series 413 (6)	8 - 10	10 - 12
Others	1 - 2	2 - 3
International Art. Pub. Co. S/Clapsaddle		
Angels, Cherubs	4 - 6	6 - 8
Greetings	4 - 6	6 - 8
Children	8 - 9	9 - 18
E. Nash Many Series	1 - 2	2 - 3
P.F.B.		
Series 7185 Cupids	5 - 6	6 - 8
Samson Bros. Many Series	1 - 2	2 - 3
Raphael Tuck Signed/Brundage		
Series 102 (6)	12 - 15	15 - 18
Blacks	22 - 25	25 - 30
Series 115 (4)	8 - 10	10 - 12
Blacks	22 - 25	25 - 30
Series 11	8 - 10	10 - 12
Series 20 & 26 (unsigned)	10 - 12	12 - 15
Series 100, 101 (6) (unsigned)	10 - 12	12 - 14
Leatherette, 114, 116 (6)	3 - 5	5 - 7
Series 1033 Blacks	20 - 22	22 - 25
Other Unsigned/Brundage	8 - 10	10 - 12
Blacks	20 - 22	22 - 25
S/Outcault Series 106, 111, 112	8 - 10	10 - 12
Black Series 108 (6)	10 - 12	12 - 14
Raphael Tuck		
Series A, B, C, 5, 6 & 7	4 - 5	5 - 6

E. H. Clapsaddle, Int. Art. Pub.
"To Greet you on St. Patrick's Day"

Sigrun Steenhoff
Easter Witches, "Rolig Päsk"

Series 231, "Poster Girls	25 - 30	30 - 35
Signed/Curtis (36)	4 - 6	6 - 8
H. Wessler	5 - 7	7 - 9
Winsch, Copyright		
Common	1 - 1.50	1.50 - 2
W/Children or Ladies	4 - 5	5 - 6
W/Uns. **Schmucker** Ladies (See Schmucker)		
Booklet-types	5 - 6	6 - 8
Silk Inserts (Ladies)	10 - 12	12 - 15
W/Uns. **Schmucker** inserts (See Schmucker)		
Rose Co. Comic Series	2 - 3	3 - 4
Illustrated P.C. Co. Comics		
S/**H. Horina** Series 5004	3 - 4	4 - 5
Aurochrome Co. Comics		
S/**Meyer**	3 - 4	4 - 5
Wolf S/Clapsaddle, Uns./Clapsaddle		

Add $3-5 per card to **Int. Art Pub. Co.** prices.

BIRTHDAY

Common	0.50 - 1	1 - 1.50
With Children	2 - 3	3 - 5
S/**Clapsaddle**	7 - 9	9 - 14

BRC -- Unsigned **LD**	6 - 8	8 - 10
Raphael Tuck (American)		
"Birthday Children" Series 102 (10)	2 - 3	3 - 4
"Quaint Dutch" Series 198 (See Schmucker)		
Winsch, Copyright	4 - 5	5 - 8
Wolf S/Clapsaddle, Uns./Clapsaddle		
Add $2-3 to **Int. Art Pub. Co.** prices.		

APRIL FOOL DAY

Henderson Litho Series 102	7 - 8	8 - 10
P.C.K. (Paul C. Kober)		
S/A. Hutaf	6 - 8	8 - 10
Ullman Mfg Co. S/B. Wall		
Series 156 (6)	6 - 7	7 - 8
Winsch Backs Series 1	8 - 10	10 - 12
FRENCH 1st of Avril Fish	8 - 12	12 - 15
P.F.B.		
Series 553, 6505	10 - 12	12 - 14

LEAP YEAR

S/Brill, B&W and Red (12)	3 - 4	4 - 5
D.P. Crane S/Zim	7 - 9	9 - 12
Sam Gabriel Series 401 (12) S/Dwig	10 - 12	12 - 14
Grollman, 1908	6 - 8	8 - 10
H.T.M. 1060-1071 (12)	7 - 8	8 - 9
Henderson Litho Series 102	5 - 6	6 - 7
Illustrated P.C. Co. Series 217	6 - 7	7 - 9
P.C. Koeber S/Hutaf	8 - 10	10 - 12
B.B. London Series E44, E81	8 - 9	9 - 10
E. Nash		
"Lemon" Series 1 (12)	8 - 10	10 - 12
"Diamond Ring" Series, 1912	8 - 10	10 - 12
"Captured him in his lair"		
"Caught on the run"		
"Don't give up the ship"		
"Lay for him"		
"On the Trail"		
"Ring up the man you want"		
Rose Co. S/G. Brill (6)	6 - 8	8 - 10
P. Sanders, 1908	6 - 8	8 - 10
R. Tuck Series 7, S/Curtis (12)	8 - 9	9 - 11
S/L. Thackeray	8 - 10	10 - 12
Ullman Series 156	6 - 8	8 - 10

GROUND HOG DAY

Henderson Litho Co., Series 101 (4)	150 - 175	175 - 200
Linens	12 - 15	15 - 18

Photo Production Ltd. (England)
"You're One To-day!"

Unsigned L.D., BRC 738
"Herzlichen Glückwunsch"

MOTHER'S DAY

Metro Litho Co.		
Series 446 (6)	10 - 12	12 - 14
Anonymous		
Lady & Soldier, "Mother's Day"	8 - 10	10 - 15
Mother holds Baby, "Mother's Day"	8 - 10	10 - 15
Mother holds baby at arm's length.	20 - 25	25 - 30
Silhouette Types	10 - 12	12 - 15

GEORGE WASHINGTON'S BIRTHDAY

Anglo American (AA)		
Open Book Series 725 (6)	15 - 20	20 - 25
728 (6)	15 - 20	20 - 25
Jules Bien Series 605 (6)	6 - 8	8 - 10
760 (4)	6 - 8	8 - 10
Gottschalk, Dreyfus and Davis 216 (12)	8 - 9	9 - 10
International Art Co.		
51646 (8)	8 - 9	9 - 10
S/Clapsaddle, 16208 (4)	7 - 8	8 - 10
16209 (4)	7 - 8	8 - 9
Uns./Clapsaddle 16250 (6)	6 - 7	7 - 8
S/Clapsaddle 51896 (6)	7 - 8	8 - 9

Anonymous Mother's Day Card
"To Mother: The sweetest flowers are not as fragrant as ..."

S/Veenfliet 51766 (6)	8 - 9	9 - 10
L & E, S/H.B.G. 2242 (8)	10 - 12	12 - 15
Lounsbury 2020 (4)	10 - 12	12 - 15
E. Nash		
1 (6)	6 - 7	7 - 8
2 (6)	6 - 7	7 - 8
4 (6)	6 - 7	7 - 8
W5, W6, W7 (4)	5 - 6	6 - 7
W9 (4)	5 - 6	6 - 7
W11 (4)	5 - 6	6 - 8
W14 (4)	5 - 6	6 - 7
W15 (4)	6 - 7	7 - 8
H.I. Robbins 329 (8)	6 - 8	8 - 10
P. Sander 414 (6)	6 - 8	8 - 10
M.W. Taggart, NY 605 (6)	6 - 8	8 - 10
Raphael Tuck Series 124 (6)	6 - 8	8 - 10
156 (6)	6 - 8	8 - 10
171 (6)	6 - 8	8 - 10
178 (10)	6 - 8	8 - 10

DECORATION DAY/MEMORIAL DAY

Raphael Tuck Series 107 (12)	8 - 10	10 - 12
158 (12)	8 - 10	10 - 12
173 (12)	12 - 15	15 - 18
179 (12)	12 - 15	15 - 18
Nash		
Series 1 (6)	6 - 8	8 - 10
Series 2 (6)	6 - 8	8 - 10

Series 3 (6)	6 - 8	8 - 10
Series D4 (6)	6 - 8	8 - 10
Series 6 (6)	10 - 12	12 - 15
Series 21 (6)	8 - 10	10 - 12
Illustrated P.C. Company Series 151 (8)	6 - 8	8 - 10
Int. Art Co.		
S/Chapman Series 6 (6)	6 - 8	8 - 10
S/Clapsaddle Series 6 (6)	8 - 10	10 - 12
S/Clapsaddle 973 (6)	6 - 8	8 - 10
S/Clapsaddle 2444 (6)	7 - 8	8 - 10
S/Clapsaddle 2935 (6)	8 - 10	10 - 12
S/Clapsaddle 4397 (6)	6 - 8	8 - 10
Lounsbury, S/Bunnell		
Series 2083 (4)	10 - 12	12 - 15
A.S.B. Series 283 (6)	5 - 6	6 - 8
Conwell Series 376-381 (6)	5 - 6	6 - 8
S. Gabriel Series 150 (6)	6 - 8	8 - 10
Santway Series 157 (6)	8 - 10	10 - 12
Taggert Series 602 and 603 (6 each)	6 - 8	8 - 10
Anonymous Series No. 1	5 - 6	6 - 8
Others	4 - 5	5 - 6

Decoration Day Series No. 1
"Fraternity, Loyalty and Charity"

P. Sander Co.
George Washington

Int. Art Pub. Co., No. 51646
"I send you patriotic Greetings ..."

CONFEDERATE MEMORIAL DAY

R. Tuck's "Confederate" Series
Divided Backs (12)

"For though Conquered ..."	10 - 15	15 - 18
"Furl that Banner!"	10 - 15	15 - 18
General Joseph E. Johnson	15 - 18	18 - 22
General Robert E. Lee	20 - 25	25 - 28
General Stonewall Jackson	20 - 25	25 - 28
Headquarters, Army of N. Virginia	10 - 15	15 - 18
"In Memoriam ..." 2 flags	10 - 15	15 - 18
"In Memoriam ..." 3 flags	10 - 15	15 - 18
"The Hands that grasped ..." 4 flags	10 - 15	15 - 18
"The Warriors Banner takes its Flight"	10 - 15	15 - 18
"Twill live in Song and Story ..."	10 - 15	15 - 18
"United Daughters Confederacy ..."	10 - 15	15 - 18

R. Tuck's "Heroes of the South"

Series 2510	18 - 20	22 - 30

Souvenir P.C. Co.

With "Bee Brand" (6)	10 - 12	12 - 15

Jamestown A & V Co.

Jamestown Expo Cards (11)	30 - 40	40 - 45

Veteran Art Co.

"National Souvenir" Set	8 - 10	10 - 12
Winsch-back, No Publisher	10 - 12	12 - 15
Two Southern Generals Card	12 - 15	15 - 18

ABRAHAM LINCOLN'S BIRTHDAY

Anglo American (AA)		
Open Book Series 726 (6)	20 - 25	25 - 30
Series 727 (6)	20 - 25	25 - 30
Century Co.		
Sepia Series (6)	8 - 10	10 - 12
Int. Art Pub. Co. Series 51658 (6)	8 - 10	10 - 12
Lincoln/Contrabands (1)	10 - 12	12 - 15
Lounsbury Centennial (4)	8 - 10	10 - 12
Nash		
Series 1 (6)	7 - 8	8 - 10
Gold or Silver 2 (6)	7 - 8	8 - 10
P.F.B. Series 9463	10 - 12	12 - 15
P. Sander Series 415 (6)	7 - 8	8 - 10
Sheehan, M.A. Series (18)	7 - 8	8 - 10
Raphael Tuck Series 155 (6)	10 - 12	12 - 14

FOURTH OF JULY

Common	2 - 3	3 - 4
With Children, Ladies	5 - 6	6 - 8

Int. Art No. 51658
A. Lincoln, "Sword and Pen"

P.F.B., Series 9463
A. Lincoln, "In Memory ..."

With Uncle Sam (See Uncle Sam below)		
Jules Bien Series 700 (6)	8 - 10	10 - 12
Conwell Series 380 (6)	6 - 8	8 - 10
S. Garre Series 51668 (6)		
S/Chapman	8 - 10	10 - 12
Gottschalk, Dreyfus & Davis		
Series 2172, 2099 (6)	8 - 10	10 - 12
Int. Art Pub Co. S/Clapsaddle		
Series 974 (6)	8 - 10	10 - 15
Series 2443 (6)	8 - 10	10 - 15
Series 2936 (6)	8 - 10	10 - 15
Series 4398 (6)	8 - 10	10 - 15
S/Chapman -- Series 51668 (6)	8 - 10	10 - 12
Fred C. Lounsbury S/Bunnell		
Series 2076 (6)	8 - 10	10 - 12
Uncle Sam Series (4)	12 - 15	15 - 18
Nash Comic Series 1 (6)	6 - 8	8 - 10

     1 "How to prevent your boy..."
     2 "Ye Spit-Devil is a wily..."
     3 "The Giant Cracker..."
     4 "Photograph your boy..."
     5 "Where ignorance is bliss"
     6 "The Dog ..."

Series 4, 5 (6)	7 - 8	8 - 9
Series J6 (6)	6 - 7	7 - 8
Series J8 (6)	8 - 10	10 - 12
With Uncle Sam	15 - 18	18 - 22
P.F.B.		
Series 8252 (6)	12 - 15	15 - 18
Series 9507 (6) S/Bunnell	15 - 18	18 - 22
Rotograph Co. S/Gene Carr		
Series 219 (6)	7 - 8	8 - 10
P. Sander Series 440 (6)	8 - 10	10 - 12
Steiner Series 129 (6)	6 - 7	7 - 8
Tower Series 106 (6)	4 - 5	5 - 6
R. Tuck Series 109, 159 (12)	6 - 7	7 - 9
Ullman Co. Series 124 (6)	6 - 8	8 - 10
Wolf S/Clapsaddle, Uns./Clapsaddle		
Add $2-3 per card to **Int. Art Pub. Co.** prices.		
Anonymous		
Series 312, 752	6 - 8	8 - 10

FLAG OF THE U.S.

Jules Bien Series 710, 716	5 - 6	6 - 8

Anonymous
"July 4"

Anonymous, 752
"Fourth of July Greetings"

Ill. P.C. Co. Series 207	5 - 6	6 - 7
Souvenir P.C. Co.	4 - 5	5 - 7

HALLOWEEN

AUBURN POSTCARD CO.

S/Weaver	8 - 10	10 - 12
Unsigned	6 - 8	8 - 10

AA (Anglo American)

Witch Series (6)	12 - 15	15 - 18
AMP CO.	10 - 12	12 - 15
B.B., LONDON (Birn Bros.)	12 - 15	15 - 18
BANKS, E.C.	12 - 15	15 - 18
BERGMAN CO.	8 - 10	10 - 12
A.C. BOSSELMAN	12 - 15	15 - 18
JULES BIEN & CO.	12 - 15	15 - 18
R.L. CONWELL CO.	10 - 12	12 - 15
A.M. DAVIS	8 - 10	10 - 12
FAIRMAN CO.	10 - 12	12 - 15

SAM GABRIEL or GABRIEL & SONS

Series 120, 121, S/Brundage	15 - 18	18 - 20
Series 122, 124	12 - 15	15 - 18
Series 123, 125, S/Brundage	15 - 18	18 - 25

GIBSON ART

S/Kathryn Elliott, Sepia (10)	8 - 10	10 - 12
S/Bernhardt Wall, Sepia (12)	8 - 10	10 - 12
Others	6 - 8	8 - 10

GOTTSCHALK, DREYFUSS & DAVIS

Series 2010A, 2097, 2171	12 - 15	15 - 18
Series 2243, 2279		

INTERNATIONAL ART MFG. CO.

No No. S/Clapsaddle (12)	15 - 18	18 - 22
Series 501 S/Clapsaddle (4)	15 - 20	20 - 25
Series 978 S/Clapsaddle (6)	15 - 18	18 - 22
Series 1002 S/Aleinmuller (6)	12 - 15	15 - 18
Series 1236 Mechanicals (4)		
White Children	175 - 200	200 - 225
Black Child	300 - 350	350 - 400
Series 1237, 1238 S/Clapsaddle (4)	15 - 18	18 - 22
Series 1301 S/Clapsaddle (12)	12 - 15	15 - 18
Series 1393 S/Clapsaddle (6)	12 - 15	15 - 18
Series 1667 S/Clapsaddle (12)	12 - 15	15 - 18
Series 1815 Unsigned (6)	10 - 12	12 - 15
Series 4439 S/Clapsaddle (6)	12 - 15	15 - 18
No No. S/Berhnardt Wall (12)	10 - 12	12 - 15
S/A.L. JACKSON	18 - 20	20 - 22

L & E

Series 2214, 2215 (6) S/HBG	15 - 18	18 - 22
Series 2216	20 - 25	25 - 28

Raphael Tuck & Sons
"Hallowe'en" Series No. 174

Stecher Series 216-C
"Hallowe'en"

R.Tuck, "Hallowe'en" Series 188
"Good Gracious, Witch ..."

Series E2231, 2262 (12) S/HBG	14 - 16	16 - 20
Unsigned	12 - 14	14 - 16
S/R.H. LORD	10 - 12	12 - 15
FRED LOUNSBURY CO.		
Series 2052 (6)	15 - 18	18 - 20
C. MARKS		
S/Dwig (12)	22 - 25	25 - 28
E. NASH		
Series 1, 2, 3, 4, and 5		
Series H-6 through H-46, H-426, H-430	12 - 15	15 - 20
F.A. OWEN	6 - 8	8 - 10
S/OUTCAULT Buster Brown Calendar	20 - 25	25 - 30
P.F.B. (Paul Finkenrath, Berlin)		
Series 9422	18 - 20	20 - 25
G.K. PRINCE		
Series 421 S/M.M.S.	10 - 12	12 - 15
SAS CO.	10 - 12	12 - 15
SB	10 - 12	12 - 14
SAMSON BROS.	10 - 12	12 - 15
P. SANDER	8 - 10	10 - 12
S/A.B.C. SANFORD	8 - 10	10 - 12
STECHER LITHO CO.		
Series 226	15 - 18	18 - 22

S/M.E.P. (Margaret E. Price)	15 - 18	18 - 22
Others	12 - 15	15 - 18
T.P. & CO.	6 - 8	8 - 10
M.W. TAGGART		
Series 803, 806 (6)	10 - 12	12 - 14
TAYLOR ART	15 - 18	18 - 20
TOWER CO.	6 - 8	8 - 10
RAPHAEL TUCK		
Series 100 Uns/Schmucker	80 - 90	90 - 100
Series 150, 160 (12)	15 - 18	18 - 20
Series 184 Uns/Brundage (12)	18 - 20	20 - 22
Series 181 (10) S/C.B.T.	12 - 14	14 - 16
Series 174, 183, 190, 197, 803	10 - 12	12 - 15
Series 188	15 - 18	18 - 22
Series 807 Uns/Wiederseim (6)	30 - 35	35 - 40
ULLMAN MFG. CO.		
S/Bernhardt Wall	8 - 10	10 - 12
VALENTINE & SONS	12 - 15	15 - 18
P.F. VOLLAND & CO.	15 - 18	18 - 22
S/E. WEAVER, Series 2335	6 - 8	8 - 10
GEORGE C. WHITNEY	12 - 15	15 - 18
Stand-up, S/Schmucker (See Schmucker)	100 - 110	110 - 125
JOHN WINSCH, COPYRIGHT		
1911, 1912, 1913 Copyright (See Schmucker)		
1912 German, Unsigned (6)	60 - 75	75 - 90
German, smaller variations	90 - 100	100 - 140
1913 German, Unsigned	60 - 80	80 - 90
Smaller variations	60 - 70	70 - 80
1914, Copyright, Children, Uns./J. Freixas	70 - 80	80 - 90
Variations	70 - 80	80 - 90
1914, Copyright Unsigned Witches, owls	65 - 75	75 - 95
Variations	50 - 60	60 - 70
1915, Copyright, Children, Uns./Freixas		
and other artists	100 - 120	120 - 140
Black Checkered Border, no copyright		
Uns./Freixas	70 - 80	80 - 90
Orange Border, Children, no copyright	100 - 125	125 - 150
Series 4975, No copyright, cats,		
goblins (4)	50 - 60	60 - 70
H.L. WOHLER	8 - 10	10 - 12

A great checklist-price list, *"Winsch Hallowe'en Post Card Check List"* (including Schmucker cards) is available from **Hazel Leler,** 12327 Windjammer, Houston, TX 77072-3241. It is 27 pages, fully illustrated, revised April, 1994, and priced at $9.98 postpaid.

THANKSGIVING

Common	0.50 - 1	1 - 1.50
W/Turkeys	1 - 1.50	1.50 - 2
W/Children, Ladies, etc.	2 - 3	3 - 5
A.S.B. Series 282, 290 (6)	0.50 - 1	1 - 3
AA (Anglo American) Series 875	0.50 - 1	1 - 3
B.B. London 2700, 2701 (6)	1 - 2	2 - 4
Conwell Series 637 (6)	0.50 - 1	1 - 2
Sam Gabriel S/Brundage		
Series 130, 132, 133 (10)	8 - 12	12 - 15
Series 135 (6)	8 - 10	10 - 12
Others	0.50 - 1	1 - 2
Ill. P.C. Co.	0.50 - 1	1 - 2
International Art. Pub. Co.		
S/Ellen H. Clapsaddle		
Series 1311, 1660, 1817	5 - 6	6 - 9
Series 2445, 4154, 4440, 51670	6 - 8	8 - 10
W/Children	5 - 6	6 - 9
W/Pilgrims, Turkeys, Corn	3 - 4	4 - 5
Others	1 - 2	2 - 3
L. & E. S/H.B.G.		
Series 2212, 2213, 2233	6 - 8	8 - 10
Series 2263, 2273 (6)	6 - 8	8 - 10
P.F.B.		
Series 8429, 8857 (6)	6 - 7	7 - 8
Taggart		
Blacks (6)	8 - 9	9 - 10
Others	2 - 3	3 - 5
Raphael Tuck (American)		
Series 101	2 - 3	3 - 4
Whitney	5 - 6	6 - 8
Winsch, Copyright		
Common	1 - 1.50	1.50 - 2
Indians	3 - 4	4 - 6
Ladies	5 - 7	7 - 10
Wolf S/Clapsaddle, Uns./Clapsaddle		

Add $2-3 per card to **Int. Art Pub. Co.** prices.

LABOR DAY

Lounsbury Series 2046 (4)	250 - 275	275 - 325
"Our Latest Holiday"	325 - 375	375 - 425
Nash Labor Day Series 1	80 - 100	100 - 120
1 "Service Shall With Steeled ..."		
2 "Labor Conquers Everything"		

CHRISTMAS

Common	0.50 - 1	1 - 2
W/Children, Animals	2 - 3	3 - 4
W/Children, w/Toys	4 - 5	5 - 7
Small Santas, Red Suit	4 - 5	5 - 6
Large Santas, Red Suit	6 - 9	9 - 12
Lady Santa	10 - 20	20 - 40
Sam Gabriel		
S/Frances Brundage		
Series 200, 208, 219 (10)	10 - 12	12 - 15
Santa	15 - 18	18 - 22
International Art Pub. Co. S/Clapsaddle		
Children	7 - 9	9 - 12
Wolf S/Clapsaddle	10 - 12	12 - 15
P.F.B.		
Series 7143 Boy/Girl (6)	7 - 8	8 - 10
Series 7422 Children/Tree (6)	10 - 12	12 - 14
Raphael Tuck (American)		
"Playtime" Series 550 (10)		
"A Christmas Message" Series (10)		
"Holly Landscape" Series (10)		
"Glad Christmas" Series (10)		
"Christmas Greetings" Series 555 (10)		
(Identical to New Year Series 620)		
"Long Ago Children" Series (10)		
"Joys of Youth" Series (10)		
"Christmas Poinsettia" Series 558		
"Muff Kiddies" Series 559		
"Christmas Symbols" Series 560		
S/E. von H. (Evelyn Von Hartmann)		
Winsch, Copyright		
Common	1 - 1.50	1.50 - 2
W/Children	4 - 5	5 - 7
W/Ladies	8 - 10	10 - 12
W/Silk Inserts, Common	3 - 5	5 - 7
W/Silk Ladies	12 - 15	15 - 20
Booklets, Common	3 - 5	5 - 7
Booklets W/Ladies	5 - 7	7 - 10
Copyright, 1913 (4) (Non-Schmucker)	18 - 22	22 - 25
Copyright, 1914 (4) (Non-Schmucker)		

SANTA CLAUS (See Santas)

KRAMPUS (See Santas)

John Winsch, Copyright 1911
"A Peaceful Thanksgiving"

Whitney Made, Worcester, Mass.
"Thanksgiving"

UNCLE SAM

Common	6 - 7	7 - 9
Better Publishers	10 - 12	12 - 18
Franz Huld Installment Set	20 - 22	22 - 25
See Fourth of July		
Uncle Sam Santa (See Santas)		

YEAR DATES

1894-1895	75 - 85	85 - 100
1896	50 - 60	60 - 75
1897	40 - 50	50 - 65
1898	35 - 40	40 - 50
1899	30 - 35	35 - 45
1900 Common	20 - 25	25 - 30
W/Animals, People	25 - 30	30 - 35
Hold-To-Light	50 - 55	55 - 65
1901 Common	15 - 20	20 - 25
W/Animals, People	20 - 25	25 - 28
Hold-To-Light	50 - 55	55 - 65
1902 Common	10 - 12	12 - 15
W/Animals, People	15 - 18	18 - 22
Hold-To-Light	30 - 35	35 - 40

Nash Labor Day Series 1
"Service shall with steel and ..."

Nash Labor Day Series 1
"Labor conquers everything"

1903 Common	8 - 10	10 - 12
W/Animals, People	10 - 12	12 - 15
Hold-To-Light	25 - 30	30 - 35
1904 Common	7 - 9	9 - 12
W/Animals, People	9 - 12	12 - 14
Hold-To-Light	22 - 25	25 - 28
1905 Common	5 - 6	6 - 8
W/Animals, People	6 - 8	8 - 10
Hold-To-Light	20 - 22	22 - 25
1906-1911 Common	4 - 5	5 - 6
W/Animals, People	6 - 7	7 - 8
1912-1914 Common	8 - 10	10 - 12
W/Animals, People	12 - 14	14 - 16
1915-1918 Common	10 - 12	12 - 14
W/Animals, People	12 - 14	14 - 16
1919-1925	20 - 25	25 - 30
1926-1930	25 - 28	28 - 32

RELIGIOUS, VIRTUES, ETC.

CHILD'S PRAYER

Cunningham (6)	8 - 10	10 - 12
Geo. F. Holbrook (4)	10 - 12	12 - 15

Christmas Fantasy
Anonymous No. 53

Signed P.E. (Pauli Ebner)
P.P., German Greeting

George F. Holbrook, 1909
"I Pray the Lord my Soul to Keep"

A.S.B. Series 350
"Hallowed be thy Name!"

Signed F.B. (Fritz Baumgarten)
M.B. No. 3312

GUARDIAN ANGEL

A.S.B. Series 250 (4)	8 - 10	10 - 12
Mark Emege Series 178 (4)	8 - 10	10 - 12
Birn Bros. Series 2109 (4)	7 - 8	8 - 10
PFB		
Series 8618, 8621 (4)	10 - 12	12 - 15

THE HOLY SCRIPTURE

S/Leinweber, Old Testament	4 - 5	5 - 6

LORD'S PRAYER

A.S.B. Series 264, 350 (8)	5 - 7	7 - 8
DB Series 350 (8)	6 - 8	8 - 10
I.S. Co. Series (8)	6 - 7	7 - 8
PFB Series 7064-7070, Series 8415 (8)	10 - 12	12 - 15
Unknown Publisher		
Series N-700 G (8)	6 - 8	8 - 10

TEN COMMANDMENTS

PFB Series 163, 8554 (10)	8 - 10	10 - 12
Taggart Series (10)	8 - 10	10 - 12
Rose Series (10)	10 - 12	12 - 15
R. Tuck Series 163 (10)	8 - 10	10 - 12

VIRTUES - FAITH, HOPE, CHARITY

A.S.B. Series 178 (6)	6 - 8	8 - 10
E.A.S. Series	7 - 8	8 - 12
G.B. Series (6)	8 - 10	10 - 12
Langsdorf Series	7 - 9	9 - 12
PFB Series 8797, 8798	10 - 12	12 - 14
Rotograph P.96	5 - 6	6 - 7

Krampus.

KRAMPUS ... *was the impish devil, with one cloven hoof, who traveled with St. Nicholas as he distributed toys and gifts to children at Christmas. He was good to the children who had been good, but those who had been bad quickly scurried away.*

Krampus chased them, and when they were caught he put them in the bucket or basket on his back. Usually, he punished them with his bundle of switches. The crying children were later released after promising to be good during the next year.

He was very suave and debonair around the pretty ladies, and many cards imply that they liked his advances. However, to the older and ugly ladies he was very mean and usually threw them into the burning flames.

8
Sets & Series

Whether there were two, six, or fifty, early publishers saw the great benefit of producing cards in sets or series. They commissioned artists and photographers to submit their works in series and package them to appeal to the customers. This method, as history has proven, turned out to be a good merchandising scheme, and greatly enhanced the interest and collectibility of postcards at that time, as well as today.

Collectors have been known to pay double or triple value for that last elusive card. *What a thrill it is to finally find the sixth and final card to complete the set!*

Because of the comprehensive listings in this price guide, this section lists only a small number of the more important sets and series. Over 1700 others are listed in other sections, either under artist or motif.

PUBLISHER SETS & SERIES

	VG	EX
Acmegraph Co. "Lovelights" (20)	3 - 4	4 - 5
American Colortype, 1909		
"American Beauty" Series 12	6 - 8	8 - 10
American Historical Art Co.		
"Colonial Heroes" (40)	5 - 6	6 - 8
American Souvenir Co.		
"Patriographics" Views 15 sets of 12 each	8 - 10	10 - 12
Boston Series	12 - 15	15 - 18

Austin "Famous American" Series (12)		
Theodore Roosevelt	10 - 12	12 - 14
Mark Twain	6 - 8	8 - 10
Robert Perry	6 - 8	8 - 10
George Dewey	6 - 8	8 - 10
John G. Whittier	6 - 8	8 - 10
U.S. Grant	10 - 12	12 - 15
Robert E. Lee	12 - 15	15 - 18
John Philip Sousa	6 - 8	8 - 10
Luther Burbank	6 - 8	8 - 10
Benjamin Franklin	6 - 8	8 - 10
Andrew Carnegie	6 - 8	8 - 10
George Washington	10 - 12	12 - 14
Austin "Tours of the World" (100)	0.25 - 0.50	0.50 - 1
A. Bauman "Homely Girl" Series (6)	5 - 6	6 - 8
Bergman "College Girls"	8 - 10	10 - 12
Cunningham College Girls	6 - 8	8 - 10
Donaldson, H.M.		
"American Heroes" (13)	10 - 12	12 - 15
David Farragut		
Sam Houston		
Andrew Jackson		

Donaldson's Heroes
Bamforth Co., "Israel Putnam"

Raphael Tuck's State Belles
"Montana"

John Paul Jones
Gen. Robert E. Lee*
Abraham Lincoln
William Penn
Oliver H. Perry
Israel Putnam
Paul Revere
Winfield Scott
Philip Sheridan*
Capt. John Smith
George Washington
*Add $8 for Lee and $5 for Sheridan.

Ferloni, L.

"Ferloni Popes" 1903	5 - 6	6 - 8

P. Gordon, 1908 Ladies (10)

Golf Girl, Tennis Girl	15 - 18	18 - 22
Others	6 - 8	8 - 10
Grollman, I. "Merry Widow Hat" Series (16)	4 - 5	5 - 6
Hill University Girls, Series 8	6 - 8	8 - 10

Hillson, D., 1907

American Beauty Series (Red) (23)	6 - 8	8 - 10

      The Auto Girl
      The Broadway
      The College Widow
      The Debutante
      The Girl from Golden West
      Golf Girl
      Hello Girl
      Lady of the Lake
      Lady of the Wind
      The Matinee Girl
      My Coy Maiden
      My Lady Fair
      A Society Bud
      My Southern Rose
      Naughty
      Queen of Sports
      "Smile"
      Stingy
      Sweet Sixteen

College Girls, Ivy League	10 - 12	12 - 15

Kober, P.C. (PCK)

Butterflies with Views in Wings	15 - 18	18 - 22
"Diabolo" S/Hutaf	10 - 12	12 - 14
Pansies with Views in Petals	12 - 15	15 - 18

Koehler, J. "Hold-To-Light" Series

New York City (24)	30 - 35	35 - 40
Coney Island (12)	35 - 40	40 - 45
"Fighting the Flames"	1500 - 1750	1750 - 2000

Washington, D.C. (12)	25 - 28	28 - 32
Hudson River (12)	25 - 28	28 - 32
Philadelphia (12)	30 - 32	32 - 35
Boston (12)	30 - 32	32 - 35
Chicago (12)	30 - 35	35 - 40
Atlantic City (6)	32 - 35	35 - 40
Buffalo (6)	30 - 32	32 - 35
Niagara Falls (6)	22 - 25	25 - 30

K.V.i.B. National Flag Series

Woman in Flag Dress Series 80 200+	6 - 8	8 - 10

Langsdorf, S. & Co.

Alligator Borders (165)		
Blacks	35 - 40	40 - 45
Views	25 - 30	30 - 35
Shell Border Views	10 - 15	15 - 20
State Capitals	8 - 10	10 - 12
State Girls (30)	12 - 15	15 - 18
Embossed	15 - 18	18 - 22
Puzzles	30 - 35	35 - 40
Silk Applique	35 - 40	40 - 45
Military Series	10 - 12	12 - 15

Hugh Leighton & Co.

Bathing Beauties Series (12)	6 - 8	8 - 10

B.B. London

Playing Cards Series E47 (6)	4 - 5	5 - 6

Fred C. Lounsbury, 1908 National Girls (4)

The American Girl	12 - 14	14 - 16
Others	6 - 8	8 - 10

Illustrated Postal Card Company, State Capitals
State House, Boston, Mass.

Oliver Wendell Holmes
Winsch Famous Authors' Series

Harry Payne, Raphael Tuck
Series 4 - 9139, "Military Life"

E. Nash Months of the Year, Series 37 (12)	6 - 8	8 - 10
National Art Co.		
National Girls	6 - 8	8 - 10
State Girls (46)	6 - 7	7 - 8
P.F.B. (Paul Finkenrath, Berlin)		
Series 5563 Girl and Cat (6)	6 - 8	8 - 10
Series 5897 Mother-in-Law (6)	8 - 10	10 - 12
Series 6307 Comic Lovers (6)	6 - 8	8 - 10
Series 9327 "Diabolo" 6)	10 - 12	12 - 15
Series 6538 "Domestic Squabbles" (6)	8 - 10	10 - 12
Series 6800 Children and Roosters (6)	8 - 10	10 - 12
Series 6943 "Children's Games ..." (6)	8 - 10	10 - 12
Series 6949 Bride & Groom (6)	8 - 10	10 - 12
Series 7185 Cupids & Large Hearts (6)	8 - 10	10 - 12
Series 7318 Children in Vehicles (6)	10 - 12	12 - 14
Series 8120 Nymph and Shell (6)	10 - 12	12 - 15
Series 8180 Two Mischievous Boys (6)	8 - 10	10 - 12
Series 8403 Dressed Rooster or Hen (6)	10 - 12	12 - 15
Platinachrome Co.		
National Girls (23)	8 - 10	10 - 12
State Girls (45)	5 - 7	7 - 8
Charles Rose, 1908		
Rose Song Cards (24)	6 - 8	8 - 10
"Maids" Series	5 - 6	6 - 8

"The Cake Walk"

"Jolly Comrades"

"Belle of the Ball"

"A Gallant"

"Music Hath Charms"

"Harlequin and ..."

"At the Carnival," Postcard Series No. 117 by Raphael Tuck
With Advertising Overprint of the 1909 Portola Festival

Rotograph College Girls Series FL100 (6)   8 - 10   10 - 12
Samson Brothers
    Series 86 "Vegetables" (12)   3 - 4   4 - 6
    "Uneedn't" (12)   3 - 4   4 - 6
Souvenir Post Card Co., 1905
    College Girl Series 4 (6)   6 - 8   8 - 10
Raphael Tuck
    Series 117 "At the Carnival" (6)   15 - 18   18 - 22
        "Belle of the Ball"
        "A Gallant"
        "Harlequin and Columbine"
        "Jolly Comrades"
        "Music Hath Charms"
        "The Cake Walk"

"Characters from Dickens" S/Kyd
Series 540, 541, 856, 5441 (6)	10 - 12	12 - 14
College Girls "Football," Series 2344 (6)	10 - 12	12 - 15
"Diabolo," Series 102, Uns./Brundage (6)	10 - 12	12 - 15
"Greetings from the Seaside," Series 116 (12)	5 - 7	7 - 8
Heraldic Series, 3308-3331 (24)	16 - 18	18 - 22

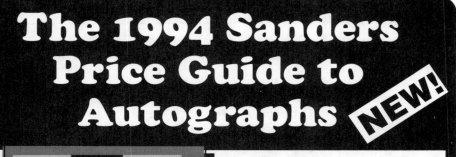
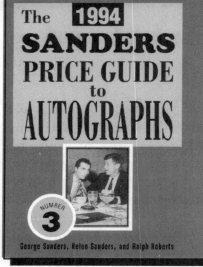
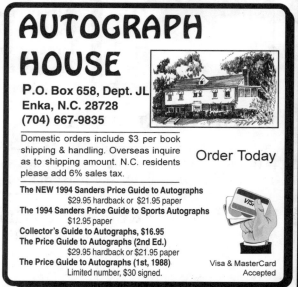

G
Advertising

The tiny advertising trade card was introduced in the early 1870's to increase business for manufacturers. Salesmen carried them to be distributed by local merchants who then gave them to customers as a means of advertising and glorifying products and services. This method worked wonders, and greatly enhanced the sales of many products.

The success of the trade card prompted the start of the letter, or cover, advertising. and millions were sent through the mail. The cost of three cents for mailing the letter was deemed rather high by businessmen, and thus came the advent of the now famous advertising postcard.

The postcard, as an advertising medium, began in 1893 when cards were printed for vendors at the Colombian Exposition in Chicago. Those visiting the Exposition purchased these cards and sent them back home to friends as proof of their attendance at the gala event. Most of the cards issued showed buildings of the Expo. However, there were many issues by the exhibitors showing their products and telling of their services.

This first special trial was extremely successful and prompted manufacturers and service orientated businesses throughout the U.S. to "jump on the bandwagon." The great acceptance by the public and the reduced postage rates for postcards made the difference.

Millions of advertising postcards, both color and black and white, were printed and mailed during the first year alone. Advertisers either mailed their own cards or gave them to customers to distribute.

High competition in all modes of product manufacturing and services prompted advertisers and merchants to publish high quality and beautiful sets and series by the artists of the day. As can be seen from the following listings, some of the companies are still in business and this alone makes them more collectible. The beauty and elusiveness of many of these cards have played a major role in making advertising postcards one of the favorites by many in the hobby.

ADVERTISING

	VG	EX
A.B.A. Travelers' Cheques	$ 6 - 8	$ 8 - 10
Absorbine Pain Killer	6 - 8	8 - 10
Albert Hosiery Co. (12)	6 - 8	8 - 10
Alexander, M.H. Co., Molasses	6 - 8	8 - 10
Allentown Adpostals (7)	35 - 40	40 - 45
American Enamel Co., 1906	5 - 6	6 - 7
American Journal Examiner Comics, by many artists	8 - 10	10 - 12

A.B.A. Travelers' Cheques, No. 3921

American Fence Co.	4 - 5	5 - 6
American Lady Corsets	6 - 7	7 - 8
American Motor Co. (B&W)		
Motor Cycle Ad w/Miles per gallon	30 - 35	35 - 40
American Thermos Bottles (10)	5 - 6	6 - 7
American Woolen Co.	6 - 8	8 - 10
Anheuser-Busch Brewing Co.(Western)	6 - 8	8 - 10
Anheuser-Busch Brewery Scenes	6 - 8	8 - 10
Anheuser-Busch Beer Wagon/Horses	8 - 10	10 - 12
Argand Stoves	5 - 6	6 - 8
Armour & Co. American Girl Series (12)		
German Publisher, (B&W)		
The Karl Anderson Girl	12 - 15	15 - 18
The Walter A. Clark Girl	12 - 15	15 - 18
The John C. Clay Girl	12 - 15	15 - 18
The Howard C. Christy Girl	15 - 20	20 - 25
The Harrison Fisher Girl	40 - 45	45 - 50
The C. Allen Gilbert Girl	15 - 20	20 - 25
The Henry Hutt Girl	15 - 20	20 - 25
The Hamilton King Girl	15 - 20	20 - 25
The F. S. Manning Girl	10 - 12	12 - 15
The Thomas M. Pierce Girl	10 - 12	12 - 15
The W. T. Smedley Girl	10 - 12	12 - 15
The G. G. Wiederseim Girl	30 - 35	35 - 40
Armour Star - "The Ham What Am"	6 - 7	7 - 8

The Albertype Company, View Post Cards of Quality

Arbuckle Coffee	5 - 6	7 - 8
Do-Wa-Jack Paintings, S/Souler	12 - 15	15 - 18
Asbestos Sad Irons	6 - 8	8 - 10
5 A Horse Blankets	12 - 15	15 - 18

    "Athol"   "Bouncer"
    "Briar"   "Buster"
    "Essex"   "Fashion"
    "Myrtle"   "Paris Faun"
    "Stratton"   "Plush Robe" 1300
    "Plush Robe" 1652
    "Plush Robe" 1853
    Promotional Cards

"Great For Wear"	15 - 18	18 - 22
"They Make Philadelphia Famous"	15 - 18	18 - 22
Bacardi Rum	10 - 15	15 - 18
Bakers Chocolate	6 - 7	7 - 8
Bear Brand Hosiery	6 - 8	8 - 9
Bell Telephone (12)	15 - 18	18 - 22

    R1 "Announces Unexpected Guests"
    R2 "The Convenience of Marketing"
    R3 "Keeps the Traveler in Touch"
    R4 "Into the Heart of Shopping District"
    R5 "When Servants Fail You"
    R6 "The Social Call"
    R7 "A Doctor Quick"
    R8 "Guards the Home"
    R9 "In Household Emergencies"
    R10 "Relieves Anxieties"

Blue Label Ketchup, Allentown Adpostal Company

The Denver Zephyrs
"Chicago ... Denver"

Cracker Jack Bears No. 4
"Hurray for Liberty"

Burlington Zephyr
"America's First Diesel ..."

R11 "Gives Instant Alarms"		
R12 "When the Elements are Against You"		
Ben-Hur Book	4 - 5	5 - 6
Ben-Hur Flour	6 - 7	7 - 8
Ben-Hur (Sears-Roebuck)	4 - 5	5 - 6
Bensdorp's Royal Dutch Cocoa (Dutch Life)	4 - 5	5 - 6
Costumed Children Series	10 - 12	12 - 15
Benjamin Suits	4 - 5	5 - 6
Berry Brothers Varnishes (18)	10 - 12	12 - 15
Bester Dairy Appliances	5 - 6	6 - 8
Bismark Beer	8 - 10	10 - 12
Blatchford Calf Meal Co.	4 - 5	5 - 6
Blatz Beer (S/Drayton)	70 - 80	80 - 90
Borden's (Elsie Says)	5 - 6	6 - 7
Boston Rubber Shoe Co. (10)	3 - 4	4 - 5
Boy's Newspaper	3 - 4	4 - 5
Brockton Shoe Industry	5 - 6	6 - 7
Brodrick Buggies	8 - 10	10 - 12
Brown's Bronchial Trochs	3 - 4	4 - 5
Brown Shoes		
Buster Brown, S/Outcault (12)	10 - 12	12 - 15
Buchan's Soap (6)		
White Bears and Children	10 - 12	12 - 15

Buckbee's Seeds (6)	2 - 3	3 - 4
Buchan's Soaps (6) W/White Bears	10 - 12	12 - 14
Budweiser Anheuser-Busch Beer Wagon (2)	10 - 12	12 - 15
Budweiser Barley Malt Syrup	12 - 15	15 - 18
Budweiser Beer (early)	12 - 15	15 - 18
Budweiser Yeast	8 - 10	10 - 12
Buffalo Bill's Wild West (6)	15 - 18	18 - 22
Bull Durham, S/Outcault (33 Countries)	60 - 70	70 - 80
Bulte's Best Flour (6) Kids	6 - 8	8 - 10

    1. "Bulte's Best"
    2 "Homeward Bound ..."
    3 "Into the Oven ..."
    4 "Of All the Flour ..."
    5 "Out Piping Hot ..."
    6 "Patty Cake"

Burke's Medicine	5 - 6	6 - 8
Burke's Whiskey	6 - 8	8 - 10
Burlington Zephyr (Train)	15 - 18	18 - 22
Busch Extra Dry Ginger Ale	20 - 25	25 - 30
Calumet Powder	4 - 5	5 - 6
Calumet Baking Powder, S/Outcault	10 - 12	12 - 15
Campbell Soup, (10 Cents a can) -- 24	100 - 120	120 - 150
Uns. G. Wiederseim, large image (4)	30 - 35	35 - 40
Other Wiederseim, w/jingles (12)	50 - 55	55 - 60
Carnation Milk	6 - 8	8 - 10
Carnation Milk (A.Y.P. Expo)	8 - 10	10 - 12
Carswell Horse Shoe Nails	5 - 6	6 - 8
Canadian Club Whiskey	8 - 10	10 - 12
Candee Rubber Co. (Comics)	5 - 6	6 - 8
Case Steam Engines	8 - 10	10 - 12
Case Threshing Machines	8 - 10	10 - 12
Cauchois' Fulton Mills Coffee	5 - 6	6 - 8
Chase & Sanborn Co.	8 - 10	10 - 12
Cherry Ripe Ice Cream Gum	8 - 10	10 - 12
Cherry Smash (On Lawn at Mt. Vernon)	70 - 75	75 - 85
Chesterfield Cigarettes		
Servicemen, Uns./Leyendecker	75 - 100	100 - 125
Chesterfield Cigarettes - Poster, Man Smoking	18 - 20	20 - 25
Chicago, Milwaukee, and St. Paul R.R.	8 - 10	10 - 12
Chocolate Lombart, Air Plane Series	8 - 10	10 - 12
Cleveland Six Automobile	15 - 18	18 - 22
Coca Cola (Girl Driving)	1000 - 1200	1200 - 1500
Coca Cola (Girl's Head) S/H. King	700 - 900	900 - 1000
Cole Mercantile Co.	4 - 5	5 - 6
Continental Rubber Tires (Bike)	15 - 20	20 - 25
Continental Rubber Tires (Tennis)	20 - 25	25 - 30
Community Silver	3 - 4	4 - 5
Continental Pneumatic Tires	15 - 18	18 - 25
Corbin Coaster Brakes (Bicycles)	12 - 15	15 - 18

Bacardi Rum, "The Perfect Duet"

Cook Beer	5 - 6	6 - 7
Cracker Jack Bears		
1 - 16	30 - 35	35 - 45
Creamlac, Bicycle Cleaner (1898)	40 - 45	45 - 50
Crescent Flour	4 - 5	5 - 6
Crocker & Best Flour	4 - 5	5 - 6
Crown Millinery Co., 1910	4 - 5	5 - 6
Crown Flour	5 - 6	6 - 8
Curtis Publishing Co.	4 - 5	5 - 6
Daniel Webster Cigars	8 - 10	10 - 12
Daniel Webster Flour	4 - 5	5 - 6
Dannemiller's Royal Coffee	4 - 5	5 - 6
Denver Zephyrs (Train)	15 - 20	20 - 25
Derby's Croup Mix (w/Children)	5 - 6	6 - 7
Devars Whiskey	12 - 15	15 - 18
De Laval Cream Separator	6 - 7	7 - 8
Diamont Rubber Co., Akron	4 - 5	5 - 7
Disinfectine Soap (Whole Dam Family) - 1905	12 - 15	15 - 18
Domino Sugar	6 - 8	8 - 10
Do-Wah-Jack, w/Indians - Months of Year Ser.	12 - 15	15 - 18
Dutch Boy Paints	7 - 8	9 - 12
Dunlop Tires (Inventor/Elves)	30 - 40	40 - 45
DuPont Bird & Wild Game (12)	30 - 35	35 - 40

      "Blue Wing Teal"   "Mallards"
      "Canada Goose"   "Prairie Chicken"
      "Canvas Back"   "Quail"
      "Gray Squirrel"   "Ruffled Grouse"
      "Jack Rabbit"   "Wild Turkey"
      "Jack Snipe"   "Woodcock"

Wyeth Painting Card	30 - 35	35 - 40
DuPont Dogs (13)	80 - 100	100 - 120

"Joe Cummings"	"Mohawk II"
"Allmabagh"	"Monora"
"Count Gladstone IV"	"Pioneer"
"Count Whitestone"	"Prince-Whitestone"
"Geneva"	"Sioux"
"Lady's Count Gladstone"	"Tony's Gale"
"Manitoba Rap"	

Eastman Cameras	10 - 12	12 - 15
Eclipse Coaster Brakes (Bicycles)	12 - 15	15 - 18
Edison Phonograph (Famous Singers)	10 - 12	12 - 15
Egg Climax Incubator	4 - 5	5 - 6
Egg-O-See Cereals	6 - 7	7 - 8
Eiffel Hosiery	5 - 6	6 - 8
Eldredge Rotary Sewing Machines	6 - 8	8 - 10
Elgin Watch Co.	12 - 15	15 - 18
Emerson Plows	6 - 7	7 - 8
Erasmic Soap - Beautiful Girl	6 - 8	8 - 10
EMF Auto (Glidden Tour)	12 - 15	15 - 18
Eskay's Foods	4 - 5	5 - 7
Evinrude Motor Girl, Real Photo	40 - 50	50 - 60
Excelsior Pneumatic Tires	15 - 20	20 - 25
Excelsior Stove & Mfg. Co.	5 - 6	6 - 7
F. A. Whitney Carriage Co.	5 - 6	6 - 7
Falstaff Beer	8 - 10	10 - 12
Faun Butters	4 - 5	5 - 6
Federal Cord Tires (3 1/2" x 6")	7 - 8	8 - 10
Firestone Tires	10 - 12	12 - 15
Fisk Tires	8 - 10	10 - 12
Fisk Red Top Tires	12 - 15	15 - 18
Fisk Removable Rims	8 - 10	10 - 12
Fitz Overalls	5 - 6	6 - 8
Fleischmann Co. Yeast	3 - 4	4 - 5
Flexible Flyer Sleds	5 - 7	7 - 8
Flexible Flyer Sleds (Government Postal)	10 - 12	12 - 15
Flood & Conklin & Co., Varnish		
P. Boileau Ladies' Calendars	100 - 125	125 - 150
Flower City Stoves and Ranges	8 - 10	10 - 12
Formosa Oolong Tea	4 - 5	5 - 6
Force Food Co.	4 - 5	5 - 7
Foss Orange Extract	8 - 10	10 - 12
Foss Pure Extract	6 - 8	8 - 10
Fowler's Cherry Smash		
W/George Washington	200 - 250	250 - 275
Fox Head Lager Beer	5 - 8	8 - 10
Fralinger's Original Salt Water Taffy		
Beach Series	4 - 5	5 - 6
Nursery Rhymes (24), S/Burd	20 - 22	22 - 25

Others, S/Burd	10 - 12	12 - 15
Fralingers Salt Water Taffy - others	5 - 7	7 - 9
Franklin Davis Nursery Co.	2 - 3	3 - 4
Free Sewing Machine Co.	7 - 8	8 - 10
Frog in the Throat Lozenge Co.		
(PMC, 12, oversized)	50 - 55	55 - 60
1 "A Social Success"		
2 "A Universal Favorite"		
3 "Don't Be Without It"		
4 "Favorite at all Times"		
5 "Fore Everybody"		
6 "For Singers"		
7 "Innocent and Instantaneous"		
8 "My Old Friend Dr. Frog"		
9 "Needs No Introduction"		
10 "Nothing Better"		
11 "Pleasant to Take"		
12 "Popular Everywhere"		
Cartoons (10) 3" x 5"	20 - 25	25 - 30
Fry's Chocolates, S/Tom Browne	10 - 12	12 - 15
Fry's Cocoa	5 - 6	6 - 7
Fuller Brush Co.	3 - 4	4 - 5

The Chesterfield Coat
Strauss Brothers, No. 905

Eiffel Hosiery
"Hosiery for Men, Women ..."

*Fall River Line
New England Steamship Co.*

*Lekko Hand Soap
Calendar for February, 1912*

Fuller Floor Wax	4 - 5	5 - 6
Gaar-Scott & Co. (Tractor)	10 - 12	12 - 15
Gales Chocolates (4" x 6")	4 - 6	6 - 8
Gates Tires	10 - 12	12 - 15
G.E. Refrigerator Drowned in Water (30's)	20 - 25	25 - 30
German-American Coffee	10 - 12	12 - 15
Gilles Coffee	3 - 4	4 - 5
Gillette Safety Razor Co. (Child Shaving)	10 - 12	12 - 15
Gladwell's Lawn Mowers	10 - 12	12 - 15
Glidden Tour Autos	10 - 15	15 - 20
Globe-Wernicke Bookcases	4 - 6	6 - 7
Gold Dust Twins Wash Powders	20 - 25	25 - 30
Billboard Signs	8 - 10	10 - 15
Gold Label Beer	6 - 8	8 - 10
Golden Tree Syrup	3 - 4	4 - 5
Gold Medal Flour	3 - 4	4 - 5
Good Luck Baking Powder (Jamestown Expo)	15 - 18	18 - 22
Goodrich Silvertown Tires	8 - 10	10 - 12
Gorham Silver Polish (1903)	8 - 10	10 - 12
Grande Ronde Meat Co., LaGrande, Oregon	6 - 8	8 - 10
Great Northern Railway	5 - 7	7 - 8
Greenfield's Chocolate Sponge	5 - 7	7 - 8
Grollman Hats, 1918	3 - 4	4 - 5
Gulf Refining Co. (Typical Filling Station)	12 - 15	15 - 20

Hackett Carbart & Co. Clothing	3 - 4	4 - 5
Happy Day Washers	5 - 7	7 - 8
Happy Thought Chewing Tobacco (12)	6 - 8	8 - 10
Hamm Brewing Co.	8 - 10	10 - 12
Hart Hats, S/Hoffman	4 - 5	5 - 6
Harley Davidson Motorcycles (6) - Govt. Postals	15 - 18	18 - 22
Hart-Parr Co. (Tractors)	10 - 12	12 - 15
Hart Schaffner & Marx		
S/Ed. Penfield	12 - 15	15 - 18
Hathaway's Bread	3 - 4	4 - 5
Havana Club Rum	7 - 8	8 - 10
Heather Bloom Petticoats (E. Barrymore)	6 - 8	8 - 10
Heinz Foods, 57 Varieties (w/Product on Front)	12 - 15	15 - 18
Heinz Foods - others	3 - 4	4 - 5
Hendel Motorcycles	8 - 10	10 - 12
Herman Reel Co. (Indians)	6 - 7	7 - 10
Hershey's Cocoa & Chocolates	2 - 3	3 - 4
High Life Beer	8 - 10	10 - 12
Hinds Honey and Almond Cream	6 - 8	8 - 9
Hiram Walker & Sons Liquors	8 - 10	10 - 12
Hires Root Bear	5 - 8	8 - 10
Holsum Bread (Cartoons)	8 - 10	10 - 12
Holsum Bread, w/Billy Baker	8 - 10	10 - 12
Hoods Sarsaparilla	6 - 8	8 - 10
Humpty-Dumpty Stockings (N. Rhymes)	5 - 6	6 - 8
Humphrey's Witch Hazel Oil	5 - 6	6 - 8
Hupmobile, 1911	20 - 25	25 - 28

Havana Cruises, Lumitone Photo, "The Morro Castle"

Plymouth Four-Door Sedan for 1940
"The Low Priced Beauty with the Luxury Ride"

Huyler's Candy (w/Children)	8 - 10	10 - 12
S/Von Hartman	10 - 12	12 - 14
I. X. L. Tamales	3 - 4	4 - 5
Imperial Diamond Needles	3 - 4	4 - 5
Independent Wall Paper Co.	3 - 4	4 - 5
India & Ceylon Tea	7 - 8	8 - 10
India Tea Growers	7 - 8	8 - 10
International Harvester, 1909 (12)	5 - 6	6 - 7
International Harvester, 1910 (12)	5 - 6	6 - 7
Iowa Seed Co.	2 - 3	3 - 4
Jack Sprat Oleomargarine	6 - 8	8 - 9
Japan Tea	4 - 5	5 - 6
Joplin Overalls (Girl)	5 - 6	6 - 8
Juniata Horse Shoes, w/Indian Girl	8 - 10	10 - 12
Kalodont Toothpaste & Mouthwash (German)	15 - 18	18 - 25
Kansas City Casket & Furniture Co.	5 - 6	6 - 8
Kaufman & Strauss F.G. Long Black Cartoons	12 - 15	15 - 18
Kelloggs Corn Flakes (Allentown Adpostal)	35 - 40	40 - 45
Kelloggs Corn Flakes, others	5 - 6	6 - 7
Kineto Clocks	15 - 18	18 - 22
Kinsey Pure Rye Whiskey	5 - 6	6 - 8
Klumbacher Beer (German Beer)	15 - 18	18 - 25
Knapp Calendars (See Artist-Signed Section)		
Frank Desch, Lester Ralph		
Kodak Cameras	15 - 18	18 - 20
Kohler Sewing Machine (German)	20 - 22	22 - 26
Kohn Brothers Fine Clothing	3 - 4	4 - 5
Koch, W.J. Seed Co. (Dutch Kids)	3 - 4	4 - 5

Korn Kinks, H.O. Company	20 - 22	22 - 25
The Jocular Jinks of Kornelia Kinks		
1 "Said Momma to Me ..."		
2 "Man, Whar's Your Politeness"		
3 "Gran'pa done say dat ..."		
4 "I'se a going to be ..."		
5 "It ain't a bit o'use ..."		
6 "Susie done 'through' ..."		
Rare Variation (Kite in Air; no 5¢ on building)	40 - 50	50 - 60
The Korn Kink Advertising cards (2)	15 - 18	18 - 22
Korvin Ice Cream, Jersey Shore Creamery	6 - 8	8 - 9
Kulmbacher Export Beer, Gruss Aus	20 - 25	25 - 30
Kuppenheimer Suits, Uns./Leyendecker	10 - 12	12 - 15
Laco Lamps (Children/Bulbs)	8 - 10	10 - 12
Lady Like Shoes (Beautiful Girls' Heads)	15 - 20	20 - 25
Lash Bitters (Laxative) Drunks	10 - 12	12 - 15
Lehr Pianos	3 - 4	4 - 5
Lekko Hand Soap	8 - 10	10 - 12
Lemp Beer	12 - 15	15 - 20
Leonard's Bulk Seed	2 - 3	3 - 4
Lindholm Piano Co.	4 - 5	5 - 6
Lindsay Gas Light Mantles	4 - 5	5 - 6
Lipton Tea (6)	5 - 6	6 - 7
Listerated Pepsin Gum (10), Bears	12 - 15	15 - 18
London & Northwestern R.R. Promotional Issues		
Promotional Issues, 28 sets of 6 each (1905)	6 - 7	7 - 8
01 Railways in the "Thirties"		
02 Old Locomotives		
03 Bridges		
04 Royal Saloons		
05 Royal Trains		
06 Express Trains		
07 Places of Interest		
08 Places of Interest		
09 Modern Locomotives		
10 Modern Steamships		
11 Famous Locomotives		
12 Exhibition Engines		
13 Carriages		
14 Miscellaneous		
15 Old London & Birmingham		
16 Tunnels		
17 Locomotives		
18 The London & Birmingham R.R. in 1837-8		
19 Signal Boxes, etc.		
20 Old & New Steamships		
21 Railway Cuttings		
22 Rolling Stock		
23 Goods & Passenger Trains		

24 Stations
25 Miscellaneous
26 Old Railway Views
27 Road Vehicles
28 Old Railway Prints

Lowney's Chocolates (Indians)	8 - 10	10 - 12
Girl Golfers, S/Archie Gunn	18 - 22	22 - 25
Magic Curlers	3 - 4	4 - 5
Majestic Stove Ranges	6 - 8	8 - 10
Malt Breakfast Food	4 - 5	5 - 6
Malted Cereal Co.	4 - 5	5 - 6
Mansville & Sons Pianos	6 - 8	8 - 10
Mason & Hanson Woolens, w/Pretty Girls	6 - 8	8 - 10
Men in mode of dress by century	8 - 10	10 - 12
Masons Automobile	15 - 18	18 - 22
Mauser's Best Flour	8 - 10	10 - 12
Maxwell Exclusive Line Wall Paper	3 - 4	4 - 5
McCallum, D. & J. "Perfection" Scotch Whiskey	8 - 10	10 - 12
McPhail Pianos (Boston Views)	2 - 3	3 - 4
Mecca Cigarettes	18 - 22	22 - 25
Meier & Frank Dept. Store (set of flags)		
Portland, Oregon	10 - 12	12 - 15
Men-tho-la-tum Salve	6 - 7	7 - 9
Metz Motorcycles	18 - 22	22 - 25
Michelin Tires	15 - 18	18 - 22
Michelin Tires, s/Vincent	8 - 10	10 - 12
Middlebrook Razors	5 - 6	6 - 8
Miller High Life Beer - Kids in Auto	15 - 20	20 - 25
Minneapolis Knitting Works (Fairy Tales)	10 - 12	12 - 15
Mistletoe Margarine	12 - 15	15 - 18
Mogul Egyptian Cigarettes (La. Purch. Expo)	12 - 15	15 - 18
Monarch Typewriters	8 - 10	10 - 12
The Monon R.R. (Signed Palenske, 1991)	15 - 18	18 - 22
Moxie	30 - 35	35 - 40
20 Mule Team Borax	7 - 8	8 - 9
Mulford, H. K., Vaccine	5 - 6	6 - 7
Murad Cigarettes (Views)	4 - 5	5 - 6
Niagara Maid Silk Gloves	8 - 10	10 - 12
National Girls	4 - 5	5 - 6
National Biscuit Co.	4 - 5	5 - 6
National Cash Register	4 - 5	5 - 6
National Cloak & Suit Co.	5 - 6	6 - 8
National Light Oil	5 - 6	6 - 8
National Lead Paint (Dutch Boy)	10 - 12	12 - 14
Others	4 - 5	5 - 6
National Phonograph Co.	5 - 6	6 - 8
National Recording Safe Co.	4 - 5	5 - 6
Nestle's Baby Food	6 - 7	7 - 8
Nestle's Chocolate	6 - 7	7 - 8

M & H Fine Woolens
Mason & Hanson, N.Y., 1909

M & H Fine Woolens
Mason & Hanson, N.Y., 1909

New Departure Brakes (Jack & Jill)	12 - 15	15 - 18
New Idea Manure Spreader	12 - 15	15 - 18
New Home Sewing Machine	6 - 8	8 - 10
Northern Pacific R.R.	5 - 6	6 - 8
Northwestern Hide & Fur Co.	8 - 10	10 - 12
Nu-Life Cereal	5 - 6	6 - 7
Nuvida Springs, California (Indian Girl)	7 - 8	8 - 10
Nylo Chocolates	5 - 6	6 - 7
Ocherade Drink	5 - 6	6 - 7
Oil Pull Tractors	12 - 15	15 - 18
Old Style Lager	6 - 8	8 - 10
Oliver Farm Machinery	5 - 6	6 - 7
Old Prentice Whiskey	6 - 8	8 - 9
Omega Watch (French Poster)	35 - 40	40 - 45
Osborne Calendar Co. (See Artist-Signed Arthur, Boileau, Underwood, Vernon)		
Overland 83B Touring Car	12 - 15	15 - 18
Pabst Breweries (Views)	6 - 7	7 - 8
Pacific Mail Steamship Co.	5 - 6	6 - 8
Pacific Tank & Pipe Co.	6 - 8	8 - 10
Palmolive Soap (Govt. Postal)	5 - 6	6 - 8
Parisian Belle Perfume	7 - 8	8 - 10
Parker Guns	15 - 20	20 - 25

Osborne Calendar Co.
Vernon No. 2729, "Corrine"

Stetson Shoes
The Stetson Blucher Oxfords

Parker Shot Guns	15 - 18	18 - 22
Pears Soap	6 - 7	7 - 8
Peter's Weatherbird Shoes (Months of Year)	8 - 10	10 - 12
Seasons	8 - 10	10 - 12
Halloween	15 - 18	18 - 22
Philadelphia Lawn Mowers	8 - 10	10 - 12
Phillips Arga - Poster	20 - 25	25 - 30
Phillips Lamps, w/Dutch Girl	15 - 18	18 - 22
Pillsbury Flour	4 - 5	5 - 6
Pinkham, Lydia E., Medicine Co.	4 - 5	5 - 6
Piso's Cure for Colds	4 - 5	5 - 6
Polarine Oil	6 - 8	8 - 9
Post Toasties Cereal	7 - 8	8 - 9
Ponds Bitters	6 - 7	7 - 8
Post Toasties Corn Flakes	8 - 10	10 - 12
Postum Cereal	3 - 4	4 - 5
Powell's N.Y. Chocolates	3 - 4	4 - 5
Premier Bicycles	20 - 25	25 - 30
Prisco Lantern	6 - 7	7 - 8
Private Estate Coffee	6 - 7	7 - 9
Purina Chick Chow	5 - 6	6 - 8
Puritan Blouses and Shirts	3 - 4	4 - 5
Purity Salt, PMC	15 - 18	18 - 20
Quaker Oats, w/B&W foreign views	8 - 10	10 - 12

Quick Meal Gas Stoves	12 - 15	15 - 18
R. B. Cigars	10 - 12	12 - 15
RCA, Dog & Mule Calendars	4 - 5	5 - 6
Rat Bis-Kit (Dog/Cat)	5 - 6	6 - 8
Red Bird Coffee	10 - 12	12 - 15
Red Cross Cotton	6 - 8	8 - 10
Red Horse Tobacco	8 - 10	10 - 12
Red Pig Knives (Posters)	20 - 25	25 - 30
Red Star Lines, S/Cassiers	12 - 15	15 - 20
Regal Shoe Co. (La. Purchase Expo)	8 - 10	10 - 12
Reliance Baking Powder	5 - 6	6 - 8
Remington Arms	15 - 18	18 - 22
Remy Magnettos, 1910	4 - 5	5 - 6
Richardson Skates	6 - 8	8 - 10
Ringling Bros. Animals	4 - 5	5 - 6
Ringling Bros. Circus Ads	8 - 10	10 - 12
Robeson Cutlery		
"Red Pig" Knives	20 - 25	25 - 30
Rockford Watches Calendars, S/Outcault	20 - 25	25 - 30
Round Up Cigars	5 - 6	6 - 8
Rumford Baking Powder	5 - 6	6 - 8
Rumley Tractors	6 - 8	8 - 10
Samoset Chocolates (8) Indians		
S/Elwell	12 - 15	15 - 18
Sandeman Scotch Whiskey	9 - 10	10 - 12
San Felice Cigars	8 - 10	10 - 12
Sanitol Girl	8 - 10	10 - 12
Santa Fe R.R.	6 - 8	8 - 10
Savannah Line, Coast Steamers	10 - 12	12 - 15
Sawyer Crystal Blue Laundry Soap	5 - 6	6 - 8
Schlitz Beer	8 - 10	10 - 12
Schraffts Chocolate	5 - 6	6 - 8
Schulze's Butter-Nut Bread	6 - 8	8 - 10
Scull, William S. Co., Coffee	6 - 8	8 - 10
Seattle Ice Co.	6 - 8	8 - 10
Selz Liberty Bell Shoes	5 - 6	6 - 8
Sen Sen Gum	10 - 12	12- 15
Sharples Cream Separator		
1 Boy and Girl	12 - 15	15 - 18
2 Cow and Ladies	12 - 15	15 - 18
3 Mother and Child	12 - 15	15 - 18
4 Farm Pleasures	12 - 15	15 - 18
5 Helping Gramma	12 - 15	15 - 18
6 Teddy	15 - 18	18 - 22
7 Modern Way	12 - 15	15 - 18
8 Dairyman's Choice	12 - 15	15 - 18
Shredded Wheat Cereal	6 - 8	8 - 10
Shredded Wheat (Factory)	3 - 5	5 - 6
Simple Simon Oleo	6 - 7	7 - 8

USM City Collections
Agent No. 3

The Sanitol Girl
The Sanitol Company

Woonsocket Rubber Company
Footwear of Nations - Russia

Simplex Cream Separators	5 - 6	6 - 8
Simplex Typewriters	6 - 8	8 - 10
Singer Sewing Machines	6 - 8	8 - 10
Sleepy Eye Milling Co. (9) Indians	90 - 100	100 - 120
"A Mark of Quality"		
"Chief Sleepy Eye Welcomes Whites"		
"Indian Artist"		
"Indian Canoeing"		
"Indian Mode of Conveyance"		
"Pipe of Peace"		
"Sleepy Eye Mills"		
"Sleepy Eye Monument"		
"Sleepy Eye, The Meritorious Flour"		
Monument	30 - 35	35 - 40
Snow Drift Cotton Oil Co.	5 - 6	6 - 8
Snow Drift Hogless Lard (Bunny & Pail of Lard)	15 - 18	18 - 22
Socony Gasoline	5 - 7	7 - 9
Sonora Phonographs	8 - 10	10 - 12
Solis Cigar Co. (Columbian Expo)	12 - 15	15 - 20
South Bend Lathes	5 - 6	6 - 8
Southern Cotton Oil Co. (Snowdrift)	5 - 6	6 - 8
Southern Pacific R.R .	5 - 6	6 - 8
Sperry Flour Co. (sketch by Malloy, signed)	10 - 12	12 - 15
Spillers Victorian Dog Food	8 - 10	10 - 12

Stacey-Adams (shoe) Company	6 - 8	8 - 10
Stanley Belting Corp. (B&W)	4 - 5	5 - 6
Sterling Ranges	5 - 6	6 - 8
Stiletto Lawn Mowers	6 - 8	8 - 10
Strauss Brothers Overcoats	4 - 5	5 - 6
Studebaker Jr. Wagons	25 - 30	30 - 35
Stukenbrok's Teutonia-Pneumatic Bicycles		
W/Golliwog, Gruss aus with und/back	35 - 40	45 - 50
Suchard Cacao, Color Product, w/B&W views	10 - 12	12 - 15
Summit Shirts	5 - 6	6 - 8
Sunny Jim Whiskey	6 - 7	7 - 9
Swift & Co., 6-Horse Team	6 - 8	8 - 10
Swift's Premium Butterine	5 - 6	6 - 8
Swift's Premium Oleomargarine		
"Children of World"	6 - 8	8 - 10
Swift's Pride, S/Grace Wiederseim	35 - 40	40 - 45
Swift's Pride Soap (6) Shadows on Wall	6 - 8	8 - 10
Taylor's Headache Cologne	6 - 8	8 - 10
Templin's "Idea" Seeds	4 - 6	6 - 8
Teutonia-Pneumatic Bicycles (w/Golliwog)	35 - 40	40 - 50
Texaco Axle Grease	8 - 10	10 - 12
Texaco Motor Oils	6 - 8	8 - 10
Thomas Brau Beer	10 - 12	12 - 15
Toledo Metal Wheel Co.	7 - 8	8 - 10
Toledo Scales	5 - 6	6 - 8
Troy Detachable Collars	4 - 5	5 - 6
True Fruit Flavors	5 - 6	6 - 8
Tudor Lights - Foreign Poster Style	10 - 12	12 - 15
Uhlen Baby Carriages	6 - 8	8 - 10
Uncle John's Syrup (Poster)	20 - 25	25 - 30
Underwood Typewriters	5 - 6	6 - 8
Union Pacific R.R.	5 - 6	6 - 8
Universal Regulators	4 - 5	5 - 6
USM City Collections	10 - 12	12 - 15
Utopia Yarns (Dutch Children)	5 - 6	6 - 7
Valentine's Varnishes (Auto)	10 - 12	12 - 15
Velvet Candy (Kissing on Joy Ride)	40 - 45	45 - 50
Velvetlawn Seeders	6 - 8	8 - 10
Verbeck & Lucas Stoves	5 - 6	6 - 8
Vick's Quality Seeds, Rochester	4 - 5	5 - 6
Voss Brothers Washing Machine	8 - 10	10 - 12
Wales-Goodyear Bear Brand Rubbers	5 - 8	8 - 10
Walker House, Toronto	5 - 6	6 - 8
Walk-Over Shoes, Famous Men (24)	6 - 8	8 - 10
Walk-Over Shoes, Dutch Children	4 - 5	5 - 6
Walk-Over Shoes, Pilgrim Series	4 - 5	5 - 6
Walk-Over Shoes, Scenes from Shakespeare (8)	6 - 8	8 - 10
"Beatrice" - *Romeo and Juliet*		
"Miranda" - *The Tempest*		

"Ophelia" - *Hamlet*
"Portia" - *Merchant of Venice*
"Rosalind" - *As You Like It*
"Titania" - *Midsummer Night's Dream*
"Viola" - *Twelfth Night*

Walk-Over Shoes, Western Series	4 - 6	6 - 8
Watkins, J. R., Medical	5 - 6	6 - 8
Watson-Plummer Shoe Co.	5 - 6	6 - 8
Weatherbird Shoes	5 - 6	6 - 8
Westinghouse Cooper Hewitt Mercury Rectifier	8 - 10	10 - 12
Westinghouse Electric Iron	6 - 7	7 - 8
Weyerheuser Lumber Co.	5 - 6	6 - 8
White Brothers Bread	6 - 7	7 - 8
White House Coffee & Tea	6 - 8	8 - 10
Whitney, F.A. Carriage Co.	8 - 10	10 - 12
Wilbur Chocolates, S/Henkels (6)	10 - 12	12 - 14
Willys Overland, Model 59T	22 - 25	25 - 30
Wilson & Co., Meat Packers	6 - 8	8 - 10
Winchester Arms & Ammo, Folding card, 1906	10 - 12	12 - 15
Witch Hazel Ointment	5 - 6	6 - 8
Woods Electrics (Auto)	15 - 18	18 - 22
Woodstock Typewriters	6 - 7	7 - 9
Woonsocket Rubber Co. (10), Footwear of Nations	8 - 10	10 - 12
Rubber Shoe Boat	12 - 15	15 - 18
Wyandotte Cleaner & Cleanser	5 - 6	6 - 8
Youth's Companion Magazine	4 - 5	5 - 6
Zang's Beer	8 - 10	10 - 12
Zeiss Ikon Camera (20's)	15 - 18	18 - 20
Zeiss Ikon Film, (20's)	15 - 18	18 - 20
Zenith Watches	5 - 8	8 - 10
Zeno Gum Co.	5 - 6	6 - 8

Although there are around 500 listings in our Advertising Postcards
section, this by no means includes all that were issued. For a more
comprehensive listing we suggest that you obtain a copy of Fred and
Mary Megson's fine book, **American Advertising Postcards, Sets
and Series, 1890-1920, Catalog and Price Guide.** It may be
obtained from the Postcard Lovers, Box 482, Martinsville, NJ 08836
at $21.50 postpaid.

LINEN ADVERTISING

Alamito Golden Guernsey Milk	6 - 8	8 - 10
Bouquet Brand Rock Lobster	8 - 10	10 - 12
Buick Auto, 1939-41	10 - 12	12 - 15
Buster Brown Shoes, P/Curt Teich	10 - 12	12 - 15
Chevrolet Auto, 1938-41	10 - 12	12 - 15

Kippendorf Foot Rest Shoes
"Style for Autumn Comfort"

Tropic Isle Restaurant
"Brooklyn's Elite Night Club"

C. T. (Curt Teich) Art Colortone
"Pictorial Post Cards"

Chicken in the Rough	6 - 8	8 - 10
Griswold Cast Ware	8 - 10	10 - 12
Habler Bros. Brush Paint Remover	10 - 12	12 - 15
Harvey Brothers Shirts & Ties	8 - 10	10 - 12
Himmel & Sons Furriers, P/Curt Teich	6 - 8	8 - 10
Johnson Candies (with Santa)	8 - 10	10 - 12
Kahn Tailors	6 - 8	8 - 10
Love's Finer Candies, Rochester, NY	8 - 10	10 - 12
Maytag Kitchen Washers	6 - 8	8 - 10
Meco Kiln and Man Koolers (fans), P/C. Teich	8 - 10	10 - 12
Mitchell Mortuary Stretcher	8 - 10	10 - 12
Oster "Stim-u-Lax" Massager	12 - 15	15 - 20
Ozark Pencil Company	6 - 8	8 - 10
Plymouth Auto, 1939-41	10 - 12	12 - 15
Soapine Soap Powder	8 - 10	10 - 12
Storiettes-Books	6 - 8	8 - 10
Tredstep Shoes	8 - 10	10 - 12
Tropic Isle Restaurant, Embossed Breasts Nude	8 - 10	10 - 12
Weather Shield for Autos - Wilson Company	6 - 8	8 - 10
Wellco House Slippers	6 - 8	8 - 10

Kalodont Zahn-Creme und Mundwasser
(German)

Bensdorp's Cacao
(Holland)

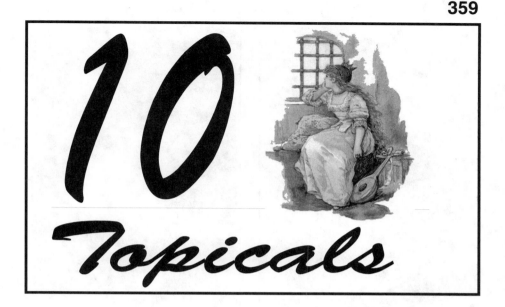

Topical postcards, as the name implies, are those of a particular place or subject and are any type not listed in a specific section of this publication. They are very special to the collecting fraternity, and make up a large part of every collection.

There were thousands of topics printed on postcards, and many are sure to appeal to any collector's fancy. As a general rule, collectors "specialize" in a particular subject or theme and try to obtain every card available, old or modern, until the collection is complete. Usually, because of their profound interest, they will also research the subject and become very knowledgeable about it and its history. This, in part, is one of the things that makes the collecting of postcards so interesting, and provides the momentum for the hobby to continue to grow and prosper.

Unless definite cards or sets are listed, values are for a generalized selection in each particular topic. There may be cards in each topic that will command higher, or even lower, prices.

TOPICALS

ACTORS AND ACTRESSES	VG	EX
Astaire, Fred	$ 5 - 6	$ 6 - 8
Baker, Josephine	40 - 60	60 - 80
Bogart, H.	8 - 10	10 - 12
Bergman, I.	4 - 6	6 - 7
Cagney, J.	4 - 6	6 - 7
Chaplin, Charles	5 - 6	6 - 8

Catherine Klein
Alphabet Series 48, "B"

Real Photo, United Artists
Rudolph Valentino

Crosby, Bing	4 - 6	6 - 7
Davis, Bette	4 - 6	6 - 7
Dean, James	10 - 12	12 - 15
Dietrich, Marlene	8 - 10	10 - 12
Fields, W. C.	4 - 6	6 - 7
Flynn, Errol	4 - 6	6 - 7
Gable, Clark	4 - 6	6 - 7
Garbo, Greta	8 - 10	10 - 12
Garland, Judy	5 - 6	6 - 8
Harlow, Jean	5 - 6	6 - 8
Laurel & Hardy	10 - 12	12 - 15
Lloyd, Harold	4 - 6	6 - 7
Marx Brothers	8 - 10	10 - 12
Monroe, Marilyn	8 - 10	10 - 12
Rogers, Ginger	3 - 4	4 - 5
Temple, Shirley	6 - 8	8 - 10
Valentino, R.	8 - 10	10 - 15
Wayne, John	8 - 10	10 - 15
West, Mae	6 - 8	8 - 10

AESOP'S FABLES
Raphael Tuck

"Aesop's Fables Up to Date" (6)	20 - 25	25 - 30
AIRPLANES, Military	5 - 6	6 - 8

AIRPLANES   (See Transportation)

Jack Rabbit Race, "Amusements at Long Beach, California"

Celluloid	2 - 3	3 - 4
Felt	2 - 3	3 - 4
Flowers	1 - 2	2 - 3
Glitter (Distracting on most cards)	1 - 2	2 - 3
Hair (On Beautiful Ladies)	15 - 18	18 - 25
Metal	3 - 4	4 - 5
Silk (See Santas, Langsdorf Ladies, E. Christy)		
Others	4 - 5	5 - 8
ART MASTERPIECES		
Stengel	1 - 2	2 - 3
Nudes	5 - 6	6 - 8
Sborgi	1 - 2	2 - 3
ASTROLOGY	3 - 4	4 - 6
ASYLUMS	5 - 7	7 - 8
AUTHORS	3 - 4	4 - 5
John Winsch (Author Series)	6 - 7	7 - 8
AUTO RACING, Early	15 - 20	20 - 25
AUTO SERVICE STATIONS See R. Photos, Views.		
BALLET DANCING	4 - 5	5 - 7
BALLOONS, Flying, Early	8 - 10	10 - 15
Real Photo	15 - 20	20 - 25
BANDS, Musical	6 - 8	8 - 10
Military	5 - 6	6 - 8
BANDSTANDS	3 - 4	4 - 6
BANKS (See Views and Real Photos)		
BASEBALL PARKS (See Baseball, Etc.)		
BASEBALL PLAYERS (See Baseball, Etc.)		
BASKETBALL PLAYERS, Home Teams, Schools	8 - 10	10 - 12
Real Photo	12 - 15	15 - 18
BATHING BEAUTIES		
Illustrated P.C. Co. Series 80	7 - 8	8 - 10
Langsdorf & Co. (10)	6 - 7	7 - 9
Leighton & Co. (10)	6 - 7	7 - 8
J. Marks "Summer Girl" Series 155	6 - 7	7 - 8
P.F.B. Series 6271 (6)	7 - 8	8 - 10
Souvenir Postcard Co. Series 526 (6)	6 - 7	7 - 8
E.L. Theochrome Series 1035	5 - 6	6 - 7
W.M. Taggert Series 25	6 - 8	8 - 10
R. Tuck		
Ser. 116, 1363 (6)	8 - 9	9 - 10
Ser. 9414, E9466, 9494 (6)	8 - 9	9 - 10
Ullman Mfg. Co. "Seashore Girls" Series 90	7 - 8	8 - 9
Foreign Series 583 (6)	6 - 7	7 - 8
Foreign Series 1070 (6)	6 - 7	7 - 8
Tinted Photos	10 - 12	12 - 15
Others	4 - 6	6 - 8
BATTLESHIPS (See Transportation)		
BEACH SCENES	1 - 2	2 - 4
W/Bathers	3 - 4	4 - 6

"*Basket Ball Team, Cavite High School*" -- 258
Real Photo, The Philippines, ARTURA Photo

Real Photo	6 - 8	8 - 12
BEARS	1 - 2	2 - 3
Teddy Bears, Artist-Signed	10 - 12	12 - 15
Teddy Bears W/Children, Artist-Signed	10 - 12	12 - 16
Real Photo, Large Image W/Children	20 - 25	25 - 35
Real Photo, Small Image W/Children	10 - 12	12 - 18
See Teddy Bear Section.		
BICYCLES	3 - 4	4 - 6
Real Photo	8 - 10	10 - 15
Advertising	10 - 15	15 - 20
BILLIARDS	4 - 6	6 - 8
Artist-Signed	8 - 10	10 - 12
BIRDS	2 - 3	3 - 4
Signed C. Klein	5 - 6	6 - 8
Audubon Society	1 - 2	2 - 3
BIRTH ANNOUNCEMENTS	4 - 5	5 - 6
BIRTHSTONES		
E. Nash Series 1	5 - 6	6 - 7
E.P.C. Co. Series 100, 200	2 - 3	3 - 4
BLACKS, U.S.A. (See Artist-Signed, Uns. Blacks)	5 - 6	6 - 10
Foreign	4 - 5	5 - 6
BOATS, Large Image	2 - 3	3 - 4
Small	1 - 1.50	1 - 50 - 2
BOER WAR	8 - 10	10 - 15
BOOKS	1 - 1.50	1.50 - 2
BOWLING	3 - 4	4 - 6
BOXING (See Baseball, Etc.)		
BOY SCOUTS		

A. E. Marty, Hemostyl Adv. Scout Card	35 - 40	40 - 45
Colortype Co., Chicago Sepia	12 - 15	15 - 18
Gartner & Bender, Chicago	12 - 15	15 - 18
Henninger Co., N.Y.		
Scouts Law (12)	12 - 15	15 - 20
Scouts Gum Co. S/H.S. Edwards (12)	18 - 20	20 - 25
1 "Bugle Calls"		
2 "The Diving Board"		
3 "Fire Without Matches"		
4 "Blazing a Trail"		
5		
6 "Hiding a Trail"		
7 "Vaulting a Stream"		
8 "Loading a Canoe"		
9 "Toting"		
10 "First Aid"		
11 "Flag of Salute"		
12 "The Camp Fire"		
R. Tuck Boy Scout Series 9950 (6)	125 - 150	150 - 175
Series 8745 S/Shepheard		
"Advice to Scouts" (6)	15 - 20	20 - 25
BREWERIES - Exteriors	6 - 8	8 - 12
Interiors	10 - 12	12 - 14
BROOKLYN EAGLE VIEWS	2 - 3	3 - 5
BULL FIGHTS	2 - 3	3 - 5
BUS DEPOTS	4 - 5	5 - 8
See Views and Real Photos.		
BUSES - 1900-1920	12 - 15	15 - 25
1920-1940	10 - 12	12 - 20
BUTTERFLIES	1 - 2	2 - 3
On Greetings	2 - 3	3 - 5
BUTTON FACES - BUTTON FAMILY		
George Jervis	18 - 20	20 - 25
CALCIUM LIGHTS		
J. Plant "Army-Navy Series"	3 - 4	4 - 5
CALENDARS, Pre-1904	8 - 10	10 - 12
1905-1910	4 - 6	6 - 8
1910-1915	3 - 5	5 - 7
1915-1940	2 - 3	3 - 4
CAMERAS		
Kodak Advertising	15 - 18	18 - 25
Artist-Signed	7 - 10	10 - 16
CANALS	1 - 2	2 - 3
Panama Canal Construction Views	5 - 7	7 - 10
CANOEING	1 - 2	2 - 3
CAPITALS See Sets & Series		
State Capitals & Seals.		
CARNIVAL		
Raphael Tuck "Carnival" Series 117 (6)	15 - 18	18 - 22

Oilette Series 6435 (6)	12 - 15	15 - 18
Oilette "Mardi Gras" Ser. 2551 (6)	7 - 8	8 - 10
T. Gessner "Mardi Gras" Series	6 - 7	7 - 8
Real Carnivals		
Sideshows, Color	6 - 8	8 - 10
Sideshows, Real Photo	15 - 18	18 - 25
CAROUSELS Color	10 - 12	12 - 15
Real Photo	15 - 20	20 - 30
CARTS		
Goat, Pony	10 - 12	12 - 15
Horse, Oxen	8 - 10	10 - 12
See Real Photos		
CASTLES	1 - 2	2 - 3
CATHEDRALS	1 - 1.50	1.50 - 2
CATS See Artist-Signed Cats		
CATTLE	1 - 2	2 - 3
CAVES	1 - 2	2 - 3
CEMETERIES	1 - 2	2 - 3
CHESS/CHECKERS	5 - 7	7 - 12
CHICKENS	1 - 3	3 - 6
Dressed like people.	6 - 8	8 - 12
CHILDREN, Foreign	1 - 2	2 - 4
Playing	2 - 3	3 - 5
W/Dolls, Toys	7 - 8	8 - 15
W/Animals	6 - 7	7 - 10
See Real Photos		
CHINESE PEOPLE	2 - 3	3 - 5
CHRISTMAS TREES		
Raphael Tuck Series 529 (6)	7 - 8	8 - 10
CHURCHES (See Views)		
CIGARETTES, CIGARS	4 - 5	5 - 8
CIRCUS		
Barnum & Bailey - 1900-1920	25 - 30	30 - 35
Posters	30 - 35	35 - 40
1920-1940	15 - 20	20 - 25
Other Circus	10 - 15	15 - 20
CIVIL WAR		
Raphael Tuck Series 2510		
"Heroes of the South"	22 - 25	25 - 30
1. General Lee & Traveler		
2. General Robert E. Lee		
3. Lee in Confederate Uniform		
4. Gen. Thomas J. "Stonewall" Jackson		
5. Lee and Jackson		
6. Prayer in "Stonewall" Jackson's Camp		
Jamestown A&V Co., 1907		
Jamestown Expo Series 50-367		
Confederate Cards	15 - 20	20 - 25
CLOCKS	1 - 2	2 - 3

CLOWNS - Barnum & Bailey	15 - 20	20 - 25
Others	10 - 12	12 - 14
COAT-OF-ARMS	3 - 4	4 - 6
COCA COLA SIGNS		
Small	4 - 6	6 - 8
Large	8 - 10	10 - 15
COIN CARDS, Embossed		
Walter Erhard	8 - 10	10 - 12
Flat Printed	7 - 9	9 - 12
H. Guggenheim	6 - 7	7 - 9
H.S.M.	10 - 12	12 - 14
COLISEUMS (See Views)		
COLLEGES (See Views)		
COMETS		
Halley's	10 - 12	12 - 16
COMPOSERS	2 - 3	3 - 5
CONFEDERATE STATES		
"Sheridan's Ride" (10)	8 - 10	10 - 12
CONVENTS	2 - 3	3 - 4
CORPSE, In Casket		
Real Photo	6 - 8	8 - 10
COSTUMES, Native	1 - 2	2 - 3
COURT HOUSES (See Views)		
COVERED BRIDGES	5 - 6	6 - 8
COWBOYS	3 - 5	5 - 8
R. Tuck "Among the Cowboys" Ser. 2499	8 - 10	10 - 12
Real Photos	8 - 10	10 - 12
COWGIRLS	6 - 7	7 - 8
Real Photos	8 - 10	10 - 12
CRADLES	2 - 3	3 - 4
CROSSES	1 - 2	2 - 3
CUPIDS	2 - 3	3 - 5
DAIRIES (See Views)		
DAMS	2 - 3	3 - 4
DANCING	3 - 5	5 - 6
Artist-Signed	6 - 8	8 - 12
DAYS OF WEEK (See Teddy Bears, Sunbonnet)	2 - 3	3 - 5
DEATH	2 - 3	3 - 5
DEER	1 - 2	2 - 3
DENTAL	12 - 15	15 - 18
Artist-Signed	12 - 15	15 - 18
DEPARTMENT STORES	4 - 5	5 - 7
Interiors	5 - 6	6 - 8
Interiors, Real Photos	8 - 10	10 - 12
DETROIT PUB. CO. VIEWS		
Early PMC Cards -- Better Views	15 - 20	20 - 25
Common	5 - 6	6 - 8
Others - Better Views	6 - 8	8 - 10
Common	1 - 2	2 - 3

DEVIL	4 - 5	5 - 8
DIABOLO		
Davidson Ser. 2627 S/Tom Browne	12 - 15	15 - 16
Langsdorf Ser. 711 S/Kinsella (6)	14 - 16	16 - 18
R. Tuck Ser. N49 S/G.E. Shepherd	12 - 14	14 - 15
LOUIS WAIN Ser. 9563, 9564 (6)	45 - 50	50 - 55
DICE	3 - 4	4 - 6
DIME STORES	2 - 3	3 - 5
DINERS (See Views, R. Photos, Roadside America)		
DIONNE QUINTUPLETS	15 - 18	18 - 20
DIRIGIBLES, AIRSHIPS, ZEPPELINS	10 - 12	12 - 20
(See Real Photos)		
DISASTERS	6 - 8	8 - 12
(See Real Photos)		
DIVERS	2 - 3	3 - 5
DOG CARTS	6 - 8	8 - 12
Sleds	6 - 8	8 - 10
DOGS (See Artist-Signed Dogs)	2 - 3	3 - 5
A.S.B. Series 245	6 - 7	7 - 8
A. & M. B. Series 54	6 - 7	7 - 8
B.B. London Series E32	6 - 7	7 - 8
H.S.M. Series 719	6 - 7	7 - 8
P.F.B. Series 8163 (6) Large Image	15 - 17	17 - 20
Raphael Tuck "Art" Series 855 (6)	10 - 12	12 - 15
"Connoisseur" Series 2546 (6)	10 - 12	12 - 15
DOLLS (See Golliwogs, Real Photos, Children)		
Gartner & Bender		
Rag Doll Series	5 - 6	6 - 8
"A Wise Guy" (6)		
"Amybility" (6)		
"Antie Quate" (6)		
"Dolly Dimple" (6)		
"Epi Gram" (6)		
"Gee Whiz" (6)		
"Gee Willikens" (6)		
"Heeza Korker" (6)		
"Jiminy" (6)		
"Optomistic Miss" (6)		
"Phil Osopher" (6)		
DONKEYS, MULES, BURROS	1 - 2	2 - 3
DOVES	0.50 - 1	1 - 1.50
DREAMING	2 - 3	3 - 4
DRINKS Beer, Drunk Comics	2 - 3	3 - 4
DRUG STORES (See Views and Real Photos)		
DRUNKS	2 - 3	3 - 4
DUCKS, GEESE	1 - 2	2 - 3
EARTHQUAKES	4 - 6	6 - 12
ELEPHANTS	4 - 5	5 - 6
Artist-Signed	8 - 9	9 - 12

Coca Cola Sign, "Boardwalk and Steel Pier, Atlantic City, NJ"

Dressed like People	12 - 15	15 - 20
Raphael Tuck S/Ellam		
Series 9684	15 - 18	18 - 22
Series 9553 (6)	15 - 18	18 - 22
ELKS	2 - 3	3 - 4
Fraternal, Artist-Signed	6 - 7	7 - 10
EXAGGERATED		
Big Fish, Rabbits, Vegetables	3 - 5	5 - 8
Big Grasshoppers	5 - 6	6 - 9
Add $2-3 each to prices for Real Photos.		
FAB PATCHWORK SILKS		
W.N. Sharpe		
Kings & Queens	25 - 30	30 - 35
Scenes	20 - 25	25 - 28
FACTORIES, PLANTS (See Views and Real Photos)		
FAIRY TALES (See Fairy Tales)		
FAIRS, FESTIVALS	5 - 6	6 - 10
(See Views)		
FAMOUS PEOPLE'S HOMES		
Movie Stars	2 - 3	3 - 5
FANS	2 - 3	3 - 4
FARMING	2 - 3	3 - 5
FARMING EQUIPMENT		
Horse-Driven	6 - 8	8 - 10
Motor-Driven	6 - 8	8 - 10
(See Real Photos)		
FASHIONS	3 - 5	5 - 10
FAT PEOPLE, Real	6 - 8	8 - 10
Circus Side Shows (See Real Photos)	7 - 8	8 - 10

COMICS	1 - 2	2 - 3
FELIX THE CAT	15 - 20	20 - 25
FENCING	3 - 4	4 - 6
FERRY BOATS (See Real Photos)	6 - 7	7 - 10
FIRE ENGINES, Horse	8 - 9	9 - 12
Motor driven (See Real Photos)	12 - 15	15 - 20
FIRE HOUSES and/or Equipment		
(See Real Photos)	10 - 12	12 - 15
R. Wilkenson, Providence, R.I. (38)	10 - 12	12 - 15
FIRES (Disasters)	5 - 6	6 - 8
Named -- See Real Photos.	6 - 8	8 - 15
FIREWORKS	4 - 5	5 - 6
FISH, FISHING	2 - 3	3 - 6
FLAGS, USA	4 - 5	5 - 6
Jules Bien Series 710	6 - 8	8 - 10
Ill. Post Card Co. Series 207	6 - 8	8 - 10
National Art Co. "Hands Across the Sea"	7 - 8	8 - 9
Real Photo	8 - 10	10 - 12
Foreign	2 - 3	3 - 4
FLOODS (Disasters)	5 - 6	6 - 8
Named (See Real Photos)	8 - 10	10 - 12
FLOWERS		
C. Klein (See Artist Signed, Misc.)	3 - 4	4 - 5
FLOWER FACES	6 - 7	7 - 8
FOOTBALL Players	6 - 8	8 - 10
FORTS	2 - 3	3 - 4
FOREIGN VIEWS	0.50 - 1	1 - 1.50
FORTUNE TELLING	3 - 4	4 - 6
FRATERNAL		
Ullman Mfg. Co. Series 199	7 - 8	8 - 9
FREAKS, Animal	6 - 7	7 - 9
People	8 - 9	9 - 12
FROGS (See Dressed Animals)	1 - 2	2 - 3
FRUIT	1 - 1.50	1.50 - 2
FUNERAL HOMES (See Views)		
GAMBLING	4 - 5	5 - 6
GEYSERS	1 - 2	2 - 3
GHOSTS (See Fantasy)		
GIANTS, MIDGETS	5 - 8	8 - 10
GIRL SCOUTS		
BALLINGER, E.		
Girl Scout Laws Series M572	10 - 12	12 - 15
GILLESPIE, JESSIE		
Silhouettes of Scout Activities (6)	12 - 14	14 - 18
EDITH B. PRICE		
The Four Seasons (4)	10 - 12	12 - 15
MARGARET EVANS PRICE		
Girl Scout Laws Series M-578	12 - 15	15 - 18

GOATS	1 - 2	2 - 3
Bergman Ser. 1052 Billy Goat Comics (6)	5 - 6	6 - 8
GOLF Players	3 - 4	4 - 5
Courses	3 - 4	4 - 5
Golf Comics	10 - 12	12 - 15
Artist-Signed Beautiful Ladies	18 - 22	22 - 28
EARL CHRISTY		
Knapp Co.		
"Always Winning"	18 - 22	22 - 25
"Goodbye Summer"	18 - 22	22 - 25
R&N		
367 "The Day's Work"	15 - 18	18 - 22
CORBELLA		
Series 316 (6)	15 - 18	18 - 22
GUTTANY		
E. Gross "A Tee Party"	12 - 15	15 - 18
NANNI Series 309 (6)	18 - 22	22 - 25
RELYEA		
W.C. 9, 10	12 - 15	15 - 18
UNDERWOOD, C.		
M. Munk "Lost"	12 - 14	14 - 16
Raphael Tuck		
Ser. 697 "Golf Hints" (6)	15 - 18	18 - 22
Ser. 9499 "Humorous Golf" (6)	15 - 18	18 - 22
Ser. 3600 "Golf Humor" (6)	15 - 18	18 - 22
S/Thackeray Ser. 9304, 9305 (6)	15 - 18	18 - 22
Ser. 1627, 1628 (6)	15 - 18	18 - 22
Ladies/Men Artist-Signed	12 - 14	14 - 18
Raphael Tuck		
Series 9427 Blacks, "More Coons" (1)	22 - 26	26 - 30
Valentine & Co. S/C. Crombie		
"Etiquette," "Local Rule," etc. (6)	15 - 18	18 - 22
Advertising, product	15 - 25	25 - 40
GOOD LUCK SYMBOLS		
Horseshoes, Four-leaf Clover	1 - 2	2 - 3
Swastikas	4 - 5	5 - 6
GYMNASIUMS (See Views)		
GYMNASTICS	3 - 4	4 - 5
GYPSIES	5 - 6	6 - 8
HANDBALL	3 - 4	4 - 6
HARBORS	2 - 3	3 - 4
W/Ships, Busy	4 - 5	5 - 7
HATS		
Ladies Big Hats	3 - 4	4 - 6
Real Photos	4 - 6	6 - 8
HERALDIC	4 - 5	5 - 10
Paul Kohl (84)	8 - 10	10 - 12
Raphael Tuck		
"Boston"	8 - 10	10 - 12

Real Photo of Hitler and His Staff by Hoffmann
(Taken at the Sternecker Bräu in München)

"Philadelphia"	8 - 10	10 - 12
"Washington, D.C." PMC's	10 - 12	12 - 14
HITLER, Real Photo		
Postmarked	15 - 18	18 - 22
Unused	12 - 15	15 - 18
Color, Continental size, Common	15 - 18	18 - 25
Color, Continental size, Rarer issues	50 - 75	75 - 100
HOLD-TO-LIGHT, Die-Cut Issues		
Koehler (See Sets & Series)		
Other Publishers		
Santa Claus (See Santas)		
Year Dates - See Year Dates		
Children	20 - 25	25 - 30
Christmas Scenes	20 - 22	22 - 25
Easter, New Year	15 - 20	20 - 25
Statue of Liberty	25 - 30	30 - 35
Trains, Ships	30 - 35	35 - 40
Other Views, Bldgs., etc.	15 - 20	20 - 30
Comics	15 - 20	20 - 25
Foreign Gruss Aus City Views	20 - 25	25 - 30
Paris Exposition (12)	30 - 35	35 - 40
Foreign War Issues (Belgian)	12 - 15	15 - 20
H-T-L See-Through Issues		
Comics	12 - 15	15 - 20
1900 Year Date	20 - 25	25 - 30
Fairy Tales	15 - 20	20 - 25
Others	12 - 15	15 - 20

HOROSCOPE
Dietrich & Co.	5 - 6	6 - 8
Williamson-Haffner Ser. 985	6 - 7	7 - 8
Others	5 - 6	6 - 7
HORSE & BUGGIES, Large Image, Color	8 - 10	10 - 12
Small Image	5 - 6	6 - 7
See Real Photos.		
HORSES, Unsigned - Heads	5 - 6	6 - 8
Large Images	5 - 6	6 - 8
Small Images	2 - 3	3 - 4
See Artist-Signed Horses.		
Dan Patch		
Wright, Barnett, & Stilwell Co.	15 - 18	18 - 22
V.O. Hammond 155	15 - 18	18 - 22
T.P. & Co.	12 - 15	15 - 20
Real Photos	35 - 40	40 - 45
HOSPITALS (See Views, Real Photos)		
HOTELS (See Views, Real Photos)		
HOURS OF THE DAY		
Rose Co.	3 - 4	4 - 5
Warwick Co.	3 - 4	4 - 5
HOUSEBOATS	4 - 5	5 - 6
HUNTING	1 - 2	2 - 3
ILLUMINATED WINDOWS	5 - 6	6 - 8
ILLUSTRATED SONGS		
Bamforth Many different.	2 - 3	3 - 5
E. Nash "National Song" Series (6)	6 - 8	8 - 10
E.L. Theochromes	2 - 3	3 - 4
INCLINE RAILWAYS (See Transportation)		
INDIANS, Chiefs	8 - 10	10 - 12
Others	4 - 6	6 - 8
Real Photos	25 - 35	35 - 45
See Cowboys and Indians.		
INDUSTRY, Exterior	3 - 5	5 - 8
Interior	5 - 6	6 - 10
See Views and Real Photos.		
INSECTS (See Fantasy, Artist-Signed)	2 - 3	3 - 5
INSTALLMENT CARDS		
W.M. Beach		
Cow (4)	15 - 20	20 - 25
Others	15 - 20	20 - 25
Huld		
1 Alligator (4)	25 - 30	30 - 35
2 Dachshund (4)	25 - 30	30 - 35
3 Uncle Sam (4)	40 - 50	50 - 60
4 Fish (4)	25 - 30	30 - 35
5 Sea Serpent (4)	25 - 30	30 - 35
6 Mosquito (4)	25 - 30	30 - 35
7 Rip Van Winkle (4)	25 - 30	30 - 35

8 New York City (4)	25 - 30	30 - 35
9 Santa (4)	100 - 150	150 - 200
10 Christmas Tree (4)	30 - 35	35 - 40
11 Fisherwoman (4)	25 - 30	30 - 35
12 Fisherman (4)	25 - 30	30 - 35
14 Rabbit (4)	25 - 30	30 - 35
15 Teddy Bear (4)	60 - 70	70 - 80
N.Y. Journal-American Comic Characters	6 - 8	8 - 9
H.M. Rose	6 - 7	7 - 8
Wildwood Co.	6 - 7	7 - 8
Wrench & Co.	6 - 7	7 - 8
Ottmar Zieher	8 - 9	9 - 10
Standup Napoleon (10) Sepia	10 - 12	12 - 14
Albert of Belgium (10) B&W	8 - 10	10 - 12
Joan of Arc (10) B&W	10 - 12	12 - 14
JAILS	4 - 5	5 - 8
JAPANESE GIRLS **P.C.K.** Series	3 - 4	4 - 5
JAPANESE NAVY		
R. Tuck Oilette Series 9237 (6)	6 - 8	8 - 10
JERUSALEM		
R. Tuck Oilette Series 3355 (6)	6 - 8	8 - 10
JEWISH NEW YEAR		
Hebrew Pub. Co.	6 - 7	7 - 8
Others	4 - 5	5 - 6
JEWISH PEOPLE	3 - 5	5 - 8
Comics	8 - 10	10 - 15
JEWISH SYNAGOGUES	10 - 12	12 - 15
KU KLUX KLAN		
Printed	50 - 75	75 - 100
Real Photo	150 - 175	175 - 200
LAKES, Named	1 - 2	2 - 3
LANGUAGE OF FLOWERS	1 - 2	2 - 3
LARGE LETTERS, Cities, States (Early)	2 - 3	3 - 6
Linens	1 - 2	2 - 3
Names Early	5 - 6	6 - 8
Letters of Alphabet	4 - 5	5 - 6
LEATHER		
Greetings, Humor	3 - 5	5 - 8
Others, add $3-5 to card values of other topics.		
LESBIAN-RELATED	12 - 15	15 - 18
Real Photo Nudes	25 - 30	30 - 35
LIBRARIES (See Views)		
LIFE SAVING STATIONS	3 - 4	4 - 6
LIGHTHOUSES	2 - 4	4 - 5
LINENS		
Advertising, Product (See Advertising)		
Blacks	3 - 4	4 - 10
Comics, Unsigned	.50 - 1	1 - 1.50
Comics, Signed	1 - 1.50	1.50 - 2

Comics, WW2	3 - 4	4 - 6
Hitler	2 - 3	3 - 5
Indians	1 - 2	2 - 3
Large Letters	1 - 1.50	1.50 - 2
Army Bases	3 - 4	4 - 5
Pin-up Girls	2 - 3	3 - 5
Political, Presidential	2 - 3	3 - 6
Court House, Post Office, etc.	1 - 1.50	1.50 - 2
Depots	2 - 3	3 - 4
Street Scenes, Small Town	1 - 2	2 - 3
See **Roadside America** for others.		
LIONS	1 - 2	2 - 3
LITERARY CHARACTERS	2 - 3	3 - 4
LOVERS	2 - 3	3 - 4
MACABRE	5 - 6	6 - 8
MAGICIANS	5 - 6	6 - 8
MAIN STREETS See Views and Real Photos.		
MAPS	1 - 2	2 - 4
MASONIC	3 - 4	4 - 6
National Art Co.		
Series 679	5 - 6	6 - 8
Series 1444	5 - 6	6 - 8
MECHANICALS, DIE-CUT		
Circle H 100 Series	15 - 20	20 - 25
P.F.B. Ser. 9526 Day-Month-Date	40 - 45	45 - 50
See Clapsaddle Halloween Mechanicals, others.		
MERRY WIDOW HATS		
Grollman	3 - 4	4 - 5
METAMORPHICS, Real Photos		
Skulls, "Diabolo"	25 - 30	30 - 35
Bismarck, Napoleon	15 - 20	20 - 25
Others	15 - 20	20 - 25
MEXICAN REVOLUTION	4 - 5	5 - 6
Real Photos	10 - 15	15 - 20
Pancho Villa	20 - 22	22 - 25
W.H. Horne - Add $2-3 per card.		
MIDGETS, GIANTS	5 - 8	8 - 10
MILITARY, Battles	2 - 3	3 - 4
Comics	3 - 4	4 - 5
Officers	3 - 5	5 - 8
Soldiers	2 - 3	3 - 4
Valentine Co.	4 - 5	5 - 6
R. Tuck "Military Life" Series (6)	6 - 8	8 - 10
"Military in London" (6)	6 - 8	8 - 10
Gale & Polden "Military Uniforms"	5 - 6	6 - 8
Langsdorf & Co. "Military Officers"	10 - 12	12 - 14
MILK CARTS	3 - 6	6 - 8
Real Photo	8 - 10	10 - 15
MILK WAGONS, TRUCKS See Real Photo		

MILLS, Industry	3 - 4	4 - 6
Real Photo Interior	10 - 15	15 - 20
Real Photo Exterior	8 - 10	10 - 15
MINING	5 - 6	6 - 8
Real Photo	8 - 10	10 - 12
MINING DISASTERS	8 - 10	10 - 15
MIRRORS	1 - 2	2 - 3
MONKEYS, APES	2 - 3	3 - 4
See Dressed Animals		
MONTHS OF YEAR	3 - 4	4- 6
MONUMENTS	1 - 2	2 - 3
MOTHER & CHILD	4 - 5	5 - 7
MOTORCYCLES	6 - 8	8 - 10
NAMED	10 - 12	12 - 15
Others	6 - 8	8 - 10
See Real Photos.		
MOTTOES	0.50 - 1	1 - 2
MOVIE STARS (See Actors/Actresses)		
MUSHROOMS	1 - 2	2 - 3
MUSICAL INSTRUCTORS	2 - 3	3 - 5
MYTHOLOGY	5 - 6	6 - 9
NAMES		
R. Tuck Series 131	5 - 6	6 - 7
Rotograph Co. Real Photos	5 - 6	6 - 7
NATIONAL SOCIALISM	12 - 15	15 - 25
NATIVES	3 - 4	4 - 6
SEMI-NUDES	8 - 10	10 - 14
NAVY		
R. Tuck		
U.S. Navy Series 2326	8 - 10	10 - 12
Illustrated P.C. Co.	8 - 10	10 - 12
NESBITT, EVELYN	10 - 12	12 - 15
NEWSPAPER	3 - 4	4 - 6
NORTH POLE EXPEDITION	10 - 15	15 - 25
NOVELTY		
APPLIQUED MATERIALS		
Feathered Birds, Feathered Hats	4 - 5	5 - 6
Flowers	1 - 2	2 - 3
Jewelry	3 - 4	4 - 5
Metal Models	7 - 8	8 - 10
Real Hair	10 - 15	15 - 20
Silk	3 - 4	4 - 10
Shells	2 - 3	3 - 4
Velvet	3 - 4	4 - 10
Miscellaneous	1 - 2	2 - 3
NOVELTY PAPER CUT-OUTS		
R. Tuck 3381, Series 1, S/M. E. Banks (6)	100 - 110	110 - 125
R. Tuck 3382, Series 2 (6)	100 - 110	110 - 125
"Baby Bunting"		

Mechanical Kaleidoscope
International Art Pub. Co., 51788

Day-Date-Month Mechanical
P.F.B., 7452

"Little Bo Beep"
"Little Jack Horner"
"The Knave of Hearts"
"Mary, Mary Quite Contrary"
"Little Miss Muffet"

R. Tuck 3383, Series 3 (6)	100 - 110	110 - 125
R. Tuck 3384, Series 4 S/M. E. Banks (6)	100 - 110	110 - 125
R. Tuck 3385, Series 5 S/Louis Wain (6)	200 - 250	250 - 300
MECHANICALS		
Special Types	20 - 30	30 - 40
Kaleidoscopes	15 - 20	20 - 30
Lever-pull	5 - 10	10 - 15
Rotating Wheels	10 - 15	15 - 20
Miscellaneous	8 - 10	10 - 15
See Halloween.		
TRANSPARENCIES		
"Meteor"	10 - 15	15 - 30
Exhibitions	8 - 10	10 - 15
Comics, Views	8 - 10	10 - 15
Fairy Tales	10 - 15	15 - 18
Year Dates	10 - 15	15 - 20
MISCELLANEOUS		
Aluminum	4 - 6	6 - 10
Bas Relief	3 - 4	4 - 5

Royalty	10 - 12	12 - 18
Book Marks		
Common	1 - 2	2 - 3
Artist-Signed	3 - 5	5 - 10
Celluloid	5 - 6	6 - 8
Glass Eyes	2 - 3	3 - 4
Glitter	.50 - 1	1 - 1.50
Hold-to-Light (See Koehler, Christmas, etc.)		
Jig Saw Puzzles	7 - 8	8 - 15
Leather	2 - 3	3 - 5
Specials	6 - 10	10 - 20
Miniature Cards	4 - 5	5 - 8
Easter Witches	12 - 15	15 - 20
Peat	6 - 8	8 - 12
Perfumed	3 - 4	4 - 5
Photo Inserts	1 - 2	2 - 3
Pull-outs	2 - 3	3 - 4
Records	10 - 12	12 - 20
Satin Finish	4 - 5	5 - 6
Specials	8 - 10	10 - 20
Squeakers	2 - 3	3 - 4
Stamp Montage	6 - 7	7 - 10
Wire Tales	6 - 8	8 - 12
Wood	5 - 7	7 - 10
NUDES (See Nudes)		
NURSERY RHYMES (See Fantasy)		
NURSES	5 - 6	6 - 8
OCEAN LINERS (See Transportation)		
OCCUPATIONS	6 - 8	8 - 12
R. Tuck -- A. Selige		
E. Curtis	8 - 10	10 - 12

"A cobbler sweetheart ..."
"All a-tiptoe ..."
"Be a baker ..."
"Come let me whisper ..."
"Cupid said you melted ..."
"Dear little teacher, ..."
"If I a sweetheart had ..."
"If you can heal a wounded ..."
"Just a line o'type ..."
"Links of love ..."
"My heart is nailed ..."
"O, queen of cooks, ..."
"O, would I were an artist ..."
"Pray if you love me, ..."
"Punch, punch, punch ..."
"The lark with notes ..."
"'Tis needless to try ..."
"What a bargain ..."

"When you're a grown-up ..."
"You may add to ..."
"You serve me kindly, ..."
"You'd keep the peace, ..."
"A little soldier ..."

OIL WELLS	3 - 4	4 - 6
OPERA SINGERS	4 - 6	6 - 8
OPIUM SMOKERS	4 - 6	6 - 8
ORANGES	1 - 2	2 - 3
ORCHESTRAS	5 - 6	6 - 8
ORGANS, MUSICAL	4 - 5	5 - 6
ORPHANAGES	4 - 5	5 - 8
OSTRICHES	2 - 3	3 - 4
OWLS	6 - 8	8 - 12
PALACES	2 - 3	3 - 4
PAPER DOLL CUT-OUTS		
R. Tuck "Window Garden" Ser. 3400 (6)	50 - 75	75 - 100
PARADES, Color	4 - 5	5 - 6
Real Photo	8 - 10	10 - 12
PASSION PLAY		
Conwell Red Borders	5 - 6	6 - 7
Others	4 - 5	5 - 6
PATRIOTIC (See Greetings)	4 - 5	5 - 8
National Song Series (6)	4 - 6	6 - 8
PENITENTIARIES	4 - 5	5 - 6
PENNANTS	1 - 2	2 - 3
PERSONALITIES		
Buffalo Bill	10 - 12	12 - 15

Real Photo, Joseph Stalin

French Lindbergh, "Traverse de L'Atlantique" -- 21 May 1927

Calamity Jane	6 - 8	8 - 10
Winston Churchill	8 - 10	10 - 12
Elvis	5 - 8	8 - 12
Wild Bill Hickock	6 - 8	8 - 10
Elbert Hubbard	5 - 6	6 - 8
Charles Lindbergh	10 - 15	15 - 20
Benito Mussolini	10 - 15	15 - 20
Wally Post	6 - 8	8 - 10
Will Rogers	8 - 10	10 - 15
Billy Sunday	6 - 8	8 - 10
Joseph Stalin	12 - 15	15 - 20
PHONOGRAPHS	5 - 6	6 - 7
PHYSICIANS	5 - 6	6 - 8
Comics	6 - 8	8 - 10
PIANOS	3 - 4	4 - 5
PIGEONS	2 - 3	3 - 5
PIGS (See Dressed Animals)	3 - 4	4 - 5
PILGRIMS	2 - 3	3 - 4
PIN-UP GIRLS	3 - 4	4 - 7
PLAYING CARDS	4 - 6	6 - 7
POLICEMEN	4 - 5	5 - 7
POLITICAL		
"Billikens" (Bryan & Taft)	175 - 200	200 - 225
Others	8 - 10	10 - 12
AMP CO.		
Ethel DeWees		
"Billy Possum" Series (6)		
"Just a few lines..."	15 - 18	18 - 22
"It's a bad thing to ..."		

Mutoscope Glamour Series

Glamour Girls: Rarity 2-4; 32-card set by various artists
All-American Girls: Rarity 2-5; 33-card set by various artists
Yankee Doodle Girls: Rarity 2-5; 32-card set by various artists
Follies Girls: Rarity 4-6 (most are 5); 32-card set by various
   artists
Hotcha Girls: Rarity 3-5 (*My Diver's License* only R-10 and
   Golden Hour R-8 are also in this set); 65-card set, all by
   Earl Moran.
Artist Pin-Up Girls: Rarity 1-4; 64-card set by various artists

<u>Values:</u>   Rarity 1 to 10 for cards in NM condition; Mint cards
will command a premium as lesser grades will cost less than
prices below.*

R-1	$10	<u>Note:</u> Artists of these sets were Elvgren,
R-2	$11	Moran, Frahm, Armstrong, D'ancona, Layne,
R-3	$13	Showalter, del Masters, Leslie, Devorss,
R-4	$16	Connally, Harris, GCA, Alden, Earl Christy,
R-5	$20	Russ, Mozert, Munson and Unknowns.
R-6	$25	
R-7	$30	
R-8	$40	
R-9	$55-75	
R-10	$180-220	

Exhibit Supply Company made 4 sets; cards will have either
"Litho USA" or "Litho in USA" on them, but will not say
Exhibit Supply or Mutoscope anywhere on cards. All these
cards are rare or scarce.

Calendar Girls I: Rarity 7-9; 32-card set by various artists.
Calendar Girls II: Rarity 6-8; 32-card set by various artists
Slick Chicks (Dipsy Doodles): Rarity 6-7; 32-card set by
   various artists.
Slick Chick Twins: Rarity -- 5 on all; 32-card set by various
   artists. Feature 2 girls on each card, horizontal format.

* Rarity system designed by Robert L. Schulhof, Publisher of
   Penny Arcade in Acton, California.

❖❖❖

Article by Gordon L. Gesner, 1800 24th Street N.E., Salem,
Oregon 97303; phone (503)371-3998 and fax (503)371-4154.

"The Nation's Choice"
Bryan-Kern, M.M. Rose Company

E.F.D. (Ethel DeWees)
A.M.P. Co., "Billy Possum Series"

"At the right is Willie B. ..."
I. Grollman, 1908

"Yale's Favorite Son"
"Arrived here just..."
"I'm going to make..."
"I'll make another..."

HSV CO.
Crite

"Billy Possum" Series (12)	15 - 20	20 - 25

"Are You Dead..."
"Aw, don't play possum..."
"The Boogie Man'll Get You..."
"Dear Friends..."
"Dear, Am unavoidably detained..."
"Do it Now!"
"Give my regards to Bill!"
"Good eating here"
"I'm having a high old time..."
"It's a Great Game..."
"Oo's 'ittle' possum is 'oo'?"
"Very Busy, Both Hands Full..."

Lounsbury, Fred C.

Billy Possum Series 2515, Emb., Sepia (4)

1. "The only Possums that escaped"	18 - 20	20 - 22

2. "Billy Possum and Jimmie Possum..."
3. "Moving day in Possum Town"

4. "Good bye Teddy"
Billy Possum Series 2517 (4)
1. "Uncle Sam's new toy"   15 - 18   18 - 20
2. "Columbia's latest possum..."
3. "Billy Possum to the front"
4. "The Nation's Choice"

Fuller & Fuller Co.
Grollman Political Set
Bryan and Taft, 1908 (16) with Uncle Sam
Presidential Race, Baseball Game,
Winners & Losers   45 - 50   50 - 55

Miscellaneous

1896 Campaign

William McKinley-Hobart	50 - 55	55 - 60
William J. Bryan	40 - 50	50 - 55

1900 Campaign

Eugene V. Debs, Socialist Party	600 - 650	650 - 700
Roosevelt-Fairbanks	35 - 40	40 - 45
McKinley & Roosevelt Jugates, PMC	40 - 45	45 - 50

1904 Campaign

Eugene V. Debs, Socialist Party	600 - 650	650 - 700
Parker-Davis	100 - 150	150 - 200
"Teddy Roosevelt, He's Good Enough for Me", P/Huld	20 - 25	25 - 30
Roosevelt-Fairbanks	20 - 25	25 - 30

1908 Campaign

Eugene V. Debs, Socialist Party	500 - 550	550 - 600
Taft-Sherman Jugates	15 - 18	18 - 22
William H. Taft	15 - 18	18 - 22
William Jennings Bryan	18 - 22	22 - 25
I. Grollman "Willie B. and Willie T. ..."	18 - 22	22 - 25

1912 Campaign

Eugene V. Debs, Socialist Party	500 - 550	550 - 600
Champ Clark	35 - 40	45 - 50
Woodrow Wilson-Marshall	15 - 18	18 - 22
Democratic Wire Tail Donkey-Wilson	30 - 35	35 - 40
Republican Wire Tail Donkey-Taft	30 - 35	35 - 40
T. Roosevelt-Johnson (Progressive Party)	40 - 50	50 - 60
Taft-Roosevelt Mechanical	50 - 55	55 - 65
Prohibition Candidates		
Eugene Chafin/Aaron Watkins	80 - 90	90 - 100

1916 Campaign

Eugene V. Debs, Socialist Party	300 - 350	350 - 400
Progressive party (Roosevelt)	35 - 40	40 - 50
Charles E. Hughes (Republican)	30 - 35	35 - 40
Wilson-Taft	18 - 20	20 - 22
Wire-tail Political (Roosevelt)	75 - 85	85 - 100

1920 Campaign

Eugene V. Debs, Socialist Party	100 - 125	125 - 150

Harding-Coolidge	15 - 20	20 - 25
Cox-Roosevelt	20 - 25	25 - 28
1924 Campaign		
Coolidge-Dawes (w/borders), post election	20 - 25	25 - 30
John W. Davis	20 - 25	25 - 30
LaFollette-Wheeler (Progressive)	50 - 60	60 - 75
1928 Campaign		
Hoover-Curtis	12 - 15	15 - 20
Al Smith	20 - 25	25 - 28
1932 Campaign		
Roosevelt-Garner	12 - 15	15 - 20
Herbert Hoover	15 - 20	20 - 25
1936 Campaign		
Landon-Knox	20 - 25	25 - 30
Roosevelt	15 - 18	18 - 22
1940 Campaign		
Wilkie-McNary	15 - 18	18 - 22
Roosevelt-Wallace	15 - 18	18 - 22
"Franklin Roosevelt, Our Next President"	20 - 25	25 - 30
1944 Campaign		
Thomas Dewey, "Vote Republican Nov. 7"	15 - 18	18 - 22
Roosevelt-Truman	10 - 12	12 - 15
1948 Campaign		
Truman-Barkley	12 - 15	15 - 18
Thomas E. Dewey	12 - 15	15 - 18
Wallace-Taylor (Progressive)	20 - 25	25 - 28
1952 Campaign		
Eisenhower-Nixon	12 - 15	15 - 18
Adlai Stevenson	10 - 12	12 - 15
1956 Campaign		
Eisenhower-Nixon	6 - 8	8 - 10
Stevenson	6 - 8	8 - 10
1960 Campaign		
Nixon-Lodge	6 - 8	8 - 10
Kennedy-Johnson	6 - 8	8 - 10
1964 Campaign		
Johnson-Humphrey	5 - 6	6 - 8
Barry Goldwater	4 - 5	5 - 6
1968 Campaign		
Nixon-Agnew-Humphrey	4 - 5	5 - 6
1972 Campaign		
McGovern-Eagleton	8 - 10	10 - 12
Nixon-Ford	4 - 5	5 - 6
1976 Campaign		
Jimmy Carter	6 - 8	8 - 10
1980 Campaign		
Carter-Mondale	4 - 5	5 - 6
Reagan	2 - 3	3 - 4
POSTCARD SHOPS	15 - 20	20 - 25

Advertising Postcards	12 - 15	15 - 20
POSTMEN	6 - 7	7 - 9
POULTRY		
H.K. & Co., Series 356	4 - 5	5 - 7
T.S.N., Series 540	4 - 5	5 - 7
PRESIDENTS, SETS/SERIES		
Cromwell "Roosevelt in Africa" (16)	7 - 8	8 - 10
Hugh C. Leighton		
Unnamed Series		
Similar to **Tuck's** below. (25)	6 - 7	7 - 9
W.R. Gordon, Phila. Unnumbered (25) B&W	4 - 5	5 - 6
M.A. Sheehan (1940's) (32)		
Serigraphs by Paul Dubosclard (32)	4 - 5	5 - 6
R. Tuck Series 2328		
S/L. Spinner		
"Presidents of the United States" (24)	6 - 8	8 - 10
President Taft - Added Later	12 - 15	15 - 18
"President Theodore Roosevelt" Ser. 2333	15 - 18	18 - 22
Underwood & Underwood		
"Roosevelt's African Hunt" (40)	5 - 6	6 - 7
PRISONS	5 - 6	6 - 7
PROPAGANDA	7 - 9	9 - 12
German	10 - 15	15 - 20
Russian	15 - 20	20 - 30
PUZZLES	3 - 4	4 - 5
QUEEN'S DOLL HOUSE		
R. Tuck		
Series 4500 Set 1 (8)	6 - 8	8 - 9
Series 4501 Set 2 (8)	6 - 7	7 - 8
Series 4502 Set 3 (8)	6 - 7	7 - 8
Series 4503 Set 3 (8)	6 - 7	7 - 8
Series 4504 Set 4 (8)	6 - 7	7 - 8
Series 4505 Set 5 (8)	6 - 7	7 - 8
QUOTATIONS	1 - 2	2 - 3
RABBITS	1 - 2	2 - 3
Dressed	5 - 8	8 - 12
RACING, Auto	8 - 10	10 - 12
Dog	5 - 6	6 - 7
Horse	7 - 8	8 - 10
RADIO STARS, Early Years	6 - 7	7 - 8
RAINBOWS	3 - 4	4 - 6
REBUS CARDS	5 - 6	6 - 8
REGIMENTAL BADGES	4 - 6	6 - 8
RELIGIOUS (See Religious)	1 - 3	3 - 5
REPTILES	2 - 3	3 - 4
RESTAURANTS (See Views and Real Photos)		
RETIREMENT HOMES	2 - 3	3 - 4
RIVERS	0.50 - 1	1 - 1.50
RODEOS	3 - 4	4 - 5

Her Majesty Queen Alexandra
Stewart & Woolf Series 105

Her Majesty Queen Elizabeth II

Real Photos	6 - 8	8 - 10
ROWING	3 - 4	4 - 5

ROYALTY, EUROPEAN

GREAT BRITAIN

QUEEN VICTORIA
1897 DIAMOND JUBILEE

Postally Used, 1897	200 - 220	220 - 235
Unused	100 - 110	110 - 125
Raphael Tuck & Sons		
Portraits	20 - 22	22 - 28
Family Groups	8 - 10	10 - 12
Foreign Issues	12 - 15	15 - 18
Mourning Issues	12 - 15	15 - 18

KING EDWARD VII
1901 ROYAL TOUR
Wrench "Links of Empire" (20)

Postally Used from Tour Cities	30 - 35	35 - 40
Unused	20 - 25	25 - 30

1902 CORONATION SERIES
Raphael Tuck & Sons

Color/Embossed	15 - 20	20 - 25

Series 655, B&W	10 - 12	12 - 15
Stewart & Woolf, Series 105 (10)	12 - 15	15 - 20
S/H. Cassiers, Views	8 - 10	10 - 14
Other Publishers	6 - 8	8 - 12
Views of Coronation Procession	3 - 6	4 - 6
Royal Visits to Foreign Countries	12 - 15	15 - 20
Royal Visits ot Great Britain	10 - 12	12 - 15
Mourning Cards	5 - 6	6 - 8
Portraits	5 - 6	6 - 8
Family Groups	4 - 5	5 - 6
Children	4 - 5	5 - 6

KING GEORGE V

Souvenir Cards	10 - 12	12 - 15
Coronation Procession	2 - 3	3 - 4
Rotary Photo, Real Photos	8 - 10	10 - 12
Others	6 - 8	8 - 10
1935 SILVER JUBILEE		
Souvenir Cards	6 - 8	8 - 10
Portraits & Family Groups	2 - 3	3 - 5
Visits	10 - 12	12 - 15
Mourning & Funeral Cards	2 - 4	4 - 7

KING EDWARD VIII

Wedding Souvenir	30 - 35	35 - 40
Coronation Souvenir	6 - 8	8 - 10
Portraits	3 - 5	5 - 7
King Edward w/Mrs. Simpson	30 - 35	35 - 40
Visits	10 - 12	12 - 18

KING GEORGE VI

1937 Coronation Souvenir Card	4 - 5	5 - 7
Visits	8 - 10	10 - 15
Mourning Cards, 1952	5 - 6	6 - 8
Others	2 - 3	3 - 6

QUEEN ELIZABETH II

Wedding, 1947 Souvenir Cards	5 - 6	6 - 8
Coronation Souvenir Cards	3 - 4	4 - 6
Raphael Tuck & Sons	5 - 6	6 - 8
Children	2 - 3	3 - 4
Portraits	2 - 3	3 - 4
Visits	7 - 8	8 - 10

MISCELLANEOUS BRITISH

Raphael Tuck & Sons		
Kings & Queens of England		
Series 614, 615, 616 (12)	10 - 12	12 - 15
Series 617 (1)	12 - 14	14 - 18
Faulkner Series	8 - 10	10 - 12

RUSSIA

Color Portraits	30 - 35	35 - 40
B&W Portraits	20 - 25	25 - 30

Coronation Souvenir 1902
R. Tuck Coronation 608 II

King George V & Queen Mary
Rotary Photo 41H

Family Groups	30 - 35	35 - 40
Children of the Czar	40 - 45	45 - 50
Rasputin	6 - 8	8 - 12
Comical/Propaganda	12 - 15	15 - 20
Czar Nicholas, 1896 Visit to France	35 - 40	40 - 45
Others	6 - 8	8 - 10
GERMANY		
Portraits	8 - 10	10 - 15
Family Groups	6 - 8	8 - 10
Comical/Propaganda	10 - 12	12 - 15
OTHER EUROPEAN	4 - 7	7 - 10
EASTERN EUROPE	5 - 8	8 - 10
P/AULT		
"RULERS OF THE WORLD" Series	8 - 10	10 - 12
OTHER RULERS	3 - 4	4 - 6
SAILORS	2 - 3	3 - 5
SAILBOATS	1 - 2	2 - 3
SALVATION ARMY	3 - 4	4 - 5
SAN FRANCISCO EARTHQUAKE	3 - 4	4 - 10
SANTA CLAUS (See Santas)		
SCHOOLS (See Views)		
23 SKIDDO	3 - 4	4 - 6
SCULPTURE	1 - 2	2 - 3
SCOUTS (See Boy Scouts)		

SEA SHELLS	1 - 2	2 - 3
SEPTEMBER MORN		
Various Cards	2 - 3	3 - 8
SHAKESPEARE		
C.W. Faulkner Series	6 - 7	7 - 9
SHEEP	1 - 2	2 - 3
SHIP WRECKS	5 - 8	8 - 15
SHIP YARDS	3 - 4	4 - 6
SHOES	2 - 3	3 - 4
SHOPS, Industry Exteriors	4 - 6	6 - 7
Interiors Real Photo	8 - 10	10 - 15
SILKS		
Beautiful Ladies, Children	15 - 18	18 - 25
Cats, other animals	10 - 12	12 - 15
Greetings	5 - 6	6 - 8
Woven Silks		
Glasgow Exhibition, 1911	45 - 50	50 - 55
"Hands Across the Sea" (19)	40 - 45	45 - 50
The Million Dollar Pier, Atlantic City	45 - 50	50 - 55
Presidential - Taft, Roosevelt, Wilson	150 - 175	175 - 200
St. Louis 1904 World's Fair (14)	300 - 325	325 - 350
Ships - "Mauretania," Others	35 - 40	40 - 45
See "P. Boileau" for most expensive silk card.		
SINGERS	2 - 3	3 - 5
SKATING, Ice	3 - 6	6 - 8
Roller	4 - 6	6 - 10
SKELETONS, SKULLS	4 - 6	6 - 10
SKIING	3 - 5	5 - 7
SLEDDING	3 - 4	4 - 5
SNAKES	3 - 4	4 - 6
SNOWMEN (See Fantasy)		
SONGS Charles Rose Series #11 (24)	6 - 8	8 - 10
SPOONS	3 - 4	4 - 5
STADIUMS, Football, Early	6 - 7	8 - 15
Others (See Baseball, Etc.)	3 - 4	4 - 8
STAGE		
Maude Adams	8 - 10	10 - 12
Lillian Russell	12 - 14	14 - 18
Others	4 - 5	5 - 8
SPANISH AMERICAN WAR	5 - 8	8 - 10
STAMP CARDS		
Kunzli Bros., Paris Series	10 - 12	12 - 15
Maduro, Jr., Panama Series	7 - 8	8 - 10
Menke-Huber Series	10 - 12	12 - 15
P/Piero, Luigi, Italy Series	7 - 8	8 - 10
P/Stengel Series (12)	8 - 9	9 - 10
P/VSM Series	7 - 8	8 - 10
P/Muller, s/Zieher	8 - 10	10 - 14
P/Zieher, Ottmar (add $2 if embossed)	8 - 10	10 - 14

Others	7 - 8	8 - 10
STAMP MONTAGE	5 - 6	6 - 8
STATE GIRLS (See Sets & Series)		
STATE CAPITALS & Seals (See Sets & Series)		
STATUE OF LIBERTY	2 - 4	4 - 8
Hold-To-Light	35 - 40	40 - 50
STATUES	1 - 2	2 - 4
STORKS	2 - 3	3 - 5
STREET SCENES (See Views and Real Photos)		
STRIKES, Labor	8 - 10	10 - 12
STUDENTS	2 - 3	3 - 5
STUNTMEN	4 - 5	5 - 8
SUBMARINES	4 - 6	6 - 10
SUBWAYS	3 - 5	5 - 10
SUFFRAGETTES		
AA Pub. Co.		
698/12 "Stumping For Votes"	10 - 12	12 - 15
Attwell, Mabel Lucie		
Little Girl, "Where's My Vote"	18 - 20	20 - 25
H.B.G. "Votes for Women"	60 - 70	70 - 80
LEVI, C.		
"Komical Koons" Series 210, 3308	20 - 22	22 - 25
Bergman Co.		
Series 6342, S/B. Wall	12 - 14	14 - 16
Cargill Co, Michigan		
Series 103-129	12 - 15	15 - 18
Campbell Art Co. S/Chamberlin (6)	15 - 18	18 - 22
Clapsaddle	60 - 70	70 - 80
Dunston-Weiler Litho Co.		
1 "Suffragette Madonna"	18 - 20	20 - 25
2 "Electioneering"	18 - 20	20 - 25
3 "Pantalette Suffragette"	18 - 20	20 - 25
4 "Suffragette Vote-Getter"	18 - 20	20 - 25
5 "Suffragette-Coppette"	18 - 20	20 - 25
6 "Uncle Sam-Suffragette...Easiest Way"	20 - 25	25 - 30
7 "Election Day"	18 - 20	20 - 25
8 "I Don't Care"	18 - 20	20 - 25
9 "Queen of the Poll"	18 - 20	20 - 25
10 "Where, Oh Where is My ..."	18 - 20	20 - 25
11 "I Want to Vote ..."	18 - 20	20 - 25
12 "I Love My Husband, But Oh You Vote"	18 - 20	20 - 25
L. & E., New York S/H.B.G.	40 - 50	50 - 60
Nash Suffragette Madonna		
"Crop of 1910"	12 - 16	16 - 20
GRACE O'NEILL		
Campbell Art Card	110 - 125	125 - 140
National Woman Suffrage Card	225 - 250	250 - 275
Roth & Langley, 1909 Issues	12 - 15	15 - 18

C. Twelvetrees, Unsigned
  Reinthal & Newman
  716 "I'll get that vote yet!!!" — 20 - 25 — 25 - 28
WELLMAN, WALTER, Artist & Publisher
  The Suffragette Series — 20 - 25 — 25 - 30
  "Bar"
  "Copess"
  "Every Year Will be Leap Year"
  "For Speaker of the House"
  "Generaless of the Army"
  "I Can Heartily Recommend My Wife"
  "Judgess"
  "Just Politics"
  "Letter Carrier"
  "Morning Suffragette Bulletin"
  "Our Choice, Miss Taffy"
  "Secretaryess of Treasury"
  "Should Women Mix in Politics"
  "Studentess"
  "To Whom It May Concern"
SUNBONNET BABIES
  Ullman, Day-of-theWeek (Uns/B. Wall) (7) — 12 - 15 — 15 - 18
SUPERLATIVES - Largest-Smallest — 2 - 3 — 3 - 5
SWANS — 1 - 2 — 2 - 3
SYNAGOGUES — 8 - 10 — 10 - 12
TARTANS — 3 - 4 — 4 - 5
TELEGRAMS — 1 - 2 — 2 - 3
TELEPHONES — 5 - 7 — 7 - 12
TEMPERANCE — 4 - 6 — 6 - 10
SHIRLEY TEMPLE
  Real Photos — 6 - 8 — 8 - 10
  Black & White, Color — 10 - 12 — 12 - 14
TENNIS, Courts — 5 - 6 — 6 - 8
  Matches in progress — 6 - 7 — 7 - 8
  Advertising Tennis Product — 12 - 15 — 15 - 25
  See Artist-Signed for Others.
THEATRES   (See Views and Real Photos)
THEATRICAL
  Maude Adams — 6 - 8 — 8 - 10
  Sarah Bernhardt (See A. Mucha) — 10 - 15 — 15 - 20
  Enrico Caruso — 8 - 10 — 10 - 12
  Zena Dare — 6 - 8 — 8 - 10
  Evelyn Nesbitt — 8 - 10 — 10 - 12
TIGERS — 2 - 3 — 3 - 5
TOLL GATES — 3 - 4 — 4 - 6
TORNADOES — 6 - 8 — 8 - 12
TRAINS AND TROLLEYS
  (See Transportation and Real Photos)
TRAMPS — 2 - 3 — 3 - 4

Suffrage, C. Twelvetrees
R&N 716, "I'll get that vote yet!!!"

"Day-of-the-Week" Sunbonnet
Ullman 1493, "Saturday"

TUNNELS	2 - 3	3 - 4
TURKEYS	1 - 2	2 - 3
TYPEWRITERS	3 - 4	4 - 6
UMBRELLAS	2 - 3	3 - 4
UNCLE SAM (See Greetings)		
U.S. NAVY (See Transportation)		
R. Tuck Series 2326	5 - 6	6 - 8
Illustrated P.C. Co.	4 - 5	5 - 6
U.S. NAVY LIFE & MISCELLANEOUS		
Mitchell, Edw. H.		
No. 1316 - 1329 (Color)	2 - 3	3 - 5
No. 4314 - 4318 (Black & White)	2 - 3	3 - 5
VIEWS (See Views and Real Photos)		
VOLCANOS	2 - 3	3 - 4
WANTED POSTERS	8 - 12	12 - 15
WAR BOND CAMPAIGNS POSTERS	12 - 15	15 - 20
Russian	30 - 35	35 - 45
WEDDINGS	3 - 5	5 - 6
Real Photos	5 - 6	6 - 8
Jewish	6 - 7	7 - 9
WHALES	3 - 5	5 - 8
WHOLE DAM FAMILY (Many)	4 - 5	5 - 7
WINDMILLS	2 - 4	4 - 6

WINERIES	3 - 5	5 - 8
WITCHES	4 - 6	6 - 8
Artist-Signed	8 - 10	10 - 15
Easter Witches, Scandinavian	10 - 12	12 - 14
Miniature cards	15 - 18	18 - 22
WORLD WAR 1	3 - 5	5 - 10
Daily Mail Series I thru XX (100)	4 - 6	6 - 8
Kavanaugh War Postals	3 - 5	5 - 7
Comics, Common	3 - 4	4 - 6
Comics, Bamforth	6 - 8	8 - 12
Camp Scenes	3 - 4	4 - 8
U.S.O./Salvation Army	4 - 5	5 - 6
Red Cross	5 - 6	6 - 8
War Scenes	4 - 5	5 - 6
W.C.A. Series 145-146	3 - 5	5 - 10
WORLD WAR II		
Comics, Linen	1 - 2	2 - 4
Hitler, Tojo, Mussolini Comics	3 - 5	5 - 10
Private Breger Comics	5 - 6	6 - 8
Camp Scenes	2 - 3	3 - 4
Army/Navy Air Force Bases	2 - 3	3 - 4
Third Reich Photos	10 - 12	12 - 20
Third Reich Black & White	8 - 10	10 - 15
(See Hitler)		
WRESTLING	3 - 5	5 - 6
YACHTING	2 - 3	3 - 5
YMCA	3 - 5	5 - 6
YWCA	4 - 5	6 - 7
ZODIAC		
P/Aenz	5 - 6	6 - 7
Jules Bien		
"Your Fortune" Series 37 (12)	5 - 6	6 - 8
P/Edw. H. Mitchell	12 - 15	15 - 19
P/R. Tuck, Series 128, s/DWIG	10 - 12	12 - 14
P/Paris Expo, 1900	100 - 125	125 - 150
P/Anon. 1970 Zodiac Series (12)	5 - 6	6 - 7
ZOOS	2 - 3	3 - 4

Collectors of transportation motifs were extremely active in the late 70's and 80's, but the activity abated until recently. Spiralling values of the ocean liner "Titanic" have fueled a surge in sales of Ocean Liners and other shippers. This action has brought out some good quality collections, and interest is currently very high.

The big market in Railway and Trolley depots has also activated good movement in the rails and rail-related issues. There was some wonderful material, including great advertising, published in these fields, and collectors are now able to take advantage of the current low values.

RAIL TRANSPORTATION

TRAINS

ENGINES	VG	EX
IDENTIFIED CLOSE-UP IMAGES*		
Real Photos	$ 12 - 15	$ 15 - 20
Color	8 - 10	10 - 12
Black & White	6 - 8	8 - 12
Advertising	10 - 15	15 - 20
Linens	2 - 3	3 - 5

"The Overland Limited," R. Tuck
2458, Famous American Expresses

"Delaware and Hudson Railroad"
Locomotive 653

Real Photo "Wellsburg-Bethany"
No. 3, Wellsburg, Virginia

Real Photo, Schenectady, N.Y.
United Publishing Company

Chromes or Reproductions	.50 - 1	1 - 1.50
Foreign, pre-1930	2 - 3	3 - 5
*Unidentified - deduct 25-50%.		
ENGINES AND CARS		
Real Photos	10 - 12	12 - 15
Color	6 - 8	8 - 10
Black & White	5 - 6	6 - 8
Advertising	6 - 10	10 - 15
Interiors, Advertising	10 - 12	12 - 18
Linens	1 - 2	2 - 3
Chromes or Reproductions	.50 - 1	1 - 1.50
Foreign, pre-1930	1 - 2	2 - 3
*Unidentified - deduct 25-50%.		
WRECKS, Real Photo		
Identified	10 - 15	15 - 25
Unidentified	5 - 8	8 - 12
RAIL YARDS, Repair Areas, etc.		
Real Photo	8 - 10	10 - 12

Color	3 - 5	5 - 8
Black & White	2 - 3	3 - 5
Linens	1 - 2	2 - 3
Chromes	.50 - 1	1 - 1.50

TRAIN STATIONS, DEPOTS

SMALL TOWNS

Color	5 - 8	8 - 12
Color, W/Train in Station	6 - 10	10 - 15
Real Photo	10 - 15	15 - 25
Real Photo W/Train in Station	12 - 18	20 - 30
Linens	3 - 4	4 - 6
Chromes	1 - 2	2 - 3
Foreign, pre-1930	2 - 3	3 - 6

LARGE CITIES

Color	1 - 2	2 - 3
Color, W/Train in Station	2 - 3	3 - 4
Real Photo	4 - 5	5 - 7
Real Photo W/Train in Station	5 - 6	6 - 8
Linens	1 - 1.50	1.50 - 2
Chromes	.50 - .75	.75 - 1
Foreign, pre-1930	1 - 2	2 - 3

ELEVATED RAILWAYS

LARGE CITIES (N.Y., Chicago, etc.)

Close-up Images	2 - 3	3 - 4
Small Images	1 - 2	2 - 3
Linens	1 - 1.50	1.50 - 2
Chromes	.50 - 1	1 - 1.50

SMALLER CITIES

Close-up Images	3 - 4	4 - 6
Small Images	2 - 3	3 - 4
Linens	1.50 - 2	2 - 2.50
Chromes	.75 - 1	1 - 1.50

INCLINE RAILWAYS

IDENTIFIED CLOSE-UP IMAGES*

Mauch Chunk, Pikes Peak, Mt. Washington	2 - 3	3 - 5
Mt. Tom, Un-Ca-Noo-Nuc Mt., Lookout Mt.	2 - 3	3 - 5
Angel's Flight, Mt. Penn, Mt. Beacon	2 - 3	3 - 5
Other, lesser known	3 - 4	4 - 6

Bowery and Doubledeck Elevated R. R., New York City.

"The Bowery and Doubledeck Elevated R.R., New York City"

IDENTIFIED SMALL IMAGES*

Most well known inclines	1 - 2	2 - 3
Other, lesser known	2 - 3	3 - 4

REAL PHOTOS, IDENTIFIED - Add 50%

*Unidentified - deduct 25-50%.

SUBWAYS

Large Car Images	6 - 8	8 - 10
Cars at Loading Platform	4 - 6	6 - 8
Linens	3 - 5	5 - 8
Chromes	1 - 2	3 - 4

ELECTRIC TROLLEYS

IDENTIFIED CLOSE-UP IMAGES*

Real Photo	15 - 20	20 - 25
Color	8 - 10	10 - 15
Black & White	6 - 8	8 - 12
Linens	3 - 4	4 - 6
Chromes and Reproductions	1 - 1.50	1.50 - 2
Foreign	3 - 4	4 - 6

* Unidentified - deduct 25-50%.

MEDIUM SIZE IN STREET SCENES

Real Photos	8 - 10	10 - 15
Color	5 - 8	8 - 10
Black & White	2 - 4	4 - 6
Linens	2 - 3	3 - 4

Chromes and Reproductions	.50 - 1	1 - 1.50
Foreign	1 - 2	2 - 3
WRECKS, REAL PHOTO		
Identified	12 - 15	15 - 18
Unidentified	6 - 8	8 - 10
TROLLEY STATIONS		
Small Towns		
Color	8 - 10	10 - 12
Color, W/Trolley in Station	10 - 12	12 - 14
Real Photo	9 - 12	12 - 16
Real Photo W/Trolley in Station	10 - 14	14 - 18
Linens	3 - 4	4 - 6
Chromes	1 - 2	2 - 3
Foreign, pre-1930	3 - 4	4 - 6
Large Cities		
Color	1 - 2	2 - 3
Color, W/Trolley in Station	2 - 3	3 - 4
Real Photo	4 - 5	5 - 6
Real Photo, W/Trolley in Station	5 - 6	6 - 7
Linens	.75 - 1	1 - 1.50
Chromes	.50 - .75	.75 - 1
Foreign, pre-1930	.50 - .75	.75 - 1
HORSEDRAWN TROLLEYS		
Color	10 - 12	12 - 15
Black & White	6 - 8	8 - 10
Real Photo	15 - 20	20 - 25
Linens, Chromes, Reproductions	1 - 2	2 - 3
Foreign, pre-1930	3 - 4	4 - 6

AIR TRANSPORTATION

AIRPLANES		
Pioneer, Named (1896-1910)	15 - 25	25 - 35
Early 1910-1914	12 - 25	25 - 35
Langley Plane (Real Photos)	30 - 40	40 - 60
Wright Flyers (Real Photos)	20 - 30	30 - 50
1910 Los Angeles Meet	12 - 18	18 - 30
Aeroplane Meet, Venice, CA	12 - 15	15 - 30
"Hoxsey Death Flight, Dec. 31, 1910"	20 - 25	25 - 30
"Louis Paulman making record flight altitude"	15 - 20	20 - 25
"Graham-White starting engine, 1910"	12 - 15	15 - 18
MAX RIGOT, CHICAGO		
1911 Chicago Aviation Meet	12 - 15	15 - 25

"Aeroplano Sommer," Fototlpia Alterocca - Terni, 7421

NC-4	30 - 40	40 - 60
"Spirit of St. Louis"	2 - 18	18 - 25
With Lindbergh	20 - 30	30 - 50
Air Meet, Compton, CA - 1910	15 - 18	18 - 22
Identified Accidents	30 - 40	40 - 50
Air Meet, Reims, France - 1909	20 - 25	25 - 30
MISCELLANEOUS		
French Aviation Set		
Glenn Curtis	30 - 35	35 - 40
De la Grange	25 - 30	30 - 35
Henri Demanest	25 - 30	30 - 35
Hubert Latham	30 - 35	35 - 40
Orville Wright	30 - 35	35 - 40
Bleriot	25 - 30	30 - 35
Voisin	25 - 30	30 - 35
Roger Sommer	25 - 30	30 - 35
Santo Dumont	25 - 30	30 - 35
Robert E. Pelterie	25 - 30	30 - 35
Anonymous Sepia Series 39424		
Glenn H. Curtis	20 - 25	25 - 30
Others	15 - 20	20 - 25
Raphael Tuck & Sons		
Aviation Series 406 (6)	18 - 20	20 - 25
Famous Aeroplanes Ser. 9943 (6)	18 - 20	20 - 25
Series 3101, 3103 (6)	12 - 15	15 - 18
Series 3144 (6)	15 - 18	18 - 22
DIRIGIBLES		
Pioneer, Named	20 - 30	30 - 50
La France Airship	20 - 40	40 - 60

Early 1898-1924	15 - 25	25 - 40
"Akron"	10 - 12	12 - 18
"Hindenberg"	20 - 30	30 - 50
Los Angeles (Real Photos)	15 - 20 .	20 - 30
Macon	12 - 18	18 - 25
R-34	20 - 30	30 - 40
R101	20 - 30	30 - 40
"Shenandoah"	15 - 20	20 - 30
Goodyear (Early)	12 - 18	18 - 25
Goodyear (Linen)	6 - 10	10 - 15
"Astra Torres" P/John Drew Real Photo	12 - 15	15 - 20
"Baby" P/John Drew Black & White	8 - 10	10 - 12
"Beta II" and "Gamma II" P/Mays Real Photo	12 - 14	14 - 18
"LeViolle de Paris, 1908" Real Photo	15 - 20	20 - 25

ZEPPELINS

Experimental Era 1898-1910	18 - 25	25 - 40
1910-1934	12 - 18	18 - 30
"Graf Zeppelin"	20 - 30	30 - 50

WAR PLANES

Early	10 - 15	15 - 25
W.W. I	I8 - 12	12 - 18
1918-1939	5 - 8	8 - 12
W.W. II	3 - 5	5 - 8
Post 1945 (Real Photos)	5 - 8	8 - 12

COMMERCIAL AIRLINES **(Usually Advertising)**

Identified, Pre-1930		
Western Airlines (earliest - 1929)	15 - 20	20 - 25
Others	12 - 15	15 - 20
1930's-1940's Linens, Black & White		
Penn Central	10 - 12	12 - 15
Central Airlines	10 - 12	12 - 15
Midwest Airlines	8 - 10	10 - 12
Pan Am, Delta, Continental, TWA,		
United, Pacific Southwest, Braniff,		
Catalina, Eastern, Northwest, Mohawk,		
North American, National, Island Air,		
American, Northwest Orient, Texas,		
International, Trans-Ocean, and		
Others	6 - 8	8 - 10
Real Photos - Add 25-50%.		
Chromes	1 - 2	2 - 5
Airfields, Linens	2 - 3	3 - 5
Advertising, without plane image	3 - 5	5 - 8
Advertising Interiors	4 - 5	5 - 10

Le "Titanic"
French Memorial Card

"Red Star Line"
Poster B-2 Series, S/H. Cassiers

Poster Card of the "Lloyd
Italiano" Line

The Cunard Line, "R.M.S.
Lusitania" - Published by P.C.S.

WATER TRANSPORTATION

OCEAN LINERS

Immigrants from all over Europe, Asia, Scandinavia and the British Isles headed for America, South America and Canada in search of a new life in the lands of plenty. These immigrants, many taking their life savings just to buy a ticket, were the main cause of the tremendous growth of the ocean liner trade, and were the leading passengers on all ships on the Atlantic Routes throughout the 1900-1940 era. Being very poor, these immigrants always traveled in the lower decks in 2nd and 3rd class.

On the other hand, the return trips to Europe were filled with prosperous Americans, among them the Rockefellers, Astors, and other millionaires of the times, for luxury vacation visits to the fashionable cities of their choice. To accommodate the elite upper class, owners of the various lines commissioned their shipbuilders to build the finest, most comfortable and most luxurious 1st class accommodations that money could buy.

Industrial advances in America and British Colony expansion buoyed the growth of British lines, while interests in East and Central Africa and commercial interests in South America led to great growth by the German shipping lines. America and other countries, viewing their early prosperity, began building ships so that they too could take advantage of the immigration to America. All tried to outdo the other by building bigger, faster, and more luxurious ships.

The British shipper, Cunard Lines, was the first and foremost in the industry. One of their liners, the "Mauretania," became the fastest ship to cross the Atlantic and held the record for 22 years. The "Titanic," of the White Star Lines and also from Britain, was destined to be the world's most famous ship after a disaster on it's maiden voyage in 1912. It sunk after hitting an iceberg in the North Atlantic, taking with it more than 1,500 rich and famous passengers, and many immigrants who were unable to get out of the lower decks because of the influx of water.

The advent of two World Wars was a great detriment to the growth of all the shipping and passenger lines. German submarines made the waters extremely treacherous. After the Cunard Liner "Lusitania" was sunk in 1914, shipping came to a standstill. Many of the great liners became troop ships to carry U.S. and other troops to battle. During the war many of the great liners were sunk on the open seas as well as in port. When the war was over, the various lines built new fleets and business prospered as before.

The same was true at the start of World War II. When war was declared, shipping ceased and many of the great liners, such as "The Queen Mary" and "The Queen Elizabeth," carried hundreds of thousands of U.S. troops to Europe...and back after the war was won. As in the first war, the casualty rate was tremendous on the ocean liners of the world. However, those that escaped were placed back in service, new ones were built, and the liner trade again prospered.

Two important factors caused the demise of the great luxury liners beginning in the late 1950's. First, immigration to North America came to a standstill and the rich and famous began flying to the beautiful cities of Europe. The liners all began losing money and one by one they were scuttled and sold for scrap. Now only a few remain of the tremendous number that once ruled the seas.

Postcard collectors have benefitted throughout the Ocean Liner period as most all the various lines advertised their ships and luxurious service to the utmost. Hundreds of beautiful advertising

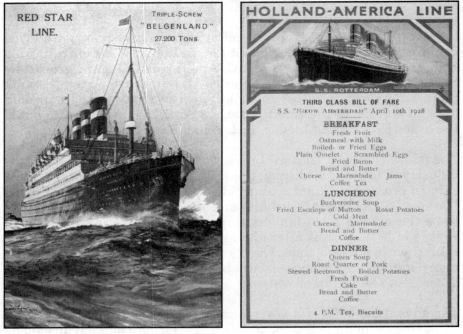

"Red Star Line"
Triple-Screw "Belgenland"

"Holland-America Line"
Third Class Menu

cards, showing magnificent ships at the docks and on the open seas, have survived and are among the most collectible in the hobby. There are reports, almost monthly, of big advances in the auction values of most all "Titanic" cards and early Poster Advertising. These big gains are helping to elevate prices on all of the other beautiful Ocean Liner material.

AMERICAN EXPORT LINES (1950's-1960's)	1 - 2	2 - 3
AMERICAN LINE		
"Haverford," "Kroonland," "Merian,"		
"New York," "Philadelphia,"		
"St. Louis," "Westernland"		
Color	10 - 12	12 - 15
Black & White	5 - 7	7 - 9
Interiors	10 - 15	15 - 18
Real Photos	12 - 15	15 - 20
Advertising	10 - 15	15 - 18
ANCHOR LINE*		
"Athenia," "Bolivia," "Caledonia,"		
"City of Rome," "Columbia," "Olympia,"		
"Transylvania," "Tuscania"		
Color	10 - 12	12 - 15

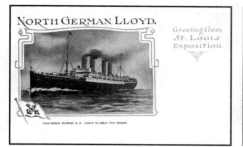 

"Kaiser Wilhelm der Gross"   *U.S. Navy Battleship "Iowa"*
St. Louis Exposition Poster   *Raphael Tuck 2324 Series*

Black & White	6 - 8	8 - 10
Interiors	12 - 15	15 - 18
Real Photos	12 - 15	15 - 20
Artist-Signed by W.T.N.	12 - 15	15 - 18
Advertising	12 - 15	15 - 18

*Purchased by CUNARD LINE in 1912.

BERGEN LINE (Norway)	2 - 3	3 - 4

CANADIAN PACIFIC

Color	6 - 8	8 - 10
Black & White	4 - 5	5 - 6
Real Photos	10 - 12	12 - 15
"Empress of Ireland" - Disaster	12 - 15	15 - 18
Advertising	12 - 15	15 - 18

CUNARD LINES*

    "Adriatic," "Alaunia" 1925, "Andavia,"
"Andonia," "Ansonia," "Antonia,"
"Aquiatania"1907, "Arabic," "Ascania,"
"Athenia" first ship torpedoed in WW2,
"Berengaria" 1918, "Britannic" 1934,
"Bothnia," "Campania" 1893, "Canopic,"
"Caronia" 1948 "Carpathia" 1903, "Catalonia,"
 "Cedric," "Celtic," "Cephalonia," "Corinthia,"
"Coronia," "Cymbric," "Etruria," "Folia,"
 "Franconia," "Gaelic," "Ivirnia," "Lancastria"
"Laurentic," "Luciana" 1893, "Lusitania"
1907, "Majestic," Mauretania" 1907, "Media"
1947, "Meganic," "Olympia," "Orduna,"
"Parthia" 1948, "Pavonia," "Persic,"
"Pittsburgh," "Republic," "Royal George,"
"Russia," "Saxonia," "Scythia," "Servia,"
"Teutonic," "Umbria," Others

*Artist-Signed cards by James S. Mann,
C.E. Turner, O. Rosenvenge and Walter
Thomas - add $2-3 per card.

Pre-1920 issues

Color	8 - 10	10 - 12
Black & White	3 - 4	4 - 5
Real Photo	10 - 12	12 - 18
Interior Views	10 - 12	12 - 15
Poster Advertising	20 - 25	25 - 35

Sunk in WW I
"Aurania," "Campania," "Franconia"

Color	10 - 12	12 - 15
Black & White	4 - 5	5 - 6
Real Photo	10 - 15	15 - 20
Interiors	10 - 15	15 - 20

"Lusitania" Sunk by Germans

Color	12 - 15	15 - 20
Black & White	6 - 8	8 - 10
Real Photos	15 - 20	20 - 30
Interiors	10 - 15	15 - 18
Interior Real Photos	15 - 20	20 - 25
Memorial Issues	15 - 20	20 - 25
Disaster Sketches	12 - 15	15 - 18

"Carpathia" 1903 Rescuer of Titanic

Color, telling of rescue	12 - 15	15 - 18
Real Photo, telling of rescue	20 - 25	25 - 30

CUNARD-WHITE STAR LINE, 1934-1948
New "Mauretania"
"Queen Elizabeth" 1938, "Queen
Mary" 1936, "Georgic" 1934, Others

Color	4 - 5	5 - 6
Black & White	2 - 3	3 - 4
Interiors	5 - 6	6 - 8
Advertising	10 - 12	12 - 15

CUNARD LINE, AFTER 1948
"Caronia" 1948, "Queen E. II" 1969

DOMINION LINE (Hands Across the Sea)	8 - 10	10 - 12

FRENCH LINE

Color	5 - 8	8 - 10
Black & White	3 - 5	5 - 7
Advertising	10 - 12	12 - 15
GDYNIA AMERICA LINE (Poland)	2 - 3	3 - 4
THE GRACE LINE	3 - 4	4 - 6
GREAT WESTERN ("Grand Trunk" R.R. Ferry)	4 - 5	5 - 6
GREEK LINE (1940-1970's)	1 - 2	2 - 3

HAMBURG-AMERICA LINE
"Alb. Ballin," "Amerika," "Belgravia,"
"Bismarck" 1914, "Blucher," "Caribia,"

"Cleveland," "Columbia" 1889, "Cordillera," "Deutchland" 1898, "Furst Bismarck," "Graf," "Hamburg," "Hansa," "Iberia," "Imperator" 1913, "Kaiser Friedrich," "Kaiserin Auguste Victoria" 1889, "Milwaukee" 1929, "Moltke," "New York," "Oceana," "Orinco," "Palatia," "Patricia," "Phoenicia," "Pres. Grant," "Princess Victoria Luise," "Reliance," "Pres. Lincoln," "Pennsylvania," "St. Louis" 1929, "Vaterland" 1914, "Waldersee," Others	10 - 12	12 - 15
Early Chromolithos, S/W. Stower & H. Buzrdt, P/Muhlmeister & Johler	20 - 22	22 - 28
Black & White Steel Engravings, S/W. Stower, P/Kutzner & Berger	12 - 15	15 - 18
Color	10 - 12	12 - 15
Black & White	6 - 8	8 - 10
Real Photos	15 - 20	20 - 25
Early Menus w/postcard attached	20 - 25	25 - 30
Poster Advertising	18 - 22	22 - 25
HAMBURG-SOUTH AMERICA LINE	5 - 7	7 - 10
HOLLAND-AMERICA LINE		
"Edam" 1921, "Maasdam" 1952, "Niew Amsterdam" 1906,"Nieuw Amsterdam II" 1938, "Potsdam" 1900, "Rotterdam" 1908, "Rotterdam II" 1959,"Ryndam," "Statendam" 1914, "Statendam II" 1929 - Bombed in 1940, "Statendam IV" 1957, "Veendam" 1923, "Volendam" 1920, "Werkendam," "Westdam" 1946, "Zaandam" 1938 - Torpedoed in war; Others		
Early Chromolithos S/C. Dixon and F. Parsing	10 - 12	12 - 15
Color	8 - 10	10 - 12
Black & White	4 - 5	5 - 7
Real Photos	12 - 15	15 - 18
Poster Advertising	15 - 20	20 - 25
After 1935	2 - 3	3 - 5
HOME LINES (1939-1970's)	2 - 3	3 - 4
ITALIAN LINE		
Color	5 - 7	7 - 10
Black & White	3 - 4	4 - 5
Poster Advertising	15 - 18	18 - 25

After 1935	2 - 3	3 - 4
MATSON LINE (1920-1930's)		
Color	5 - 7	7 - 10
Black & White	3 - 4	4 - 6
MOORE-McCORMICK LINES, INC.		
"Brazil" and "Argentina"	4 - 5	5 - 6

NORDDEUTSCHER LLOYD, Bremen
(North German Lloyd Lines)
"Amerika," 1903, "Alb. Ballin" 1923,
"Elbe," 1900, was sunk in collision,
"Imperator" 1913,
"Aller," "Barbarossa," "Berlin" 1955,
"Bremen" 1928, "Bulow," "Coblenz,"
"Columbus" 1922, "Dresden," "Eider,"
"Ems,""Europa" 1929, "Eitel Friedrich,"
"Fried. der Grosse," "Fulda," "Gen.
 v. Steuben," "George Washington,"
"Goeben," "Grosser Kurfurst," "Havel,"
"Kaiser Wilhelm II," "Kleist,"
"Konig Albert," "Kronprinz Wilhelm,"
"Kronprinze. Cecille" 1904, "Muenchen,"
"Orotava" "Prinzess Alice," "Prinzess
 Irene," "Prinz Regent Luitpold,"
"Roon," "Saale," "Scharnhorst," "Spree,"
"Trave," "Werra," "Wilh. Gostloff" was
 torpedoed in 1945 (6,096 died),
"York," Others

Early Chromoliths, S/T.v.E.	18 - 22	22 - 26
Black & White vignettes, S/T.v.E.	12 - 15	15 - 18
Black & White Engravings	10 - 12	12 - 18
Color	10 - 12	12 - 15
Black & White	6 - 8	8 - 10
Real Photos	15 - 18	18 - 22
Early Menus with postcard attached	20 - 25	25 - 30
Poster Advertising	20 - 25	25 - 35
St. Louis Exposition	15 - 20	20 - 25
BECAME HAPAG-LLOYD LINE IN 1932	4 - 5	5 - 6
BECAME BREMEN-AMERICAN LINE IN 1954	2 - 3	3 - 4
N.Y.K. LINE		
Color	8 - 10	10 - 12
Black & White	4 - 6	6 - 7
NORWEGIAN-AMERICAN LINE (1940-1980's)	1 - 2	2 - 3
O.S.K. LINE		
Color	8 - 10	10 - 12

Hamburg Amerika Linie
"President Lincoln"

Hamburg Amerika Linie
Real Photo,Tourist Class Cabin

Black & White	4 - 6	6 - 7
ORIENT LINE (Britain)	3 - 4	4 - 5
P & O LINE		
Color	6 - 8	8 - 10
Black & White	3 - 4	4 - 5
PANAMA-PACIFIC LINE	4 - 5	5 - 6
RED STAR LINE		
"Belgenland," "Finland," "Friesland,"		
"Kensington," "Kroonland," "Lapland,"		
"Marquette," "Noordland," "Pennland,"		
"Westernland," "Vaderland," "Zeeland"	8 - 10	10 - 15
P/American Litho Co. PMC's	15 - 18	18 - 22
Chromolitho Posters, S/H. Cassiers		
A Ser., B&W, of Ships & Dutch People	15 - 18	18 - 22
B Ser., Color, of Ships & Dutch People	20 - 25	25 - 30
C Ser., Color	20 - 25	25 - 30
H Ser., Color, of Ships in Harbor	20 - 25	25 - 30
Others S/H. Cassiers	10 - 12	12 - 15
Posters, S/V. Greten, K Series	12 - 15	15 - 18
Wood Engravings, S/Edw. Pellens		
L Ser., View and People of Antwerp	10 - 12	12 - 15
Art Deco O & P Series, P/J.L. Goffart	30 - 35	35 - 40

Poster Advertising	20 - 25	25 - 35
ROYAL MAIL LINE Britain-South America	5 - 6	6 - 8
SUD-ATLANTIQUE LINE		
"L'Atlantique"		
Color	8 - 10	10 - 12
Black & White	5 - 6	6 - 8
The L'Atlantique disaster	12 - 15	15 - 18
Others	6 - 7	7 - 9
SVENSKA (SWEDISH) AMERICA LINE		
Color	6 - 8	8 - 10
Black & White	4 - 5	5 - 6
Advertising	10 - 12	12 - 15
UNITED STATES LINE		
"Geo. Washington," "Leviathan,"		
"Manhattan," "Pres. Harding,"		
"Pres.Roosevelt," "Republic, "United States"		
1952, "The America" 1940		
S/Willy Stover	10 - 12	12 - 15
Color	8 - 10	10 - 12
Black & White	4 - 6	6 - 8
Real Photos	10 - 14	14 - 18
Advertising	10 - 12	12 - 15
UNITED FRUIT CO. (Great White Fleet)	1 - 2	2 - 3
WHITE STAR LINES*		
"Adriatic" 1902, "Albertic,"		
"Baltic" 1902, "Britannic" 1914 lost		
in WWI, "Britannic II" 1930,"Canopic,"		
"Cedric" 1902, "Celtic" 1901, "Ceramic,"		
"Cretic," "Doric" 1923, "Georgic,"		
"Germanic," "Homeric," "Lapland,"		
"Laurentic," "Majestic," "Megantic,"		
"Oceanic" 1899,"Olympic" 1911,		
"Republic" Rammed and sunk 1909,		
"Runic," "Suevic," "Vedic," Others		
Color	8 - 10	10 - 15
Black & White	5 - 7	7 - 10
Real Photos	10 - 15	15 - 20
S/Norman Wilkinsen or M. Black	10 - 15	15 - 20
Poster Advertising	20 - 30	30 - 40
Titanic - 1912		
Postally Used before 4/15/12	1,000 - 1250	1250 - 1500
Woven Silk	1,300 - 1500	1500 - 1750
Sea Trials - Belfast, Austrian R.P.	375 - 425	425 - 500
Pre-Sinking Real Photos	325 - 350	350 - 400

Real Photo Memorial Cards	100 - 125	125 - 150
Tucks	65 - 75	75 - 90
"Among the Icebergs," Valentine Pub.	75 - 85	85 - 100
"Steamer Titanic," Tichnor Bros. Pub.	75 - 85	85 - 100
"Nearer My God to Thee," Bamforth (6)	40 - 50	50 - 75
Australian, French, Misc. Publishers	100 - 150	150 - 200
Titanic/Olympic	30 - 40	40 - 50
Olympic	15 - 20	20 - 35
AFTER 1934	2 - 3	3 - 4
*White Star Lines and Cunard Lines		
merged in 1934.		

CELEBRATED LINERS SERIES
RAPHAEL TUCK (Oilette 6-Card sets)

3378, 3379, 6228 "White Star Lines"	10 - 12	12 - 15
3592	6 - 8	8 - 10
6229 "Orient-Pacific Line"	8 - 10	10 - 12
6230, 8960, 8961	8 - 10	10 - 12
9106 "The Cunard Line"	10 - 12	12 - 15
9121, "Canadian-Pacific Line"	8 - 10	10 - 12
9112, 9124, 9125	6 - 8	8 - 10
9126 "Atlantic Transport Line"	8 - 10	10 - 12
9133 "Union Castle Line"	8 - 10	10 - 12
914 "American Line"	10 - 12	12 - 15
9151, 9155, 9213	6 - 8	8 - 10
9215 "White Star Line"	10 - 12	12 - 15
9268 "Cunard Line"		
"Mauretania" (Image 1)	10 - 12	12 - 15
"Lusitania" (Image 1)	18 - 22	22 - 25
"Carmania"	8 - 10	10 - 12
"Lusitania" (Image 2)	18 - 22	22 - 25
"Mauretania" (Image 2)	10 - 12	12 - 15
"Carpathia"	12 - 15	15 - 18
9503 "White Star Line"	10 - 12	12 - 15
9625 "Canadian Pacific," Series II	8 - 10	10 - 12
9808 "White Star Line"		
"Titanic" (2)	65 - 75	75 - 90
Others	10 - 12	12 - 15

OTHER LINERS
PRE - 1930

Color	6 - 7	7 - 9
Black & White	4 - 5	5 - 7
Interiors, Real Photos	8 - 10	10 - 12
AFTER 1930	2 - 3	3 - 4

OCEAN COAST LINERS
CANADIAN PACIFIC RAILROAD
 "Princess Charlotte"   8 - 10 10 - 12
 "Princess Charlene"
 "Princess Victoria"
CLYDE STEAMSHIP LINE
 E. Coast, NY - Miami
 Early Vignettes, Black & White 10 - 12 12 - 15
 Color   8 - 10 12 - 15
 Real Photo   12 - 15 15 - 20
EASTERN STEAMSHIP LINES
 "Boston," "New York"
 Color   4 - 6 6 - 8
 Black & White   3 - 4 4 - 5
 Real Photo   8 - 10 10 - 15
FURNESS-BERMUDA LINE 1 - 2 2 - 3
MAINE STEAMSHIP CO.
 Color   4 - 6 6 - 8
 Black & White   3 - 4 4 - 5
 Real Photos   8 - 10 10 - 12
MATSON NAVIGATION CO. (San Francisco) 3 - 4 4 - 6
MERCHANTS & MINERS LINE (Atlantic Coast)
 Color   4 - 6 6 - 8
 Black & White   3 - 4 4 - 5
 Real Photos   8 - 10 10 - 12
  Old Dominion Line   6 - 8 8 - 10
PACIFIC MAIL CO. LINE (Pacific Coast)
 Color   4 - 6 6 - 8
 Black & White   3 - 4 4 - 5
 Real Photo   8 - 10 10 - 12
PANAMA PACIFIC LINE
  "City of Baltimore," "Newport News,"
  "Norfolk," "L.A.," "S.F.," "Calif.," "Penna."
  "Virginia"
 Color   5 - 7 7 - 10
 Black & White   3 - 5 5 - 7
 Real Photos   8 - 10 10 - 12
SAVANNAH LINE (NY-Boston-Miami)
  "City of Birmingham," "City of Chattanooga,"
  "City of Savannah," Others
 Color   5 - 7 7 - 10
 Black & White   3 - 5 5 - 7
 Real Photos   6 - 8 8 - 10
WARDS LINE New York-Havana

Color	6 - 8	8 - 10
Black & White	4 - 5	5 - 6
Real Photo of "Morro Castle" Wreck	10 - 12	12 - 15

WOVEN SILKS OF SHIPS

Stevensgraphs

"S. S. Haverford" and "R.M.S. Baltic"	70 - 80	80 - 90
"R.M.S. Mauretania"	80 - 90	90 - 100
Others	70 - 80	80 - 90

Hands Across the Sea/With Flags

"R.M.S. Victorian" and "S.S. Romanic"	40 - 50	50 - 60
Others	40 - 50	50 - 60

GREAT LAKES AND RIVER STEAMERS

HUDSON RIVER DAY LINE	4 - 6	6 - 7
"Robert Fulton," "New York"		
"Hendrick Hudson"		
Color	3 - 5	5 - 7
Black & White	2 - 3	3 - 4

D & C LINE

"City of Cleveland," Others

Color	3 - 4	4 - 6
Black & White	1 - 2	2 - 4

BATTLESHIPS/CRUISERS/NAVAL VESSELS

Arthur Livingston PMC's

"Maine"	12 - 15	15 - 20
Others	8 - 10	10 - 12
H.A. Rost, Pioneers & PMC's	15 - 20	20 - 30
American News Co.	4 - 5	5 - 7
American Souvenir Card Co.		
The White Squadron (12) "Patriographic"	10 - 12	12 - 15
A.C. Bosselman	5 - 7	7 - 9
Boston P.C. Co. (Brown-tint)	4 - 5	5 - 7
Britton & Rey	4 - 5	5 - 7
Brooklyn Eagle, Black & White	3 - 4	4 - 6
E.P. Charlton	5 - 7	7 - 9
Detroit Photographic Co.	5 - 7	7 - 9
Allen Fanjoy	3 - 4	4 - 5
Henderson Litho		
S/Enrique Muller	5 - 7	7 - 9
Illustrated P.C. Co.	5 - 7	7 - 9
L. Kaufmann & Sons	4 - 6	6 - 8

Hugh C. Leighton	5 - 7	7 - 9
Lowman & Hanford	5 - 7	7 - 9
Metropolitan News Co.	4 - 6	6 - 8
Edward H. Mitchell	5 - 7	7 - 9
Enrique Muller, P/Rotograph Co.		
Real Photos, 1904	6 - 8	8 - 10
Real Photos, 1910	6 - 8	8 - 9
Prudential Insurance Co. (U.S. & Foreign)	3 - 4	4 - 5
Rotograph Co.	5 - 6	6 - 8
Souvenir Postcard Co.	5 - 7	7 - 9
State of Washington, Puget Sound Ferries	5 - 7	7 - 9
Tichnor Bros.	5 - 6	6 - 8
S/Enrique Muller	6 - 8	8 - 10
Raphael Tuck		
1076 "U.S. Navy"	7 - 8	8 - 12
9082 "Our Ironclads"	5 - 7	7 - 10
1223 "U.S. Navy Cruisers"	7 - 8	8 - 12
2324 "U.S. Navy-Battleships"	7 - 8	8 - 12
4484 "U.S. Ironclads"	7 - 8	8 - 12
Valentine Series	4 - 5	5 - 7
C.E. Waterman, 1909	4 - 5	5 - 6

Battleship USS Utah, Real Photo

12

Baseball, Etc.

BASEBALL

Baseball enjoys the distinction of having two major collector groups, postcard and sports, who are vying for a great shortage of material. Therefore, any cards that surface are quickly purchased and, just as quickly, taken out of circulation again. Values vary widely, especially in some of the early 1900-1920 issues, and it is extremely difficult to value individual cards when so few are available.

Newer issues, especially those of Hall of Famers and those published by Perez Galleries, are enjoying much success because of the sports autograph craze. The cards are purchased by collectors and are signed by the players at sportscard and autograph shows.

We feel the values listed here are rather conservative, as prices realized on some issues may have been somewhat higher. Hopefully, greater numbers of these cards will surface so that a more accurate listing can be made in future editions.

A.C. DIETSCHE, 1907-09, B&W, Detroit Tigers	VG	EX
Series I, 1907		
Tyrus Cobb	$ 200 - 250	$ 250 - 300
Hughie Jennings	100 - 125	125 - 150
Others	70 - 80	80 - 90

Series II, 1908-09

Tyrus Cobb	200 - 250	250 - 300
Hughie Jennings	80 - 90	90 - 100
Team Picture	200 - 250	250 - 300
Others	70 - 80	80 - 90

A.C. DIETSCHE, 1907, B&W, Chicago Cubs

Tinker, Evers, Chance, Brown	200 - 250	250 - 300
Others	70 - 80	80 - 90

AMERICAN LEAGUE PUB. CO., 1908, (7)
Cleveland, B&W, Action + Oval Shots

Ty Cobb, Honus Wagner	200 - 250	250 - 300
Nap Lajoie	100 - 150	150 - 200

H.H. BREGSTONE, 1909-11 (40) Unnumbered

St. Louis Browns & Cardinals	90 - 100	100 - 125

BOSTON AMERICAN SERIES, 1912
Cream color w/Sepia Photos, Red Sox

Tris Speaker	90 - 100	100 - 125
BOSTON DAILY AMERICAN, 1912, B&W (3)	60 - 70	70 - 80

CINCINNATI REDS CHAMPIONS,
1920, B&W, (24)

Edd Roush	100 - 110	110 - 125
Others	50 - 60	60 - 70

EXHIBIT SUPPLY CO., Chicago, 1921-66
Postcard Backs only, 50's (32?)

Mantle, Mays	80 - 100	100 - 120
Musial, Campanella, Berra	30 - 40	40 - 50
Feller, Lemon, Kaline, Snider	20 - 30	30 - 40
Others	10 - 15	15 - 18

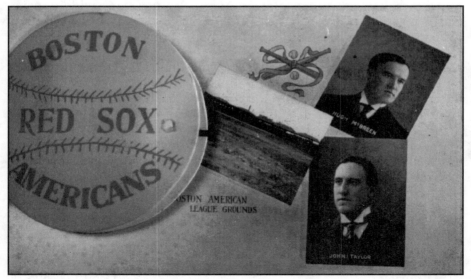

Section of Double-Fold by P. Furlong (Realized $3,520 at Auction)

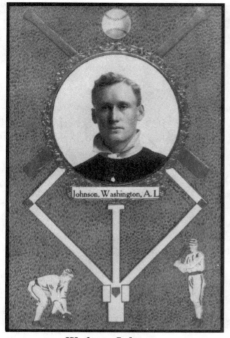

Walter Johnson
The Rose Company, 1909

Tyrus R. Cobb
A. C. Dietsche, 1907, Detroit

G.F. GRIGNON CO., 1907, Green Chicago Cubs
　Player Inset & Big Teddy Bear

Tinker, Evers, Chance	150 - 175	175 - 200
Others	75 - 85	85 - 100

GEORGE W. HALL, 1907, Black & White, (12)
　World Champs Chicago White Sox players

in ovals on socks on clothesline	100 - 125	125 - 150

V. O. HAMMON

Chicago Cubs Team	100 - 125	125 - 150

MORGAN STATIONERY CO., Cincinnati, 1907

Unnumbered Issues	150 - 175	175 - 200

NOVELTY CUTLERY CO., 1910, Sepia, (25)
　Players enclosed in frame

Wagner, Cobb, Johnson, Mathewson	175 - 200	200 - 225
Cobb/Wagner	225 - 250	250 - 300

E.J. OFFERMAN, 1908, Buffalo Players (20)

Action shot & photo inset	75 - 85	85 - 100

THE ROSE CO., 1909
　Players in Gold Frame above Diamond
　on yellow/green field (200+)

Hall of Famers	150 - 175	175 - 200
Scranton Players	60 - 70	70 - 80
Others	40 - 50	50 - 60

THE ROTOGRAPH CO., 1905, B&W Photos

John McGraw, Clark Griffith	150 - 175	175 - 200
Others	100 - 120	120 - 140

SOUVENIR POSTCARD SHOP OF CLEVELAND (17+)

Cleveland Players, B&W Photos

Lajoie	150 - 175	175 - 200
Others	100 - 125	125 - 150

A.W. SPARGO, 1908, Black & White

Hartford Players (4?)	80 - 90	90 - 100

SPORTING NEWS, 1915, Color (6)

Ty Cobb	200 - 225	225 - 250
Walter Johnson	150 - 175	175 - 200
Others	75 - 100	100 - 125

MAX STEIN, P/U.S. PUB. HOUSE, 1909-16

35 Unnumbered, Sepia, "Noted People"

Cobb, Wagner	150 - 175	175 - 200
Mathewson	125 - 150	150 - 175
Speaker, Tinker, Evers, Chance	75 - 100	100 - 125
Others	40 - 50	50 - 60

H.M. TAYLOR, 1909-11, D. Tigers (7) B&W

Ty Cobb	200 - 225	225 - 150
Others	100 - 125	125 - 150

Ed Lopat (1950's P.C. Back)
Exhibit Supply (Mutoscope)

Jack Dempsey
Spanish Real Photo

Jim Thorpe   *Otto Graham (1950's P.C. Back)*
Real Photo   *Exhibit Supply (Mutoscope)*

ANONYMOUS SEPIA SET, 1910 (25)

Wagner, Cobb, Johnson, Mathewson	150 - 175	175 - 200
Cobb/Wagner	175 - 200	200 - 225
Others	75 - 100	100 - 125

TOPPING & CO., 1909, "Tiger Stars" (20)
Black & yellow - Head in big star.

Ty Cobb	150 - 175	175 - 200
Others	100 - 125	125 - 150

WOLVERINE NEWS CO., 1909, Tiger Players

(2) Ty Cobb	150 - 175	175 - 200
Others	80 - 90	90 - 100

MISCELLANEOUS

Boston Red Sox, **P/Furlong 1908**

Mechanical, Cobb/Wagner	3000 - 3250	3250 - 3700

Boston Red Sox, 1915

Team, Real Photo (including Babe Ruth)	6000 - 6250	6250 - 6750

Art P.C. Company

Fold-out Cards, 1907-1910	2000 - 2500	2500 - 3000
Baseball Comics, Many Publishers	10 - 15	15 - 20

Baseball Parks, Major Leagues

1900-1920	20 - 30	30 - 40
1920-1940	15 - 20	20 - 25
Linens, 1945-1949	8 - 10	10 - 15
Chromes	2 - 4	4 - 6

Baseball Parks, Minor Leagues, 1900-1935	10 - 12	12 - 15
Others	5 - 8	8 - 10

BOXING

Early 1900-1930

Jim Jeffries	25 - 28	28 - 32
Jeffries-Johnston Fight	30 - 35	35 - 40
Dempsey-Carpentier Fight	30 - 35	35 - 40
Dempsey, Real Photos	20 - 25	25 - 30
Heavyweight Champions	10 - 20	20 - 30
Other Champions	5 - 10	10 - 15
Exhibit Supply Company Issues	5 - 10	10 - 15
Semi-Pro, High School	3 - 5	5 - 10

FOOTBALL

EXHIBIT SUPPLY CO. B&W, Tints (32)

Postcard Backs only

Baugh, Graham, Connerly, Waterfield	30 - 40	40 - 50
Hirsch, Matson, Layne, Ratterman,		
Fears, Motley, Matson, Trippi	20 - 25	25 - 30
Others	10 - 15	15 - 20
Red Grange	25 - 30	30 - 40
Jesse Owens	20 - 25	25 - 30
Real Photo	40 - 50	50 - 60
Jim Thorpe	30 - 40	40 - 50
Jim Thorpe, Real Photo	50 - 70	70 - 90
Professional Stars	15 - 20	20 - 30
College Players	10 - 15	15 - 20
High School Players	8 - 10	10 - 12

GOLF

Pre-1930 Stars	20 - 25	25 - 40
1930-1960 Stars	15 - 20	20 - 25
Artist-Signed	15 - 20	20 - 35
Real Photos, Identified	12 - 15	15 - 25
Golf Advertising, Artist-Signed	25 - 35	35 - 60

TENNIS

Artist-Signed	15 - 20	20 - 30
Tennis Advertising	20 - 25	25 - 35
Real Photos, Identified	10 - 15	15 - 20

U.S. VIEWS

From their beginning as the "Pioneers" in the 1890's through the "chromes" of today, view cards have been the dominant collectible type in the postcard hobby. Other types have always had periods of high interest only to level off and even lose popularity at times. Not so with view cards. The biggest majority of all postcard collectors begin their participation in the hobby by collecting views of their home town. They have this interest because of their familiarity with the city, town, or community as it is today...and the desire to know what it was like in the early growth years.

This desire prompts each collector-historian to search every possible avenue for these collectible gems of the early years. The more views they find of the court house, post office, etc., the more they wonder if there was one of the depot, a barber shop, a meat market, and others. As the search continues the interest expands to other views, possibly of a nearby town, a once visited memorable city, and finally for those from all over their state. The fever elevates until the home town collector has become a full-blown postcard collector who will travel hundreds of miles and spend countless hours to enhance his collection.

Although small town views are the most popular and, therefore, command the highest prices, they, plus large town and city views of busy main streets, trolleys, depots, banks, etc., are continually pursued by topical collectors who care not whether the town is large or small, whether in Missouri or North Carolina...it just doesn't really matter. This elevates the price of topicals and also makes the small town views much dearer.

On the negative side, however, views of large cities such as New York, Washington, Philadelphia, etc., and tourist attractions such as Niagara Falls, Mount Vernon, Watkins Glen, Grand Canyon, Yellowstone Park and others, have very little value because of the millions produced for the people who visited. Only special views in these areas are of any value. Scenic views of mountains, rivers, etc., and unnamed views also are shunned by collectors.

THE VIEW PUBLISHER

There were many great and illustrious publishers of views in the early years. Among the great early Pioneer publishers were **The Albertype Co., American Souvenir Co., E.C. Kropp, Arthur Livingston, Ed. Lowey, H.A. Rost, Souvenir Postal Card Co.,** and **Walter Wirth**. Views by these, plus those by anonymous publishers pre-1900, are extremely scarce and are rarely found.

More familiar to today's view collector are names like **Albertype Co., A.C. Bosselman, Detroit Publishing Co., Illustrated Postcard Co., Kraemer Art, Hugh Leighton, Rotograph Co., Edw. H. Mitchell, Curt Teich, Raphael Tuck,** and **Valentine & Sons**. These names are among the most prolific of the era and most noted on cards that remain today. They usually sent representatives to all areas several times each year to take photos of the principal street scenes, statues, schools, and buildings. On the return trip, the representative would bring the photos and printing proofs and take orders from the drugstores and other postcard sellers. Each photo was retouched (power lines, obstructions, etc., removed) and colored to conform with the natural shade as nearly as possible. Resulting orders were returned to the merchant by mail. File copies of each card were retained by the merchant for future orders.

Basically, this is how the tremendous view card business was handled throughout the U.S. Thanks to these photographers, publishers and distributors, histories of small town America have been recorded for future generations and have made it possible for the postcard hobby to attain unbelievable heights.

VIEWS

View cards are classified as to Era for this listing.

1 = Postcard Era - 1900-1915
2 = White Border Era - 1915-1930
3 = Linen Era - 1930's-1940's

The values listed are for general views of the particular topic. Outstanding, or special subject matter, may be valued higher. On the other hand, a poorly printed image would lessen the value.

According to the majority of dealers and collectors, the actual selling prices of view cards have basically the same value structure in all states of the U.S. It all depends on the particular view and how much the collector is willing to pay. For instance, a collector in North Carolina will pay much more for a North Carolina view that a collector from Florida would pay for the same view.

	VG	EX
Airports-1	$ 5 - 6	$ 6 - 8
Airports-2	4 - 5	5 - 6
Airports-3	1 - 2	2 - 3
Amusement Parks-1	8 - 10	10 - 15
Amusement Parks-2	6 - 7	7 - 10
Amusement Parks-3	2 - 3	3 - 4
Banks-1	2 - 3	3 - 5
Banks-2	1 - 2	2 - 3
Banks-3	0.50 - 1	1 - 1.50
Birds Eye View-1	3 - 4	4 - 6
Birds Eye View-2	2 - 3	3 - 4
Birds Eye View-3	1 - 1.50	1 .50 - 2
Bridges-1	1 - 2	2 - 3
Bridges-2	1.50 - 2	2 - 2.50
Bridges-3	0.50 - 1	1 - 1.50
Bus Stations-1	N/A	N/A
Bus Stations-2	4 - 5	5 - 7
Bus Stations-3	2 - 3	3 - 4
Cemetery-1	5 - 6	6 - 8
Cemetery-2	4 - 5	5 - 6
Cemetery-3	2 - 3	3 - 4
Churches-1	2 - 3	3 - 4
Churches-2	1 - 2	2 - 3
Churches-3	1 - 1.50	1.50 - 2
Colleges-1	2 - 3	3 - 5

Colleges-2	1 - 2	2 - 4
Colleges-3	1 - 1.50	1.50 - 2
County Fair-1	6 - 7	8 - 12
County Fair-2	5 - 6	6 - 8
County Fair-3	3 - 4	4 - 6
Court House-1	3 - 4	4 - 6
Court House-2	2 - 3	3 - 4
Court House-3	1 - 1.50	1.50 - 2
Depots-1	5 - 6	6 - 10
Depots-2	3 - 5	5 - 7
Depots-3	2 - 3	3 - 4
Diners-1	N/A	N/A
Diners-2	N/A	N/A
Diners-3	10 - 12	12 - 25
Fire Department-1	6 - 8	8 - 12
Fire Department-2	5 - 6	6 - 8
Fire Department-3	3 - 4	4 - 5
Funeral Homes-1	7 - 8	8 - 12
Funeral Homes-2	6 - 7	7 - 9
Funeral Homes-3	4 - 5	5 - 6
Garages/Gas Stations-1	6 - 7	8 - 12
Garages/Gas Stations-2	5 - 6	6 - 8
Garages/Gas Stations-3	4 - 5	5 - 7

Bijou Theatre, Chattanooga, TN
International P.C. Company

Am. Thread Co., Willimantic, CT
Hugh C. Leighton Co.

St. Paul's Episcopal Church
Chester, PA, Valentine & Sons

First Ave., Atlantic Highlands, NJ
Valentine & Sons

G. P. Smith, "Harness . Buggies"
Store Front & Indian Bicycle

Evaul Brothers
Haddon Heights, NJ (1898)

Locust Valley Long Island Depot
Long Island Railroad

R.R. Station
Greensboro Bend, Vermont

General Stores-1	5 - 6	6 - 10
General Stores-2	4 - 5	5 - 7
General Stores-3	2 - 3	3 - 4
Gymnasiums-1	4 - 5	5 - 7
Gymnasiums-2	3 - 4	4 - 5
Gymnasiums-3	1 - 2	2 - 3
Hospitals-1	3 - 4	4 - 6
Hospitals-2	2 - 3	3 - 4
Hospitals-3	1 - 1.50	1.50 - 2
Hotels-1	3 - 4	4 - 6
Hotels-2	2 - 3	3 - 4
Hotels-3	1 - 2	2 - 3
Library-1	3 - 4	4 - 5
Library-2	2 - 3	3 - 4
Library-3	1 - 2	2 - 3
Main Streets-1	5 - 6	6 - 10
Main Streets-2	4 - 5	5 - 7
Main Streets-3	1 - 2	2 - 3
Mills/Plants-1	4 - 5	5 - 10
Mills/Plants-2	3 - 4	4 - 6
Mills/Plants-3	1 - 2	2 - 4
Motels-1	N/A	N/A
Motels-2	4 - 5	5 - 7
Motels-3	1 - 2	2 - 4

Malamute Dog Team, Valdez, Alaska
Portland Postcard Company

Opera-1	5 - 7	7 - 12
Opera-2	4 - 5	5 - 7
Opera-3	2 - 3	3 - 5
Parks-1	1 - 2	2 - 3
Parks-2	1 - 1.50	1.50 - 2
Parks-3	0.50 - 1	1 - 1.50
Post Office-1	3 - 4	4 - 6
Post Office-2	2 - 3	3 - 4
Post Office-3	1 - 1.50	1.50 - 2
Restaurants-1	6 - 7	7 - 10
Restaurants-2	3 - 4	4 - 6
Restaurants-3	2 - 3	3 - 4
Rivers, Creeks-1	1 - 2	2 - 3
Rivers, Creeks-2	1 - 1.50	1.50 - 2
Rivers, Creeks-3	0.50 - 1	1 - 1.50
Roadside Stands-1	N/A	N/A
Roadside Stands-2	4 - 5	5 - 8
Roadside Stands-3	3 - 4	4 - 6
Schools-1	2 - 3	3 - 5
Schools-2	1 - 2	2 - 3
Schools-3	1 - 1.50	1.50 - 2
Statues-1	1 - 2	2 - 3
Statues-2	1.50 - 2	2 - 2.50
Statues-3	0.50 - 1	1 - 1.50
Street Scenes-1	4 - 5	5 - 7
Street Scenes-2	3 - 4	4 - 5
Street Scenes-3	1 - 2	2 - 4
W/Parades-1	6 - 7	7 - 10
W/Parades-2	5 - 5	6 - 8
W/Parades-3	2 - 3	3 - 5

Tennis Courts-1	7 - 8	8 - 12
Tennis Courts-2	6 - 7	7 - 9
Tennis Courts-3	3 - 4	4 - 5
Theatres-1	8 - 10	10 - 15
Theatres-2	7 - 8	8 - 10
Theatres-3	4 - 5	5 - 6

FOREIGN VIEWS (Topographical)

Just as the hobby in the U.S. grows yearly by leaps and bounds, postcard collecting is also thriving in the other countries of the world. Great Britain, France, Germany and Italy are the leaders in Europe, but others are not far behind. Called Topographicals by most foreigners, which simply are view cards showing all the various motifs of almost every description, are the rage.

Much like the U.S. collector, foreigners also collect cards of their home towns and soon expand to views of other towns, cities, and countries searching for motifs of their choice. Therefore, the search for good material now includes most all countries, large and small,

Avignon-Dominion Hotel, Paris
R.C. Seine, No. 207-029B

Meissen, Germany
Meissner & Buch, Series 4, No. 1

Gruss Aus Bremerhaven
(Germany), O.Z.M. Publisher

Gruss Aus Bremen (Germany)
Rathaus und Dom

throughout the world. Collectors will do well to reevaluate the contents of those boxes and albums of old foreign cards they believed worthless. Of special interest are early pre-1905 Chromo-Lithographic Gruss Aus and vignette views of all countries. These early chromo-lithographs, usually multi-views, were printed by a special process where the design was etched on soft stone and printed in the various colors. Large irregular dots can be seen, usually with a magnifying glass, throughout the image surface as opposed to dots all the same size in the regularly printed lithograph cards.

After the chromo-lithograph cards, the most desired are identified topographicals...of people doing things, occupations, events, happenings, disasters, store and business fronts, exceptional busy street scenes, etc. These types, of course, are also those most desired by like collectors in the U.S., and the values are comparable in most instances. Therefore, the value to a collector of a small town depot in England or Germany would have a relative value to an American collector of a depot in a small town in the U.S.

The rarest and most highly valued foreign views are those of the tiny and thinly populated countries, colony possessions, and islands. Rarer still, with even higher valuations are "postally used in country of origin" views of these cards. The philatelic value can be many times that of the image or scene. An unused view of tiny Bhutan is valued at around $6 while the same card stamped and postmarked in Bhutan commands $40 or more.

Special events also make many cards much more valuable. For instance, the Royal Visit to Ascension brings $40-45 unused and up to $250 if postmarked in Ascension during the visit. As can be seen from these examples, a thorough examination of all those seemingly "worthless" foreign views could prove to be most rewarding. Many foreign dealers are now appearing at postcard shows in the U.S., and most will be happy to purchase worthwhile views.

Most views taken in larger cities, especially those generated for the tourist trade, have little value. The hordes of visitors to Paris, Rome, London, Brussels, Venice, Vienna, and other cities during the golden years of the postcard purchased tons of views of museums, churches, statues, buildings, landmarks, etc., so that many still exist today. Many of these were the poorly printed black and white or sepia tones. However, many were beautifully printed with radiant colors and can often be purchased for under $1.00 each by the patient collector.

FOREIGN VIEWS

The listings below should only be used as a guide to average values of views. It must be realized that views of various images could be valued much higher or lower, depending on the motif, the publisher, whether it is black and white, in color, a real photo, and other factors. Also, the demand by collectors in the city, town, or country of origin would determine whether the value is higher or lower.

EARLY CHROMO-LITHOGRAPHS, Pre-1910
    ALL COUNTRIES

Gruss Aus/Vignettes Single & Multi-views	5 - 7	7 - 10
Named Landscapes	4 - 5	5 - 6
Exhibitions	12 - 15	15 - 30
Festivals	15 - 18	18 - 35
Heraldic	8 - 10	10 - 15
Royalty Commeratives	12 - 15	15 - 30
Town/City Views, Color	6 - 8	8 - 10
Town/City Views, B&W or Sepia	3 - 4	4 - 5
Views in Shells, Fish, Leaves, etc.	5 - 7	7 - 9

PRINTED, Color, B & W and Real Photo, 1900-1920
    EUROPEAN COUNTRIES

Costumes	1 - 2	2 - 3
Disasters	2 - 5	5 - 10
Industrial	2 - 4	4 - 8
Occupations	3 - 5	5 - 10
Small Town Street Scenes	3 - 4	4 - 6
Large City Views, Street Scenes	0.50 - 1	1 - 1.50
Synagogues	8 - 10	10 - 12

Exceptional views can be much higher.
French Occupational views valued higher.
    AFRICAN NATIONS

Early Cards	2 - 4	4 - 8
Ethnic	1 - 2	2 - 5

    AUSTRALIA

Early Cards	8 - 10	10 - 12
Aborigines	5 - 7	7 - 9
Animal Carts, Teams, Etc.	4 - 6	6 - 8
Gold Mining	4 - 6	6 - 8
Railway Stations, Works	6 - 8	8 - 10
Street Scenes	2 - 3	3 - 4

    CANADA
Most values compare to those in U.S.
Central and South America, Cuba, Costa Rica,
Bahamas, Barbados, Bermuda, Puerto Rico,
Dominican Republic, etc.

Early Cards	5 - 6	6 - 8

Costumes	1 - 2	2 - 2.50
Cities	1 - 1.50	1.50 - 2
Small Towns, Street Scenes, etc.	2 - 3	3 - 5
Industrial	2 - 3	3 - 4
Occupations	2 - 4	4 - 6
Railways, Stations	4 - 5	5 - 7
Ethnic	3 - 5	5 - 7

Exceptional views can be much higher.

RUSSIA & EASTERN EUROPE

Early Cards, Gruss Aus, etc	.4 - 6	6 - 10
Costumes	2 - 3	3 - 4
Cities	1 - 2	2 - 3
Small Towns, Street Scenes, etc.	4 - 5	5 - 6
Industrial	3 - 5	5 - 7
Occupations	4 - 6	6 - 8
Railways & Other Transportation	4 - 5	5 - 10
Ethnic	3 - 4	4 - 6

Exceptional views can be much higher.

FAR EASTERN COUNTRIES   1 - 10

ISLANDS AND COLONIES, ETC., Early Cards*

Aldabra	10 - 15
Andaman	8 - 10
Canary	3 - 6
Caroline	8 - 10
Cayman	20 - 25
Christmas	25 - 30
Coscos Keeling	25 - 30
Cook	12 - 15
Eastern	12 - 15
Falkland	10 - 35
Fanning	15 - 20
Faroe	12 - 15
Gilbert Isle and Lord Howe Isle	12 - 15
Mafia	8 - 12
New Guinea	8 - 12
Norfolk	20 - 25
Ocean	10 - 15
Perim	8 - 12
Pitcairn	15 - 20
Solomon	10 - 15
Thursday	15 - 20
Turks	15 - 20
Virgin	15 - 20
Others	1 - 10

* Cards stamped & postmarked in country of origin
  can have much higher values.

BRITISH, FRENCH, GERMAN, ETC. COLONIES,
Early Cards   4 - 15

14
Real Photos

Real-Photo cards are still among the popular groups as they continue their long climb from obscurity to the top of the view and topical fields. As stated earlier, their authenticity and portrayal of life and living as it actually was, plus the fact that many are one-of-a-kind, are determining factors to collectors.

It is important in most instances that the image be identified. Clarity and sharpness in the photo image is extremely important so that all detail can be seen and the time era can be determined. This is equally important if the photo is not identified. Each card must be judged on its own qualities and, therefore, it is extremely hard to base values on the auction price of another card. For instance, an ice delivery wagon which is close-up, has sharp and clear features with legible name of the ice company and the city location could bring (**to a person who really wanted it**) up to $300. If another collector **"really wanted it"** the card could be bid up to $500. This euphoria, however, does not make all ice delivery wagons worth $500...the image, the location and the desire make the price.

Photo cards most sought after are those taken by amateur photographers of everyday life and "happenings" such as accidents, disasters, etc. However, there were those taken by professionals, signed by them, and distributed to the wholesale and retail trade that are also widely collected. Real-photo collectors seek cards by these photographers just as avidly as a "beautiful lady" collector would seek cards of Harrison Fisher or Philip Boileau.

Various papers and processes were used for producing real photo postcards. AZO and VELOX were the most dominant with EKC, KRUXO, KODAK, CYKO, DARKO, EKKP and DOPS following. The process is usually notated in the stamp box on the reverse side although not all real photos have these listings. Most European real photos have no process byline listed.

Collectors of real photos should be wary of reproductions. This is true mainly in the modes of transportation fields. Although these are usually very easily spotted by the seasoned collector, some are actually being sold as originals to those who can not spot the difference.

> For any transportation-related subjects, please refer to the chapter entitled "Transportation."

Automobiles	VG	EX
Identified --Large Image	$ 18 - 20	$ 20 - 25
Small Image	5 - 10	10 - 12
Unidentified -- Large Image	12 - 15	15 - 18
Small Image	5 - 8	8 - 10

Gas Pump
Newark, New Jersey

P.H. 2123
Child Playing Diabolo

Douglas Fir Log Truck -- Seattle, Washington (by AZO)

Gas Pumps
<u>Note:</u> Gas Pump Pictured Auctioned for $85.

Trucks

Identified -- Large Image	20 - 25	25 - 30
Small Image	10 - 15	15 - 18
Unidentified -- Large Image	10 - 12	12 - 15
Small Image	6 - 8	8 - 10

Delivery Trucks

Large Image, with Advertising	40 - 50	50 - 60
Small Image, with Advertising	30 - 35	35 - 40

Farm Trucks

Large Image	15 - 20	20 - 25
Small Image	10 - 12	12 - 15

Service Vehicles

Dump Trucks, etc., Large Image	25 - 30	30 - 35
Small Image	15 - 18	18 - 22
Mail Trucks -- Large Image	15 - 20	20 - 25
Small Image	10 - 15	15 - 20
Fire Engines -- Large Image	35 - 40	40 - 45
Small Image	12 - 15	15 - 18
Paddy Wagons	20 - 25	25 - 30

Farm Tractors

Identified -- Large Image	20 - 25	25 - 30
Small Image	10 - 12	12 - 15
Unidentified -- Large Image	12 - 16	16 - 20
Small Image	8 - 12	12 - 15

Race Cars

Large Image	15 - 20	20 - 25
Small Image	10 - 12	12 - 16

Fox Hill Fruit Farm
McNightstown, Pennsylvania (?)

World War I
Soldier and Flag (by AZO)

Vernia Burnette Huskey, Age 17
1908-1974

Cook Mercantile Company Store Front -- Cook, Minnesota (by AZO)

With Driver Identified -- Large Image	20 - 25	25 - 30
Small Image	15 - 18	18 - 22
Motorcycles		
Identified -- Large Image	25 - 30	30 - 35
Small Image	15 - 18	18 - 22
Unidentified -- Large Image	15 - 18	18 - 22
Small Image	8 - 10	10 - 12
Bicycles		
Identified -- Large Image	25 - 30	30 - 35
Small Image	15 - 18	18 - 22
Unidentified -- Large Image	15 - 18	18 - 20
Small Image	10 - 12	12 - 15
Horse-Drawn Delivery Wagons		
Ice -- Large Image	50 - 60	60 - 75
Small Image	20 - 25	25 - 35
Mail -- Large Image	50 - 60	60 - 70
Small Image	20 - 25	25 - 30
Coal -- Large Image	50 - 60	60 - 70
Small Image	20 - 25	25 - 30
Others -- Large Image	40 - 50	50 - 60
Small Image	20 - 25	25 - 30
Moving Vans/Freight Wagons -- Large Image	40 - 50	50 - 60
Small Image	20 - 25	25 - 30
Horse-Drawn Sales Wagons		
Ice Cream -- Large Image	60 - 70	70 - 85
Small Image	35 - 40	40 - 50
Bakery -- Large Image	50 - 60	60 - 70
Small Image	30 - 35	35 - 40
Grocery -- Large	50 - 60	60 - 70

U.S. Mail Truck (H.R. Smith, Photographer)
"Our Mail Man" - Anna Maria Island, Florida

Small Image	30 - 35	35 - 40
Others -- Large Image	45 - 50	50 - 60
Small Image	25 - 30	30 - 40
Horse & Buggy -- Large Image	12 - 15	15 - 18
Small Image	8 - 10	10 - 12
Horse & Wagon, Carts -- Large Image	12 - 15	15 - 20
Small Image	8 - 10	10 - 12
Goat Carts, With Children -- Large Image	15 - 20	20 - 25
Oxen-Driven Wagons	12 - 15	15 - 20
Fire Engines		
Hose Trucks	15 - 18	18 - 22
Horse-Driven Fire Engines	25 - 30	30 - 35
Horse-Driven Equipment	20 - 22	22 - 30
Trains, With Engine		
Identified -- Large Image	15 - 20	20 - 25
Unidentified -- Large Image	10 - 12	12 - 15
Passenger Car Interiors	20 - 25	25 - 30
Repair Shop Interiors	18 - 20	20 - 25
Train Wrecks		
Identified -- Large Image	10 - 15	15 - 25
Small Image	8 - 10	10 - 15
Unidentified -- Large Image	10 - 12	12 - 15
Small Image	6 - 8	8 - 10
Train Depots		
Small Town, East	10 - 15	15 - 20
With Train in Station	15 - 20	20 - 25
Large Town, East	5 - 8	8 - 12

Small Town, West	15 - 18	18 - 22
With Train in Station	15 - 20	20 - 30
Large Town, West	10 - 12	12 - 15
Trolley Cars		
Identified -- Large Image	20 - 25	25 - 30
Small Image	12 - 15	15 - 18
Unidentified -- Large Image	12 - 15	15 - 20
Small Image	8 - 10	10 - 12
Airplanes		
Identified -- Large Image (1896-1910)	15 - 25	25 - 35
Small Image	10 - 12	12 - 15
With Pilot	20 - 25	25 - 30
Balloons		
Identified Large Image	20 - 25	25 - 30
Small Image	15 - 20	20 - 25
Unidentified -- Large Image	15 - 20	20 - 25
Small Image	10 - 12	12 - 15
Dirigibles (See Zeppelins)		
Identified -- Large Image (1898-1924)	20 - 30	30 - 50
Small Image	15 - 20	20 - 25
Unidentified -- Large Image	15 - 20	20 - 25
Small Image	10 - 12	12 - 15
Ships, Interior Views	10 - 15	15 - 20
Small Business Buildings, Identified		
Bakeries -- Exteriors	15 - 20	20 - 25
Interiors	20 - 25	25 - 30
Banks -- Exteriors	10 - 12	12 - 15

Maryville Street, Galmar, Iowa (by AZO)

Interiors	15 - 18	18 - 20
Billiard Parlors -- Exteriors	20 - 25	25 - 30
Interiors	25 - 30	30 - 35
Bowling Alleys -- Exteriors	10 - 12	12 - 18
Interiors	18 - 20	20 - 25
Cigar/Tobacco Stores -- Interiors	50 - 55	55 - 60
Dairies -- Exteriors	10 - 15	15 - 20
Drug Stores -- Exteriors	12 - 15	15 - 20
Interiors	20 - 25	25 - 30
Fish/Meat Markets -- Exteriors	20 - 25	25 - 30
Interiors	30 - 35	35 - 40
General Stores -- Exteriors	15 - 20	20 - 25
Interiors	25 - 30	30 - 35
Grocery Stores -- Exteriors	15 - 20	20 - 25
Interiors	25 - 30	30 - 35
Ice Cream Parlors -- Exteriors	30 - 35	35 - 40
Interiors	40 - 45	45 - 50
Post Office -- Exteriors	10 - 12	12 - 15
Restaurants -- Exteriors	10 - 12	12 - 15
Interiors	15 - 18	18 - 22
Service Stations -- Exteriors	18 - 22	22 - 25
Soda Fountains	15 - 18	18 - 22
With Ice Cream or Coca Cola Signs	20 - 25	25 - 35
Taverns -- Exteriors	12 - 15	15 - 18
Interiors	15 - 20	20 - 25
Theaters -- Exteriors	20 - 25	25 - 30
Toy Store -- Exteriors	20 - 25	25 - 30
Interiors, Showing Toys	35 - 40	40 - 50

Street Scenes

Main Streets -- Small Towns	8 - 15	15 - 25
Large Towns	6 - 10	10 - 20
Others -- Small Towns	6 - 12	12 - 18
Large Towns	5 - 8	8 - 12

Bathing

Attractive Ladies	8 - 10	10 - 12
Groups	7 - 8	8 - 10

Blacks

Children	5 - 8	8 - 10
Men/Women	4 - 7	7 - 8
Blacks Working in Fields, etc.	10 - 12	12 - 15
Musical Groups	10 - 15	15 - 25
Black-Face Minstrels	28 - 32	32 - 35
Bands	20 - 25	25 - 30
Baseball Team	25 - 30	30 - 35

Children

Common	3 - 4	4 - 7
With Animals	7 - 8	8 - 12
With Dolls	15 - 18	18 - 22
With Dolls in Doll Carriage	18 - 22	22 - 26

Sailor Boy and Toy Tin Automobile

With Toys	10 - 15	15 - 18
With Large Teddy Bears	25 - 30	30 - 40
With Small Teddy Bears	15 - 18	18 - 22
In Classroom/School	10 - 12	12 - 15
In Costumes	15 - 18	18 - 25
Christmas Trees	15 - 18	18 - 22
With Gifts Under Tree	20 - 25	25 - 30
Circus-Related		
Trapeze Artist, Identified	15 - 20	20 - 25
Other Performers	10 - 15	15 - 20
Fat Ladies	15 - 18	18 - 22
Giants, Midgets, Strongmen, etc.	12 - 15	15 - 20
Advertising Circus	20 - 25	25 - 30
Animals -- Elephants, etc.	20 - 25	25 - 30
Add $5-8 for Barnum & Bailey Circus.		
Exaggerated		
Big Fish	10 - 12	12 - 15
Big Grasshoppers	12 - 14	14 - 18
Farm Products	6 - 8	8 - 12
Big Fruit	6 - 8	8 - 10
Big Animals	7 - 9	9 - 12
Hangings/Lynchings	25 - 30	30 - 40
Adolf Hitler (By **Hoffman**)		
Used, With Postmark	15 - 18	18 - 22
Unused, No Postmark	12 - 15	15 - 18
Other Publishers		
Used, With Postmark	16 - 20	20 - 25
Unused, No Postmark	12 - 15	15 - 18

Indians
   Identified Chiefs   20 - 25   25 - 30
   Others   12 - 15   15 - 18
   Unidentified   8 - 10   10 - 12
Nudes (See "Real Photo Nudes")
Plants, Mills
   Small Town -- Exteriors   20 - 25   25 - 35
   Large Town -- Exteriors   10 - 15   15 - 20
Political
   Presidents   15 - 18   18 - 25
   President and Running Mate   20 - 22   22 - 30
   Losing Candidates   18 - 20   20 - 35
   Governors   20 - 25   25 - 30
River Ferries   20 - 25   25 - 30
Billy Sunday   10 - 12   12 - 14
U.S. Flag
   People Dressed or Wrapped in Flag   35 - 40   40 - 50
   Uncle Sam in Flag   40 - 45   45 - 55
   Rallies, Showing Flag   15 - 20   20 - 25
   Orations or Debates, Showing Flag   20 - 25   25 - 30
   Patriotic Children   20 - 25   25 - 30
Zeppelins   20 - 25   25 - 30

"Glen Shulz Ford Special" No. 24 (by AZO)

15
Roadside America

The collecting of Roadside America material has grown dramatically as many collectors have become aware of the outstanding cards involved, and the possibility of getting into postcard groups where prices are still low and availability is good. Diners, gas stations, and drive-in restaurants are the most sought after, and are becoming very elusive.

To those who may be unfamiliar with cards of Roadside America, they consist of cards that were published to advertise a place of business on or near a busy highway during the 30's, 40's, and 50's. The cards were usually given to travelers when they stopped by, or were mailed to prospective customers.

Most Roadside America cards were issued in the Linen and early Chrome Eras. There has, however, been some overlapping from the White Border Era, especially with cards of filling stations and restaurants. Real-photo views, and any views of diners, are always in great demand and command the highest prices.

Chromes, as many dealers attest, are also becoming popular. Those new to the hobby, usually 30-40 years of age, can identify with cards of the 50's and are seeking them for their collections. Chrome prices on many topics are not much below those of linens. In the final analysis, however, the particular view, its location, and the person buying it will determine the value.

Gator Diner, St. Petersburg, Florida (Linen)
Curt Teich
(Sold at Auction for $200)

Values are listed as follows:
1 Linens
2 Real Photos
3 Chromes

Shadrick's Candy and Gift Shoppe, Jennings, Florida (R.P.)

	VG	EX
AUTOMOBILE DEALERSHIPS		
1	$ 4 - 6	$ 6 - 8
2	8 - 10	10 - 12
3	1 - 2	2 - 3
BAR & GRILL		
1	5 - 6	6 - 8
2	6 - 8	8 - 10
3	1 - 2	2 - 3
CAFE		
1	5 - 6	6 - 8
2	6 - 8	8 - 12
3	1 - 2	2 - 3
COFFEE POT CAFE TYPES		
1	5 - 7	7 - 10
2	8 - 10	10 - 12
3	2 - 3	3 - 4
DINERS		
1	12 - 15	15 - 20
2	20 - 25	25 - 28
3	5 - 6	6 - 8
DRIVE-IN RESTAURANTS		
1	8 - 10	10 - 12

Paul Bunyan
Bemidji, Minn.

Hotel Laughlin, El Paso, Texas
Exterior and Lobby, E. C. Kropp

Multi-View of Bon-Ette Motel, "In the Heart of Statesboro, Georgia"
Nationwide Specialty Company

2	10 - 12	12 - 15
3	2 - 3	3 - 5
DRIVE-IN THEATERS		
1	8 - 10	10 - 12
2	12 - 15	15 - 18
3	4 - 6	6 - 8
EXAGGERATED BUILDINGS		
1	5 - 8	8 - 10
2	10 - 12	12 - 15
3	2 - 3	3 - 4
FILLING STATIONS/SERVICE STATIONS		
1	8 - 10	10 - 12
2	10 - 15	15 - 18
3	3 - 4	4 - 5
FOOD MARKETS		
1	5 - 6	6 - 8
2	8 - 10	10 - 12
3	2 - 3	3 - 4
FRUIT, VEGETABLE STANDS		
1	5 - 6	6 - 8
2	8 - 10	10 - 12
3	2 - 3	3 - 4
GAS PUMPS		
1	5 - 6	6 - 8
2	8 - 10	10 - 12
3	2 - 3	3 - 4

A Typical Late 1930s Service Station, including Gas Pumps and
Coca Cola Sign
"Scheibel's Service Station" by Silvercraft, No. 12412

A Service Station and Auto Camp with Modern Cabins
"Sorrensen's Auto Camp" -- Sisters, Oregon
Silvercraft No. 12558

HOTELS
1	1 - 2	2 - 3
2	3 - 4	4 - 5
3	0.50 - 1	1 - 1.50

ICE CREAM SHOPS
1	8 - 10	10 - 12
2	12 - 14	14 - 18
3	3 - 4	4 - 5

MINIATURE GOLF
1	6 - 8	8 - 10
2	10 - 12	12 - 15
3	2 - 3	3 - 4

MOTELS, MOTOR COURTS, Single View
1	1 - 2	2 - 3
2	4 - 5	5 - 6
3	0.50 - 1	1 - 1.50

MOTELS, MOTOR COURTS, Multiple Views
1	4 - 5	5 - 8
2	5 - 7	7 - 10
3	2 - 3	3 - 4

PECAN STANDS
1	6 - 8	8 - 10
2	10 - 12	12 - 14
3	2 - 3	3 - 4

RESTAURANTS
1	4 - 5	5 - 6
2	5 - 6	6 - 8
3	1 - 2	2 - 3

SANDWICH SHOPS
1	6 - 8	8 - 10
2	8 - 10	10 - 12
3	2 - 3	3 - 4

SKATING RINKS
1	4 - 5	5 - 7
2	8 - 10	10 - 12
3	1 - 2	2 - 3

SOUVENIR SHOPS, TRADING POSTS
1	4 - 6	6 - 8
2	8 - 10	10 - 12
3	1 - 2	2 - 3

SWIMMING POOLS, COMMERCIAL (Not Motels)
1	6 - 8	8 - 10
2	8 - 10	10 - 12
3	2 - 3	3 - 4

TRAILER PARKS, COMMERCIAL
1	6 - 8	8 - 10
2	8 - 10	10 - 12
3	2 - 3	3 - 4

16 Expositions

Collectors are starting to become more interested in exposition postcards. They were heavily collected in the 1970s, but interest abated until recently. Leading the way are early hold-to-lights and woven silk issues. Interest will continue to grow as more of these fine collectibles appear.

1893 COLUMBIAN EXPOSITION

	VG	EX
Goldsmith Pre-Official, no Seal	$100 - 125	$125 - 150
Officials, Series 1	15 - 20	20 - 25
J. Koehler B&W Issues	35 - 40	40 - 45
PMC or Post Card Backs	15 - 20	20 - 30
Puck Magazine Advertising Cards	135 - 140	140 - 145
Other Advertising Cards	100 - 120	120 - 150
Signed **R. SELINGER**	100 - 115	115 - 140
Anonymous Publishers	100 - 150	150 - 175
1894 CALIFORNIA MID-WINTER EXPO	150 - 200	200 - 250
1895 COTTON STATES & INT. EXPO	150 - 175	175 - 200
Negro Building	200 - 225	225 - 275
1897 TENNESSEE CENTENNIAL EXPO	160 - 170	170 - 190
1898 TRANS-MISSISSIPPI EXPO		
Trans-Mississippi Official Cards	30 - 35	35 - 45
Albertype Co. Views	90 - 100	100 - 110
1898 WORCESTER SEMI-CENTENNIAL	70 - 80	80 - 90
1900 PARIS EXPOSITION		
Scenes	10 - 12	12 - 15
Hold-To-Light	20 - 25	25 - 30

Official Souvenir Mail Card of World's Fair, St. Louis, 1904
Large 6x9" Hold-to-Light, Cascade Gardens and Grand Basin

1901 PAN AMERICAN EXPOSITION

Niagara Envelope Co. B&W	5 - 6	6 - 8
Color	6 - 7	7 - 9
Oversized	70 - 80	80 - 90

1902 SOUTH CAROLINA INTERSTATE

Albertype Co. Issues	100 - 125	125 - 150
Others	80 - 90	90 - 110

1903 20TH TRIENNIAL NAT. SANGERFEST

Franz Huld	15 - 20	20 - 25

1904 ST. LOUIS WORLD'S FAIR

Buxton & Skinner	6 - 8	8 - 10
Chisholm Bros.	4 - 5	5 - 6
Samuel Cupples	4 - 5	5 - 6
Jumbo 6 x 9" H-T-L	200 - 225	225 - 250
Transparencies	5 - 6	6 - 8
Hold-To-Light	30 - 32	32 - 35
V.O. Hammon	4 - 5	5 - 6
The Inside Inn H-T-L	200 - 250	250 - 275
E.C. Kropp	3 - 4	4 - 5
Raphael Tuck	5 - 8	8 - 12
Woven Silks (14)	250 - 400	400 - 500
Advertising Cards	6 - 7	7 - 10

1905 LEWIS & CLARK EXPOSITION

E.P. Charlton	6 - 7	7 - 8
Edw. H. Mitchell	6 - 7	7 - 8
B.B. Rich (10)	8 - 10	10 - 12

1907 Jamestown Exposition
T. A. Bramberry

1907 Jamestown Exposition
M. L. Leigh

1915 San Francisco Panama
Pacific Expo, Int. Novelty Co.

Hold-to-Light of "The Inside Inn" at the St. Louis World's Fair, 1904

Portola Festival, San Francisco
Pacific Novelty Co., 1909

Portola Festival, San Francisco
Pacific Novelty Co., 1909
(Copyright by George Gordon)

Portola Festival, San Francisco, 1909
(Copyright 1907 by George Gordon)

A. Selige (10)	7 - 8	8 - 10
Advertising Cards	6 - 7	7 - 8
1907 JAMESTOWN EXPOSITION		
A.C. Bosselman	7 - 8	8 - 10
Illustrated Post Card Co.	25 - 30	35 - 40
Jamestown A&V	10 - 12	12 - 14
Battleships	12 - 15	15 - 20
H.C. CHRISTY		
Army Girls	200 - 225	225 - 250
Navy Girls	200 - 225	225 - 250
Raphael Tuck Oilettes	6 - 8	8 - 10
Silver Issues (10)	12 - 14	14 - 15
1908 PHILADELPHIA FOUNDERS WEEK		
Illustrated Post Card Co. (10)	6 - 7	7 - 8
Fred Lounsbury (10)	6 - 8	8 - 10
1908 APPALACHIAN EXPO, Knoxville, TN	8 - 10	10 - 15
1909 ALASKA YUKON-PACIFIC EXPOSITION		
Edw. H. Mitchell	3 - 4	4 - 5
Portland Post Card Co.	2 - 3	3 - 4
Advertising Postcards	4 - 5	5 - 8
1909 HUDSON-FULTON CELEBRATION		
J. Koehler	4 - 5	5 - 6
Fred Lounsbury	7 - 8	8 - 10
Redfield Floats (72)	5 - 6	6 - 7
Raphael Tuck, Series 164 (6)	5 - 7	7 - 8
Valentine & Co., S/Wall (6)	5 - 6	6 - 8
1909 PORTOLA FESTIVAL	8 - 10	10 - 12
1911-1912 GOLDEN POTLATCH-SEATTLE		
Edw. H. Mitchell (Sepia)	18 - 20	20 - 22
1915 PANAMA-PACIFIC EXPOSITION	3 - 4	5 - 6
Advertising Poster Cards	8 - 10	10 - 12
1915 PANAMA-CALIFORNIA EXPOSITION	3 - 4	5 - 6
Pre-Issues	5 - 6	6 - 8
Advertising Poster Cards	8 - 10	10 - 12
1933 CENTURY OF PROGRESS		
Exhibits	1 - 2	2 - 3
Advertising	2 - 3	3 - 5
Comics	2 - 3	3 - 5
1936 TEXAS CENTENNIAL	2 - 3	3 - 5
1939 NEW YORK WORLD'S FAIR	1 - 3	3 - 6
1939 SAN FRANCISCO EXPOSITION	1 - 3	3 - 6

"THE OTHER SIDE OF THE CARD"

By Vernon Ham

Dealers and collectors can benefit from the "other side" of the postcard if a little effort is made to learn what is interesting to other collectors -- not necessarily of postcards. Postcards give collectors of stamps and paper memorabilia an interesting and colorful addition to their hobbies.

It is possible to make the hobby of card collecting "pay its own way." This effort sometimes takes on the appearance of a hobby in itself. Stamps and postal markings are two of the selections that are worthy of comment.

There is sometimes a mistaken notion among many that if a stamp is old it is valuable; however, scarcity plays a far bigger part in pricing. Demand, of course, is also considered. Listed below are a few of the more often seen U.S. "rare" commemoratives and their catalog value (used) as listed in the *"1995 Scott Standard Postage Stamp Catalogue, Volume I."*

The one cent Trans-Mississippi Expo stamp of June 17, 1898 is the oldest and the used valuation is only $4.00. Others, including the regular 1901 Pan Am Expo, The 1904 Louisiana Purchase, the 1907 Jamestown, the 1909 Alaska-Yukon, Hudson-Fulton, 1913 Panama-Pacific, 1920 Pilgrim Tercentenary, the 1924 Huguenot-Walloon Tercentenary, the 1925 Lexington-Concord and the Parcel Post stamp are all valued in used condition from $0.85 to $4.00. Exceptions are the Pan-Am inverted center stamp valued at $5500, and the 1909 Alaska-Yukon and the Hudson-Fulton (both without perforations), valued at $20 and $22 respectively.

One item of interest on foreign cards is the use of "semi-postal" stamps. These are often the country's official solicitation for funds for some specific project -- either a tax or a donation. Many foreign Red Cross (TB) stamps are semi-postal. Cuba used funds collected in this way to build a number of public buildings. These stamps are highly regarded in stamp circles, especially the early ones, because of their relative scarcity.

To discourage theft in 1929, Kansas and Nebraska overprinted regular issue stamps with "Kans." or "Nebr." Scott values the 1 cent denomination at $1.35 and $1.50 respectively (used). Similarly, other public and private users of stamps have resorted to the use of perforated initials, referred to as "perfins."

The final stamp variety discussed here is the coil stamp. The first of the coil stamps to see extensive use because of the "postcard craze" was the 1908 issue. There are two varieties--those with vertical and those with horizontal perforations. Remember that a collectible stamp has perforations on four sides (except coil), is well centered, and if postally used is lightly cancelled. The value of a card is determined by the combined values of the view side, the stamp and the postal cancel.

"Cancellations" is a field in itself, or rather several fields in themselves. Probably the most obvious cancels are the "flag cancellations." There are two types that are scarcer than the usual, and both are easily recognized. One is the "ovate" with 12 stars in an oval with the 13th star inside the oval. The other is the "involute" which shows the flag not only wavy but folded. The flag cancel may also be from a discontinued post office.

A popular collectible topic requires many active participants. One of the most popular is Discontinued Post Offices (DPOs), which is a segment of the Postal History Society of any stamp club. A nationally recognized journal, "La Posta," publishes checklists of DPOs and conducts reputable mail auctions for its members. A Zip Code directory can be used as a guide for collecting (in reverse, you might say), but the La Posta checklists scales the scarcity of each cancel and applies an evaluation. They also handle information on Railroad Post Offices (RPOs) and Highway Post Offices (HPOs). The Mobile Post Office Society has the recognized catalog in these fields.

The final aspect of the "other side" collecting concerns a topical interest highly regarded by the stamp enthusiast. These are cards postally flown by the Graf Zeppelin (Zeppelin #Z-130) on its successful flights from Germany to North and South America and the North Pole. The American Mail Catalog (AAMC) details quite extensively the various flights and mailing combinations used. Look for Zeppelin stamps of any country, as well as the four from the United States. These four are listed in the "*1995 Scott's Standard Postage Stamp Catalog, Volume I*":

Denomination	Date of Issue	Withdrawn from Sale	Used Value
$0.65	04/19/30	6/30/30	$150.00
$1.30	04/19/30	6/30/30	$350.00
$2.60	04/19/30	6/30/30	$500.00
$0.50	10/02/33	--	$65.00

References:
American Air Mail Society, Steven Reinhard, P. O. Box 110, Mineola, NY 11501
American Philatelic Society, P. O. Box 8000, State College, PA 16803
American First Day Cover Society, P. O. Box 65960, Tucson, AZ 85728
Christmas Seal & Charity Stamp Society, Joseph S. Wheeler, P. O. Box 41096, Sacramento, CA 95841
Perfins Club, Kurt Ottenheimer, 462 West Walnut St., Long Beach, NY 11561
Postal History Society, Kalman V. Illyefalvi, 8207 Daren Court, Pikesville, MD 21208
Mobile Post Office Society, Douglas N. Clark, P. O. Box 51, Lexington, GA 30648
La Posta, P. O. Box 135, Lake Oswego, OR 97034

POSTCARD PUBLISHERS & DISTRIBUTORS

Following are some of the major publishers of postcards world-wide. Minor publishers can be found under each particular listing throughout this book.

A.M.B. -- Meissner & Buch, Quality Greetings, Artist-Signed
A.S.B. — Greetings
Ackerman — Pioneer Views of New York City
Albertype Co. — Pioneer & Expo Views; Local Views
Am. Colortype Co. — Expositions
Am. News Co. — Local Views
Am. Post Card Co. — Comics
Am. Souvenir Co. — Pioneers
Anglo-Am. P.C. Co. (AA) — Greetings, Comics
Art Lithograph Co. — Local Views
Asheville P.C. Co. — Local Views, Comics
Auburn P.C. Mfg. Co. — Greetings, Comics
Austin, J. — Comics
Ballerini & Fratini, Italy — Chiostri, Art Deco
BKWI, German — Artist-Signed, Comics
Bamforth Co. — Comics, Song Cards
Barton and Spooner — Comics, Greetings
Bergman Co. — Comics, Artist-Signed Ladies, etc.
Julius Bien — Comics, Greetings, etc.
B.B. (Birn Brothers) — Greetings, Comics
Bosselman, A.C. — Local Views, Others
Britton & Rey — Expositions, Battleships, etc.
Brooklyn P.C. Co. -- Views
Campbell Art Co. — Comics Rose O'Neill, etc.
Chapman Co. — Greetings, College Girls, etc.
Charlton, E.P. — Expositions, Local Views

Chisholm Bros. — Expositions, Local Views
Colonial Art Pub. Co. -- Scenics, Comics, Sepia Lovers
Conwell, L.R. — Greetings
Crocker, H.S. — Local Views
Davidson Bros. — Greetings, Artist-Signed
Dell Anna & Gasparini, Italy — Art Deco
Delta, Paris — French Fashion
Detroit Pub. Co. — Prolific Publisher, All Types
Faulkner, C.W., British — Artist-Signed, Greetings
Finkenrath, Paul, Berlin (PFB) — Greetings
Gabriel, Sam — Greetings
German-American Novelty Art — Greetings, Comics
Gibson Art Co. — Comics, Greetings
Gottschalk, Dreyfus & Davis — Greetings
Gross, Edward — Artist-Signed
Hammon, V.O. — Local Views
Henderson & Sons — Artist-Signed, Comics
Henderson Litho — Greetings, Comics, Local Views
Huld, Franz — Installment Sets, Expositions, etc.
Ill. Postal Card Co. — Greetings, Artist-Signed and Many Others
Int. Art Publishing Co. — Greetings by Clapsaddle, etc.
Knapp Co. — Artist-Signed
Koeber, Paul C. (P.C.K.) — Comics, Artist-Signed
Koehler, Joseph — H-T-L, Expositions, Local Views
Kropp, E.C. — Local Views, Battleships, etc.
Langsdorf, S. — Alligator and Shell Border Views, Local Views, Greetings
Lapina, Paris — Color Nudes and French Fashion
Leighton, Hugh — Local Views
Leubrie & Elkus (L.&E.) — Artist-Signed
Livingston, Arthur — Pioneers, Local Views
Lounsbury, Fred — Greetings, Local Views, etc.
Manhattan P.C. Co. — Local Views, Comics
Marque L-E, Paris — French Fashion
Meissner & Buch, German — Artist-Signed, Greetings
Metropolitan News Co. — Local Views
Mitchell, Edward H. — Expositions, Battleships, Local Views
Munk, M., Vienna — Artist-Signed, Comics, etc.
Nash, E. — Greetings
National Art Co. — Artist-Signed, Greetings, etc.
Nister, E., British — Artist-Signed, Greetings
Novitas, Germany — Artist-Signed
Noyer, A., Paris — Nudes and French Fashion
O.P.F. -- Quality German Artist-Signed
Owen, F.A. — Greetings, Artist-Signed
Phillipp & Kramer, Vienna — Artist-Signed, Art Nouveau
Platinachrome — Artist-Signed, Earl Christy, etc.
Reichner Bros. — Local Views
Reinthal & Newman — Artist-Signed, Greetings
Rieder, M. — Local Views
Rose, Charles — Greetings, Song Cards, Artist-Signed, Comics
Rost, H.A. — Pioneer Views, Battleships
Roth & Langley — Greetings, Comics
Rotograph Co. — Local Views, Expostiions, Battleships, Artist-Signed, etc.
Sander, P. — Greetings, Comics, Artist-Signed

Santway — Greetings
Sborgi, E., Italy — Famous Art Reproductions
Selige, A. — Expositions, Western Views, People, etc.
Sheehan, M.T. — Local Views, Historical, Artist-Signed
Souvenir Post Card Co. — Local Views, Greetings, etc.
Stecher Litho Co. — Greetings, Artist-Signed
Stengel & Co., Germany — Famous Art Reproductions
Stewart & Woolf, British — Comics, Artist-Signed
Stokes, F.A. — Artist-Signed, Comics
Strauss, Arthur — Local Views, Historical, Expositions
Stroefer, Theo. (T.S.N.), Nürnburg — Artist-Signed, Animals, etc.
Taggart Co. — Greetings
Tammen, H.H. — Expositions, Historical, Local Views
Teich, Curt — Local Views, Artist-Signed, Comics
Tichnor Bros. — Later Local Views, Comics
Tuck, Raphael & Sons, British — Artist-Signed, Views, Comics, Greetings, etc.
Ullman Mfg. Co. — Greetings, Artist-Signed, Comics
Valentine & Sons, British — Artist-Signed, Comics, Views, etc.
Volland Co. — Artist-Signed, Greetings
Whitney & Co. — Greetings, Artist-Signed
Winsch, John — Greetings, Artist-Signed
Wirths, Walter — Pioneer Views

BIBLIOGRAPHY

The following publications, all related to the collection and study of postcards, are recommended for further reading.

American Advertising Postcards, Sets and Series, 1890-1920, Fred and Mary Megson, Martinsville, NJ, 1987.

American Postcard Collectors Guide, 1981, Valerie Monahan.

The American Postcard Guide to Tuck, Sally Carver, Brookline, MA, 1979.

The American Postcard Journal, Roy and Marilyn Nuhn, New Haven, CT .

The Artist-Signed Postcard Price Guide, J. L. Mashburn, 1993, Colonial House.

Art Nouveau Post Cards, Alan Weill, Image Graphics, NY, 1977.

Bessie Pease Gutmann, Published Works Catalog, Victor J.W. Christie, Park Avenue Publishers, NJ, 1986.

The Collector's Guide to Post Cards, Jane Wood, Gas City, IN.

A Directory of Postcard Artists, Publishers and Trademarks, 1975, Barbara Andrews.

Encyclopedia of Antique Postcards, S. Nicholson, Wallace-Homestead, 1994.

Guide to Artists' Signatures & Monograms on Postcards, Nouhad A. Saleh.

Minerva Press, Boca Raton, FL 33429-0969, USA.

Neudin Cartes Postales de Collection, 1991, 35 rue G. St-Hilaire, 75005 Paris.

How to Price and Sell Old Picture Postcards, Roy Cox, Baltimore, 1992.

Harrison Fisher, David Bowers, Ellen H. Budd, George M. Budd, 1984.

Official Postcard Price Guide, Dianne Allman, NY, 1990.

Philip Boileau, Painter of Fair Women, D. Ryan, Gotham Book Mart, NY, 1981.

The Postcard Catalogue, 1993, Venman, Smith, Mead, IPM, U.K.

Picture Postcards in the U.S., **1893-1918,** Dorothy Ryan.

Picture Postcards of the Golden Age, Tonie & Valmai Holt, U.K.

Pioneer Postcards, J.R. Burdick, Nostalgia Press, 1956.

Prairie Fires & Paper Moons: The American Photographic Postcard, 1902-1920, Hal Morgan, Andreas Brown, Boston, 1981.

The Postcards of Alphonse Mucha, Q. David Bowers, Mary Martin.

Reklame Postkarten, Peter Weiss, Karl Stehle, Munich, Birkhauser Verlag, Basel, Switzerland.

The 1994 Sanders Price Guide to Autographs, Sanders, Sanders, Roberts, Alexander Books, Asheville, NC.

Standard Postcard Catalog, James L. Lowe, PA.

The Super Rare Postcards of Harrison Fisher, J.L. Mashburn, Enka, NC, Colonial House, 1992.

What Cheer News, Mrs. E.K. Austin, Editor, Rhode Island Postcard Club, RI.

PERIODICALS

The Antique Trader Weekly, P.O. Box 1050, Dubuque, IA 52004

Antiques & Auction News, P.O. Box 500, Mt. Joy, PA 17552

Barr's Post Card News, 70 S. 6th St., Lansing, IA 52151

Paper Collectors Marketplace, P.O. Box 127, Scandinavia, WI 54977

Paper Pile Quarterly, P.O. Box 337, San Anselmo, CA 94979

Picture Post Card Monthly, 15 Debdale Ln, Keyworth, Nottingham NG12 5HT, U.K.

The Postcard Album, H. Luers, Anton-Gunther-Str. 12, W-2902, Rastede, Germany

Postcard Collector, P.O. Box 337, Iola, WI 54945

Index